Seventh Edition

CORNERSTONES
FOR COLLEGE SUCCESS

Robert M. Sherfield
College of Southern Nevada

Patricia G. Moody
University of South Carolina

Boston • Columbus • Indianapolis • New York • San Francisco • Upper Saddle River
Amsterdam • Cape Town • Dubai • London • Madrid • Milan • Munich • Paris • Montreal • Toronto
Delhi • Mexico City • Sao Paulo • Sydney • Hong Kong • Seoul • Singapore • Taipei • Tokyo

Editor-in-Chief: Jodi McPherson
Acquisition Editor: Katie Mahan
Managing Editor: Karen Wernholm
Associate Managing Editor: Tamela Ambush
Senior Development Editor: Shannon Steed
Editorial Assistant: Erin Carreiro
Executive Marketing Manager: Amy Judd
Senior Production Project Manager: Peggy McMahon
Senior Procurement Specialist: Megan Cochran
Project Coordination, Editorial Services, and Text Design: Electronic Publishing Services
Inc., NYC
Art Rendering and Electronic Page Makeup: Jouve
Cover Designer: Barbara T. Atkinson
Associate Director of Design, USHE EMSS/HSC/EDU: Andrea Nix
Image Manager: Rachel Youdelman
Permissions Manager: Carol Besenjak
Permissions Project Manager: Pam Foley

Credits and acknowledgments borrowed from other sources and reproduced, with permission,
in this textbook appear on page 381. Also, p. xxv (wooden bridge), Fotolia.

Library of Congress Cataloging-in-Publication Data
Sherfield, Robert M.
    Cornerstones for college success / Robert M. Sherfield, Patricia G. Moody. — 7th ed.
        p. cm.
    ISBN 978-0-321-86047-7
    ISBN 0-321-86047-0
    1. College student orientation–United States.   I. Moody, Patricia G.   II. Title.
    LB2343.32.S54 2014
    378.1'98–dc23

                                                                            2012028080

1 2 3 4 5 6 7 8 9 10—CRK—15 14 13 12

ISBN 10: 0-321-86047-0
ISBN 13: 978-0-321-86047-7

ROBERT M. SHERFIELD, PH.D.

Robert Sherfield has been teaching public speaking, theater, technical writing, and student success, as well as working with first-year success programs, for 30 years. Currently, he is a professor at the College of Southern Nevada, teaching student success, technical writing, and drama.

An award-winning educator, Robb was named Educator of the Year at the College of Southern Nevada. He twice received the Distinguished Teacher of the Year Award from the University of South Carolina at Union, and has received numerous other awards and nominations for outstanding classroom instruction and advisement.

He has extensive experience with the design and implementation of student success programs, including one that was presented at the International Conference on the First-Year Experience in Newcastle upon Tyne, England. He has conducted faculty development keynotes and workshops at over 400 institutions of higher education across the United States. He has spoken in 46 states and several foreign countries.

In addition to his coauthorship of *Cornerstones for Community College Success* (Pearson, 2012), he has authored or coauthored *Cornerstones for Professionalism* (Pearson, 2013), *Cornerstone: Discovering Your Potential, Learning Actively, and Living Well* (Prentice Hall, 2008), *Roadways to Success* (Prentice Hall, 2001), the trade book *365 Things I Learned in College* (Allyn & Bacon, 1996), *Capstone: Succeeding Beyond College* (Prentice Hall, 2001), *Case Studies for the First Year: An Odyssey into Critical Thinking and Problem Solving* (Prentice Hall, 2004), and *The Everything Self-Esteem Book* (Adams Media, 2004).

Robb's interest in student success began with his own first year in college. Low SAT scores and a dismal high school ranking denied him entrance into college. With the help of a success program, he was granted entrance into college and went on to earn five college degrees, including a doctorate. He has always been interested in the social, academic, and cultural development of students, and sees this book as his way to help students enter the world of work and establish lasting, rewarding careers and productive lives. For more information, visit www.robertsherfield.com.

PATRICIA G. MOODY, PH.D.

Patricia G. Moody is Dean Emerita of the College of Hospitality, Retail, and Sport Management at the University of South Carolina, where she served on the faculty and in administration for over 30 years. An award-winning educator, Pat was honored as Distinguished Educator of the Year at her college, and as Collegiate Teacher of the Year by the National Business Education Association. She was also a top-five finalist for the Amoco Teaching Award at the University of South Carolina. She received the prestigious John Robert Gregg Award, the highest honor in her field of over 100,000 educators.

Pat has coauthored many texts and simulations, including *Cornerstones for Professionalism* (Pearson, 2013), *Cornerstones for Community College Success* (Pearson, 2012), *Cornerstone: Discovering Your Potential, Learning Actively, and Living Well* (Prentice Hall, 2008), *365 Things I Learned in College* (Allyn and Bacon, 1996), *Capstone: Succeeding Beyond College* (Prentice Hall, 2001), and *Case Studies for the First Year: An Odyssey into Critical Thinking and Problem Solving* (Prentice Hall, 2004). Prior to writing in the student success field, Pat published several business books and simulations.

A nationally known motivational speaker, consultant, and author, she has spoken in most states, has been invited to speak in several foreign countries, and frequently keynotes national and regional conventions. Pat has presented her signature motivational keynote address, "Fly Like an Eagle," to tens of thousands of people, from Olympic athletes, to corporate executives, to high school students.

As the dean of her college, she led international trips to build relationships and establish joint research projects in hospitality. Under her direction, faculty members in her college began a landmark study of Chinese tourists. She now travels the country delivering workshops, keynotes, and presentations on topics such as Managing Change, Working in the New Global Community, the Future of the Future, Student Motivation, and Emotional Intelligence. Moody also serves as a personal coach for business executives.

ACKNOWLEDGMENTS and GRATITUDE

We would like to acknowledge with earnest gratitude the following individuals at **The College of Southern Nevada** for their support:

Dr. Michael Richards, *President*
Dr. Darren Divine, *Vice President for Academic Affairs*
Dr. Hyla Winters, *Associate Vice President for Academic Affairs*
Professor James McCoy, *Associate Vice President for Academic Success*
Dr. Levia Hayes, *Department Chair—English*
Dr. Katherine Baker, *Assistant Chair—English*
Professor Linda Gannon, *Lead Faculty—Academic and Life Strategies*

We would also like to thank individuals at **The University of South Carolina,** and faculty members and staff in the Department of Hospitality, Retail, and Sport Management.

Our fondest gratitude to the following **colleagues and friends** who recommended individuals for the features, *How College Changed My Life* and *from Ordinary to Extraordinary:*

Shannon McCasland, *Aims Community College*
Steve Piscitelli, *Florida State College at Jacksonville*
Donna J. McCauley, *Moraine Valley Community College*
Colin Crick, *The University of South Carolina*
Melanie Deffendall, *Delgado Community College*
Robin Jones, *West Virginia University*
Rhonda R. Black, *West Virginia University*
Tina Eliopulos, *The College of Southern Nevada*
Karen Morris, *North Central Texas College*
Ryan Messatzzia, *Wor-Wic Community College*
Jana Schwartz, *University of Northern Colorado*
Nancy Gerli, *SUNY–Suffolk Community College*
Deanna Beachley, *The College of Southern Nevada*
Lya Redmond, *The Art Institute of Philadelphia*

To the **amazing individuals** who shared their life stories with us for the feature, *from Ordinary to Extraordinary:*

Bill Clayton
Derwin Wallace
Lydia Hausler Lebovic
Luke Bryan
Dino J. Gonzalez, M.D.
Odette Smith-Ransome
H.P. Rama
Sylvia Eberhardt
Vivian Wong
Matt Karres

Leo G. Borges
Dr. Wayne A. Jones
Maureen Riopelle
Catherine Schleigh
Mark Jones

To **the marvelous students (current and former)** who shared their advice and experiences for *How College Changed My Life:*

Brandon Sellers, *Aims Community College*
Jennifer Adams, *Florida State College at Jacksonville*
Mark D. Weber, *Moraine Valley Community College*
Erin Phillips, *The University of South Carolina*
Alencia Anderson, *Delgado Community College*
Diana Daugherty, *West Virginia University*
Pat Walls, *The College of Southern Nevada*
Kayla Stevens, *North Central Texas College*
Jeffrey Steele, *Wor-Wic Community College*
Biatriz Portillo, *University of Northern Colorado*
Gregg Gudelinis, *SUNY–Suffolk Community College*
Kerie F. Grace, *The University of Nevada–Las Vegas*
Zack Karper, *The Art Institute of Philadelphia*

Reviewers for this new edition and previous editions of *Cornerstones,* whom we recognize with deep appreciation and gratitude:

Christian M. Blum, Bryant and Stratton College; James Briski, Katherine Gibbs School; Christina Donnelly, York Technical College; Connie Egelman, Nassau Community College; Amy Hickman, Collins College; Beth Humes, Pennsylvania Culinary Institute; Kim Joyce, Art Institute of Philadelphia; Lawrence Ludwig, Sanford-Brown College; Bethany Marcus, ECPI College of Technology; Kate Sawyer, Pittsburgh Technical Institute; Patricia Sell, National College of Business and Technology; Janis Stiewing, Pima Medical Institute; June Sullivan, Florida Metropolitan University; Pela Selene Terry, Art Institute of New York City; Fred Amador, Phoenix College; Kathy Bryan, Daytona Beach Community College; Dorothy Chase, Community College of Southern Nevada; JoAnn Credle, Northern Virginia Community College; Betty Fortune, Houston Community College; Doroteo Franco Jr., El Paso Community College; Cynthia Garrard, Massasoit Community College; Joel Jessen, Eastfield College; Peter Johnston, Massasoit Community College; Steve Konowalow, Community College of Southern Nevada; Janet Lindner, Midlands Technical College; Carmen McNeil, Solano College; Joan O'Connor, New York Institute of Technology; Mary Pepe, Valencia Community College;

Bennie Perdue, Miami Dade Community College; Ginny Peterson-Tennant, Miami Dade Community College; Anna E. Ward, Miami Dade Community College; Wistar M. Withers, Northern Virginia Community College; Marie Zander, New York Institute of Technology; Joanne Bassett, Shelby State Community College; Sandra M. Bovain-Lowe, Cumberland Community College; Carol Brooks, GMI Engineering and Management Institute; Elaine H. Byrd, Utah Valley State College; Janet Cutshall, Sussex County Community College; Deborah Daiek, Wayne State University; David DeFrain, Central Missouri State University; Leslie L. Duckworth, Florida Community College at Jacksonville; Marnell Hayes, Lake City Community College; Elzora Holland, University of Michigan–Ann Arbor; Earlyn G. Jordan, Fayetteville State University; John Lowry-King, Eastern New Mexico University; Charlene Latimer; Michael Laven, University of Southwestern Louisiana; Judith Lynch, Kansas State University; Susan Magun-Jackson, The University of Memphis; Charles William Martin, California State University, San Bernardino; Jeffrey A. Miller; Ronald W. Johnsrud, Lake City Community College; Joseph R. Krzyzanowski, Albuquerque TVI; Ellen Oppenberg, Glendale Community College; Lee Pelton, Charles S. Mott Community College; Robert Rozzelle, Wichita State University; Penny Schempp, Western Iowa Community College; Betty Smith, University of Nebraska at Kearney; James Stepp, University of Maine at Presque Isle; Charles Washington, Indiana University–Purdue University; Katherine A. Wenen-Nesbit, Chippewa Valley Technical College; Fred Amador, Phoenix College; Barbara Auris, Montgomery County Community College; Elvira Johnson, Central Piedmont Community College; Peter Johnston, Massasoit Community College; Steve Konowalow, Community College of Southern Nevada; Janet Lindner, Midlands Technical College; Joel V. McGee, Texas A&M University; Carmen McNeil, Solano College; Ryan Messatzzia, Wor-Wic Community College; Jan Norton, University of Wisconsin–Osh Kosh; Joan O'Connor, New York Institute of Technology; Bennie Perdue, Miami-Dade Community College; Ginny Peterson-Tennant, Miami Dade Community College; Todd Phillips, East Central College; Pela Selene Terry, Art Institute of NYC; Kate Saywer, Pittsburg Technical Institute; Sarah K. Shutt, J. Sergeant Reynolds Community College; Pamela Stephens, Fairmont State University; and Angela Vaughan, University of Northern Colorado.

Our Creative and Supportive Team at Pearson

Without the support and encouragement of the following people at Pearson, this book would not be possible. Our sincere thanks to:

Greg Tobin
Jodi McPherson
Amy Judd
Shannon Steed
Peggy McMahon
Karla Walsh
Erin Carreiro

Your constant belief in us has been a most cherished gift. We are lucky to know you and are better people because of you. Thank you!

Pearson Course Redesign

Did You Know?

Course Redesign is the process of restructuring the way course content is delivered with the goal of increasing both student achievement and institutional productivity. Pearson has successfully partnered with colleges and universities engaged in Course Redesign for over ten years through workshops, Faculty Advisor programs, and online conferences.

Take Action!

Get involved by attending a Pearson-hosted Course Redesign event. Hear from Faculty Advisors already involved in course redesign at various stages and in a variety of disciplines. Our Faculty Advisors are experienced in implementing MyLab/Mastering for redesign. They are ready to share what they have learned and offer advice.

Learn More

Learn more about Pearson Course Redesign resources and events at www.pearsoncourseredesign.com

Pearson MyStudentSuccessLab
Faculty Advisor Network

What is F.A.N.?
The Faculty Advisor Network is Pearson's peer-to-peer mentoring program in which we ask experienced MyStudentSuccessLab users to share their best practices and expertise with current and potential customers.

How do they help?
Our Faculty Advisors are experienced in supporting new and potential MyStudentSuccessLab users in a variety of ways such as:

• One-on-one phone and email coaching

• Webinars and presentations

• Live workshops and training sessions

Learn More
Contact your Pearson representative to connect with a Faculty Advisor or learn more about the FacultyAdvisory Network.

MyStudentSuccessLab™

MyStudentSuccessLab is an online solution designed to help students acquire the skills they need to succeed for ongoing personal and professional development. They will have access to peer-led video interviews and develop core skills through interactive practice exercises and activities that provide academic, life, and professionalism skills that will transfer to ANY course.

How can "skills" be measured – and what can you do with the data?

Measurement Matters – and is ongoing in nature. No one is ever an "expert" in 'soft skills' - something students learn once and never think about again. They take these skills with them for life.

Learning Path Diagnostic

- For the course, 65 Pre-Course questions (Levels I & II Bloom's) and 65 Post-Course questions (Levels III & IV Bloom's) that link to key learning objectives in each topic.

- For each topic, 20 Pre-Test questions (Levels I & II Bloom's) and 20 Post-Test questions (Levels III & IV Bloom's) that link to all learning objectives in the topic.

What gets your attention?

It's about engagement. Everyone likes videos.
Good videos, conveniently organized by topic.

FinishStrong247 YouTube channel

- Best of 'how to' for use as a practical reference
  (i.e. - manage your priorities using a smart phone)

- Save time finding good video.

- All videos have been approved by members of our student
  advisory board and peer reviewed.

How can everyone get trained?

We all want a 'shortcut to implementation'.
Instructors want to save time on course prep.
Students want to know how to register, log in, and know 'what's due, and when'.
We can make it easy.

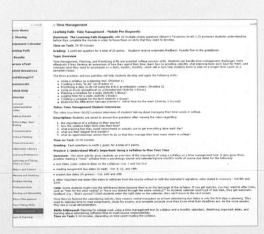

Implementation Guide

- Organized by topic, provides time on task, grading rubrics,
  suggestions for video use, and more.

- Additional videos and user guides, registration and log in guides,
  and technical support for instructors and students at www.mystudentsuccesslab.com

MyStudentSuccessLab Feature set:

Learning Path provides:
- 65 Pre-Course (Levels I & II Bloom's) and 65 Post-Course (Levels III & IV Bloom's)
- 20 Pre-Test (Levels I & II Bloom's) and 20 Post-Test (Levels III & IV Bloom's)
- Overview (ie. – Learning Outcomes)
- Student Video Interviews (with Reflection questions)
- Practices and Activities Tied to Learning Path
- FinishStronger247 YouTube channel with student vetted supporting videos

Student Inventories:
1. **Golden Personality**—Similar to Meyers Briggs–it offers a personality assessment and robust reporting for students to get actionable insights on personal style. www. talentlens.com/en/employee-assessments/golden.php
2. **ACES (Academic Competence Evaluation Scales)**—Strength inventory which identifies and screens students to help educators prioritize skills and provides an overview of how students see themselves as learners. Identifies at-risk. www.pearsonassessments.com/HAIWEB/Cultures/en-us/ Productdetail.htm?Pid=015-8005-805
3. **(Watson-Glaser) Thinking Styles**—Helps students understand their thought process and how they tend to approach situations. Shows how you make decisions. www.thinkwatson.com/mythinkingstyles

Student Resources:
Pearson Students Facebook page, FinishStrong247 YouTube channel, MySearchLab, Online Dictionary, Plagiarism Guide, Student Planner, MyProfessionalismKit resources including video cases, job search documents, and interview FAQ's. GPA, Savings, Budgeting, and Retirement Calculators.

Instructor Resources:
Instructor Implementation Guide supports course prep with Overview, Time on Task, Grading rubric, etc.

MyStudentSuccessLab Topic List:

A First Step: Goal Setting	Memory and Studying
Communication	Problem Solving
Critical Thinking	Reading and Annotating
Financial Literacy	Stress Management
Information Literacy	Teamwork
Interviewing	Test Taking
Job Search Strategies	Time Management
Learning Preferences	Workplace Communication (formerly 'Professionalism')
Listening and Taking Notes in Class	Workplace Etiquette
Majors/Careers and Resumes	

MyLabsPlus Available upon request for MyStudentSuccessLab

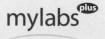

MyLabsPlus service is a dynamic online teaching and learning environment designed to support online instruction programs with rich, engaging customized content. With powerful administrator tools and dedicated support, MyLabsPlus is designed to support growing online instruction programs with an advanced suite of management tools. Working in conjunction with MyLabs and Mastering content and technology, schools can quickly and easily integrate MyLabsPlus into their curriculum.

Custom Publishing

As the industry leader in custom publishing, we are committed to meeting your instructional needs by offering flexible and creative choices for course materials that will maximize learning and engagement of students.

The Pearson Custom Library

Using our online book-building system, **www.pearsoncustomlibrary.com**, create a custom book by selecting content from our course-specific collections which consist of chapters from Pearson Student Success and Career Development titles and carefully selected, copyright cleared, third-party content, and pedagogy.
www.pearsonlearningsolutions.com/custom-library/pearson-custom-student-success-and-career-development

Custom Publications

In partnership with your Custom Field Editor, modify, adapt and combine existing Pearson books by choosing content from across the curriculum and organize it around your learning outcomes. As an alternative, work with them to develop your original material and create a textbook that meets your course goals.
www.pearsonlearningsolutions.com/custom-publications

Custom Technology Solutions

Work with Pearson's trained professionals, in a truly consultative process, to create engaging learning solutions. From interactive learning tools to eTexts, to custom websites and portals we'll help you simplify your life as an instructor.
www.pearsonlearningsolutions.com/higher-education/customizable-technology-resources.php

Online Education

Offers online course content for online learning classes, hybrid courses, and enhances the traditional classroom. Our award-winning product CourseConnect includes a fully developed syllabus, media-rich lecture presentations, audio lectures, a wide variety of assessments, discussion board questions, and a strong instructor resource package.
www.pearsonlearningsolutions.com/higher-education/customizable-online-courseware.php

For more information on how Pearson Custom Student Success can work for you,

please visit **www.pearsonlearningsolutions.com** or call 800-777-6872

ALWAYS LEARNING

PEARSON

Student Success CourseConnect

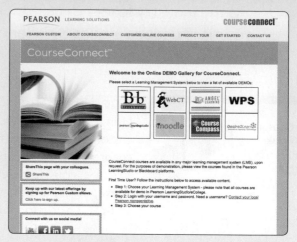

Student Success CourseConnect (http://www.pearsonlearningsolutions.com/courseconnect) is one of many award-winning CourseConnect customizable online courses designed by subject matter experts and credentialed instructional designers, and helps students 'Start strong, Finish stronger' by building skills for ongoing personal and professional development.

Topic-based interactive modules follow a consistent learning path, from Introduction, to Presentation, to Activity, then Review. Student Success CourseConnect is available in your school's learning management system (LMS) and includes relevant video, audio, and activities. Syllabi, discussion forum topics and questions, assignments, and quizzes are easily accessible and it accommodates various term lengths as well as self-paced study.

Course Outline (ie 'Lesson Plans')

1. Goal setting, Values, and Motivation
2. Time Management
3. Financial Literacy
4. Creative Thinking, Critical Thinking, and Problem Solving
5. Learning Preferences
6. Listening and Note-Taking in Class
7. Reading and Annotating
8. Studying, Memory, and Test-Taking
9. Communicating and Teamwork
10. Information Literacy
11. Staying Balanced: Stress Management
12. Career Exploration

"What makes my CourseConnect course so successful is all the engagement that is built-in for students. My students really benefit from the videos, and all the interactivity that goes along with the classes that I've designed for them."

—Kelly Kirk, Director of Distance Education, Randolph Community College

"It's truly great that Pearson is invested in using the latest technologies to reach me in ways beside the traditional educational model. This innovative approach is one of the best ways to facilitate the education of students of my generation."

—Zach Gonzales, Student, University of Denver

ALWAYS LEARNING

PEARSON

Resources for Online Learning or Hybrid

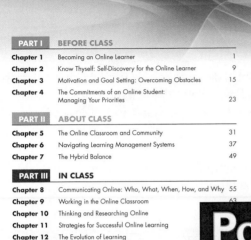

Power Up: A Practical Student's Guide to Online Learning, 2/e

Barrett / Poe / Spagnola-Doyle

©2012 • ISBN-10: 0132788195 • ISBN-13: 9780132788199

Serves as a textbook for students of all backgrounds who are new to online learning and as a reference book for instructors who are also novices in the area, or who need insight into the perspective of such students. Provides readers with the knowledge and practice they need to be successful online learners.

"We have used this excellent text with all cohorts of the last two years, as the text is an integral part of the first course in our graduate online program. Students love that its user-friendly and practical. Instructors see this text as a powerful learning tool that is concise yet is able to be comprehensive in its coverage of critical skills and knowledge that support online student success."

—Dr. William Prado
Associate Professor & Director,
Business Program, Green Mountain College

Introducing CourseSmart, The world's largest online marketplace for digital texts and course materials.

A Smarter Way for Students

CourseSmart is convenient. Students have instant access to exactly the materials their instructor assigns.

CourseSmart offers choice. With CourseSmart, students have a high-quality alternative to the print textbook.

CourseSmart saves money. CourseSmart digital solutions can be purchased for up to 50% less than traditional print textbooks.

CourseSmart offers education value. Students receive the same content offered in the print textbook enhanced by the search, notetaking, and printing tools of a web application.

CourseSmart is the Smarter Way

To learn for yourself, visit
www.coursesmart.com

Resources

Online Instructor's Manual – This manual is intended to give instructors a framework or blueprint of ideas and suggestions that may assist them in providing their students with activities, journal writing, thought-provoking situations, and group activities.

Online PowerPoint Presentation – A comprehensive set of PowerPoint slides that can be used by instructors for class presentations and also by students for lecture preview or review. The PowerPoint Presentation includes bullet point slides with overview information for each chapter. These slides help students understand and review concepts within each chapter.

Assessment via MyStudentSuccessLab – It is an online solution—*and powerful assessment tool*—designed to help students build the skills they need to succeed for ongoing personal and professional development at www.mystudentsuccesslab.com

Create tests using a secure testing engine within MyStudentSuccessLab (similar to Pearson MyTest) to print or deliver online. The high quality and volume of test questions allows for data comparison and measurement which is highly sought after and frequently required from institutions.

- Quickly create a test within MyStudentSuccessLab for use online or to save to Word or PDF format and print

- Draws from a rich library of question test banks that complement course learning outcomes

- Like the option in former test managers (MyTest and TestGen), test questions in MyStudentSuccessLab are organized by learning outcome

- On National average, Student Success materials are customized by 78% of instructors—in both sequence and depth of materials, so organizing by learning outcomes (as opposed to 'chapter') saves customers time

- Questions that test specific learning outcomes in a text chapter are easy to find by

  using the ACTIVITIES/ASSESSMENTS MANAGER in MyStudentSuccessLab

- MyStudentSuccessLab allows for personalization with the ability to edit individual questions or entire tests to accommodate specific teaching needs

- Because MyStudentSuccessLab is written to learning outcomes, this technology has breadth across any course where 'soft skills' are being addressed

LASSI – The LASSI is a 10-scale, 80-item assessment of students' awareness about and use of learning and study strategies. Addressing skill, will and self-regulation, the focus is on both covert and overt thoughts, behaviors, attitudes and beliefs that relate to successful learning and that can be altered through educational interventions.

Noel Levitz/RMS – This retention tool measures Academic Motivation, General Coping Ability, Receptivity to Support Services, PLUS Social Motivation. It helps identify at-risk students, the areas with which they struggle, and their receptiveness to support.

Premier Annual Planner – This specially designed, annual 4-color collegiate planner includes an academic planning/resources section, monthly planning section (2 pages/month), and weekly planning section (48 weeks; July start date). The Premier Annual Planner facilitates short-term as well as long-term planning. This text is spiral bound and convenient to carry with a 6x9 inch trim size.

IDentity Series—which will you choose?

Our consumer flavored "IDentity" Series booklets are written by national subject matter experts, and offer strategies and activities for immediate application. These essential supplements can be packaged with any text or purchased individually. Additional information is available at www.pearsonhighered.com/educator/series/IDentity-Series/12561.page

Now Featuring: IDentity Series: *Ownership*

Do you remember how you learned to ride a bike? It probably went something like, 'put on the training wheels, learn to brake/steer; remove training wheels, try to ride with a strong hand on the back to keep you balanced, try on your own as you wobbled along; then fell a few times before you...rode away and never looked back'.

If you teach students ownership of concepts in class, they are more likely to take responsibility for their successes and failures and "own" their learning. First, we offer a multimedia professional development course on Ownership in an easy-to-use online format that walks through teaching methods and includes ready-to-use activities, coaching tips, assessments, animations, and video on a topic. Second, we provide a short, affordable student booklet covering ownership essentials and the topic that can be used independently or as part of your course.

Instructors will learn how to use this groundbreaking four-step process to teach ownership to any student in any class. Students will learn how to take ownership over their education and ultimately their life path.

Complete list of current and forthcoming IDentity Series publications:

TOPIC	SKILLS	ISBN	TITLE	AUTHOR (S)
CAREER	Key Cognitive	0132819678	Now You're Thinking About Your Career	Chartrand et. al.
COLLEGE	Key Cognitive	0132825740	Now You're Thinking About College	Chartrand et. al.
CRITICAL THINKING	Key Cognitive	013286908X	Ownership: Critical Thinking	Stone
FINANCES (brief)	Contextual Skills & Awareness	0132819694	Financial Literacy	Torabi
FINANCES (comprehensive)	Contextual Skills & Awareness	0132819651	Financial Responsibility	Clearpoint Financial Solutions, Inc.
IDENTITY	Contextual Skills & Awareness	0321883330	Identity: Passport to Success	Graham
VETERANS	Contextual Skills & Awareness	0132886952	Finding Success as a Military Student	McNair/Stielow
GOAL SETTING	Academic Behaviors	0132868792	Ownership: Effective Planning	Stone
TEST TAKING	Academic Behaviors	0132869063	Ownership: Study Strategies	Stone
TIME MANAGEMENT	Academic Behaviors	0132869500	Ownership: Accountability	Stone

Pearson Success Tips
Which will you choose for your students?

Success Tips provides information 1-page highlights on critical topics, available in three formats:

- *Success Tips* (6-panel laminate) includes: MyStudentSuccessLab, Time Management, Resources All Around You, Now You're Thinking, Maintaining Your Financial Sanity, Building Your Professional Image

- *Success Tips for Professionalism* (6-panel laminate) includes: Create Your Personal Brand, Civility Paves the Way Toward Success, Succeeding in Your Diverse World, Building Your Professional Image, Get Things Done with Virtual Teams, Get Ready for Workplace Success

- Choose pages from the list below to insert into a custom text via Pearson Custom Library.

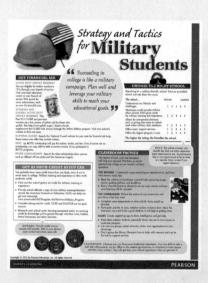

Blackboard	0132853159	Success Tips: Welcome to Blackboard!
Brand U	0132850788	Success Tips: Create Your Personal Brand
Campus Resources	0132850605	Success Tips: Resources All Around You
Civility	0132853140	Success Tips: Civility Paves the Way Toward Success
Critical Thinking	0132850729	Success Tips: Now You're Thinking
Diversity	0132850753	Success Tips: Succeeding in Your Diverse World
eCollege	0132850664	Success Tips: Welcome to eCollege!
Finances	0132850710	Success Tips: Maintaining Your Financial Sanity
Goal Setting	0132850702	Success Tips: Set and Achieve Your Goals
Information Literacy	0132850613	Success Tips: Information Literacy is Essential to Success
Moodle	013285077X	Success Tips: Welcome to Moodle!
MyStudentSuccessLab	0132850745	Success Tips: MyStudentSuccessLab
Note Taking	0132850672	Success Tips: Good Notes Are Your Best Study Tool
Online Learning	013298153X	Success Tips: Power Up for Online Learning
Privacy	0132850796	Success Tips: Protect Your Personal Data
Professional Image	0132850826	Success Tips: Building Your Professional Image
Service Learning	0132886316	Success Tips: Service Learning What You Learn Helps Others
Stress Management	0132852071	Success Tips: Stay Well and Manage Stress
Test Taking	0132850680	Success Tips: Prepare for Test Success
Time Management	0132850842	Success Tips: Time Management
Veterans	013285080X	Success Tips: Veterans/Military Returning Students
Virtual Teams	0132850761	Success Tips: Get Things Done with Virtual Teams
Workplace Success	0132850834	Success Tips: Get Ready for Workplace Success

PEARSON

BRIEF CONTENTS

CONTENTS

chapter 4

CONNECT 70

CONNECTING WITH TECHNOLOGY, RESEARCH, AND INFORMATION LITERACY

chapter 5

THINK 101

BUILDING CRITICAL THINKING, EMOTIONAL INTELLIGENCE, AND PROBLEM SOLVING SKILLS

chapter 6

PRIORITIZE 128

PLANNING YOUR TIME AND REDUCING STRESS

chapter 7

LEARN 154

DISCOVERING YOUR LEARNING STYLE, DOMINANT INTELLIGENCE, AND PERSONALITY TYPE

chapter 8
READ 179

BUILDING SUCCESSFUL READING
STRATEGIES FOR PRINT AND
ONLINE MATERIAL

chapter 9
RECORD 202

CULTIVATING YOUR LISTENING SKILLS
AND DEVELOPING A NOTE-TAKING
SYSTEM THAT WORKS FOR YOU

chapter 10
STUDY 225

DEVELOPING YOUR
MEMORY, STUDY, AND
TEST-TAKING SKILLS

chapter 15

PLAN 341

FOCUSING ON YOUR FUTURE AND PROFESSIONAL CAREER

Cornerstones Speaks to Where You Are

Why?

You and Your Students Have Unique Needs.

Cornerstones recognizes how student and instructor needs have evolved, and have made the change from editions that catered to *all* institutions to specific programs (four year, two year, and blended and online). In learning environments, it is important to get relevant information—at the time you need it. Now you can select course materials from *Cornerstones* that reinforce your institution's culture (four year, two year, or blended and online) and speak directly to your specific needs.

Choice is Yours.

Cornerstones is known for concrete and practical strategies that students can apply to all college classes, the world of work, and life in general, and addresses the "why" of learning and the power of positive change. It offers coverage of Bloom's taxonomy, SQ3R integration, and information and financial literacy. Defining topics include first generation students, adult learners, making successful transitions, and planning for success in the second year and beyond. The ancillary materials are designed to assist instructors in delivering a top-level student success course.

Choose the version of *Cornerstones* that aligns best with your institution and student population, all while getting the hallmark features and content you've come to expect.

Four Year

Cornerstones for College Success 7e (formerly *Cornerstone: Creating Success Through Positive Change* 6e, and *Cornerstone: Creating Success Through Positive Change Concise* 6e). Written specifically for students attending four year programs, it addresses today's college students.

Two Year

Cornerstones for Community College Success 2e (formerly *Cornerstones for Community College Success*). Written specifically for students attending two year programs, it addresses students in community and technical colleges.

Blended and Online

Cornerstones for College Success Compact (new offering). Written specifically for blended and online environments, it addresses students as digital learners and aligns with learning outcomes from MyStudentSuccessLab (http://www.mystudentsuccesslab.com), and Student Success CourseConnect (http://www.pearsonlearningsolutions.com/courseconnect). This makes it ideal as a print companion paired with one of these technologies to actively augment learning with activities, assessments, and critical thinking exercises to apply concepts.

NEW TO THE SEVENTH EDITION OF
CORNERSTONES FOR COLLEGE SUCCESS

How College Changed My Life showcases stellar graduates who used their challenges and strengths as motivational forces in obtaining degrees and entering their professions. These engaging stories help students understand the importance of their own college experience and how to apply skills gained during their college experience to their professional and personal lives. See these features at the beginning of every chapter.

CONNECT Chapter on Technology helps students master the ever-changing skills of information literacy, understand today's technology "language," conduct effective online searches, and monitor their online behavior and actions. This chapter also introduces the basics of the most popular computer programs and social media platforms used in education today. To explore further, see Chapter 4.

The D.A.R.T.S. Information Literacy System developed specifically for the Cornerstones franchise introduces students to an effective, useful, and easy-to-remember formula for conducting online research and evaluating sources. The D.A.R.T.S. Information Literacy System involves D*etermining* the information needed, A*ccessing* the appropriate information, R*eading* and evaluating the information carefully, T*ransforming* the information into a dynamic project, and S*electing* appropriate documentation styles. To learn more see Chapter 4.

Writing a Research Paper using D.A.R.T.S. Information Literacy System makes dreaded research projects easier for students. This system walks students through the research process to narrow the topics, develop an effective thesis, conduct meaningful and useful research, test the validity of sources, and use proper documentation styles. To review this new coverage, see Chapter 4.

PRESENT Chapter on Oral Communication focuses on the importance of oral communication in the digital age. The major types of speeches-Informative, Demonstrative, and Persuasive-are discussed. Students will learn skills crucial for future career success including effective oral communication in teleconferencing, telephone etiquette, personal introductions, and selling your ideas. See Chapter 13 for this new coverage.

Higher Education and the Adult Learner helps students who are returning to college after an extended absence. Tips and advice are provided to help returning students make the most of college services and relationships. See Chapter 3 for this new coverage.

Conquering the First Generation Student Gap helps students who are first generation college students understand more about college life and how to adjust to their changing world. See Chapter 3 for this new coverage.

Developmental and Remedial Classes coverage is included to reflect the importance of having a firm foundation in English, reading and mathematics, this section stresses the importance of registering for and completing developmental classes that may have been identified as necessary based on placement testing. See Chapter 3 for this new coverage.

Working in Teams and Studying in Groups shows students the importance of establishing, working in, and maintaining effective study, learning, and working teams. Coverage includes strategies to use in creating effective virtual teams. See Chapters 10 and 12 to learn more.

BEGIN

"Talent alone won't make you a success. Neither will being in the right place at the right time, unless you are ready. The most important question is: 'Are you ready?'" —Johnny Carson

 If you look at the figure printed here you will see the Chinese symbol meaning *to change*. It is made up of two symbols—the first means *to transform* or to be flexible. The second means *to do* or *to deliver*. In its purest form, the symbol means *to deliver transformation*. That is what *Cornerstones* is all about: helping you deliver or bring about transformation, positive change if you will, to your life. It is about helping you discover ways to change your thoughts, change your performance, and change your life.

Our goals in writing *Cornerstones* are to help you discover your academic, social, and personal strengths so that you can build on them, and to provide concrete and useful tools that will help you make the changes necessary for your success. We believe that in helping you identify and transform areas that have challenged you in the past, you can *discover your true potential, learn more actively, and have the career you want and deserve.*

Cornerstones for College Success is written with three major areas of self-development in mind. These three areas will help you create positive change that can help you become the individual you would like to be. These areas are:

CHANGING YOUR THOUGHTS	addresses a broad spectrum of topics that begins with a focus on change as it relates to becoming a college student in a different culture and setting than you may have known before. In this section, you will be introduced to tools of self-management as they relate to your academic success. You will be exposed to a variety of new terms, ideas, and thoughts—all of which begin your journey of change. You will learn to enhance your communication skills, improve your self-concept, and manage conflict, all valuable tools on the road to change. You will become more adept at critical thinking and problem solving. When you have mastered these areas, you should notice a difference in the way you approach tasks and think about subjects, challenges, and people.
CHANGING YOUR PERFORMANCE	focuses on you and how you physically and mentally manage yourself. You will begin this part of the journey to change by learning to manage your time while controlling the inherent stress that accompanies being a student. You will realize that you have a dominant intelligence, learning style, and personality type, and learn how to use them to your advantage. Even though you have been reading for some time, you will be shown strategies to improve both your speed and comprehension because reading is a major part of your studies. You will be shown several note-taking systems designed to improve your ability to record what your instructors are teaching. Finally, you will be taught strategies for empowering your memory, learning to study more effectively, and taking tests with confidence. When you master these areas, you should be able to perform most tasks more effectively and confidently.
CHANGING YOUR LIFE	is designed to round out your total personal profile and springboard you to success as you move into a different realm. To be a completely successful student, you need to address all these areas because they are significant to the changes you need to embrace. You will learn to manage your money and your debts wisely. So many students are burdened with astronomical financial debts when they graduate; our desire is for you to have accumulated as little debt as possible, while at the same time taking advantage of all that your college has to offer. On this important journey to change, you will learn how to immerse yourself in many categories of diversity while you celebrate all kinds of people. You will be taught to be responsible for your own wellness and how to exercise personal responsibility. Finally, you will be introduced to techniques for planning your professional career in the face of dramatic global changes. When you master these areas, you should be prepared to move through the next few years of school and beyond with confidence and optimism.

We know that your time is valuable and that you are pulled in countless directions with work, family, school, previous obligations, and many other tasks. For this reason, we have tried to provide only the most concrete, useful strategies and ideas to help you succeed in this class and beyond.

We have collectively spent over 60 years gathering the information, advice, suggestions, and activities on the following pages. This advice and these activities have come from trial and error, colleagues, former students, instructors across the United States, and solid research. We hope that you will enjoy them, learn from them, and, most of all, use them to change your life and move closer to your dreams.

Let the journey to positive change begin!

IMPORTANT FEATURES OF CORNERSTONES FOR COLLEGE SUCCESS

Throughout the text, you will find several common features to help you master the material. We hope you will use these features to become more engaged with the book, test your mastery, and practice what you have learned. The common features include:

- How College Changed My Life
- From Ordinary to Extraordinary
- Scan and Question
- Bloom's Taxonomy triangles
- Successful Decisions: An Activity for Critical Reflection
- Knowledge in Bloom

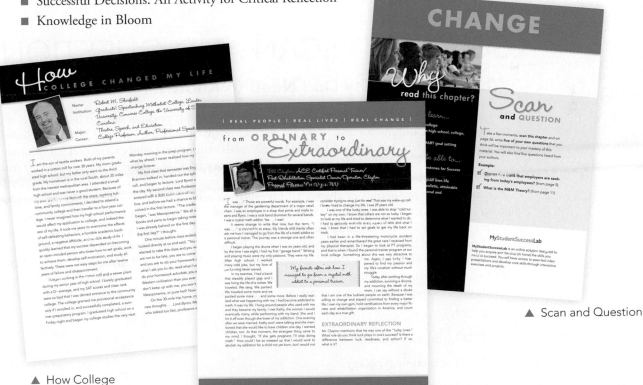

▲ How College Changed My Life

▲ From Ordinary to Extraordinary

▲ Scan and Question

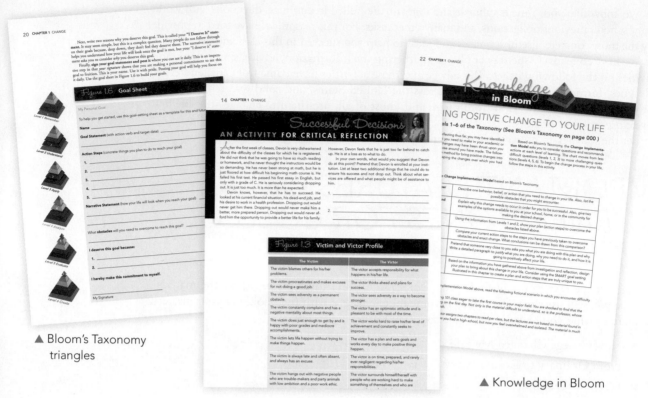

▲ Bloom's Taxonomy triangles

▲ Successful Decisions: An Activity for Critical Reflection

▲ Knowledge in Bloom

SQ3R AND SCAN AND QUESTION

What Is It and Why Do I Need to Know It?

You may be asking, "What does SQ3R mean and what could it possibly have to do with me, my text, this course, and my success?" The answer: SQ3R (S: Scan, Q: Question, 3R: Read, Recite, Review) is one of the most successful and widely used learning and study tools ever introduced.

This simple yet highly effective mnemonic (memory trick) asks that *before you actually read the chapter,* you look over the contents, check out the figures and photos, look at section headings, and review any graphs or charts. This is called *scanning.* Step 2, *question,* asks that you jot down questions that you think you will need to answer about the chapter's content in order to master the material. These questions might come from charts or figures, but most commonly, they come from the chapter's section headings. Examine the questions below derived from a section of *Criminal Justice: A Brief Introduction* (6th ed.) by Frank Schmalleger (Prentice Hall, 2006) on the next page.

Some of the questions you may ask based on the content shown here are:

1. What are the categories of crime?

2. Why do they matter?

3. What is crime typology?

4. When categories of crime are most often used?

After writing these questions from the section heading, you will read this section and then answer those questions. This technique gives you more focus and purpose for your reading. Each chapter in *Cornerstones* begins with this technique in the feature called **Scan and Question.**

We included this feature in *Cornerstones* to help you become a more active reader with greater comprehension skills in all of your classes. This technique is fully discussed in Chapter 8 of this text.

Excerpt From Text

reported data.[64] Crimes that result from an anomalous event, but which are excluded from reported data, highlight the arbitrary nature of the data-collection process itself.

Special Categories of Crime

crime typology

A classification of crimes along a particular dimension, such as legal categories, offender motivation, victim behavior, or the characteristics of individual offenders.

A **crime typology** is a classification scheme that is useful in the study and description of criminal behavior. All crime typologies have an underlying logic, and the system of classification that derives from any particular typology may be based on legal criteria, offender motivation, victim behavior, the characteristics of individual offenders, or the like. Criminologists Terance D. Miethe and Richard C. McCorkle note that crime typologies "are designed primarily to simplify social reality by identifying homogeneous groups of crime behaviors that are different from other clusters of crime behaviors."[65] Hence one common but simple typology contains only two categories of crime: violent and property. In fact, many crime typologies contain overlapping or nonexclusive categories—just as violent crimes may involve property offenses, and property offenses may lead to violent crimes. Thus no one typology is likely to capture all of the nuances of criminal offending.

BLOOM'S TAXONOMY OF THINKING AND LEARNING

Level 1 Remember

What Are All of Those Little Triangles Throughout My Book?

Another feature that you will notice throughout your text is a series of small triangles followed by questions pertaining to the content. These triangles help you recognize which of the six levels of learning from Bloom's Taxonomy is being used. See the quick reference chart of Bloom's Taxonomy (Revised) at the front of this text.

Bloom's Taxonomy (also called Levels of Thinking and Learning) is simply a way of explaining the stages at which we all acquire information. These levels progress from simple learning and thinking (levels 1, 2, 3) to more complex learning and thinking (levels 4, 5, 6). In addition to having correlations to Bloom's Taxonomy throughout your text, each chapter will end with an exercise called ***Knowledge In Bloom***. This chapter-end activity is included to help you process and apply the information from the chapter.

SO, WHY USE BLOOM'S IN THE CORNERSTONES TEXT?

Bloom's Taxonomy is important because it helps us determine the level at which we understand important information. For example, it is important to be able to answer questions at level 1, such as:

Abraham Lincoln was the _____ president of the United States.

Abraham Lincoln's wife's name was _____ _____ Lincoln.

However, it is also important to be able to answer questions at levels 4, 5, and 6, such as:

Compare and contrast the differences between the Union and Confederate military structure, conditions, and leadership.

Based on your knowledge of the American Civil War era, predict what would have happened to the United States without the Emancipation Proclamation. Justify your answer.

Summarize the main events that led to the American Civil War.

As you can clearly see, there is a great difference between these levels of learning. The higher the level, the more information and knowledge you need to be able to understand to respond to the question or problem.

The chapter-end activity, ***Knowledge In Bloom***, will help you process and demonstrate your knowledge at different levels. This is important because you will have professors who teach and test at levels 1, 2, and 3, and others who teach and test at levels 4, 5, and 6. Learning to process and demonstrate your knowledge at every level can assist you in:

- Doing well in other classes by providing a foundation for effective studying and learning
- Learning to solve problems more thoroughly
- Predicting exam questions
- Learning how to critically evaluate and assess ideas and issues
- Learning to thoroughly and objectively research topics for papers and presentations
- Testing your own reading comprehension

A WORD ABOUT READING AND USING *CORNERSTONES*

We encourage you to read this text (and every text) with great care so that you can learn from the ideas presented within its pages. We also encourage you to *use* this book!

- Write in the margins
- Circle important terms
- Highlight key phrases
- Jot down word definitions in the margins
- "Dog-ear" the pages
- Write questions that you have in the spaces provided

Review the following page from another *Cornerstones* text to see how one student used the book to its fullest.

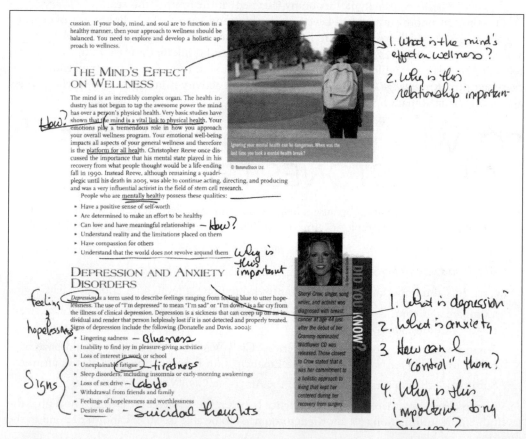

By treating this book like your "foundation to success," you will begin to see remarkable progress in your study practices, reading comprehension, and learning skills.

chapter one

CHANGE

CREATING SUCCESS, GUIDING CHANGE, AND SETTING GOALS

"The greatest reward of an education is to be able to face the world with an open mind, a caring heart, and a willing soul." —Robert M. Sherfield

CHANGE

Why read this chapter?

Because you'll learn...

- The basic truths about college
- The differences between high school, college, and career
- The nuts and bolts of SMART goal setting

Because you'll be able to...

- Apply the Essential Cornerstones for Success in a Changing World
- Create positive change in your own life
- Set, evaluate, and adjust realistic, attainable SMART goals for your personal and academic life

Scan and QUESTION

Take a few moments, **scan this chapter** and on page 26, write **five of your own questions** that you think will be important to your mastery of this material. You will also find five questions listed from your authors.

Example:

☑ **Discuss two traits that employers are seeking from today's employees?** (from page 5)

☑ **What is the M&M Theory?** (from page 11)

MyStudentSuccessLab

MyStudentSuccessLab is an online solution designed to help you acquire and develop (or hone) the skills you need to succeed. You will have access to peer-led video presentations and develop core skills through interactive exercises and projects.

How

Name: Robert M. Sherfield

Institution: Graduate! Spartanburg Methodist College, Lander University, Converse College, the University of South Carolina

Major: Theatre, Speech, and Education

Career: College Professor, Author, Professional Speaker

I am the son of textile workers. Both of my parents worked in a cotton mill for over 30 years. My mom graduated high school, but my father only went to the third grade. My hometown is in the rural South, about 35 miles from the nearest metropolitan area. I attended a small high school and was never a good student. Because of my poor performance through the years, working full-time, and family commitments, I decided to attend a community college and then transfer to a four-year college. I never imagined how my high school performance would affect my application to college, and indeed the rest of my life. It took me years to overcome the effects of self-defeating behaviors, a horrible academic background, a negative attitude, and terrible study skills. I quickly learned that my success depended on becoming an open-minded person who knew how to set goals, work to achieve them, develop self-motivation, and study effectively. These were not easy steps for me after twelve years of failure and disappointment.

I began working in the cotton mill and a sewer plant during my senior year of high school. I barely graduated with a D– average, and my SAT scores and class rank were so bad that I was denied entrance to the community college. The college granted me provisional acceptance only if I enrolled in, and successfully completed, a summer preparatory program. I graduated high school on a Friday night and began my college studies the very next

Monday morning in the prep program. I never realized what lay ahead. I never realized how my life was about to change forever.

My first class that semester was English. Professor Brannon walked in, handed out the syllabus, called the roll, and began to lecture. Lord Byron was the topic for the day. My second class was Professor Wilkerson. She entered with a dust storm behind her, went over the syllabus, and before we had a chance to blink, she was involved in the first lecture. "The cradle of civilization," she began, "was Mesopotamia." We all scurried to find notebooks and pens to begin taking notes. I could not believe I was already behind on the first day. "Who teaches on the first day?" I thought.

One minute before class ended, she closed her book, looked directly at us and said, "You are in history now. You elected to take this class and you will follow my rules. You are not to be late, you are to come to this class prepared, and you are to do your homework assignments. If you do what I ask you to do, read what I've assigned to you, and do your homework activities, you will learn more about Western civilization than you ever thought possible. If you don't keep up with me, you won't know if you are in Egypt, Mesopotamia, or pure hell! Now get out!"

On the 30-mile trip home, my mind was filled with new thoughts . . . *Lord Byron, Mesopotamia, professors who talked too fast, professors who did not talk at all,* tuition, parking, and the size of the library. I knew that something was different, *something had changed in me.* In one day at my college, I had tasted something intoxicating, something that was addictive. *I had tasted a new world.* My college experience changed my life in so many ways, but the number one thing that happened to me was that I learned how to be more comfortable in more places. Because of my experiences at Spartanburg Methodist College, I began to be as comfortable in New York City at a Broadway play as I was at my job in the cotton mill. I learned to be as comfortable sailing the River Thames past Big Ben and Parliament as I was working at the Buffalo Sewer District. I learned to appreciate the fjords of Norway as much as the cool stream on my daddy's farm. My college experience taught me to appreciate the joys and wonders of travel, learning, and meeting new people. I had never known this before. My college experience changed my life, and I will be forever grateful to those instructors who opened the door to the world for me.

Five college degrees and 30 years later, as I coauthor your *Cornerstones* text, I am still addicted to that new world I first experienced in college. Higher education changed my life, and I am still changing—with every day I live, every new book I read, every new class I teach, every new person I meet, and every new place to which I travel, I am changing. I wish the same for you.

THINK a b o u t *it*

1. What adversities in your past will you have to work to overcome to persist in your current studies?

2. What changes and adjustments do you think you are going to have to make in your personal and academic life to reach your goals, graduate, and enter the career you want?

THE TIMES . . . THEY ARE A CHANGIN'

What Is the Relationship Between Your Education and the New Global Economy?

Why do you need to consider today's global economy when thinking about your future?

Composer, singer, and activist Bob Dylan once titled a song, "The Times, They Are a-Changin'." Truer words have never been spoken—especially for anyone living during these times. This is not your daddy's economy, it is not your mama's workplace, and it certainly is not your grandfather's job market. To glide over this simple truth *could be the most costly decision of your life.*

"New global economy," you might say, "Who cares about a global economy?"

"China? Who cares about the fluctuating economy in China, Russia, South America, or India? I live in Kansas and I'm worried about America's future."

"An iPhone? A Blackberry? An iPad? I can't even afford my bus ticket this month," you may be thinking.

While you may not be alone in thinking, "*this does not matter to me,*" you would be very wrong to think that today's world affairs do not concern **you**, your **education**, and your **future**. Yes, it may be true that you are simply trying to get a degree in medical assisting to work in a doctor's office in Spokane, Washington, or obtain a degree in criminal justice to work at the police department in Union, South Carolina, or to earn a degree in business so that you can work in banking in Stockton, California. However, no certificate, no degree, no job, and certainly no person will be exempt from the changes and challenges of the new "global economy."

"*So, where does this leave ME*," you might be asking? It leaves you in an exciting, vulnerable, challenging, scary, and wonderful place. We did *not* include this information to scare you or to turn you off, but rather to give you a jolt, to open your eyes to the world in which you live and the workforce for which you are preparing. We encourage you to use *every tool* available, *every resource* possible, *every connection* imaginable, and *every ethical, moral, and legal means* possible to prepare yourself for this ever-changing world in which we live today. The present and the future may not be as rosy as you had hoped for, but it is here, it is real, and it is yours. However, you must know this: If you make strategic changes in your life now, you can have a much brighter future. No workplace will be immune from the changes facing our world today, and your very survival depends on being prepared and knowing how to quickly adapt to and change with a variety of situations.

> "When it comes to the future, there are three kinds of people: those who let it happen, those who make it happen, and those who wonder what happened."
>
> —John Richardson, Jr.

What Employers Are Saying

According to several career professionals (Hansen & Hansen, 2012; Kay, 2011; Zupek, 2011), employers want associates who are well trained in their chosen professions, have job-specific technical skills, and possess tact and sensibility, but they also look for other skills and abilities. Skills listed as vitally important to employers include:

long-term potential	strong online social media/technical skills
ability to work with others	enthusiasm and initiative
communication skills	ability to learn new skills quickly
attention to detail	self-confidence
creative problem solving skills	flexibility/adaptability

What Strategies Can I Use to Keep from Being Outsourced?

Go where the puck is going! Sound crazy? Hockey champ Wayne Gretzky made the comment that this **one step** had been his key to success. What does it mean? He said that when he was playing hockey, he did not skate to where the puck was at the moment, he skated to where the puck was *going*. He anticipated the direction of where the puck was going to be hit, and when it came his way, he was already there, ready to play.

Think of your career in this light. Go to where it will be bright in the future, not necessarily where it is bright at this moment. Look ahead and try to determine what is going to be "hot" in the coming years, not what is hot right now. Plan ahead. Look at trends. Read. Ask questions. Stay prepared. Think in the future, not the moment.

People holding degrees and certificates are a dime a dozen. This does not mean, however, that *you* are a dime a dozen. Herein lies the challenge. How do you

How does the statement "go where the puck is going" relate to your chosen profession?

distinguish yourself from the countless job seekers out there? What are you going to do that sets you apart from your competition? What do you have to offer that no one else can possibly offer to an employer? Below, we will discuss some of the talents and qualities that are becoming increasingly rare, yet constantly sought after, in today's knowledge economy. By understanding more about these qualities, you can put yourself miles ahead of the competition.

Whether we like it or not, a massive transformation is going on all around us in this country, as well as all over the world. Thriving in the coming years is going to be more difficult than in the past and will require certain new and different abilities and attitudes to be successful. You will need to learn and acquire the skills that will make you competitive, give you an edge, and help you master a life filled with changes and challenges. Many of these skills are outlined in Figure 1.1. These skills will be needed for your success, personal independence, and growth in the new economy. Study them carefully, as each one will help you create a positive transition to the world of work.

Figure 1.1   The Essential Cornerstones for Success in a Changing World

Seek Excellence as a Communicator

Writing, speaking, and listening skills are constantly listed by employers as mandatory for success in *any* profession. Few people actually possess these qualities—especially all three. If you want to put yourself ahead of the competition, then attend every class, every seminar, every meeting, and every function where you can learn more about effective writing, speaking, and listening skills.

Become a Desirable Employee

A strong work ethic will be another valuable quality that sets you apart from other job seekers. A work ethic can include a variety of characteristics, including your pride, passion, professionalism, ability to work on a team, and your ability to adapt, grow, and change. Your work ethic is how you perform at work without a job description, constant supervision, or someone threatening you.

Practice Loyalty and Trustworthiness

Loyalty to your employer is a highly valued trait. However, one's loyalty cannot be measured by a resume or determined by a simple interview. Proving that you have the characteristics of loyalty and trustworthiness comes over time. It may take years to establish loyalty and trustworthiness with your company and within your industry, but with hard work, dedication, and honesty, it can and will be achieved. Be forewarned, however, it may take years to build trust, but it only takes seconds to destroy it.

Use Critical-Thinking Skills

The ability to think your way through problems and challenges is highly valued by employers. Employers are looking for people who can distinguish fact from opinion; identify fallacies; analyze, synthesize, and determine the value of a piece of information; think beyond the obvious;

see things from varying angles; and arrive at sound solutions. They also want people who possess the emotional intelligence to critically and creatively work to resolve challenges.

Manage Your Priorities Well

Setting priorities and managing time are essential to success in today's stressful workplace. Today, maybe more than any other time in mankind's history, we are faced with more and more to do and what seems like less and less time in which to do it. Your success depends on how well you manage your priorities both personally and professionally. Priority management not only involves getting today's work accomplished, it also involves the ability to plan for your personal and professional future. Use your time wisely at work, at home, and in leisure.

Stay Current and Build Transferable Skills

Keeping your skills and knowledge current is essential to your success. Building skills that can be transferred from one position to another is essential in today's workplace. Fine-tuning your computer skills can set you apart from many of today's applicants. Your skills need to include the ability to work with word processing programs, spreadsheets, databases, PowerPoint, Prezi, social media, and document sharing programs.

Continue to Get Experience and Education

Never stop learning! You may not want to hear it, but your education will never end. You will eventually complete your formal schooling, but as long as you are working in today's global economy, you will need to keep abreast of the changes in your field. Seek out opportunities to expand your knowledge base. Get certified in areas that will make you more marketable. Take a continuing education course to brush up on changing workplace skills. Make yourself the best, most knowledgeable, well-rounded applicant in the field.

Avoid Internet and Social Media Blunders

Don't let social media mistakes come back to haunt you and cause you to miss out on your dream job! You may think that posting that photo of yourself half-naked with a bottle of Jim Beam in one hand and a stuffed poodle in the other is cute and that your friends will love it. They may. Your current or future employer may not. What you post online today may very well come back to haunt you in the future—even if you remove it, it can still be accessed. You may not lose your current position over a crazy, spur-of-the-moment posting, but it may cost you a future position. You may tell yourself that your Facebook, LinkedIn, or your web page is private and no one's business, but remember, nothing is private online and everything is someone's business in the world of business.

Watch Your Credit Rating

Building a good credit rating is one of the most important jobs you have. Really? My credit rating? What in the world does my credit score have to do with my employment. The answer? A great deal. More and more, employers are accessing your credit history and score as a part of the hiring procedure. Why? Because some employers believe that your credit history paints a clear picture of your working future. Bad credit history means a bad employee. Missed payments means missed work. Low credit score means low morale. Careless errors mean careless

job performance. This is just one of the many ways that your credit history and score can follow you for years.

Remain Openminded

Accept and appreciate a highly diverse workplace and the inherent differences and cultures that will be commonplace. You will need to develop the ability to listen to others with whom you disagree or with whom you may have little in common and learn from them and their experiences. The ability to learn a new language, even if your mastery is only at a primitive, broken, conversational level, and the ability to conduct yourself in a respectable and professional style will set you apart from other employees.

Polish Your Human Relation Skills

Polish your people skills and learn to get along with people from all walks of life. We saved this one for last, certainly not because it is least important, but because this quality is an overriding characteristic of everything listed previously. Employers are looking for individuals who have "people skills." This concept goes so much further than being a team player; it goes to the heart of many workplaces. It touches on your most basic nature, and it draws from your most inner self. The ability to get along with grouchy, cranky, mean, disagreeable, burned-out co-workers is, indeed, a rare quality. But don't be mistaken, there are those who do this, and do it well. Peak performers, or those at the "top of their game," have learned that this world is made up of many types of people and there is never going to be a time when one of those cranky, grumpy people is not in our midst. Smile. Be nice. Remain positive.

> *"You want to be the most educated, the most brilliant, the most exciting, the most versatile, the most creative individual in the world because then, you can give it away. The only reason you have anything is to give it away."*
>
> —Leo Buscaglia, Ph.D.

BUILDING LASTING SUCCESS

Can You Really Create Your Future?

Is it really possible to draft a blueprint of your own future? Is it possible to "create success"? The answer is yes. The process of creating success begins with the internal understanding that you have the power, the passion, and the capacity to **be** successful—to reach your chosen goals. It has been said that those people who are not out there creating their own future deserve the future that will be handed to them. You can be a person who creates the future for yourself and your family. Your education is one of the most important steps in this process because your education will give you options and alternatives. It will also help you create opportunities, and, according to Leo Buscaglia (1982), writer and speaker, the healthiest people in the world are the people with the most alternatives.

"*So how do I create a successful future with more options,*" you may be asking. The formula is simple, but the action required is not—and have no doubt, *action* **is** *required*. The formula consists of four steps:

1. The willingness to set clear, realistic goals and the ability to visualize the results of those goals
2. The ability to recognize your strengths and build on them
3. The ability to recognize your weaknesses or challenges and work to improve them
4. The passion and desire to work at your zenith every single day to make your goals and dreams a reality

> "*Though no one can go back and make a brand new start, anyone can start from now and make a brand new ending.*"
> —Carl Bard

Simple? The first three are rather simple. Number four is the kicker. Truthfully, most people have little trouble with the first three, it is the work involved with number four that causes most people to give up and never reach their fullest potential—and be handed a future over which they had little say in creating. You can create your own future, your own success, and your own alternatives.

Coming to the realization that there is no "easy street" and no "roads paved with good intentions" is also important to creating your success. In his landmark book, *Good to Great*, Jim Collins (2001) suggests that once you decide to be great, your life will never be easy again. Rid yourself of the notion that there is some easy way out, that school will be easy, or that your education will make your professional life easier. Success requires hard, passionate work on a daily basis. This passionate work may require you to change some of your thoughts, actions, and beliefs. That is what this chapter, and indeed this entire course, is about: creating success through positive change.

How can your college classes help you grow, change, and prosper?

YOUR EDUCATION AND YOU

Why Is It the Partnership of a Lifetime?

What can a college education do for you? The list will certainly vary depending on whom you ask, but basically, colleges can help you develop in the areas listed below. As you read through the list, place a checkmark beside the statements that most accurately reflects which skills you hope to gain from attending classes at your institution. If there are other skills that you desire to achieve from your education, write them at the end of the list.

_____ Grow more self-sufficient and self-confident.

_____ Establish and strengthen your personal identity.

_____ Understand more about the global world in which you live.

_____ Become a more involved citizen in social and political issues.

_____ Become more open-minded.

_____ Learn to manage your emotions and reactions more effectively.

_____ Understand the value of thinking, analyzing, and problem solving.

_____ Expand and use your ethical and moral thinking and reasoning skills.

_____ Develop superior computer and information literacy skills.

_____ Manage your personal resources, such as time and money.

_____ Become more proficient at written, oral, and nonverbal communication.

_____ Grow more understanding and accepting of different cultures.

_____ Become a lifelong learner.

_____ Become more financially independent.

_____ Enter a career field that you enjoy.

_____

_____

Which skill is _the_ most important to you?

_____

_____

_____

Why?

_____

_____

_____

What plans will you put into action to hone and master this skill?

_____

_____

_____

CREATING SUCCESS THROUGH POSITIVE CHANGE

How Can You Bring Positive, Lasting Change to Your Daily Life?

Why is change so important to you and your future? Quite simply, change that you direct creates opportunities for you to grow and prosper in ways you may have never imagined. It allows you to become and remain competitive. It allows you to actively live in a world that is fluid and unpredictable. There are several things you need to know about creating success in your life through positive change. Consider the following ideas:

1. **Change is a skill.** Change is a *learned skill* that any willing person can do. Period. Public speaking is a skill, learning how to drive a car is a skill, and just like those activities, learning to change is a skill, too. You'll need to familiarize yourself with the tools to learn this skill.

2. **Change takes time**. Change does not happen immediately at the snap of your fingers. If you've ever taken piano, guitar, or drum lessons, you know it took time to learn how to play these instruments because it is a skill—just like change. You did not learn to play overnight, just as you won't learn everything about math or nursing in one semester. Often, change is a slow, systematic series of events that eventually leads you to your desired end.

DID YOU

MICHAEL OHER was one of twelve children born to Denise Oher in Memphis, Tennessee. His mother was a crack cocaine addict and an alcoholic who gave her children very little attention. His father was an absentee father, in and out of prison, and murdered in prison when Michael was a high school senior. Michael had to repeat the first and second grades, and attended eleven different schools during his first nine years of education. When Michael was only seven, he was placed in foster care. He moved back and forth from homelessness to foster care during the next several years.

Michael was fortunate that an acquaintance encouraged him to apply for admission to Briarcrest Christian School. At Briarcrest, Michael was named Division II Lineman of the Year and First Team Tennessee All State. His biggest break came when Leigh Anne and Sean Tuohy, who had two children at Briarcrest, took him into their home and eventually adopted him. Not only did they give him a stable, comfortable, and loving family, they hired a private tutor who spent twenty hours a week with Michael helping him catch up. He improved his 0.76 GPA to 2.52, which allowed him to attend the University of Mississippi on a football scholarship. He excelled at Ole Miss and went on to sign a $13.8 million contract with the Baltimore Ravens and became a star in the National Football League. A movie about his life, *The Blind Side,* was a major hit for which Sandra Bullock won an Academy Award.

3. **Change requires an "attitude adjustment."** A contestant on the TV show, *America's Got Talent,* was being interviewed about her chances of success on the show. Queen Emily was an African American, single mother working full-time. She had given up her dream of being a professional singer years earlier to raise her children. She stated that before her audition, she stood and looked in the mirror crying. She thought that her time has passed and her dream was never going to happen. Then, she changed her thinking and began to say, Why not me? As corny or hokey as it may sound, her attitude adjustment was the key to her being able to change her life. She auditioned, surpassed thousands of contestants, and was invited to Los Angeles as one of five finalists. After *America's Got Talent,* she performed in a major show in Las Vegas, Nevada.

4. **Change demands action**. While circumstances and desire may drive the need for change in your life, don't lose sight of the fact that, ultimately, change is an action. It is something you must do—mentally, physically, spiritually, and intellectually. Just as Queen Emily from the previous example knew, if she didn't take action, her life was not going to change.

5. **Change is about working toward something, not running away from something**. If you want true, lasting, meaningful change in your life, you have to think about it as working toward good, positive, useful things, not as running away from bad, negative, unpleasant things. "Working toward" is *positive and internal*. "Running away from" is *negative and external*. Try to work **toward a goal** and not **run from a problem**.

6. **Change is about letting go and holding on**. As with any new endeavor, you will have to decide what is working in your life and what is not. By doing so, you can decide what you need to hold onto and what you finally need to let go of. You will want to hold onto the positive strengths and talents you have, while letting go of the negative, destructive attitudes that you may have held in the past.

7. **Change is accomplished by having a clear, focused, directed goal**. To change something in your life, you will need to develop a clear, realistic, simple path to make that change. You may need to divide the change into smaller bits so that it does not seem so overwhelming. In their book *Switch* (2010), Chip and Dan Heath support shrinking the change—that big change comes from a succession of small changes. They state, "Big problems are rarely solved with big solutions. Instead, they are most often solved by a sequence of small solutions, sometimes over weeks, sometimes over decades"(p. 44). If you want to change your life and lose 50 pounds, you should decide to lose five pounds first. *Just five pounds*—not fifty. After the first five, your goal will be to lose five more. Before you know it, you've lost 30, 40, then

50 pounds. A smaller, clearer focus helps you bring about the change and not get bogged down in the massive struggle to lose all 50 pounds.

THE M & M THEORY

What Have Your *Money* and Your *Mama* Got to Do with It?

What is the M & M Theory? It is quite simple really. We all pay attention to and try to protect the things that matter most to us. Your "**M**oney and your **M**ama" are symbolic of what you care about. Most people care deeply about what happens to their families, their income, their friends, their careers, and the environment. Most people also care and are concerned about the facts presented regarding our ever-changing world.

However, in the hustle and bustle of finding daycare, studying for classes, working a full-time job, cleaning the house, helping the kids with homework, and trying to prepare a meal from time-to-time, we may lose sight of some of the most important things in our lives. Try to keep this thought in mind: *your education is important, too*. In fact, it is of paramount importance to your future on many levels—culturally, socially, intellectually, and in preparing you for the future. Your education is a part of the M & M Theory because it involves your money—the future financial health for you and your family.

According to one of the leading research sources in higher education, *The Chronicle of Higher Education* ("A Profile of This Year's Freshmen," 2011), first-year students had a variety of thoughts regarding a college education and money. Of the 200,000 students who responded to their survey, 85 percent responded that "***the ability to get a better job***" was an essential objective for going to college. Seventy-two percent responded that an important reason for going to college was the "***ability to make more money***."

According to the United States Census Bureau, in their annual report, *Education and Training Pay* (2011), people with college degrees can earn considerably more than those who do not have a degree. For example, those with a Bachelor's degree average approximately $22,800 *more per year* in earnings than those with only a high school education. People with an Associate's degree average approximately $10,000 more per year in earnings than those with only a high school education. For a complete look at the earning power of U.S. citizens aged 25 and older, see Figure 1.2.

> "Forget mistakes. Forget failures. Forget everything except what you're going to do now...and do it."
>
> —Will Durant

Figure 1.2 Annual Earnings and Unemployment by Level of Education

Unemployment Rate	Degree	Mean Earnings
2.40%	Professional degree	$103,411
1.90%	Doctorate degree	$ 88,867
4.00%	Master's degree	$ 69,958
5.40%	Bachelor's degree	$ 57,026
7.00%	Associate's degree	$ 44,086
9.20%	Some college, no degree	$ 40,556
10.3%	High school graduate	$ 34,197
14.9%	Less than high school graduate	$ 27,470

Source: Data from U.S. Bureau of the Census, Department of Labor (2011).

By focusing on money in this section, we do not mean to suggest that the only reason for attending college is to make more money. As a matter of fact, we feel that it is a secondary reason. Many people *without college degrees* earn huge salaries each year. However, as the data above suggest, traditionally those with college degrees *earn **more** money* and *experience **less** unemployment*. Basically, college should make the road to financial security easier, but college should also be a place where you learn to make decisions about your values, your character, and your future. College can also be a place where you make decisions about the changes that need to occur in your life so that you can effectively manage and prosper in an ever-changing world, and where you learn the skills to change and continue to grow long after you graduate.

THE CULTURE OF COLLEGE

What Are the Basic Truths about College Success?

In your lifetime, you will experience many things that influence and alter your views, goals, and livelihood, including travel, relationships, and personal victories or setbacks. However, few experiences will have a greater influence than your college experience. A college education can help you realize your hopes, fulfill your dreams, and break down social and economic walls. To get the most from your college experience and to lay a path to success, it will be important to look at your expectations and the vast differences between high school, jobs you may have held, and the culture of your institution. This section will introduce you to some of the changes you can expect.

BASIC TRUTH 1

Success Is About Choices, Sacrifices, and Making Intelligent Transitions

Life is a series of choices. Hard choices. Easy choices. Right Choices. Wrong Choices. Nevertheless, the quality of *your life* is determined by the *choices you make* and your willingness to evaluate your life and determine if changes are in order. You will have many important and hard choices in the near future, such as deciding whether to devote your time to studying or partying, whether to ask for help in classes that challenge you or give up and drop out, or whether to make the sacrifices needed for your future success or take the easy road. Those choices will determine the quality of your future. Some of the choices that you make will force you to step beyond your comfort zone, to move to places that may frighten you or make you uncomfortable. That's OK. That's good. In fact, that's very good.

So what is a **comfort zone?** It sounds cozy, doesn't it? Warm and fuzzy. However, do not let the term fool you. A comfort zone is not necessarily a happy and comfortable place. It is simply a place where you are familiar with your surroundings and don't have to work too hard. It is where you feel confident of your abilities, but it is also a place where your growth stops. *It can be a prison, and staying there is a cop-out.* Successful people who have won personal and professional victories know that moving beyond one's comfort zone helps in nurturing change, reaching your potential, and creating opportunities for positive growth.

What sacrifices do you think you'll need to make in your personal life to be academically successful?

BASIC TRUTH 2

Your Education Is a Two-Way Street

Perhaps the first thing that you will notice about higher education is that you have to **give** in order to **receive**. Not only do you have expectations of your institution and instructors, but your institution and instructors also have expectations, great expectations of you. To be successful you will need to accept substantially more responsibility for your education than you may have in the past. By attending this institution, you have agreed to become a part of its community, values, and policies. You now have the responsibility to stand by its code of academic and moral conduct, and you have the responsibility of giving your very best to every class and organization in which you are involved. And, you have a responsibility to **yourself** to approach this new world with an open mind and curious enthusiasm. In return, your school will be responsible for helping you reach your fullest potential and live the life you desire.

> *"You gain strength, experience, and confidence by every experience where you stop to look fear in the face. You must do the thing that you think you cannot."*
> —Eleanor Roosevelt

BASIC TRUTH 3

You're In Charge Here—It's All About Self-Motivation and Self-Responsibility

One person and *only* one person has the power to determine your thoughts and the direction of your future. **It is you!** You will decide the direction of your future. You are *not* a victim and you will not be treated as a victim at this college. You will not be allowed to use "victim excuses" or employ the "victim mentality." This is all about you and your desire to change your life. Higher education is not about others doing the work, but rather about you finding internal motivation and accepting responsibility for your actions, your decisions, your choices, and yourself. It is not about making excuses and blaming others. *You are in charge here.* This is *your* education, and no one else will be responsible for acquiring the knowledge and skills you will need to survive and thrive. No one will be able to "give you" personal motivation.

Regardless of your circumstances, that late paper for English is not your husband's fault. That missed lab report is not your child's problem. Your tardiness is not your mother's mistake. That unread chapter is not your partner's liability. Likewise, that 98 you scored on your drug calculation test is yours. That A you got on your paper about the criminal justice system is yours. That B+ you got on your first math test is yours. This is about **you!** Your life. Your future. Your attitude is going to greatly affect your possibility of success.

Consider Figure 1.3 describing the differences between a "victim" and a "victor."

BASIC TRUTH 4

Self-Management Will Be Your Key to Success

A major transition coming your way involves the workload for your courses and the choices you will need to make regarding your schedule and time. You may be assigned a significant amount of reading as homework; in fact, the amount of reading that your classes demand is usually a shock to many students. Although you may have only two or three classes in one day, the basic guideline is that for every hour spent in class, a minimum of 2–3 hours should be spent in review and preparation for the next class.

Quick math: if you are taking 5 classes and are in class for 15 hours per week, you need to spend 30 hours studying; this makes a 45-hour week—5 hours more than a normal work week for most people! Not I, you may say, and you may be right. It all depends on how wisely you use your time, how difficult the work is, and the strength of your academic background.

Successful Decisions
AN ACTIVITY FOR CRITICAL REFLECTION

After the first week of classes, Devon is very disheartened about the difficulty of the classes for which he is registered. He did not think that he was going to have so much reading or homework, and he never thought the instructors would be so demanding. He has never been strong at math, but he is just floored at how difficult his beginning math course is. He failed his first test. He passed his first essay in English, but only with a grade of C. He is seriously considering dropping out. It is just too much. It is more than he expected.

Devon knows, however, that he has to succeed. He looked at his current financial situation, his dead-end job, and his desire to work in a health profession. Dropping out would never get him there. Dropping out would never make him a better, more prepared person. Dropping out would never afford him the opportunity to provide a better life for his family.

However, Devon feels that he is just too far behind to catch up. He is at a loss as to what to do.

In your own words, what would you suggest that Devon do at this point? Pretend that Devon is enrolled at your institution. List at least two additional things that he could do to ensure his success and not drop out. Think about what services are offered and what people might be of assistance to him.

1. _____
   _____

2. _____
   _____

Figure 1.3 Victim and Victor Profile

The Victim	The Victor
The victim blames others for his/her problems.	The victor accepts responsibility for what happens in his/her life.
The victim procrastinates and makes excuses for not doing a good job.	The victor thinks ahead and plans for success.
The victim sees adversity as a permanent obstacle.	The victor sees adversity as a way to become stronger.
The victim constantly complains and has a negative mentality about most things.	The victor has an optimistic attitude and is pleasant to be with most of the time.
The victim does just enough to get by and is happy with poor grades and mediocre accomplishments.	The victor works hard to raise his/her level of achievement and constantly seeks to improve.
The victim lets life happen without trying to make things happen.	The victor has a plan and sets goals and works every day to make positive things happen.
The victim is always late and often absent, and always has an excuse.	The victor is on time, prepared, and rarely ever negligent regarding his/her responsibilities.
The victim hangs out with negative people who are trouble-makers and party animals with low ambition and a poor work ethic.	The victor surrounds himself/herself with people who are working hard to make something of themselves and who are encouraging and motivating.

BASIC TRUTH 5

This Is Not High School

It sounds so simple, but this is perhaps the most universal and important truth discussed here. College is very different from high school *or* the world of work and perhaps one of the most different places you'll ever encounter. The expectations for four different areas are outlined in Figure 1.4. Review each area carefully and consider your past experiences as you study the differences.

Figure 1.4 · A Guide to Understanding Expectations

	High School	College	Work
Punctuality and Attendance	**Expectations** ■ State law requires that you attend a certain number of days ■ The hours in the day are managed for you ■ There may be some leeway in project dates	**Expectations** ■ Attendance and participation in class are strictly enforced by many professors ■ Most professors will not give you extensions on due dates ■ You decide your own schedule and plan your own day	**Expectations** ■ You are expected to be at work and on time on a daily basis
	Penalties ■ You may get detention ■ You may not graduate ■ You may be considered a truant ■ Your grades may suffer	**Penalties** ■ You may not be admitted to class if you are late ■ You may fail the assignment if it is late ■ Repeated tardiness is sometimes counted as an absence ■ Most professors do not take late assignments	**Penalties** ■ Your salary and promotions may depend on your daily attendance and punctuality ■ You will most likely be fired for abusing either
Teamwork and Participation	**Expectations** ■ Most teamwork is assigned and carried out in class ■ You may be able to choose teams with your friends ■ Your grade may reflect your participation	**Expectations** ■ Many professors require teamwork and cooperative learning teams or learning communities ■ Your grade will depend on your participation ■ Your grade may depend on your entire team's performance ■ You will probably have to work on the project outside of class	**Expectations** ■ You will be expected to participate fully in any assigned task ■ You will be expected to rely on coworkers to help solve problems and increase profits ■ You will be required to attend and participate in meetings and sharing sessions ■ You will be required to participate in formal teams and possess the ability to work with a diverse workforce
	Penalties ■ If you don't participate, you may get a poor grade ■ You may jeopardize the grade of the entire team	**Penalties** ■ Lack of participation and cooperation will probably cost you a good grade ■ Your team members will likely report you to the professor if you do not participate and their grades suffer as a result	**Penalties** ■ You will be "tagged" as a non–team player ■ Your lack of participation and teamwork will cost you raises and promotions ■ You will most likely be terminated

(continued)

	High School	**College**	**Work**
Personal Responsibility and Attitude	**Expectations** ■ Teachers may coach you and try to motivate you ■ You are required by law to be in high school regardless of your attitude or responsibility level	**Expectations** ■ You are responsible for your own learning ■ Professors will assist you, but there is little "hand holding" or personal coaching for motivation ■ College did not choose you; you chose it and you will be expected to hold this attitude toward your work	**Expectations** ■ You are hired to do certain tasks and the company or institution fully expects this of you ■ You are expected to be positive and self-motivated ■ You are expected to model good behavior and uphold the company's work standards
	Penalties ■ You may be reprimanded for certain attitudes ■ If your attitude prevents you from participating, you may fail the class	**Penalties** ■ You may fail the class if your attitude and motivation prevent you from participating	**Penalties** ■ You will be passed over for promotions and raises ■ You may be reprimanded ■ You may be terminated
Ethics and Credibility	**Expectations** ■ You are expected to turn in your own work ■ You are expected to write your own papers, without plagiarizing	**Expectations** ■ You are expected to turn in your own work ■ You are expected to write your own papers, without plagiarizing ■ You are expected to conduct research and complete projects based on college and societal standards	**Expectations** ■ You will be required to carry out your job in accordance with company policies, laws, and moral standards ■ You will be expected to use adult vision and standards
	Penalties ■ You may get detention or suspension ■ You will probably fail the project	**Penalties** ■ Poor ethical decisions may land you in front of a student or faculty ethics committee or result in expulsion from the college ■ You will fail the project as well as the class ■ You may face deportation if your visa is dependent on your student status	**Penalties** ■ Poor ethical decisions may cause you to be severely reprimanded or terminated, or in some cases could even result in legal consequences

BASIC TRUTH 6

Eliminating the "This Isn't Harvard Syndrome" Will Be Essential to Your Success

Some students enter college with little or no perception of how much work is involved or how much effort it is going to take to be successful. They do not think that the local college could possibly be "*that difficult*." Many even perceive his or her institution to be less rigorous than what it actually is. "It's only Grace College," or "It's only Trion State University," some might reason. They do not think that the college they are attending has the academic standards of Harvard, Yale, or Stanford University. The truth is that your college education is what *you make*

from ORDINARY to *Extraordinary*

Bill Clayton, ACE Certified Personal Trainer/ Post-Rehabilitation Specialist Owner/Operator, Clayton Personal Fitness—Las Vegas, NV

"I was . . ." Those are powerful words. For example, *I was* the manager of the gardening department of a major retail chain. *I was* an employee in a shop that prints and mails inserts and flyers. *I was* a rock band drummer for several bands. *I was* a crystal meth addict. Yes . . . *I was!*

It seems strange to write that now, but the term, "I was. . . ." is impossible to erase. My friends and clients often ask me how I managed to go from the life of a meth addict to a personal trainer. The journey was a strange one and often difficult.

I began playing the drums when I was six years old, and by the time I was eight, I had my first "garage band." Writing and playing music were my only passions. They were my life. After high school, I worked many odd jobs, but my love of performing never waned.

In my twenties, I had a band that steadily played gigs and I was living the life of a rocker. We traveled. We sang. We partied. We traveled some more and we partied some more . . . and some more. Before I really realized what was happening with me, I had become addicted to meth. It was my life. I hung around people who used with me and they became my family. I met Kathy, the woman I would eventually marry, while performing with my band. She and I hit it off even though she knew of my addiction. One evening after we were married, Kathy and I were talking and she mentioned that she would like to have children one day. I wanted children, too. At that moment, the strangest thing came to my mind. I thought, "If she gets pregnant, I'll stop doing meth." How could I be so messed up that I would work to abolish my addiction for a child not yet born, *but* I would not consider trying to stop just for **me**? That was my wake-up call. I knew I had to change my life. I was 29 years old.

I was one of the lucky ones. I was able to stop "cold turkey" on my own. I know that others are not so lucky. I began to look at my life and tried to determine what I wanted to do. I had to seriously evaluate every aspect of who and what I was. I knew that I had to set goals to get my life back on track.

I had been in a life-threatening motorcycle accident years earlier and remembered the great care I received from my physical therapist. So I began to look at PT programs, and that is when I found the personal trainer program at our local college. Something about this was very attractive to me. Again, I was lucky. I happened to find my passion and my life's vocation without much struggle.

Today, after working through my addiction, surviving a divorce, and mourning the death of my mom, I can say without a doubt that I am one of the luckiest people on earth. Because I was willing to change and stayed committed to finding a better life, I own my own gym, hold certifications from every major fitness and rehabilitation organization in America, and count each day as a true gift.

> *My friends often ask how I managed to go from a crystal meth addict to a personal trainer.*

EXTRAORDINARY REFLECTION

Mr. Clayton mentions that he was one of the "lucky ones." What role do you think luck plays in one's success? Is there a difference between luck, readiness, and action? If so, what is it?

of it. When you graduate and you are interviewing for a job, the name of your institution may hold some weight, but, your skills, passion, experiences, knowledge, and thinking abilities will be the paramount "tipping point."

True, you may not be at Harvard or Yale, but the rigor of your programs, the amount of reading required, the level of math skills needed, and the degree to which critical thinking, communication, and information literacy skills will be required may surprise you. We think that it is important to dispel the "This Isn't Harvard Syndrome" as quickly as possible so that you can prepare yourself for the coursework and requirements ahead and make the most of your college experience.

BUILDING A NEW YOU

How Can You Change Your Life Through SMART Goal Setting?

Positive change can be brought about in several ways, but the most effective ways are through SMART goal setting and having a "change plan." SMART is an acronym for goals that are **S**pecific, **M**easurable, **A**ttainable, **R**elevant, and **T**ime-Bound (Doran, 1981).

> *"Decide you want it more than you're afraid of it."*
> —Bill Cosby

Think about what you really want or what you need to change in your life. More importantly, think about why you want "this thing" and what it is going to mean to your life. By thinking about what you want, what needs to change, and where you want to be, goals become easier.

Goal setting itself is relatively easy—it is the personal commitment and self-motivation that requires detailed attention, hard work, and unbridled passion. The most vital step toward reaching your goal is making a personal commitment to yourself that you are going to achieve it and then committing all of your possible resources toward the completion of that goal.

Characteristics of SMART Goals

The following characteristics will help you in your quest to bring about change through effective goal setting. Goals should be:

- **Specific.** Your goals should have a direct purpose and direction. Your goals should not be vague but rather state what, when, where, and why.
- **Measurable.** Your goal needs to be concrete and measurable in some way. Avoid such terms as "earn a lot," or "lose some."
- **Attainable.** Your goal should be a challenge for you, but also within reason based on your abilities.
- **Relevant.** To attain a difficult goal, you must want it very badly. You should never work toward something just because *someone else* wants it. The goal must be realistic and desirable to you. To achieve a goal, you must really believe it is within your capacity to reach it.
- **Time-Bound.** Your goals may need to be adapted to changing circumstances in your life. You should also have a challenging but realistic deadline.

How to Write Your Goals to Bring About Positive Change

"I will pass my next math test with a B or better" is an example of a short-term goal. *"I will purchase my first home in seven to ten years"* is a long-term goal. During your time at school, more of your goals may be short term rather than long term, but you can certainly begin setting both. Goals can be lofty and soaring, but great goals can also be as simple as *"I will spend two hours at the park with my children tomorrow afternoon."*

Well-written, exciting, and effective goals include:

- A Goal Statement with a Target Date
- Action steps
- A narrative statement
- An "I Deserve It" statement
- A personal signature

Your **goal statement** should be specific and measurable; that is, it should entail some tangible evidence of its achievement and it should have a **target date**, or timeline for accomplishing your goal. Your goal statement *must* use an action verb. An example of a goal statement with an action verb and target date is: "I *will* lose 10 pounds in six weeks" or "I *am going to* join a campus club by the fifth week of this term." This is a much more powerful statement than: "I am thinking about joining a club" or "I wanna get a new car."

What exactly is it going to take to achieve your biggest, most important goals?

After you write the goal statement, you'll need to create **specific action steps** that explain exactly what you are going to do to reach your goal. There is no certain number of steps; it all depends on your goal and your personal commitment. An example of action steps for weight loss might be: (1) I *will* walk up three flights of steps daily, (2) I *will* meet with a personal trainer, (3) I *will* set an appointment with a nutrition counselor.

The next step is to write a **narrative statement** about what your goal accomplishment will mean to you and how your life will change because of reaching this goal. For example, if your goal is to lose 30 pounds, paint a "verbal picture" of how your life is going to look once this goal has been reached. Your verbal picture may include statements such as: "I'll be able to wear nicer clothes," "I'll feel better," "I'll be able to ride my bicycle again," and "My self-esteem will be stronger." If your goals don't offer you significant rewards, you are not likely to stick to your plan.

Figure 1.5 SMART Goals

Goal Setting

S Specific
M Measurable
A Attainable
R Relevant
T Time-bound

Next, write two reasons why you deserve this goal. This is called your **"I Deserve It" statement.** It may seem simple, but this is a complex question. Many people do not follow through on their goals because, deep down, they don't feel they deserve them. The narrative statement helps you understand how your life will look once the goal is met, but your "I deserve it" statement asks you to consider *why* you deserve this goal.

Finally, **sign your goal statement and post it** where you can see it daily. This is an imperative step in that *your signature* shows that you are making a personal commitment to see this goal to fruition. This is your name. Use it with pride. Posting your goal will help you focus on it daily. Use the goal sheet in Figure 1.6 to build your goals.

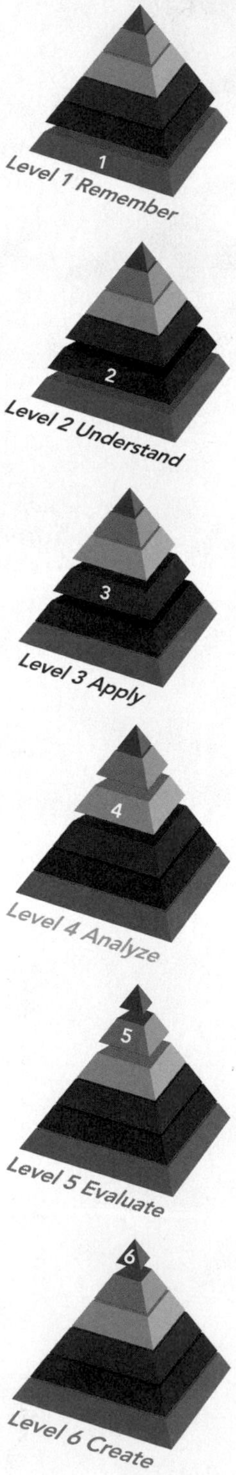

Figure 1.6 **Goal Sheet**

My Personal Goal

To help you get started, use this goal-setting sheet as a template for this and future goals.

Name _____

Goal Statement (with action verb and target date) _____
_____

Action Steps (concrete things you plan to do to reach your goal)

1. _____

2. _____

3. _____

4. _____

5. _____

Narrative Statement (how your life will look when you reach your goal) _____
_____
_____

What **obstacles** will you need to overcome to reach this goal? _____
_____

I deserve this goal because:

1. _____

2. _____

I hereby make this commitment to myself.

_____   _____
My Signature   Date

Level 1 Remember

Level 2 Understand

Level 3 Apply

Level 4 Analyze

Level 5 Evaluate

Level 6 Create

ONE LAST, IMPORTANT WORD ABOUT YOUR GOALS

What Happens When Your Aspirations and Behaviors Collide?

Earlier in the chapter you read about change and how to bring about a positive change in your life. One of the ideas discussed was "***change demands action***." Your goals demand action, too. Many students are dismayed when they realize that goals don't just happen. Dreams and plans and aspirations are fine, but the ending can be quite painful if you don't put forth the effort to bring them to fruition. To reach your goals and meet your aspirations, you may have to work harder than you've ever worked in the past. You may have to adjust the way you approach things, you may have to adjust the way you think about involvement, and, most importantly, you may have to change the level of action that you put toward your goals.

The point at which many students leave college is the point at which their aspirations and behaviors collide. They realize that monumental changes are going to have to occur before their aspirations are met and they are simply not ready, willing, or able to make these monumental adjustments. Begin today working to employ healthy study habits, get involved in your institution's activities, work to get to know your instructors, counselors, and advisors, and reach out to people in class and beyond who can help you. Build on your strengths and work tirelessly to overcome your challenges. These steps will help you reach your goals and make your future aspirations a reality.

REFLECTIONS ON CHANGE AND GOAL SETTING

The transition from one place to another is seldom easy, even when the change is what you want. Entering college has given you the opportunity to assume new roles, develop new friendships, meet new people, work under different circumstances, and create a bountiful future. It is an opportunity to improve on who you are at this moment or to build an entirely new person if you choose to do so. Going to college gives you the opportunity to reflect on your strengths and consider areas where you might need to change. These changes form the very essence of the college experience; they create wonderful new experiences and help you discover who you really are and what you have to offer the world.

As you reflect upon this chapter, keep the following pointers in mind:

- Evaluate your reason(s) for attending college and what it means to your life.
- Understand and use the Essential Cornerstones for Success In a Changing World.
- Work hard to be a victor, not a victim.
- Don't just let change happen, get involved in your own life and learning.
- Use goal setting to help you direct changes in your life.

Knowledge
in Bloom

BRINGING POSITIVE CHANGE TO YOUR LIFE

Utilizes Levels 1–6 of the Taxonomy (See Bloom's Taxonomy at the front of this text)

After reading and reflecting thus far, you may have identified several changes that you need to make in your academic or personal life. Also, changes may have been thrust upon you by choices you or those around you have made. The following model provides a method for bring positive changes into your life and/or reshaping the changes over which you had little control.

Based on Bloom's Taxonomy, the **Change Implementation Model** asks you to consider questions and recommends actions at each level of learning. The chart moves from less difficult questions (levels 1, 2, 3) to more challenging questions (levels 4, 5, 6). To begin the change process in your life, follow the steps in this activity.

STEP 1

Review the steps of the **Change Implementation Model** based on Bloom's Taxonomy.

Level 1—Remember	*Describe* one behavior, belief, or action that you need to change in your life. Also, *list* the possible obstacles that you might encounter.
Level 2—Understand	*Explain* why this change needs to occur in order for you to be successful. Also, *give* two examples of the options available to you at your school, home, or in the community for making the desired change.
Level 3—Apply	*Using* the information from Levels 1 and 2, *show* your plan (action steps) to overcome the obstacles listed above.
Level 4—Analyze	*Compare* your current action steps to the steps you have previously taken to overcome obstacles and enact change. What conclusions can be drawn from this comparison?
Level 5—Evaluate	Pretend that someone very close to you asks you what you are doing with this plan and why. Write a detailed paragraph to *justify* what you are doing, why you need to do it, and how it is going to positively affect your life.
Level 6—Create	Based on the information you have gathered above from investigation and reflection, *design* your plan to bring about this change in your life. Consider using the SMART goal setting illustrated in this chapter to create a plan and action steps that are truly unique to you.

STEP 2

After studying the Change Implementation Model above, read the following fictional scenario in which you encounter difficulty in Accounting 101.

You enter your Accounting 101 class eager to take the first course in your major field. You are shocked to find that the professor begins lecturing on the first day. Not only is the material difficult to understand, so is the professor, whose first language is not English.

For homework, the professor assigns two chapters to read per class, but the lectures are not based on material found in the text. You try to study as you had in high school, but now you feel overwhelmed and isolated. The material is much harder.

After three weeks and a failed first test, you notice that the students who passed the test had formed study groups, something that you once thought only the brightest students practiced.

Using the Change Implementation Model, you decide to make positive changes in your study habits. As an example, plans for change are shown in Step 3.

STEP 3

Review this example and determine how you might use the **Change Implementation Model** to enact changes to save your grade in Accounting 101.

Level 1—Remembering	
Identify one behavior, belief, or action that you need to change in your life. Also, *list* the possible obstacles that you might encounter.	If I could, I would change my study habits in accounting and become stronger in my math skills. Obstacles: fear of change, shyness, pride, and time constraints
Level 2—Understanding	
Explain why this change needs to occur in order for you to be successful. Also, *give* two examples of the options available to you at your institution, home, or in the community for making the desired change.	Why change is needed: weak math skills causing me to fail accounting Institution: tutoring center and math lab, professor's office hours Community: aunt works in accounting office
Level 3—Applying	
Using the information from Levels 1 and 2, *show* your plan (action steps) to overcome the obstacles listed above.	Step 1—I will join a study group. Step 2—I will make an appointment for tutoring in the math lab. Step 3—I will talk to my advisor about available services. Step 3—I will plan at least five hours per week to study for my accounting class. Step 4—I will seek help from my aunt, who is an accountant.
Level 4—Analyzing	
Compare your current action steps to the steps you have previously taken to overcome obstacles and enact change. What conclusions can be drawn from this comparison?	Past: I took notes in class and looked over them before a test. New: I will join a study group and go to tutoring center and math lab. New: I will talk with my advisor. New: I will meet with my aunt for advice and assistance. Conclusion: In taking personal responsibility for my education, taking calculated risks to bring about change, and asking for help, I'm more likely to pass accounting.
Level 5—Evaluation	
Pretend that someone very close to you asks you what you are doing with this plan and why. Write a detailed paragraph to *justify* what you are doing, why you need to do it, and how it is going to positively affect your life.	I am working so hard to pass accounting because I want this degree and I want the knowledge of how to run my own business. If I don't change my habits, I will not pass accounting and I will not have this degree. Without this degree, I will most likely have to work in low-paying jobs for the rest of my life. By asking for help, spending more time studying, and spending more time around people who have some of the same interests, I can develop the skills to graduate, start my own business, and help my family out financially.

Level 6—Creating	
Based on the information you have gathered above from investigation and reflection, *design* your plan to bring about this change in your life. Consider using the SMART goal setting illustrated in this chapter to create a plan and action steps that are truly unique to you.	Goal: I *will* get involved with a study group, schedule a tutor, and spend at least five hours per week studying for accounting. I will do this by the end of this week. **Action Steps:** Step 1—I will join a study group/get accounting tutor. Step 2—I will talk to my advisor about available services. Step 3—I will study at least five hours per week for accounting class. Step 4—I will work with my boss to design a plan for more study time. Step 5—I will meet with my aunt once a week to get her help. Narrative Statement: By getting involved and not trying to go this alone, I will begin to enjoy college more and do better in my classes. I deserve this goal because I have the courage to ask for help and the intelligence to put my pride aside and seek assistance. I deserve to learn this material so that I can successfully run my own business.

STEP 4

After studying the **Change Implementation Model** example above, focus on a few things that you might want to change about your own academic life, such as study habits, motivation level, financial or priority management, or your attitude. Now, choose **one** of these major changes you wish to incorporate into your life from the list above. Using the **Change Implementation Model**, devise a strategy to effect this change. Complete each section carefully and thoughtfully, but make sure that Level Six contains concrete, doable action steps that will help you actually bring about this change. Remember, without action steps and ACTION, this change will not occur.

Level 1—Remembering	
Identify one behavior, belief, or action that you need to change in your life. Also, *list* the possible obstacles that you might encounter.	

Level 2—Understanding	
Explain why this change needs to occur in order for you to be successful. Also, *give* two examples of the options available to you at college, home, or in the community for making the desired change.	

Level 3—Applying	
Using the information from Levels 1 and 2, *show* your plan (action steps) to overcome the obstacles listed above.	

Level 4—Analyzing	
Compare your current action steps to the steps you have previously taken to overcome obstacles and enact change. What conclusions can be drawn from this comparison?	

Level 5—Evaluating	
Pretend that someone very close to you asks you what you are doing with this plan and why. Write a detailed paragraph to *justify* what you are doing, why you need to do it, and how it is going to positively affect your life.	

Level 6—Creating	
Based on the information you have gathered above from investigation and reflection; *design* your plan to bring about this change in your life. Consider using the SMART goal setting illustrated in this chapter to create a plan and action steps that are truly unique to you.	

SQ3R MASTERY STUDY SHEET

EXAMPLE QUESTION (FROM PAGE 5) Discuss two traits employers are seeking from today's employees?	**ANSWER:**
EXAMPLE QUESTION (FROM PAGE 11) What is the M & M Theory?	**ANSWER:**
AUTHOR QUESTION (FROM PAGE 6) Identify and discuss the Essential Cornerstones for Success in a Changing World.	**ANSWER:**
AUTHOR QUESTION (FROM PAGE 7) Why is it important to avoid social media blunders?	**ANSWER:**
AUTHOR QUESTION (FROM PAGE 8) List and discuss the four steps in bring about positive change to your life.	**ANSWER:**
AUTHOR QUESTION (FROM PAGE 18) What are the characteristics of SMART goals?	**ANSWER:**
AUTHOR QUESTION (FROM PAGE 18) Why must a goal be measurable?	**ANSWER:**
YOUR QUESTION (FROM PAGE ___)	**ANSWER:**
YOUR QUESTION (FROM PAGE ___)	**ANSWER:**
YOUR QUESTION (FROM PAGE ___)	**ANSWER:**
YOUR QUESTION (FROM PAGE ___)	**ANSWER:**
YOUR QUESTION (FROM PAGE ___)	**ANSWER:**

Finally, after answering these questions, recite this chapter's major points in your mind. Consider the following general questions to help you master this material.

- What is it about?
- What does it mean?
- What is the most important thing you learned and why?
- What are the key points to remember?

ENGAGE

DEVELOPING YOUR PERSONAL AND ACADEMIC MOTIVATION

"To be successful you need to find something to hold on to, something to motivate you, something to inspire you." —Tony Dorsett

ENGAGE

Why read this chapter?

Because you'll learn...

- The difference between internal and external motivation
- How to put adversity and failure into perspective
- The impact of self-esteem on your values, motivation, and attitude

Because you'll be able to...

- Define, discuss, and use the Cornerstones for Lifetime Success
- Identify your values and use them to develop a strong "Guiding Life Statement"
- Evaluate your self-image to build healthier self-esteem

Scan and QUESTION

Take a few moments, **scan this chapter,** and on page 47, write **five of your own questions** that you think will be important to your mastery of this material. You will also find five questions listed from your authors.

Example:

☑ **What is the difference between internal and external motivation?** (from page 30)

☑ **How can overcoming self-defeating behaviors help you become a better student?** (from page 35)

MyStudentSuccessLab

MyStudentSuccessLab is an online solution designed to help you acquire and develop (or hone) the skills you need to succeed. You will have access to peer-led video presentations and develop core skills through interactive exercises and projects.

Name: Brandon Sellers
Institution: Graduate! Aims Community College, Greely, Colorado
Major: Political Science

Brandon's unplanned journey to college began when he dropped out of the seventh grade in order to get a job to help his single mother pay the bills. Fifteen years and several construction jobs later, a disabling injury brought Brandon to the stark reality that, at age 29, he didn't have a plan for taking care of his two children. Construction was all he knew.

"I didn't think I could afford college," said Brandon. "I also knew I wasn't smart enough, since I only had a seventh grade education."

I met Brandon at new student orientation at Aims Community College, where he learned about various financial aid opportunities. That was when he realized that if he managed his money right, he could do this *"college thing."*

But three weeks into the semester, Brandon came close to calling the whole thing off. He had gotten his first test grade: 73 percent. He had studied very hard for this history test. The grade sent him over the edge—sitting at home crying like a baby.

An interview conducted and written by Shannon McCasland, Assistant Director of Student Life, Aims Community College, Greely, CO

"I was thinking: is this what I have to look forward to? Is this my future in college? I felt like I had let myself and my kids down. If I can't be successful at this, what the heck am I going to do?"

For many students, this would have been the end of the story, but not for Brandon. He met with his history professor and immediately knew this man cared about his future.

"The personal attention my professor extended to me that day is **the** driving force for why I stayed in college," said Brandon. "I wasn't just a number. I was somebody to a college professor!" That was Brandon's turning point.

"Every non-traditional student will hit a bump in the road somewhere during their first semester. It's a decision point. It's critical that someone is there to help the student navigate the challenges," said Brandon. "My history professor did that for me."

Brandon decided that to be 100% successful, he needed to give college everything he had—he was going to treat it like a job, including classes and extracurricular involvement.

As Brandon's student government advisor, I watched him meet his goals both inside and outside of the class-room walls. I watched his history professor give him the coveted Aims Distinguished Scholar Award. It was one of the happiest moments in my professional career when I got to place a call to Brandon for the college president, inviting him to be the commencement speaker. His story echoed in my mind as he told the graduating class they could be anything they wanted to be. It was no longer a cliché to him.

"I was totally humbled speaking at graduation," said Brandon. "I was remembering that day I went home crying. I was remembering how close I came to giving up."

"Aims really helped me believe that. I've always heard that but never believed it. Coming away from Aims, I know that it actually is true: I **can** be whatever I want to be. Before I came to college, I felt that's for people who have money and a high school education. But it doesn't matter what your background is. If you want to succeed, the tools are there."

Many doors have opened to Brandon since his graduation from Aims. He is transferring to the University of Northern Colorado with several scholarships.

"I've been given a unique opportunity to go to school and now it is my responsibility to share that with others."

THINK about it

1. How do tests, projects, and quiz scores affect your internal motivation? Have you been able to turn negative results into stronger internal motivation? If you make a bad grade, can you overcome the temptation to quit?

2. If the time ever arises when you feel like giving up and "going home," what types of plans do you have in place to overcome these feelings and persist?

THE POWER AND PASSION OF MOTIVATION

What Is the Difference Between Internal and External Motivation?

Motivation can change your life! *Read that statement again.* Motivation can change your life! Ask any successful business person. Ask your favorite athlete or actor. Ask your classmates who pass every exam, project, or paper with an A. It is their burning desire, their aspiration to succeed, to live an exceptional life, and to reach their goals that changed their lives and got them to where they are today. Motivation is a force that can transform your attitude, alter the course of your performance, intensify your actions, and illuminate your future. Motivation can help you live a life that reflects your true potential. Motivation can help you live a life beyond your grandest dreams.

If you have a need or desire to change your motivation level or attitude toward personal and academic success, there are steps you can take to help you with this goal. Some of the steps described in this chapter will be easy to implement, and others will greatly challenge you, but taken seriously, each step can assist you in discovering who you really are, what you want in life, and how to find the motivation you need to change. No one can do this for you.

> "The moment you begin to do what you really want to do, your life becomes a totally different kind of life."
>
> —B. Fuller

There are two types of motivation: **external** and **internal**. *External motivation* is the weaker of the two because, as the title suggests, there are *external forces or people* causing you to do something. You do not own it. External motivators may be things or people, such as your parents, spouse, or partner, pushing you to complete your degree; your supervisor telling you to do "x, y, or z" or you will be fired; or even your instructors giving you an exam to make sure you have read chapter two. You may do the things asked of you, but the reason for doing them is external. You did not necessarily choose to do them on your own.

Internal motivation is uniquely yours. It is *energy* inside of you, pushing **you** to go after what **you** want. Internal motivation is a strong and driving force because you own it. There are no external forces or people telling you that you must do it—it comes from your desire *to be something, to have something, to attain a goal that you truly desire, or to solve a problem.* Successful people live in the world of internal motivation, or find ways to convert external motivation into internal motivation.

A simple example of this conversion may be that your current degree requires you to take classes of which you cannot understand their value or purpose. You may ask yourself, *"Why would an art history major have to take an algebra class?"* The class is hard, math is not your thing, the chapters are frustrating and difficult to read, and math has little to do with your interests, career goals, or overall life plan. The challenge for you is to find an internal reason to move forward, a rationale for how math is going to help you, now and in the future. This is called *internalizing*. Perhaps you want to own your own art store or appraisal business, a business that will require the use of math. Internalizing the content of this math class and its requirements can motivate you to do well.

How can doing something you love and enjoy increase your motivation level?

By converting this external motivation (a requirement for your degree) into internal motivation (something that can help you run your business), the math class will become easier and more relevant because you have found a way to link it to your success, your goals, your money, your health, your family, and your overall life plan.

Figure 2.1 Seeing the Importance

Think about a class that is required for your degree. What class, or content/assignment within that class, seems to have no relevance to you or your career field? (You may have to look at your college catalog to check your degree requirements.) What courses do you think you are going to have to work hard to convert? One example is given below. We have also provided space for you to do several conversions.

My Major Is Theatre/Acting	How Can This Class Help Me in My Chosen Profession?
Seemingly irrelevant class, content, or assignment: **History** and writing a paper on the Reformation	✓ A class in history can help me understand the historical and social context in which the plays I'm studying were written. ✓ A class in history can help me understand more about scene design and period costumes.
My Major Is _____	How Can This Class Help Me In My Chosen Profession?
Seemingly irrelevant class, content, or assignment: _____	_____
Seemingly irrelevant class, content, or assignment: _____	_____

THE NEED TO BE MORE

What Is the Relationship Between Motivation and Maslow?

> *"An ocean lies between what is said and what is done."*
>
> —Italian Proverb

One important way to think about motivation is to consider the work of Abraham Maslow, a renowned psychologist who, in 1943, introduced his hierarchy of basic needs in his landmark paper, *A Theory of Human Motivation*. His basic premise is that *every* human being is motivated by a set of basic needs, and we will do whatever it takes to have these things in our lives. The bottom four levels are what he calls *deficiency needs*, and they include things such as the need for food, air, water, security, family, health, sexual intimacy, self-esteem, achievement, and respect from others. The top level is called a *psychological need* and it involves self-actualization, personal growth, and fulfillment. See Figure 2.2.

Self-actualization, the top level, is perhaps the most obscure and abstract to understand, but it is the most important when it comes to motivation. Maslow suggests that we all have a basic, driving desire to matter, to have a life where we are doing what we were meant to do. Self-actualization can also be described as living at our "peak" and being fully ourselves. Renowned psychologist, author, and speaker Dr. Wayne Dyer describes self-actualization as meaning: *"You **must** be what you **can** be."* By this he suggests that if you know you are living a life that is "less" than what you know you are capable of living, true happiness will never be yours.

Figure 2.2 **Maslow's Hierarchy of Basic Needs Triangle**

SELF-ACTUALIZATION
Personal growth, fulfillment, reaching your potential socially, compassion

ESTEEM NEEDS
Self-esteem, achievement, recognition, earning the respect of others, independence

LOVING/BELONGINGNESS NEEDS
Friendship, family, affection, relationships, belonging in work groups, sexual intimacy

SAFETY NEEDS
Security of body, security of employment, having resources, protection from the elements, law, order, stability

PHYSIOLOGICAL NEEDS
Basic life needs such as air, food, water, sleep, shelter, warmth, sex, excretion

If, indeed, self-actualization is a basic need in all of us then the theory holds that we all have a burning desire to do our best work, to live a life that matters, and to reach our fullest potential—"to be what we can be." It means that we want to be fulfilled in our lives and experience personal growth. For example, if you are taking a class that you do not really enjoy and don't know why you have to take this class, you may not be putting your best self forward. This may seem to be OK, but deep down inside, you know that you could, and *should*, do better. You know that you are not living up to your full potential and not fulfilling your purpose in class, at college, or in life. You know in your heart that you are not living at your peak and this will begin to gnaw at you until it affects other areas of your life.

CONQUERING THE GENERATION GAP

How Do You Make It and Stay Motivated When You're the First in the Family?

Many college students are *first-generation students*, meaning that their parents' highest level of education is a high school diploma or less. This may not seem like such a big deal, but it can be on many levels. If you are a first-generation student, you may not have the support and understanding of family members who know first-hand the pressures of what you're going through. It may seem as if they are not supportive. This could be true, but more than likely, they are unaware how to offer support because college is new for them, too. Therefore, it is so very important that you find support beyond what your family may be able to offer. You will encounter many people at your college who are first generation, and they can help guide you. Many non-first-generation students, faculty, staff, and personal friends will be able to offer you support, too.

In a personal survey, first-generation students responded that their reasons for attending college were to be well off financially and provide their children with better opportunities than they had. As you begin your studies, however, you may find that you face some resistance from some friends and family members. You may even find that some relationships suffer or end because of your pursuit of self-improvement. Don't let this discourage you. Again, this is one of the many changes that may occur in your personal life as you embark upon your college journey. Before ending a relationship, try talking to the other person and let them know that you still care about them, while holding fast to the notion that your own life and your own future are of great importance, too. You may find that some people leave you. You may also find that you have to leave some people. Some friends may not be able to rejoice in the fact that you are going to college because they feel that you are leaving them behind; others will simply be jealous of the fact that you are bettering yourself and they are not. If those around you do not support you and your dreams and they cannot be reasoned with, you may have to part company for the sake of growth and future security.

As you begin your studies, let yourself undergo the whole spectrum of the college experience. Get involved with your classmates, use college resources to your best advantage, establish meaningful relationships, and enjoy the ride. Yes, you may face challenges on a day-to-day basis, but growth and change include challenges. It only means you are moving, expanding, and growing!

What support groups exist on your campus to help first-generation students?

If you are a first-generation student, you can do many things to help ensure your success and graduation. They include:

- Deal with family conflicts and misunderstandings early and quickly. Talk with them about your plans, daily schedules, and college culture. Keep family members involved so that they don't feel they are being left out or that you are abandoning them.

- Don't let feelings of guilt or "selling out" derail your goals and plans. Yes, you may be the first in your family to attend college, but with your guidance and mentoring, you will not be the last.

- Work hard to find a support group, advisor, counselor, peer, or professor who understands your situation and ask them for advice. Talk to people, make friends, and associate.

- Try to meet people who have been at your institution for at least one semester or one year so that you can learn survival tips from them.

- Immerse yourself socially and academically at your institution. Make use of every source of academic, financial, career, and cultural assistance possible.

- Find a healthy balance among work, family, and your college studies. Remember, this is your future. One way to look at this is to ask yourself, "Is my current job my future? Is it my destiny? Can I do what I am doing right now for the next 25 years?"

- Involve your family and friends in your education as much as possible. Ask them to attend events with you. Encourage them to begin their studies, too.

- Don't be ashamed of what you are doing or for trying to improve your station in life. Dimming your own light does nothing to help others see more clearly. This is a major step forward, and you should be proud of yourself for taking it.

- Have an open mind and enjoy the process. This is the time to learn, grow, explore, and prosper.

ACHIEVING YOUR POTENTIAL AND INCREASING MOTIVATION

What Are the Cornerstones for Lifetime Success?

- "I am a winner."
- "I fail at everything I do."
- "I am a dedicated person."
- "I don't really care about anything."
- "I hate getting up in the morning."
- "I can't wait for my day to start."

> "Watch your thoughts, they become words. Watch your words, they become actions. Watch your actions, they become habits. Watch your habits, they become character. Watch your character, it becomes your destiny."
>
> —Frank Outlaw

As you can see by the two different perspectives above, your attitude and perspective on how you approach life, relationships, problems, and goals can mean the difference between being a motivated, inspired, and successful person or a weary, frightened, and unsuccessful person.

The reason that we have included the *Cornerstones for Lifetime Success* in this chapter is to help you see that by focusing on you and knowing where you're going, what you want, and what you have to offer, your motivation and passion for learning and growing will flourish. By knowing more about yourself, you can then establish a clearer vision of your true potential. Take your time and read each point carefully. Consider the questions asked and complete the chapter activities to assist you with your motivation plan.

POINT 1

Develop a New Attitude

Your attitude—new or old, good or bad—belongs to you. If your attitude needs changing, no one can do it for you. Writer and speaker Stedman Graham (2009) states, "Your attitude is your altitude." Now is the perfect time to begin changing your attitude if it needs an adjustment, because small changes in the way you approach life can mean major changes to your success throughout your college career.

Just as some people embrace the attitude of *learned helplessness* (i.e. letting your past and people in your family or personal community and their failures dictate your future), you can just as easily embrace the attitude of learned optimism. A *pessimist* finds bad news in most situations; they live in a world that has a cloud over them all the time. *Optimists*, on the other hand, can better handle bad news and difficult challenges because they have a positive way of viewing the world. Optimists learn how to determine why things went wrong and can adjust and fix the underlying problem.

Do you think that surrounding yourself with optimistic, motivated people will help you succeed? Why or why not?

People actually create their own accomplishments, reach their goals, and become successful by embracing a positive outlook on life. Conversely, a great deal of personal misery and failure is caused by adopting a bad attitude and by embracing negative feelings and *self-defeating behaviors*. Take the assessment in Figure 2.3 to determine your current attitudes.

Figure 2.3 Is My Behavior Self-Defeating?

Review the checklist below of typical self-defeating habits that can be changed by adapting the right attitude. Place a check by the ones that relate to you and your behavior.

- ❏ I am frequently depressed, lonely, sad, frustrated, worried, or frightened.
- ❏ I spend a lot of time with people who aren't very motivated to excel in college.
- ❏ I waste a lot of time watching TV, playing video games, texting, scanning Facebook, etc.
- ❏ I get very uptight and negative when I have to take a test.
- ❏ I am more worried about associating with friends than I am about my grades.
- ❏ I spend money that I shouldn't spend and charge things on my credit card that I can't afford.
- ❏ I eat too much junk food when I get stressed.
- ❏ I don't exercise properly when I feel depressed.
- ❏ I procrastinate a lot and I lose my temper quickly when I am under pressure.
- ❏ I tend to give up easily when things get hard.

- ❏ I am having trouble with my living arrangement.
- ❏ I have trouble making it through the day without some form of stimulant such as coffee, cigarettes, drugs, or alcohol.
- ❏ I daydream in some of my classes.
- ❏ I turn in my assignments late and make up excuses as to why.
- ❏ I seem to daydream a lot about how things used to be.
- ❏ I cut class when I feel depressed or unprepared.
- ❏ I don't feel comfortable talking to my advisor and instructors.
- ❏ I don't feel like I am making many friends here and I often feel lonely and discouraged.
- ❏ I do not participate in any extracurricular activities.
- ❏ I spend a lot of my time doing nothing.
- ❏ I hate my job.
- ❏ Some of my classes suck and I cut them often.

If you checked off three or more statements on this chart, you may be experiencing self-defeating behavior. You will need to consider carefully how to eliminate these behaviors from your life as you work on a personal attitude adjustment.

Level 6 Create

Select one of the self-defeating habits that you checked from the list in Figure 2.3 and state your specific behavior and why you think you are experiencing this problem.

_____

_____

_____

Develop five action steps to help you change your attitude and overcome this self-defeating behavior.

1. _____

2. _____

3. _____

4. _____

5. _____

POINT 2

Make Excellence a Habit

> "Never leave well enough alone. If it ain't broke, fix it; take fast and make it faster; take smart and make it smarter; take good and make it great."
>
> —Cigna Advertisement

As you work to change some of your habits and to become a highly motivated person, one practice you need to embrace is excellence in everything you do. The average person is happy doing just enough to get by. Those who excel and succeed demand excellence from themselves in everything they do. If you don't think excellence matters, consider these points: Would you want a doctor who cheated his or her way through medical school to operate on you or your child? Would you want a pilot to fly your plane who didn't perform very well on the simulated crash test? Would you want to be the one to cross the bridge every day that was designed by an engineer who cheated his way through design class? ***Excellence matters!*** Figure 2.4 illustrates the importance of excellence in several real-life instances.

Figure 2.4 What If 99.9% Were Good Enough?

If 99.9% were good enough, then:

■ 12 newborns would be given to the wrong parents in the U.S. every day.

■ 7 people would be buried in the wrong graves or cremated incorrectly daily in the U.S.

■ 292 book titles published in the U.S. would be shipped with the wrong covers on them this year.

■ 400 entries in *Webster's Dictionary* would be misspelled.

■ 1,200,000 credit cards held in the U.S. would have incorrect cardholder information on the black magnetic strip on the back of the card.

■ 79,000 drug prescriptions would be written incorrectly this year in the United States.

■ 32,000 books in the Library of Congress would be filed on the shelves incorrectly.

EXCELLENCE MATTERS!

POINT 3

Overcome Your Doubts and Fears

Success is a great motivator, but so is fear. Actually, fear probably motivates more people than anything else. Unfortunately, fear motivates most people to hold back, to doubt themselves, to stay in their comfort zones, and to accomplish much less than they could have without the fear. Your own personal fears may be one of the biggest obstacles to reaching your potential. If you are afraid, you are not alone; everyone has fears. Isn't it interesting that *our fears are learned*? As an infant, you were born with only **two fears:** a fear of falling and a fear of loud noises. As you got older, you added to your list of fears. And, if you are like most people, you may have let your fears dominate parts of your life, saying things to yourself like: "*What if I try and fail?*" "*What if people laugh at me for thinking I can do this?*" or "*What if someone finds out that this is my dream?*" You have two choices where fear is concerned: You can let fear dominate your life, or you can focus on those things you really want to accomplish, put your fears behind you, and "*go for it.*"

"People become who they are. Even Beethoven became Beethoven."
—Randy Newman

Dr. Robert Schuller (1987), minister, motivational speaker, and author, once asked, **"What would you attempt to do if you could not fail?"** This is an important question for anyone, especially those trying to increase their motivation level. We have adapted and expanded this question for the purpose of this exercise. In the spaces below, work through this idea by answering the questions truthfully.

1. What would you attempt to do if you could not fail?

_____

_____

Level 4 Analyze

2. Beyond the answers, "I'm afraid," or "Money," or "Fear," why are you not doing this "thing"?

_____

_____

3. If you did this "thing" and were successful at "it," how would your life change? Be specific.

_____

_____

POINT 4

Put Adversity, Failure, and Challenges into Perspective

Failure is just a temporary by-product of the success that lies ahead if you persevere. A part of being motivated means learning to deal with failure and setbacks. Most people compile a string of failures before they have great success. Winning is getting up one more time than you are knocked down. Successful people

"If you fall down or if you're knocked down, try to land on your back because if you can look up, you can get up."
—Les Brown

When faced with adversity, what techniques have you used in the past to survive and move on?

are successful because they hung on *just one moment longer* than the person who gave up.

We've all had challenges and wounds. We've all made excuses because of the way life turns out sometimes. The key to success is to never let your challenges and wounds turn you into something that you are not. Never let your excuses cheat you out of having the life you deserve. You have the power if you have the will. Just because someone says something about you or does something to you does not mean you have to accept it as your fate. Just because you have a challenge or problem does not mean that it will be yours forever unless you *choose* to let it be with you forever. Consider the example below. You can see the difference between having a challenge and using an excuse. Challenges can be overcome, excuses paralyze you.

Challenge	Excuse
English is not my first language.	I refuse to take an ESL course because it is hard, it will cost money, and they should offer classes in my language.
I have many family responsibilities.	I don't like getting up early to get things done so that I can study later. I'd rather sleep in.
I have transportation problems.	I don't want to ride public transportation or ask someone for a ride.
I am having trouble understanding some of the concepts in my math class.	I don't have the time to go to the tutoring lab or math center. Math should be easier since I'm never going to use it.

POINT 5

Eliminate Negative Self-Talk and the "I Can't" Syndrome

Try as you might sometimes, harmful emotions, fear of the unknown, and that nagging little voice inside your head (negative self-talk) can cause you problems. *Negative self-talk* usually appears when you are afraid, uneasy, hurt, angry, depressed, or lonely. By the time you read this, you may have experienced these feelings. When you experience change, your body, mind, and soul typically go through a process of physical and emotional change as well. Learning to recognize these symptoms in order to control them can help you control the stress that can accompany change. You may have to develop a new attitude.

Your attitude is yours. It belongs to you. You own it. Good or bad, happy or sad, optimistic or pessimistic, it is yours and you are responsible for it. However, your attitude is greatly influenced by situations in your life and by the people with whom you associate. Developing a winning, optimistic attitude can be hard, yet extremely rewarding work, and is beneficial to the change process. Motivated and successful people have learned that one's attitude is the mirror to one's soul.

"It's not the load that breaks you down, it's the way you carry it."
—Lena Horne

Listen to yourself for a few days. Are you more of an optimist or a pessimist? Do you hear yourself whining, complaining, griping, and finding fault with everything and everybody around you? Do you blame others for things that are wrong in your life? Do you blame your bad grades on your professors? Is someone else responsible for your unhappiness? If these thoughts or comments are in your head, you are suffering from the *"I Can't" Syndrome"* (**I**rritated, **C**ontaminated, **A**ngry, **N**egative **T**houghts). This pessimistic condition can negatively influence every aspect of your life, from your self-esteem, to your motivation level, to your academic performance, to your relationships, and to your career success.

If you want to eliminate *"I can't"* from your life, consider the following tips:

- Think about the many positive aspects of your life and show gratitude for them.
- Work every day to find the good in people, places, and things.
- Eliminate negative thoughts that enter your mind before you begin your day.
- Discover what is holding you back and what you need to push you forward.
- Visualize your success—see yourself actually being who and what you want to be.
- Locate and observe positive, optimistic people and things in your life.
- Make a list of those who help you, support you, and help you feel positive, then make a point to be around them more,
- Take responsibility for your own actions and their consequences.
- Force yourself to find five positive things a day for which to be thankful.

You've seen the difference between an *optimist* and a *pessimist*. They are both everywhere—at work, at school, and maybe in your own family. Think of the optimist for a moment. You've probably sat next to them in one of your classes or seen them at work, the person who always seems to be happy, motivated, bubbling with personality, organized, and ready for whatever comes their way. They greet people as they enter the room, they respond in class, they volunteer for projects, and they have a presence about them that is positive and lively. You may even look at them out of the corner of your eye and ask, "What is he on?" Positive, upbeat, and motivated people are easy to spot. You can basically see their attitude in the way they walk, the way they carry themselves, the way they approach people, and the way they treat others.

Be wary, however, of "the others," the ones you need to avoid—whiners, degraders, attackers, manipulators, pessimists, back stabbers, abusers, cowards, two-faced racists, sexists, ageists, homophobes, and ethnocentrists. These people carry around an aura so negative that it can almost be seen as a dark cloud above them. They degrade others because they do not like themselves. They find fault with everything because their own lives are a mess. They do nothing and then attack you for being motivated and trying to improve your life. We call them *contaminated people.* Contaminated people are unhappy with who they are. To make themselves feel better, they try to tear down people who are the opposite of what they are. They belittle your positive actions and try to make your life as miserable as their lives are.

Successful Decisions

AN ACTIVITY FOR CRITICAL REFLECTION

Your friend, Jamal, is struggling with staying motivated during his first term at school. He didn't have to study much in high school and still pulled good grades, but he has been overwhelmed with the amount of work his instructors are assigning. He knows he is not doing his best work, but he can't seem to get motivated to excel. You know he is capable because he participated in your study group several times, but then stopped coming.

Lately, Jamal has begun to wake up during the night very stressed out and afraid that he is going to flunk out. His parents will be devastated if this happens because he is a first-generation student, and they have sacrificed so much for him to further his education. His fears gnaw at him all the time.

Sometimes he can see himself going home to tell his parents that he is failing. He visualizes how embarrassed he will be to tell them and his friends that he has failed. One of his instructors has told him that he has a bad attitude. He spent a long time this afternoon talking to you about his lack of motivation and is thinking of dropping out.

What advice and motivational tips would you offer Jamal to help him get on the right track?

1. _____

_____

2. _____

_____

POINT 6

Identify and Clarify What You Value in Life

If you have been highly motivated to accomplish a goal in the past, this achievement was probably tied to something you valued a great deal. Since most of what you do in life centers on what is truly important to you, you need to identify and then clarify what you value in your life, what really matters to you.

Values, self-esteem, motivation, and goal setting are all mixed up together, making it difficult to separate one from the other. The things you work to accomplish are directly connected to the things you value. Therefore, your *attitude* and *actions* are tied to your *values*. If you value an attitude or belief, your actions will be centered on these ideals. If you love to spend time with your friends and this is valuable to you, you will make the time for this on a regular basis. Why? Because your friendships are a fundamental part of your value system. You like it and get pleasure from it so you are motivated by it and you do it. It is that simple. Our values influence our actions. It is, once again, tied to Maslow's Hierarchy of Basic Needs.

> *"Our souls are not hungry for fame, comfort, wealth, or power. These rewards create almost as many problems as they solve. Our souls are hungry for meaning, for the sense that we have figured out a way to live so that our lives matter."*
>
> —H. Kushner

Honesty	Affection	Punctuality	Respect
Frankness	Open-Mindedness	Reliability	Trustworthiness
Sincerity	Wit/Humor	Spontaneity	Devotion
Frugality	Justice	Creativity	Caring
Spirituality	Friendliness	Energy	Intellect
Attentiveness	Conversational	Money	Security
Fine Dining	Beauty	Devotion	Enthusiasm
Positivism	Commitment	Foresightedness	Creativity
Organization	Learning	Listening	Giving
Control	Comfort	Knowledge	Success
Athletic Ability	Thoughtfulness	Independence	Courage
Safety	Fun	Excitement	Partying
Love	Friendship	Writing	Speaking
Reading	Family	Dependability	Teamwork
Time Alone	Time with Friends	Phone Calls	Walks
Exercise	Problem Solving	Empowerment	Integrity
Service to Others	Modesty	Strength	Tolerance
Imagination	Self-Esteem	Food	Power
Winning	Goals	Risk Taking	Change
Self-Improvement	Forgiveness	Fairness	Optimism
Successful Career	Motivation	Trust	Direction in Life
Working	Hobbies	Books	Mentoring
Stability	_____	_____	_____
_____	_____	_____	_____
_____	_____	_____	_____
_____	_____	_____	_____

Take a look at the boxed section that includes a wide and varied list of items. Read over them carefully and circle the ones you truly value. Be careful and selective—*do not* just randomly circle words. As a criterion for each word you circle, ask yourself, "Can I defend why I value this in my life?" and "Is this truly something *I value* or something I was told to value and never questioned why?" If you value something and it is not on the list, add it in the spaces at the bottom. Work on this before reading further.

Now that you have circled or written what you value, choose the five that you value the most. In other words, if you were *only* allowed to value five things in life, what five would you list below? In the space to the right of each value, rank them from 1 to 5 (1 being the most important to you, your life, your relationships, your actions, your education, and your career). Take your time and give serious consideration to this activity as you will need to refer back to this exercise later in this chapter.

LIST   **RANK**

_____   _____

_____   _____

_____   _____

_____   _____

_____   _____

Now, look at your #1. Where did this value originate?_____
_____

Defend why this is the one thing you value more in life than anything else.

_____

How does this one value motivate you?_____
_____

How can damage to your name and reputation negatively affect your overall success?

POINT 7

Take Pride in Your Name and Personal Character

"My name?" you may ask. *"What does my name have to do with anything?"* The answer: At the end of the day, the end of the month, the end of your career, and the end of your life, your name and your character are all that you have. Taking pride in developing your character and protecting your good name can be two powerful, motivational forces.

It comes down to this: Every time you make a choice, every time you complete a project, every time you encounter another person, your actions define your character and your name. People admire and respect you when you make an honorable and moral choice, especially if it is a difficult decision. Both your character and your name are exclusively yours and you are responsible for their well being.

> *"Your character is determined by how you treat people who can do you no good and how you treat people who can't fight back."*
> —Abigail Van Buren

When you care this passionately about your reputation and character, your life is governed by protecting your name. Your actions, beliefs, and decisions are all tied to this one belief: "My name and my reputation matter and I will do nothing to bring shame or embarrassment to my name."

POINT 8

Develop a Strong Personal "Guiding Statement"

You're wearing a t-shirt to class. It is not your normal, run-of-the-mill t-shirt, however. You designed this t-shirt for everyone to see and read. It is white with bright red letters. On the front of the t-shirt is written your *personal guiding statement*, the words by which you live, the words that govern your life. What would your t-shirt say? Perhaps you will use the golden rule, "Do unto others…," it might be an adaptation of the Nike® slogan, "Just Do It," or it might be something more profound, such as, "I live my life to serve others and to try to make others' lives better," or "Be a blessing," or "Live, Love, Laugh."

Whatever your guiding statement, it must be yours. It can't be your parents', or your professor's, or your best friend's statement. It must be based on something you value and it must be strong enough to motivate you in hard, tough times. Your guiding statement must be so powerful that it will literally "guide you" when you are ethically challenged, broke, alone, angry, hurt, sad, or feeling vindictive. It is a statement that will guide you in your relationships with family, friends, spouses, partners, or would-be love interests. It is a statement that gives direction to your *daily* actions. Think about how different your life would be if you woke up each morning and *lived* your guiding statement to the fullest.

One of the best places to start working on your guiding statement is to look back at those things you circled as valuable to you in Point 6 of this chapter. If you value something, it may appear in your guiding statement. For example, if you circled the words "Respect," "Giving," and "Optimistic" among those you value, this is a basis for your statement. A guiding statement based on these words might read:

"I will live my life as a positive, optimistic, upbeat, motivated person who respects others and enjoys giving to others on a daily basis."

If your circled words included "Integrity," "Truth," and "Fairness," your statement may read:

"My integrity is the most important thing in my life and I will never act in any way that compromises my integrity. I will be truthful, fair, and honest in all my endeavors."

More simply, your guiding statement may read something like:

"Be reliable," "Live optimistically," or *"Never give up."*

In the space below, transfer the most important words from your list of values on page 40 and then work to develop your guiding statement.

My most important values are:

_____

_____

_____

Guiding Statement Draft (Using the values you identified in Point Six, build your Guiding Life Statement. Take your time and be sincere. You will need this statement later in the chapter.):

_____

_____

_____

from ORDINARY to *Extraordinary*

Derwin Wallace, Director of Corporate Investor Relations, National Association of Investor Corps

Derwin was born in a ghetto on the West Side of Chicago. His father was a strict man from the Mississippi Delta and his way of disciplining his children was to beat them, Derwin included. By the sixth grade, Derwin had a job, paid rent, and bought his own school lunches and clothes. When he was 16, he had saved enough money to buy a boom box. One night he was playing the boom box, and because it was plugged into an electrical outlet, using power and increasing electrical costs, his father took the power cord and began to beat him with it. It was at this point that he knew he had to leave…and leave he did.

Derwin broke into a friend's garage and wrapped himself in blankets and paper to keep from freezing to death. Later, he hid in his basement and was nearly eaten to death by rats. He began to stop by an old bakery to get their thrown-away donuts to feed the rats so they would leave him alone. That is how he

> *Derwin broke into a friend's garage and wrapped himself in blankets and paper to keep from freezing to death. Later, he hid in his basement and was nearly eaten to death by rats.*

survived. He went on to live in busses and abandoned buildings and cars. He was on the high school tennis team and diving team so he had a key to the school gym. He took his showers in the locker room. He lived like this for two years. After high school graduation, others went out to party and Derwin found himself celebrating in an abandoned car.

After high school, he joined the military for a few years and was asked to leave due to acts of immaturity. After the military, he began his college studies, but dropped out shortly thereafter because of money and many other life situations. His life was going nowhere. He lived in rented rooms for eight years. One day Derwin decided to move to Atlanta and found himself homeless again. He began work as a telemarketer, and found another room to rent. At 28, he found himself with nothing. He had a dead end job, no education, and was dating a woman who was, unknown to him, an occasional drug user. Something had to change. His life had to change. He looked around at others and wondered why they had a nice life and he did not. Finally, he realized that he had to look at

his own life and actions before he could blame anyone else. He decided his lack of education was holding him back.

Derwin had seen an ad for DeVry University and he decided to investigate. He had been interested in math and accounting. He decided to enroll and was able to get tutoring and individual attention in the small classes. Some of his instructors worked in the accounting and investment field and shared their real-world experiences. After his first semester, he had a 4.0 GPA and received a Georgia Lottery Scholarship. He made the Dean's List and was a President's Scholar.

Because of his accounting and business classes, he began to watch the stock market. As crazy as it seems, he took the extra money from his loans and scholarships and began to invest it in stocks. After six years, he graduated with a B.S. in accounting and an MBA concentration in finance. His education assisted him in obtaining careers as a stockbroker, financial analyst, investor relations professional, and financial controller. As Director of Corporate Investor Relations, Derwin's main responsibility is to put companies that trade in the stock market in front of investors in hopes they may purchase that company's stock.

Education took Derwin from homeless in a rat-infested basement to flying in corporate jets and working with some of the most wealthy and powerful companies in America. His education gave him limitless opportunities. He has often stated that "corporate America is a battlefield and you must get your armor ready. Your education is your preparation for battle—it is your boot camp for the real world." He moved from ordinary to extraordinary!

EXTRAORDINARY REFLECTIONS

What role has your family played in shaping your experiences and future? How can you use this to your best advantage?

DID YOU *Know?*

TIM MCGRAW, recording artist and country music sensation, was born in Louisiana in 1967. When he was 11 years old, he discovered that the man he believed to be his father was not and that his father was actually the famous New York Mets baseball player, Tug McGraw. Tug denied that Tim was his son for seven years. When Tim was 18, Tug finally admitted that he was Tim's father.

During his early recording years, his first series of singles failed so badly that he was told to give up his dream of becoming a country recording artist. One producer even told him, "You'll never make it, son. Go on home and find yourself a job."

As of today, he has sold over 40 million CDs and has 31 #1 hits. His last eleven CDs debuted at #1 on the *Billboard* charts. He has won three Grammy awards, 14 Academy of Country Music Awards, 11 Country Music Association (CMA) Awards, and three People's Choice Awards. (TimMcGraw.com, n.d.; Wikipedia, n.d.)

POINT 9

Make a Commitment to Strengthen Your Self-Esteem

If you were asked to name all the areas of your life that are impacted by self-esteem, what would you say? The correct answer is "Everything." Every area of your life is affected by your self-esteem.

Self-esteem and self-understanding are two of the most important components of your personal makeup! To be truly motivated, you have got to know yourself and love yourself! Many people who are in therapy are there simply because they cannot accept the fact that they are OK. Self-esteem is a powerful force in your life and is the source of your joy, your productivity, and your ability to have good relationships with others.

You can think of self-esteem as a photograph of yourself that you keep locked in your mind. It is a collective product—the culmination of everyone with whom you have associated, everywhere you've traveled, and all of the experiences you have had. **William James** (2011), the first major psychologist to study self-esteem, defined it as, "*the sum total of all a person can call their own*: the *Material Me* (all that you have), the *Social Me* (recognition and acceptance from others), and the *Spiritual Me* (your innermost thoughts and desires)."

Stanly Coopersmith (1981), noted psychologist and developer of the most widely used self-esteem inventory in America, defined self-esteem as, "*a personal judgment of worthiness*." Psychologist and author **Nathanial Branden** (1994) defines self-esteem as, "*confidence in our ability to cope with the basic challenges of life*." Psychologist **Charles Cooley** (1981) called it "*the looking glass*." Perhaps in everyday terms we can define healthy self-esteem as, "I know who I am, I accept who I am, I am OK, and I'm going to make it."

Self-esteem has five basic characteristics based in Maslow's Hierarchy of Basic Needs. They are:

- A sense of **security** (I am safe and have the basics of life, food, water, etc.)
- A sense of **identity** (I know who I am and where I'm going.)
  - A sense of **belonging** (I know how to love and I am loved.)
  - A sense of **purpose** (I know why I'm here and what I am going to do with my life.)
  - A sense of **personal competence** (I have the ability to achieve my goals and grow.)

These characteristics are considered key to a person's ability to approach life with motivation, confidence, self-direction, and the desire to achieve outstanding accomplishments.

Tips to Enhance Your Self-Esteem

- **Take control of your own life**. If you let other people rule your life, you will always have unhealthy self-esteem. Get involved in the decisions that shape your life. Seize control—don't let life just happen to you!
- **Adopt the idea that you are responsible for you.** The day you take responsibility for yourself and what happens to you is the day you start to develop healthier self-esteem. When you can admit your

How can actively participating in class help build your self-esteem?

mistakes and celebrate your successes knowing you did it your way, loving and respecting yourself become much easier.

- **Refuse to allow friends and family to tear you down.** Combat negativity by admitting your mistakes and shortcomings to yourself (without dwelling on them) and by making up your mind that you are going to overcome them. By doing this, you are taking negative power away from anyone who would use your mistakes to hurt you.

- **Control what you say to yourself.** "Self-talk" is important to your self-esteem and to your ability to motivate yourself positively. If you allow negative self-talk into your life, it will rule your self-esteem. Think positive thoughts and surround yourself with positive, upbeat, motivated, happy people.

> "To every person there comes that special moment when he is tapped on the shoulder to do a very special thing unique to him. What a tragedy if that moment finds him unprepared for the work that would be his finest hour."
>
> —Winston Churchill

- **Take calculated risks.** If you are going to grow to your fullest potential, you will have to learn to take some calculated risks and step out of your comfort zone. While you should never take foolhardy risks that might endanger your life or cause you to lose everything you have, you must constantly be willing to push yourself.

- **Stop comparing yourself to other people.** You may never be able to beat some people at certain things. Does it really matter? You only have to beat yourself to get better. If you constantly tell yourself that you "are not as handsome as Bill" or "as smart as Mary" or "as athletic as Jack," your inner voice will begin to believe these statements, and your motivation and self-esteem will suffer. Everyone has certain strengths and talents to offer to the world.

- **Keep your promises and be loyal to friends, family, and yourself.** If you have ever had someone break a promise to you, you know how it feels to have your loyalty betrayed. The most outstanding *figure* of your character is your ability to be loyal, to keep your promises, and do what you have agreed to do. Few things can make you feel better about yourself than being loyal and keeping your word.

- **Win with grace—lose with class.** Everyone loves a winner, but everyone also loves a person who can lose with class and dignity. On the other hand, no one loves a bragging winner or a moaning loser. If you are engaged in sports, debate, acting, art shows, or academic competitions, you will encounter winning and losing. Remember, whether you win or lose, *if you're involved and active,* you're already in the top 10 percent of the population. You're already more of a winner than most because you showed up and participated.

- **Be a giver.** Author, speaker, and teacher Leo Buscaglia (1982) states: "You want to make yourself the most brilliant, the most talented, the most fabulous person that you can possibly be so that you can give it all away. The only reason we have anything is to be able to give it away." By giving to other people and sharing your talents and strengths, you begin to live on a level where kindness, selflessness, and others' needs gently collide. Whatever you want in this life, give it away and it will come back to you.

CHANGING IDEAS *to Reality*

REFLECTIONS ON MOTIVATION AND SELF-ESTEEM

Motivation can change your life. Healthy self-esteem can change your life. *You* can change your life. This chapter has been about self-discovery and defining what you value, what role your attitude plays in your motivation, and how to surround yourself with positive, optimistic people. By focusing on **you** and determining what is important to your college studies, your career, your relationships, and your personal life, you can develop a vision of your future. If you can see your future, *really see it*, then you are more likely to be motivated to achieve it. Remember, we are motivated by what we value.

As you continue on in the semester and work toward personal and professional motivation, remember the following ideas:

- Convert external motivators into internal motivation.
- Use the power of positive thinking and surround yourself with positive people.
- Step outside your comfort zone.
- Use your values to drive your life statement.

- Do one thing every day to strengthen your self-esteem.
- Turn negative thoughts into positive energy.
- View adversity as a stepping stone to strength.
- Picture yourself as optimistic and motivated.

Good luck to you as you begin developing the motivation and positive attitude you need to be successful in your studies and beyond.

Knowledge
in Bloom

USING AND EVALUATING YOUR GUIDING STATEMENT

Utilizes Levels 3 and 6 of the Taxonomy (See Bloom's Taxonomy at the front of this text)

Process: Now that you have developed your guiding statement, consider how it can be used to guide you in the following situations:

_____

Guiding statement as written on page 42 of this chapter:

_____

_____

HOW WILL YOUR GUIDING STATEMENT HELP . . .

If you have a disagreement with your supervisor at work?

_____

_____

If your class paper or project receives a failing grade from your professor?

_____

_____

If you are having a disagreement with someone for whom you care deeply (friend, spouse, partner, parent, work associate, etc.)?

_____

_____

If you see that someone is struggling and having a hard time "making it"?

_____

_____

Now that you have had a chance to apply your guiding statement to several simulations, on a scale of 1 to 10 (1 being not effective at all and 10 being very effective), how would you rate your guiding statement's effectiveness to you and to those involved? Why? Discuss.

_____

_____

SQ3R MASTERY STUDY SHEET

EXAMPLE QUESTION (FROM PAGE 30) What is the difference between internal and external motivation?	**ANSWER:**
EXAMPLE QUESTION (FROM PAGE 35) How can overcoming self-defeating behaviors help you become a better student?	**ANSWER:**
AUTHOR QUESTION (FROM PAGE 38) How can the "I Can't" Syndrome affect your classroom performance?	**ANSWER:**
AUTHOR QUESTION (FROM PAGE 40) How can identifying your values help you stay motivated?	**ANSWER:**
AUTHOR QUESTION (FROM PAGE 41) Define the word "character" and discuss how it plays a role in your motivation level.	**ANSWER:**
AUTHOR QUESTION (FROM PAGE 44) Explain how self-esteem plays a role in one's motivation.	**ANSWER:**
AUTHOR QUESTION (FROM PAGE 45) Why is loyalty important to your self-esteem?	**ANSWER:**
YOUR QUESTION (FROM PAGE ____)	**ANSWER:**
YOUR QUESTION (FROM PAGE ____)	**ANSWER:**
YOUR QUESTION (FROM PAGE ____)	**ANSWER:**
YOUR QUESTION (FROM PAGE ____)	**ANSWER:**
YOUR QUESTION (FROM PAGE ____)	**ANSWER:**

Finally, after answering these questions, recite this chapter's major points in your mind. Consider the following general questions to help you master this material.

- What is it about?
- What does it mean?
- What is the most important thing you learned? Why?
- What are the key points to remember?

chapter three

PERSIST

UNDERSTANDING THE CULTURE OF YOUR COLLEGE

"I know the price of success: dedication, hard work, and constant devotion to the things you want to see happen." —Frank Lloyd Wright

Scan and QUESTION

Take a few moments, **scan this chapter** and on page 69, write **five of your own questions** that you think will be important to your mastery of this material. You will also find five questions listed from your authors.

Example:

☑ **Why is it important to understand your college's policies?** (from page 52)

☑ **What is the difference between a BA and a BS degree?** (from page 54)

Why read this chapter?

Because you'll learn...

■ The rules of your college
■ What college professors really want
■ The value of planning for your second term

Because you'll be able to...

■ Calculate your grade point average (GPA)
■ Find and use academic, campus, and personal success centers at your college
■ Use civility, personal decorum, and self-management to guide future plans

MyStudentSuccessLab

MyStudentSuccessLab is an online solution designed to help you acquire and develop (or hone) the skills you need to succeed. You will have access to peer-led video presentations and develop core skills through interactive exercises and projects.

Name: Jennifer Adams
Institution: Graduate! Florida State College at Jacksonville, Jacksonville, FL
Major: Recreation Administration

Jenna's initial college attempt had ended after three less-than-successful semesters. So, when she decided to return, to say she had mixed emotions is an understatement. She was not only concerned about whether she would be able to handle the work, she was not sure she would fit in with the student population. After all, she was a 27-year-old divorcee—and she was nervous.

Although Jenna was not aware of it at the time, her choice to attend Florida Community College at Jacksonville proved to be the first of many wise decisions she was to make on her educational journey. She said, "The community college professors and counselors helped me see that there is not a right or wrong way to succeed, it depends on the person and her goals. The smaller-sized classes, individual attention, and campus resources were invaluable to my success. I feel like I would have been lost in a larger college. The freedoms and distractions of a university can be a lot to handle!"

An interview conducted and written by Steve Piscitelli, Professor of History and Student Success, Florida State College at Jacksonville

Jenna's age actually proved to be positive. Once again, in Jenna's words, "There were times when my maturity was able to help a classmate understand a topic as I could relate to both the professor and the student. I feel like I was able to help some of my peers understand different points of view. Many students lack confidence to enter a dialogue with a professor, as they are used to being told what they need to know and do. College offers the opportunity to question material and discover knowledge." Jenna found the college environment exhilarating. The smaller classes meant a greater opportunity to ask questions, have dialogue, and even try to debate with the professor!

After successfully completing her community college program, Jenna moved to California to attend Humboldt State University. And while she has happily adjusted to her new home and college campus, she still looks back with affection on her community college days. "Attending community college," Jenna remembers, "offered me the opportunity to avoid many of the struggles that I see students facing at my current university. College gave me the fundamental learning skills that I needed to be able to be successful without being distracted. Now that those skills are secure, I am far better at balancing tougher classes and the challenges of life in general."

THINK a b o u t *it*

1. What steps do you need to take to be able to establish better dialogue with your professors? What can you do this week to get started?

2. What kinds of skills and knowledge do you think you can learn from other students of all ages and backgrounds? How can you begin this week taking advantage of learning from your colleagues?

TO BE SUCCESSFUL, YOU HAVE TO LAST

How Can You Make It and Persist in Your Studies?

Have you ever faced adversity and heavy odds when attempting to do something? Most everyone has. If you are one of the people who refused to let adversity hold you back, faced your fears, and continued with the project at hand, then you know how it feels to survive. You know how it feels to reach a goal when the odds were not in your favor. You know the feeling of winning. You know the value of persistence.

Conversely, have you ever given up on something in the past and regretted it later? Do you ever think back and ask yourself, "What would my life be like if only I had done this or that?" Have you ever made a decision or acted in a way that cost you dearly? If you have, then you know how difficult it can be to begin new projects or face the future with motivation. You know the feeling of defeat. Know this, however: Defeat *does not* have to be a part of your life. It may be a part of your journey, but it does not have to be a permanent part of your life.

So, what is **persistence**? The word itself means that you are going to stay—that you have found a way to stick it out, found a way to make it work, and found a way *to not give up*. That is what this chapter is all about—giving you the tools to discover how your college works and what tools you will need to be successful. Self-management is about taking initiative and not waiting for someone to tell you how "it" works and not waiting until something goes wrong. Self-management is about investigating and researching ways to be successful at your college from this day forward. It is about your ability to *last during tough times*.

KNOWING THE RULES UP FRONT

Why Do You Need to Know about College Policies and Procedures?

Policies and procedures vary from institution to institution, but regardless, it is your responsibility to know what you can expect from your college and what your college expects from you. These policies can be found in your college catalog (traditional and online), your student handbook, or your schedule of classes, depending on your college.

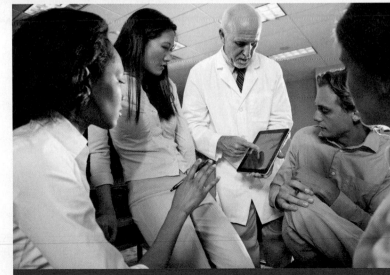

Why is it important to establish a positive relationship with your instructors?

> "The very first step toward success in any endeavor is to become interested in it."
>
> —William Osler

Universal policies include the following:

- All students are subject to the Federal Privacy Act of 1974 (this ensures your privacy, even from your parents).
- Most colleges require placement tests (these are different from admission tests). They are used to properly advise you into the correct English, math, international languages, reading, and/or vocabulary classes.
- Most colleges adhere to a strict drop/add date. Always check your schedule of classes for this information.
- Most colleges have an attendance policy for classroom instruction.
- Most colleges have a strict payment/refund/default policy.
- Almost every college in America has an Academic Dishonesty Policy.

Colleges do not put these policies and procedures in place to punish you or to make things harder; rather, they are designed to ensure that all students are treated fairly and equitably. Some of the policies are also mandated by the federal government in order for the institution to be allowed to receive federal monies. By reviewing your school's catalog, schedule of classes, or student handbook, you can familiarize yourself with your college's specific guidelines. Use these documents to complete Figure 3.1.

Level 1 Remember
1

Figure 3.1 Understanding College Policy

Policy Question	Response
What is the last day to drop a class without penalty?	
What is the grade appeal policy for your college?	
Does your college have a refund policy? If so, what is it?	
Does your college have a policy on the number of hours for which you can register in one term? If so, what is that number? Is it different for online classes?	
What is your college's religious (holy day) policy?	
What is your college's policy for placement testing?	
What is your college's policy on academic probation?	
Does your college have an attendance policy? What is it?	

I WANT A DEGREE!…I THINK

Is It Better to Earn a Certificate or a Degree?

If you are not sure about the coursework or degree in which you would like to get involved, it is advisable to consult an advisor or counselor at your school as soon as possible. If you want to obtain a two-year degree to enter the workforce or transfer to a university, you may consider an Associate of Applied Science degree. If you already have a degree or simply need to become certified in a specific area, you may want to consider a certificate. If you want a four-year degree, you'll probably be working toward a **BA** (Bachelor of Arts) or **BS** (Bachelor of Science) degree. You may also be seeking a **BAS** (Bachelor of Applied Science) or **BFA** (Bachelor of Fine Arts) degree. Most colleges offer the BA and BS degrees.

The Associate's Degree

For those of you seeking an associate's degree, it can become somewhat *confusing*. There are major differences among the **AA** (Associate of Arts), **AS** (Associate of Science), and **AAS** (Associate of Applied Science) degrees. "*What? They're really that different?*" you may be asking. *Yes, they are quite different* and knowing the difference could save you years of time, thousands of dollars, and countless headaches. If you plan to transfer to a university, you should enroll in either the AA or AS transfer degree program. Why? Because these courses are designed to transfer into a bachelor's degree and are taught by faculty with at least a master's degree. If you plan to get your two-year degree and enter the world of work, you will probably enroll in the AAS degree program. Why? Because the courses in the AAS are designed for the world of work and may be taught by faculty who are experts in their field but may not have a college degree.

The Bachelor's Degree

For those of you who are planning to seek a bachelor's degree, you will need to consider your college's catalog to determine if your major requires a **BA** (Bachelor of Arts), **BS** (Bachelor of Science), **BAS** (Bachelor of Applied Science), or **BFA** (Bachelor of Fine Arts). In some instances, you can choose the degree, but you will most likely be directed by the college into one degree or the other. The bachelor's degree can also lead to studies for a master's degree, professional degree, and/or doctoral degree. To learn more about two- and four-year degrees, consider Figure 3.2.

GREAT EXPECTATIONS

Who Are Professors and What Do They Really Want?

Many of your college professors attended college for 7 to 12+ years preparing to teach you. College professors, for the most part, must have at least a master's degree in their field, but many have a doctorate or a post-doctorate degree. A professor who has obtained a master's or a doctorate may have spent as many as 12 or more years in college. Others will have spent years and years working in their fields as experts in hospitals, engineering firms, hotels, technology companies, and police departments, to name just a few careers. Basically, your professors have spent a lifetime preparing to do what they do at your college.

The Freedom to Teach and Learn

Professors are granted something called *academic freedom*. Most high school teachers do not have this privilege. Academic freedom means that a professor has the right to teach controversial

Figure 3.2 The Differences between Types of Associate and Bachelor Degrees

Degree	Definition	Emphasis/Purpose
AA	The **Associate of Arts** degree consists of around 60–63 semester hours and most universities accept these credits as a part of your bachelor's degree.	The emphasis of the AA degree is the liberal and performing arts, history, English, literature, international languages, psychology, sociology, education, the humanities, and communication. This is a **transfer degree**.
AS	The **Associate of Science** degree consists of around 60–65 semester hours and most universities accept these credits as a part of your bachelor's degree.	The emphasis of the AS degree is math, the sciences (biology, chemistry, physics, geology, geography, astronomy), economics, and accounting. This is a **transfer degree**.
AAS	The **Associate of Applied Science** degree consists of around 60–65 semester hours and many of these credits may **not** transfer as university credit.	The emphasis of the AAS degree is employment. Students who want to get a two-year degree and **then enter the workforce** in areas such as criminal justice, nursing, dental assisting, graphic design, computers, building technologies, office technology, and medical laboratory technology should seek the AAS degree.
BA	The **Bachelor of Arts** degree consists of around 120 semester hours. In many cases, you can transfer up to 60 hours into this degree from another college.	The emphasis of the BA degree is the **liberal and performing arts,** such as history, English, literature, international languages, psychology, sociology, education, art, music, theatre, the humanities, and communication.
BS	The **Bachelor of Science** degree consists of around 120–124 semester hours. In many cases, you can transfer up to 60 hours into this degree from another college.	The emphasis of the BS degree is **math and science,** with courses such as biology, chemistry, physics, geology, geography, astronomy, economics, accounting, and many of the **professional sciences,** such as hotel administration, architecture, nursing, engineering, and computer networking.
BAS	**Bachelor of Applied Science** is a highly specialized, technical degree that usually requires more semester hours than the BA or BS because of the intense nature and application of the courses required.	The emphasis of the BAS degree is in **applied science** courses, such as applied physics, environmental engineering, industrial management, and mechanical and automotive engineering. Many people seeking this degree are already employed in their profession and need to upgrade or acquire technical skills in their areas of study.
BFA	The **Bachelor of Fine Arts** degree is a highly specialized degree in one of the fine arts. This degree is not widely offered.	The primary emphasis of a BFA is the **visual and performing arts,** such as dance, theatre, art, music, graphic and industrial arts, photography, advertising, and gaming design. About two-thirds of this degree is grounded in the visual arts, and one-third in the liberal arts.

issues, topics, subjects, pieces of literature, scientific theories, religious tenets, and political points of view that may be out of the mainstream *without* the threat of termination. However, this does not mean that a faculty member has the right to push a personal agenda or preach a religion. Teaching information that is related to the course is different than spending an hour talking about their political or religious agenda.

You may not have been able to read Mart Crowley's, *The Boys in the Band,* in your high school drama class because of its homosexual content, but you would be able to study it uncensored in a college course. You may have never engaged in a discussion on the existence of God in high school, but this may very well be a topic of debate in your logic, religion, sociology, or critical thinking class. This is the right of the college professor—to teach and guide in an unobstructed atmosphere free from parental, administrative, trustee, religious, political, or public pressure.

What Professors Expect from You

You've probably already noticed that your professors' styles, personalities, and rules are not the same. Some are very strict on tardiness and attendance, and some do not call roll. Some professors will provide the opportunity for many grades, while others will only give a midterm and a final. Some will be very friendly and helpful, while others may treat you as if you are a burden. You may leave at the end of the day wondering what these people want from you. The answers vary, but the following list will provide you with a general idea of what is expected of you by your professors.

Professors want you to:

- Come to class or log onto your online course when required

- Read the assigned materials before coming to class or participating in an online chat or discussion

- Go beyond the required readings and assignments and take the initiative to study deeper on your own

- Ask questions and participate in class or in online posts, chats, and discussions

- Turn in your assignments on time and not ask for extensions or favors

- Work to solve problems and challenges before asking for assistance or giving up

- Be respectful to them, your peers, and to yourself

- View your education and college as more than a degree mill

- Learn how to learn for the rest of your life

I CAN'T BELIEVE YOU GAVE ME AN F

What Is Your Role in Earning Grades?

There will be times when you are disappointed with a grade that *you earn* from a professor—and yes, you do *earn* an A or an F; professors do not *give* A's or F's. What do you do? Threaten? Sue? Become argumentative? Those techniques usually cost you more than you gain.

First, remember that the grade assigned by a professor can rarely be changed. If you made a less than satisfactory grade, there are several things that you need to do. First, be truthful with yourself and examine the amount of time you spent on the project. Review the requirements for the assignment. Ask yourself:

- Did I miss something or omit some aspect of the project?

- Did I take an improper or completely wrong focus?

Figure 3.3 Do I Practice Personal Responsibility?

Think about a grade or project on which you scored lower than you would have liked or expected. Answer these questions truthfully to determine your role in the grading process. Place a check mark beside the questions that truly reflect your effort. If you have not yet turned in a project or taken an exam, consider these questions as a checklist for success.

❏ I attend class regularly.
❏ I participate in class discussions and group work.
❏ I ask pointed and direct questions in class.
❏ I read my assignments, do my homework, and come to class prepared.
❏ I work with a study group.
❏ I have all of the supplies I need to be successful in this class (text, workbook, calculator, highlighters, etc.).
❏ I visit my professor during office hours to ask questions and seek clarification.
❏ I use the academic support services on my campus (tutorial services, math lab, writing center, communication lab, language lab, science lab, etc.).
❏ I use the library as a resource for greater understanding.
❏ I practice academic integrity.
❏ I bring my best to the class every time we meet.

Being able to answer these personal responsibility questions positively can mean the difference between success and failure with a project, assessment, or a class.

If you are truly concerned about the grade, talk to the professor about the assignment. Ask the professor to describe the most apparent problem with your assignment, and ask how you might improve your studying or how best to prepare for the *next* assignment.

- Did I turn the project in late?
- Did I document my sources correctly?
- Did I really give it my very best?

Answering these important questions, and the ones listed in Figure 3.3 can help you determine the extent of your personal responsibility and preparation for success.

CLASSROOM CHALLENGES

What Do You Need to Know Right Now?

WHEN YOUR PROFESSOR'S FIRST LANGUAGE IS NOT YOUR FIRST LANGUAGE. Yes, you may have professors whose first language is not your primary language. Colleges often hire professors from around the world because of their expertise in their subjects. You may find that it is difficult to understand a professor's dialect or pronunciation from time to time. If you have a professor who is difficult to understand, remember these hints:

- Sit near the front of the room so that you can see the instructor's mouth and facial expressions.
- Follow the professor's nonverbal communication patterns.
- Record the lecture if allowed (*always* ask first).
- Read the material beforehand so that you will have a general understanding of what is being discussed.
- Ask questions when you do not understand the material.

WHEN YOU AND YOUR PROFESSOR HAVE A DISAGREEMENT. There may be times when you clash with your professor. It may be over a grade, an assigned project, a topic of discussion, a misunderstanding, or a personality issue. Above all, don't get into a verbal argument or physical confrontation. This will only make matters worse for everyone involved. If you have a disagreement, make sure that *the professor is your first point of contact*. Unless you have spoken with him or her *first* and exhausted all options with him or her, approaching the department chair, the dean, the vice president, or the president will more than likely result in your being sent directly back to the professor. If you go to the professor's superiors before talking to them, this will likely result in having your professor get upset with you.

THE GOLDEN RULE— OR JUST A CROCK

Do Civility, Etiquette, and Personal Decorum Affect Success?

You may be surprised, but the way you act in (and out) of class and in online classes can mean as much to your success as what you know. No one can make you do anything or act in any way that you do not want. The following tips are provided from years of research and actual conversations with thousands of professors teaching across America. You have to be the one who chooses whether or not to use this advice.

- If you are late for class, enter quietly and take the seat nearest the door. **Do not** walk in front of the professor, let the door slam, or talk on your way in. Make every effort not to be late to class.

- Wait for the professor to dismiss class before you begin to pack your bags to leave. You may miss important information or you may cause someone else to miss important information.

- Do not carry on a conversation with another student while the professor or another student is talking.

- Don't ask your professor to break the rules just for you. The rules in your class syllabus are provided to everyone so that all students will be treated fairly. If you have a true, legitimate reason to ask for an extension or some other exception, talk to your professor *beforehand*.

- Do not sleep in class. If you are having problems staying awake, make changes in your personal life. If you're sleeping, you're wasting your money and your time.

- If for any reason you must leave during class, do so quietly and quickly. It is customary to inform the professor that you will be leaving early before class begins.

- If you make an appointment with a professor, keep it. If you must cancel, a courtesy call is in order.

- If you don't know how to address your professor, that is, by Mr., Mrs., Miss, Ms., or Dr., ask them which they prefer, or simply call them "Professor _____."

- If instructed, turn off your electronic devices. Even if the device is off, take your earbuds out of your ears; leaving them in is disrespectful.

DID YOU *Know?*

NELSON MANDELA was born on July 18, 1918, in the small village of Mvezo, South Africa. His father had four wives and he was raised in a family of 13 children. His father died when he was nine years old. When he was 20, he found that his family had arranged a marriage for him. He was displeased with this arrangement and decided to flee to Johannesburg, where he found work as a guard for a mining company. He was fired from this job because the supervisor found out that he was a runaway.

Throughout his life, he suffered abuse and discrimination. He was asked to leave college because of his beliefs and protests. He endured a 5-year trial for treason, and later spent 27 years in prison for his outspoken opinions. He was released in 1990. In 1994, at the age of 76, he became the first black president of South Africa, effectively ending "white-only rule."

In 1993, President Mandela accepted the Nobel Peace Prize on behalf of all South Africans who suffered to end apartheid. (Nobel Foundation, 1993)

"Respect your efforts, respect yourself. Self-respect leads to self-discipline. When you have both firmly under your belt, that's real power."

—Clint Eastwood

- Be respectful of other students. Profanity and obscene language may offend some people. You can have strong, conflicting views without being offensive.

- If you're taking an online class and enter a chat or discussion late, don't interrupt other members to find out what is happening. Simply skim through the discussion thread and catch up.

- Whether in class or online, never ask "are we doing anything important today?"

Remember that respect for others on your part will afford you the opportunity to establish relationships that otherwise you might never have had. Respect begets respect.

SELF-MANAGEMENT, ETHICS, AND YOUR FUTURE

Who Are You When No One Is Looking?

Think about these questions: What if there were no rules or laws to govern your behavior? What if there were no consequences or ramifications for any of your actions? Let's pretend for a moment that you could never go to jail or face fines or be shunned for your words, actions, behaviors, or thoughts. If these statements came to pass, what would your life—or the lives of those you love— look like? This is one of the best ways to offer a practical definition of ethics. Basically, ethics is the *accepted* moral code or standard by which we all live, and that code is communicated many ways, including through our relationships with others. Codes of ethics vary from culture to culture, country to country, college to college, and group to group, but each carries with them certain "rules" that members of that culture, country, college, or group are expected to follow.

Making professional or personal ethical decisions usually involves three factors or levels, as shown in Figure 3.4. They include: the ***law, fairness***, and your ***conscience*** (Anderson & Bolt, 2008). You might also consider adding three other levels; ***time***, ***pride***, and ***publicity***.

> "Have the courage to say no. Have the courage to face the truth. Do the right thing because it is right. These are the magic keys to living your life with integrity."
>
> —Clement Stone

Figure 3.4 **Six Levels of Ethical Decision Making**

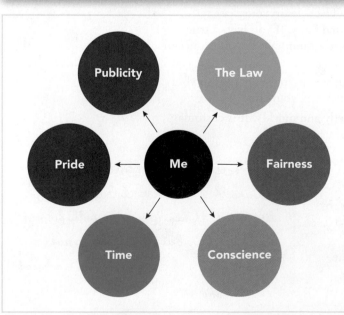

▶ Is it legal?

▶ Is it fair to me and others?

▶ Can I live with my decision?

▶ Is this decision in my long-term best interest?

▶ Could I tell my mama about it and be proud?

▶ How would I feel if this showed up on the front page of the newspaper tomorrow morning?

If you can respond positively to all six statements, this decision would most likely be in your best interest and the best interest of those around you.

MAKING MATURE DECISIONS

What Is the Importance of Academic and Personal Integrity?

As a student of higher education, you will be faced with temptations that require you to make hard choices. You have probably already been forced to make decisions based on ethics. Do I cheat and make a higher grade so I can compete with top students? Will cheating help me earn higher grades so I get a better job? Do I copy this paper from the Internet? Who will know? Why shouldn't I buy one of the term papers that is floating around my fraternity? What if I just copy someone's home-work and don't cheat on a test? What if I lie to the professor and say I was sick so I can get more time for a test for which I am not pre-pared? What if I let someone look on my paper during a test—I'm not cheating, am I? These are all ethical questions that require you to use your personal integrity to make mature decisions. Integrity is purely and simply making decisions about what is right and wrong accord-ing to your personal code of ethics and accepted social behavior.

> *"No one will question your integrity if your integrity is not questionable."*
> —Nathaniel Bronner, Jr.

CHEATING

What Do You Need to Know about Academic Misconduct?

It is important to know what constitutes dishonesty in an academic setting. The following is a list of offenses that most colleges consider academic misconduct:

- Looking on another person's test paper for answers
- Giving another student answers on tests, homework, or lab projects
- Using any kind of "cheat sheet" on a test or project
- Using a computer, calculator, dictionary, or notes when not approved
- Discussing exam questions with students who are taking the same class at another time
- "Using the words or works of others without giving proper credit, which is known as plagiarism" This includes the internet.
- Stealing another student's class notes
- Using an annotated professor's edition of a text
- Having tutors do your homework for you
- Copying files from a lab computer
- Bribing a student for answers or academic work, such as papers or projects
- Buying or acquiring papers from individuals or the Internet
- Assisting others with dishonest acts
- Lying about reasons you missed a test or a class

THE DANGERS OF USING SOMEONE ELSE'S WORK AS YOUR OWN

How Can Plagiarizing Affect Your Future?

Plagiarism is a serious offense, and you should not take it lightly—your professors do not!

Plagiarism is often defined as using another's words or ideas as your own without permission. Turnitin.com (n.d.) provides a solution to avoiding plagiarism: "Most cases of plagiarism can be avoided by citing sources. Simply acknowledging that certain material has been borrowed, and

Level 1 Remember

> "I would prefer to fail with honor than to win by cheating."
> —Sophocles

providing your audience with the information necessary to find that source, is usually enough to prevent plagiarism." Avoiding plagiarism takes a little more effort, but it saves you a great many problems.

STUDENT SERVICES AT YOUR COLLEGE

How Do College Services Affect Your Success?

Most colleges offer assistance for academic, social, cultural, spiritual, and physical enrichment outside the classroom. Your tuition or student activities fee may fund many of the centers on your campus. You've paid for them, so you should take full advantage of their services. Some college services are easier to find than others, but most are usually listed in your student handbook, college catalog, schedule of classes, or the college website. When in doubt, don't be afraid to ask your professor, advisor, or counselor if a particular service exists. It could save you time, effort, and, in many cases, money. In Figure 3.5, conduct your own campus orientation.

LET ME GIVE YOU A PIECE OF ADVICE

How Can You Make the Most of Your Advisor/Counselor Relationships?

Your academic advisor can be enormously helpful to you throughout your college career. They are usually assigned to you, although a few colleges will allow you to select your own advisor. Your advisor will help you select courses for the completion of your degree. However, you are the person most responsible for registering for classes that will count toward graduation. You should know as much as your advisor about your degree. Even though your advisor knows a great deal of information, everyone makes mistakes, so you should check to be sure you have been advised properly and that you are progressing toward graduation.

If you do not know why you have to take certain courses, or in what sequence courses should be taken, don't leave your advisor's office until you find out. Lack of understanding of your course sequence, your college catalog, or the requirements for graduation could mean the difference between a four-year degree, a five-year degree, or no college degree at all.

DEVELOPMENTAL/ REMEDIAL CLASSES

Why Is It Important to Get a Basic Foundation First?

Yes, you may need to take a developmental or remedial class. *"What is that,"* you may ask? A class in developmental/remedial education is a class that offers basic skills in areas such as math, English, vocabulary, and spelling. Most students who take these classes are directed into them by the college's placement test. Most of these classes *do not* carry academic credit, do not count toward graduation, and still cost the same amount as credit classes. Because of this, many students try very hard to avoid these classes. This can be a huge mistake on your part.

Do you think establishing a positive relationship with your advisor or counselor is really all that important? Why or why not?

Figure 3.5 Campus/Community Success Centers

Campus/Community Service	How It Can Help You	Phone Number, Physical Location, Online Resource
Academic Advisement Center	Assists in choosing classes for each semester, and offers career assessments and advice on careers	
Computer Lab	Offers students the use of e-mail, Internet services, and other on-line applications, usually free of charge	
Writing Center	Offers assistance with your writing skills; they will not rewrite your paper for you, but they can give you advice on how to strengthen your project	
Math Center	Offers help with math problems, one-on-one or group tutoring, and study sessions	
Tutoring or Mastery Learning Center	Offers assistance in almost any subject matter; many colleges offer this service free of charge (or for a very nominal fee)	
Language Lab	Offers assistance with international languages or sign language	
Library	Your college library can be the hub of your learning experience, from printed materials to Internet usage to computer assisted tutorials; your library and librarians are vital to helping you succeed in your classes and becoming information literate	
Veteran Affairs	Offers assistance to veterans, especially with government paperwork and financial aid	
Health services	Some campuses offer student services for physical and mental health, complete with a nurse and/or physician's assistant	
International Student Services	Assists international students with admissions, housing, cultural adjustment, and language barriers	
Minority Student Services	Offers services and programming for minority students on campus	
Financial Aid Office	Assists students with federal, state, and local paperwork to apply for financial aid and scholarships; they are especially helpful in assisting with your FAFSA form each year	
Student Activities	Offers a wide variety of programming in social and cultural activities	
Disabled Student Services	If you have a documented disability, colleges and universities across the U.S. are required by law to offer you "reasonable accommodations" to ensure your success (Americans with Disabilities Act, Sec. 504). Some of these accommodations include: ■ Handicapped parking ■ Special testing centers ■ Extended time on tests and timed projects ■ Textbook translations and conversions ■ Interpreters ■ Note-taking services ■ TTY/TDD services	

> "It is better to take many small steps in the right direction than to make a great leap forward only to stumble backward."
>
> —Chinese Proverb

If you really need developmental classes, they will provide a foundation for you that will make the rest of your college career much easier and more successful.

If you tested and placed in a developmental English or math class, **take it**! The assessments were put into place for your well being, not to punish you. College-level English and math classes are difficult, and if you do not know the basics, you will not do well in these and many other classes. For example, many college texts are written on the thirteenth and fourteenth grade levels. If you are reading and spelling on the seventh or even tenth-grade level, you're going to be in trouble. Therefore, do yourself a favor and take the class into which you placed. You'll save yourself money, time, and a great deal of heartache! Trust us on this one.

HOW TO CALCULATE YOUR GRADE POINT AVERAGE

Does 1 + 1 Really = 2?

The *grade point average* (GPA) is the numerical grading system used by almost every college in the nation. GPAs determine if a student is eligible for continued enrollment, financial aid, or honors. Most colleges operate under a 4.0 system. This means that:

Each A earned is worth 4 quality points, each B is worth 3 points, each C is worth 2 points, each D is worth 1 point, and each F is worth 0 points

For each course, the number of quality points earned is multiplied by the number of credit hours carried by the course. For example, if you are taking:

English 101 for 3 semester hours of credit earning an A:, $3 \times 4 = 12$

Speech 101 for 3 semester hours of credit earning a C: $3 \times 2 = 6$

History 201 for 3 semester hours of credit earning a B: $3 \times 3 = 9$

Psychology 101 for 3 semester hours of credit earning a D: $3 \times 1 = 3$

Chemistry 112 for 4 semester hours of credit earning a B: $4 \times 3 = 12$

then you are enrolled for 16 hours of academic credit and earned 42 quality points. Examine Figure 3.6 to see an example of this GPA calculation. In Figure 3.7, you will calculate a GPA.

Figure 3.6 Calculating GPA

	Grade	Semester Credit		Quality Points		Total Points
ENG 101	A	3 hours	×	4	=	12 points
SPC 101	C	3 hours	×	2	=	6 points
HIT 201	B	3 hours	×	3	=	9 points
PSY 101	D	3 hours	×	1	=	3 points
CHM 112	B	4 hours	×	3	=	12 points
		16 hours				42 Total Points

42 total points divided by 16 semester hours equals a GPA of 2.62 (or C + average).

Figure 3.7 Give It a Try—Calculating Bennie's GPA

Using the information provided below, calculate Bennie's GPA.

English 101	3 credits	Grade = A	Quality Points _____	Total _____
Chemistry 210	3 credits	Grade = C	Quality Points _____	Total _____
Chem Lab 100	1 credit	Grade = A	Quality Points _____	Total _____
Math 110	4 credits	Grade = B	Quality Points _____	Total _____
Med. Term 101	3 credits	Grade = D	Quality Points _____	Total _____
Speech 101	3 credits	Grade = B	Quality Points _____	Total _____
Total	_____ credits		Quality Points _____	Total _____

Bennie's Grade Point Average = _____

Level 3 Apply

GOING BACK TO COLLEGE AS AN ADULT STUDENT

Is Learning Now Really So Different Than When You Were Younger?

Surprisingly, yes. But, that is **not** a bad thing. Learning as an adult can certainly have its challenges, such as childcare, tending to an elderly parent, working full-time, managing a household, self-esteem issues, time management constraints, and trying to maintain healthy relationships. Take heart, however, because you are not alone. The ERIC Digest (2010) suggests that almost 50% of today's college students are classified as adult or nontraditional. Learning as an adult can also have many advantages, such as:

- More focus, drive, and motivation
- Increased career focus
- Enhanced world and life experiences
- Workplace skills and experiences

As someone who may be returning to school after a break of a few years or 30 years, keep the following tips in mind as you begin your incredible journey:

- Use your whole college: tutorial services, career counseling, library, computer centers, student activities, math and language labs. You paid for these services, don't let them go to waste.

- Quickly discover your learning style, dominant intelligence, and personality type so that you can work to adapt your learning style to various teaching styles. Basically, you will need to learn how to process information in a timely, accurate, and compelling way.

What qualities do nontraditional students bring to the college setting?

from ORDINARY to Extraordinary

Lydia Hausler Lebovic, Jewish Holocaust Survivor
Auschwitz Concentration/Extermination Camp,
Auschwitz, Poland, 1944

"Sweet Sixteen." Isn't that the moment of joy for so many female teens today? It is a milestone date when childhood passes and young adulthood arrives. One can legally drive, and in many states, "Sweet Sixteen" signifies the age of consent.

My "Sweet Sixteen" was very different. Yes, I was dating, had a somewhat rebellious relationship with my mother, and socialized with friends, but in the countryside around me, World War II raged. In 1944, when I was 16, my family and I were ordered to pack 20 pounds of personal belongings and were told that we were being taken to the "Ghetto," a holding area for Jews in my hometown of Uzhorod, Czechoslovakia, now a part of the Ukraine. I understood that the situation was not good and that things were changing, but I had no real idea of how my life would forever be altered in the coming weeks, months, and years.

After two weeks in the Ghetto, my family, friends, neighbors, and I were ordered onto cattle cars—60 to 80 per car—and told that we were being taken to Hungary to work in the corn and wheat fields. So there, in the darkness of night, our journey began—young, old, weak, strong, nursing mothers, and babies—all in the same cattle car with no water and only two buckets to use for a bathroom.

After two days of travel, the train stopped and the doors of the cattle car opened. My mother recognized that we were not in southern Hungary, but rather on the Hungary/Poland border in the north. She took us aside in the car and told us of her suspicion—that we were being taken to Auschwitz concentration camp. After another two days on the train, we arrived at Auschwitz in the early dawn hours.

The doors of the cattle cars opened and the men were quickly separated from the women, and the children from the adults. We were put into lines of five and marched forward. In front of every line was an SS officer. Quickly, I was pushed to the right and my mother and sister were pushed to the left. Little did I know at that point that those shoved to the right would be

- Don't be afraid of technology. You won't "blow up" the computer or the lab and there are people on campus to help you with your technological needs. Technology is now going to be a major part of your life.
- **Never** be afraid to ask for help from your professors, staff members, and fellow students.
- Don't let your feelings and emotions ruin your future. Yes, you may be challenged, befuddled, afraid, and even intimidated. Everyone is, regardless of age. Don't let one professor or one experience strip you of your dreams.
- Learn to delegate. It is of utmost importance that students with jobs, families, responsibilities, and relationships learn to let others do some of the work that you may have been doing for years. Delegate. Delegate. Delegate.
- Don't let the "process" ruin your dreams. Yes, there may be times when you simply don't understand why you have to take certain classes or complete certain projects. The process is a means to an end, and if you use the process well, you'll learn a great deal. Yes, you have real-world experiences, but you can still learn many valuable things from your professors, peers, and surroundings.

put to work, and those shoved to the left would be dead by the evening. I never saw my mother or sister again after that moment. I never said goodbye. I was "Sweet Sixteen."

After the separation, my group was taken to a very large building and told to undress. We were completely shaven, sponged from head to toe with a bleach-like substance, showered, and given a uniform. We were then marched to the barracks, where we would sleep 12–14 to a bed with 600 to 800 people per barracks. The black and white photo was taken as we marched toward the barracks from the shower facility and now hangs in the National Holocaust Museum in Washington, DC.

Some of the Jewish girls who had been in the camp for a while were considered "foremen." I remember approaching one such female. I asked her, "When do I get to see my mother and my sister?"

She took me by the arm and pointed me toward the billowing chimney of the crematory. "You see that smoke? You see that ash? You smell that flesh burning? That's your mother. That's your sister." Then she walked away. I did not believe her at the time, but she was absolutely right. This realization remains the most distressing of all events in my life, past and present—that my mother and sister died in such a horrific manner, gassed and cremated.

I remained in Auschwitz until I was shipped to the labor camp, Bergen-Belsen, in Germany. We were liberated on April 15, 1945. Upon liberation, I began working for the British Red Cross. Later that year, I was reunited with a friend of my brother and we were married in November of 1945. We moved to Chile in 1947, and then to Los Angeles, California, in 1963.

I now travel the nation speaking about the events of my life and delivering the message, "Never Again." I write this essay to you for many reasons, but specifically to let you know this: The Holocaust did not ruin me. They did not destroy me. They did not destroy my belief in love. They did not destroy my faith in people. They did not destroy my religion or values. The events made me a stronger, more compassionate person. I went on to become a loving wife and mother, a successful businesswoman, and, eventually, a devoted grandmother. *I refused to be ruined.* I encourage you to use the adversity in your life to make you stronger, more compassionate, more caring, and more helpful to mankind.

> *Little did I know at that point that those shoved to the right would be put to work and those shoved to the left would be dead by the evening.*

EXTRAORDINARY REFLECTION

Mrs. Lebovic suffered the death of family members during the Holocaust, but she makes the statement, "The Holocaust did not ruin me. They did not destroy me. They did not destroy my belief in love. I refused to be ruined." How can adversity in your life, like that in Mrs. Lebovic's, make you a stronger and more motivated person?

SUCCEEDING IN THE SECOND TERM AND BEYOND

What Are the Next Steps to Success?

It is never too early to begin planning for your future and the steps that will get you there successfully.

The following is a list of steps that will help you transition successfully to your second term and beyond. Put them into practice and feel the power of knowing you are ready and prepared.

Begin with the end in mind. Think about how happy you are going to be when you finish your term and you are about to go on to your next term or are getting ready to pursue a job that you really want. All the way through this venture—and any venture—work hard today, but focus on the end result and enjoy the great opportunity that you have to learn and grow.

Formulate a clear vision about what you want your life to be. This may not happen overnight, or even for a few weeks or months, but you should begin embracing certain

Successful Decisions
AN ACTIVITY FOR CRITICAL REFLECTION

JoAnne was a very shy lady who had been out of school for 27 years. When she entered her first class, she was stunned to see so many younger people and to learn that everyone seemed to have more in-depth computer skills than she did.

Horrified that her first assignment was to include a chart created in Microsoft Excel, she thought about dropping the class. "How am I going to ever learn how to turn data into a chart and insert it into a document by next week?" she thought. "I've never even heard of Excel." She even heard a classmate grumbling about dropping the class, too. Determined that she was not going to be beaten, JoAnne decided to go to the computer lab and ask for help. Within an hour, she had learned how to make a simple chart and paste it into a document.

In your own words, what advice would you give to someone who is nervous about being in school (or back in school)? List at least two things that your classmate could do to ensure his or her success.

1. _____

2. _____

thoughts, ideas, and pictures of what you want your life to be. It may sound strange, but having a visual picture of what you want actually helps you move toward it. Each transition can be looked at as another step toward getting to this beautiful vision you have created in your head.

Look inside yourself and get in touch with your inner feelings about school, work, family, and community. You will most likely never have another time when you will be as free to focus on yourself as you do right now. Even if you have a family and children, you are free to focus on you while you are in class and perhaps in between some classes.

Beware of the "second term slump." Although it is hard to pinpoint exactly what the "second term slump" really is, continuing students often find themselves confused about what they want to do, stressed because of hard decisions that need to be made, depressed because they are getting less attention in college than they did in high school, or simply tired from working, trying to spend time with a family, and keeping good grades all at the same time. This condition might invade your space early, so be prepared to combat it. Some ways to deal with the "second term slump" are:

- Interact with faculty and advisors and try to make a strong connection with at least one of them.
- Try to make connections with at least one or two fellow students with whom you have something in common.
- Realize that you may become less motivated, and that re-focusing on your purpose can help you get back on track.
- If you are not doing well in a particular subject, get help as quickly as you can. Talk to the professor, hire a tutor, start a study group, or connect with a study partner. Don't wait until it is too late!

PERSISTING FOR YOUR FUTURE

Won't You Stay for a While?

> "Striving for success without hard work is like trying to harvest where you have not planted."
>
> —David Bly

It is estimated that 30 percent of college students leave during the first year, and nearly 50 percent of the people who begin college never complete their degrees ("College Dropout Rate Climbs," 2007). The age-old scare tactic for first-year students, "Look to your left, look to your right—one of those people will not graduate with you," is not far from the truth. But the good news (actually, the great news) is that you do not have to become a statistic. You do not have to drop out of classes or college. You don't have to be the one who leaves. You have the power to earn your degree. Sure, you may have some catching up to do or face a few challenges, but the beauty of college is that if you want help, you can get help.

Below, you will find some powerful, helpful tips for persisting at your college. Using only a few of them can increase your chances of obtaining your degree or certificate. Using all of them virtually assures it!

- Visit your advisor or counselor frequently and establish a relationship with them. Take their advice and ask them questions. Use them as a mentor.
- Register for the classes in which you place when you were tested. It is unwise to register for Math 110 if you placed in Math 090 or English 101 if you placed in English 095. It will only cost you money, heartache, time, and, possibly, a low GPA.
- Make use of every academic service that you need that the college offers, from tutoring sessions to writing centers—these are essential tools to your success.
- Work hard to learn and understand your learning style. This can help you in every class in which you enroll.
- Take steps to develop a sense of community. Get to know a few people on campus, such as a special faculty member or another student—someone you can turn to for help.
- Join a club or organization. Research proves that students who are connected to the campus through activities drop out less.
- Concentrate on setting realistic, achievable goals. Visualize your goals. Write them down. Find a picture that represents your goal and post it so that you can see your goal every day.
- Work hard to develop and maintain a sense of self-esteem and self-respect. The better you feel about yourself, the more likely you will reach your goals.
- Learn to budget your time as wisely as you budget your money. You've made a commitment to college, and it will take a commitment of time to bring your degree to fruition.
- If you have trouble with a professor, don't let it fester. Make an appointment to speak with the professor and work through the problem.
- If you feel your professor doesn't care, it may be true. Some don't. This is where you have to apply the art of self-management.
- Find some type of strong, internal motivation to sustain you through the tough times—and there will be tough times.
- Focus on the future. Yes, you're taking many classes at one time while your friends are off partying, but in a few years, you'll have something that no party could ever offer, and something that no one can ever take away—your very own degree.
- Move beyond mediocrity. Everyone can be average. If getting a degree were easy, everybody would have one. You will need to learn to bring your best to the table for each class.

We wish you every success imaginable. Use us as resources, contact us, ask us questions, trust us, visit us, and allow us to help you help yourself.

CHANGING IDEAS *to Reality*

REFLECTIONS ON PERSISTENCE AND SELF-RESPONSIBILITY

Higher education is an exciting and wonderful place. You're meeting new people, being exposed to innovative ideas, and learning new ideas. There has never been a time when the old saying, "knowledge is power," is more true. By participating in your own learning, engaging in the art of self-management, and taking initiative to learn about your college, you are potentially avoiding mistakes that could cost you your education. Good for you!

Simply taking the time to familiarize yourself with the workings of your college can eliminate many of the hassles that first-year students face. By doing this, you can enjoy your experience with more energy, excitement, and optimism. As you continue on in the semester and work toward self-management, consider the following ideas:

- Determine what it is going to take for you to persist and succeed at your college.
- Practice self-responsibility.
- Guard your *ethics* and *integrity*, and use civility and personal decorum.

- Know the *policies* and *rules* of your college.
- Establish a *relationship* with your professors, advisors, and counselors.
- Join *a club* or *organization* and get involved.
- Determine if you have the time to take an online class.
- Make use of *student services*.

Knowledge in Bloom

DISCOVERING YOUR CAMPUS RESOURCES

Utilizes Level 1 of the Taxonomy (See Bloom's Taxonomy at the front of this text)

Explanation: Now that you have discovered more about your campus, professors, and the services available, complete the following Identification and Scavenger Hunt.

Question	Answer	Location	Phone Number
If you happen to fail a test, where could you go at your college to find assistance?			
If you are having trouble writing a paper or completing a written project, where could you go at your college to get assistance before you turn the paper into your professor?			
Where can you go to find out the names and meeting times of clubs and organizations at your college?			
If you need to speak to someone about a personal health issue, stress, or overwhelming anxiety, where could you go at your college or in the community to get help?			
You discover that someone broke into your car while you were in class—what should you do at this point?			
If you're having doubts about your major or what you want to do for a career, what office on your campus can help you?			
Who is your advisor advisor, counselor, or program chair?			
If you're thinking of taking an online class, where is the first place you could go to at your college to speak with someone about the technical requirements?			
If you want to read more about the penalties for academic dishonesty (cheating) at your college, where could you look?			

SQ3R MASTERY STUDY SHEET

EXAMPLE QUESTION (FROM PAGE 52) Why is it important to understand your college's policies?	**ANSWER:**
EXAMPLE QUESTION (FROM PAGE 54) What is the difference between a BA and BS degree? (from page 54)	**ANSWER:**
AUTHOR QUESTION (FROM PAGE 56) List three tips for succeeding in a class where the professor and you do not have the same first language.	**ANSWER:**
AUTHOR QUESTION (FROM PAGE 57) Why is civility and personal decorum important in a college classroom?	**ANSWER:**
AUTHOR QUESTION (FROM PAGE 60) How can I get to know my advisor or counselor better?	**ANSWER:**
AUTHOR QUESTION (FROM PAGE 60) What is an academic support service?	**ANSWER:**
AUTHOR QUESTION (FROM PAGE 66) What are two ways that I can persist in college?	**ANSWER:**
YOUR QUESTION (FROM PAGE ____)	**ANSWER:**
YOUR QUESTION (FROM PAGE ____)	**ANSWER:**
YOUR QUESTION (FROM PAGE ____)	**ANSWER:**
YOUR QUESTION (FROM PAGE ____)	**ANSWER:**
YOUR QUESTION (FROM PAGE ____)	**ANSWER:**

Finally, after answering these questions, recite this chapter's major points in your mind. Consider the following general questions to help you master this material.

- What is it about?
- What does it mean?
- What are the most important thing you learned? Why?
- What are the key points to remember?

chapter four

CONNECT

CONNECTING WITH TECHNOLOGY, RESEARCH, AND INFORMATION LITERACY

"It is so much easier to look for more and more information than to sit back and think about how it fits together." —Joanne Cantor

Scan and QUESTION

ake a few moments, **scan this chapter** and on page 100, write **five questions** that you think will be important to your mastery of this material. In addition to the two questions below, you will also find five additional questions from your authors.

Example:

☑ **Why is it important to know the different types of technology used in education?** (from page 76)

☑ **What is information literacy?** (from page 87)

Why read this chapter?

Because you'll learn...

- How technology can assist you in all classes
- How to search a topic more easily and effectively
- How to understand the rules of the Internet (netiquette)

Because you'll be able to...

- Use the steps in the information literacy process to adequately research a project
- Identify a variety of search engines and various types of educational technology
- Protect your online privacy and avoid identity theft

MyStudentSuccessLab

MyStudentSuccessLab is an online solution designed to help you acquire and develop (or hone) the skills you need to succeed. You will have access to peer-led video presentations and develop core skills through interactive exercises and projects.

Name: Mark D. Weber

Institutions: Graduate! Moraine Valley Community College, Palos Hills, IL; University of Illinois at Urbana–Champaign

Career: Management Consultant and Moraine Valley CC Trustee

The best kept secret about Moraine Valley? It's the total package, says a former student who now serves on the college's Board of Trustees.

"When folks think about a community college, it's not always looked at the same as going away to a university or college out of state," says Mark Weber, a 2003 Moraine Valley Community College graduate who was appointed to the board in 2008, and elected to a full term thereafter. "But once they're enrolled, I think people realize and can see community college is the total package."

"I was very involved while I was attending Moraine Valley," said Mark, who, in addition to his club affiliations on campus, served as a student trustee. "I really enjoyed my time here and I found it very unique to find an organization like this college that truly values people— whether students or staff."

Mark believes it was his college experience that broadened his perspective on individuals from other cultures and socioeconomic backgrounds. "I met individuals who walked into college with only the clothes on their back and graduated with the skills and opportunity

An interview conducted and written by Donna J. McCauley, Professor, Moraine Valley Community College, Palos Hills, IL

to become self-sufficient and upwardly mobile," he said. "I had a more valuable resource of knowledge and aptitude combined with access to my local community college. I had to prove myself in the university system and then the workforce, which all resulted from the foundational skills I learned at Moraine Valley."

After earning a bachelor's degree in political science with a concentration in business from the University of Illinois at Urbana–Champaign, Mark began working for the State of Illinois in Springfield, but never lost sight of his first alma mater. "I always wanted to maintain that connection to Moraine Valley, so when I heard about the referendum, I would drive back every weekend just to help out with phone calls, pass out literature, whatever was needed," he said. Mark's volunteer efforts on behalf of the $89 million bond referendum for 2006 helped the college earn voter approval for new instructional buildings, technology upgrades, and enhanced student services.

Mark, who is currently working for one of the largest professional service firms in the world, says he finds serving as a trustee for Moraine Valley very gratifying and his college experience afforded him this opportunity. "I'm very involved with one of the highest priorities for this board," Mark said. "It's seeing the capital construction come to fruition. That's very important. But also, at the end of the day, it's what the college can offer our students. Maybe it's an additional course, a new course, or an online course so a working mom can take a class. It's the personal things that resonate with me."

THINK about *it*

1. What skills do you think you are learning right now at your college that will serve you well in the world of work?

2. What could you do right now to help your college?

THE FAST, EVER-CHANGING FACE OF TECHNOLOGY

Can Anyone Possibly Keep Up?

You've probably heard the old expression, *"It's like a train wreck…you can't look at it and you can't look away."* Some people view today's technological changes and advances as something you can't look at, but if you look away for even a moment, you're lost. Between the tools of Twitter, Jing, Bing, Voice Thread, Facebook, Blackboard, streaming video, Hulu, YouTube, and countless other programs and services, it is vital that you know the basics of these tools as your instructors may use them in class or require you to use them beyond the classroom. At the very least, it is important to know they exist and how to find help in using these new, ever-changing learning tools.

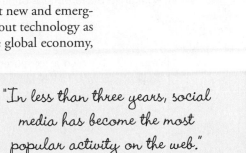

How much technology is too much?

In today's technologically driven education environment, colleges have classes, entire degrees, schedules, course listings, and other pertinent information and programs online. Office hours with faculty members are held via a learning management program, Skype, or a social networking tool. Cooperative learning activities are facilitated by programs such as dimdim, WebEx, or E-lluminate. Often, students are required to research or network with people outside their own institution—many times internationally. We have truly become a global society through technology. This is one of the main reasons we all need to learn as much about new and emerging technologies as possible. Another monumental reason to learn as much about technology as possible is the fact that almost any career you pursue will be impacted by the global economy, and the competition is brutal.

You may be saying, *"I'm online all the time—I Facebook my friends, I use Skype, e-mail my instructors, and research topics for papers and speeches."* All of this is great and we encourage you to use the technology that will help you build relationships, connect with others, and continue learning. However, if you are honest with yourself, you may have to admit that much of your time online is spent in activities that do not use the tools to your educational advantage. You may also have to admit that, sometimes, you are overwhelmed by the amount of information available on

"In less than three years, social media has become the most popular activity on the web."

—Erik Qualman

one topic. This chapter will help you learn the many technological tools available to assist you in becoming a better student, researcher, writer, and employee in the 21st century.

SPENDING TIME ONLINE

Are You Searching, Perching, or Lurking?

You get online with a purpose, a real purpose, and before you know it, hours have passed and you find that you've wasted all this time and nothing has been accomplished. This is not an uncommon occurrence. You may have had the best of intentions to go online and work or research

Figure 4.1 Are You Addicted to Technology?

The following survey will help you assess whether you use technology in a smart, healthy, useful way or whether you have an addiction to tapping, clicking, texting, searching, and tweeting. Truthfully answer the following questions using the scale provided. The results of this survey are at the bottom of the assessment.

1 = Never   2 = Sometimes   3 = Frequently   4 = Always

____ 1. I eat my meals in front of a computer, phone, or television.

____ 2. I turn on my computer or TV or check my messages immediately upon waking.

____ 3. If the power goes out or my battery goes dead, I begin to panic after 15 minutes (or sooner).

____ 4. I must check my non–work related messages, e-mails, Facebook page, Twitter account, or texts more frequently than every two hours.

____ 5. I check my e-mail, texts, or Facebook page while in class, at religious services, at the movies, or in social settings.

____ 6. I take my phone or laptop to the bathroom with me.

____ 7. I communicate more on Facebook than I do in person, over the phone, or by handwritten correspondence.

____ 8. I spend a at least a fourth of my monthly budget on technology costs (phone bill, texting plans, Internet connections, cable TV, video games, new gadgets, etc.).

____ 9. My parents, spouse, partner, and/or friends complain that I spend too much time using technology.

____ 10. I find it easier to make friends online than communicate with new people in a class or social setting.

____ 11. I lose track of time due to using technology, texting, or being online.

____ 12. I read tweets, texts, e-mails, or news, or play games while watching a movie.

____ 13. When I go out with friends (to movies, dinner, social settings), I have my phone with me at all times so that I can check my messages.

____ 14. I get halfway to my destination, realize I forgot my non–work related or non–school related technology device, and turn around and go back to get it.

____ 15. When I get an important piece of news (good or bad) I communicate this news through social media.

SCORE

15–33	You probably own a computer and cell phone but do not use them on an hourly basis. You may struggle to keep up with conversations that involve "tech speak." You may actually need to engage in the use of more technology to keep current with changing programs and social media applications for work and education. You probably have strong face-to-face relationships. **Consider this:** If you are not a member of a social media group, join one and establish a communication pattern using this technology. Sit with friends and ask them to help you learn at least one new technology application.
31–45	You are tech savvy. You use technology frequently. You have a healthy balance between the use of technology and personal relationships. You know how to use many programs, but you are not obsessed with having technology with you at all times. You can take a vacation, go to dinner, or spend time in a leisure activity without constantly thinking about a missed text message. **Consider this:** Stay the course. Continue to use technology in a healthy fashion and strive to keep your personal relations healthy via technology and with face-to-face meeting.
46–60	You are totally addicted to technology, and your cell phone has become a part of your anatomy. You probably sacrifice close, personal relationships for time online. Being without your technology is almost a life or death situation. If you had to do without it, you would be in dire straits or begin to hyperventilate. **Consider this:** Once daily, put down your computer, phone, tablet, or e-reader. Do not check messages, send texts, or e-mail anyone. Instead, use face-to-face interaction for at least one hour. After a week of doing this daily, try it for two hours in the second week.

a project, but before you know it, you've checked e-mail, watched a YouTube video, IMed three friends, Facebooked five friends, and checked your Twitter messages. This may not be the best use of your time.

How can we spend quality time online? Consider the following tips when going online to work or complete an assignment:

- Use your favorite e-tools (Twitter, Facebook, eBay, etc.) as a *reward* for getting your work done. This is a strong priority management tool. Work first, then socialize, play, and shop.
- Have a plan and a timeline before you go online. If you have a topic to research, allow yourself enough time to do your work, check your messages, and network with friends later.
- When going online, do not sign onto Facebook, Twitter, or e-mail until you have completed your work. Don't tempt yourself.
- Treat your time online as you would treat your time at work. Divide your time into work time and break time, but put your break time at the end.
- Allow yourself enough time during the day to do all of the things online that you love to do, such as network, search iTunes or Rhapsody, Google, or play games. There is nothing wrong with enjoying technology if your other work has been completed.
- Let your e-friends know when you'll be online for work and when you'll be online for socializing. Don't cross or blur the lines.

EVALUATING YOUR TECHNOLOGY SKILLS

Do You Really Need to Know Them All?

One of the most wonderful things about the world of technology is that if you have never heard of a program or don't know how to use a certain application, there is immediate, useful help online on sites such as www.butterscotch.com and www.youtube.com. If you don't know how to create a movie using Jing or Camtasia, all you have to do is go to YouTube and you'll find a tutorial to assist you. If you don't know what the Blackboard Course Management System is or how to use it for class, you can simply go to Google, type in "Blackboard Learning" and read about the program and watch a brief demo tutorial. This is the beauty of technology. The curse? It seems to change every day. Learning to keep up with the latest trends and how to apply these to your educational process is imperative. Learning the programs, applications, and terminology is also important.

> "Technology makes it possible for people to gain control over everything, except over technology."
> —John Tutor

Figure 4.2 will detail some of the major programs and applications used in today's higher education setting. You may not be required to use them all, but it will be helpful to familiarize yourself with the different applications and their websites in case the need arises.

LEARNING THE LANGUAGE OF TECHNOLOGY

What Is a Worm and Why Is It in Your Computer?

As you begin to familiarize yourself with the many aspects of computer literacy, there may be terms that pop up that you have not heard before. The list of terms defined in Figure 4.3 will help you as you discover more about the world of technology and computer literacy.

Level 2 Understand

Level 3 Apply

Figure 4.2 — Types of Technology in Education

Description	Program	Website	How Could You Use These Programs to Help with a Class or Assignment?
Software Programs Common word processing, presentation, and chart/graph creation packages used on PCs and Macs	Microsoft Office (Word, Excel, PowerPoint) Prezi Pages for Mac Google Docs	www.microsoftoffice .com www.prezi.com www.apple.com/iwork/ pages www.docs.google.com	
Popular Learning Management Systems Used to offer classes and training throughout higher education and business	Blackboard Moodlerooms E-lluminate Course Compass Desire-2-Learn Instructure	www.blackboard.com www.moodlerooms .com www.elluminate.com www.coursecompass .com www.desire2learn.com www.instructure.com	
Group Communication Tools Used to communicate in groups and share information on your computer screen with others around the world	dimdim Twitter Voicethread Go-To-Meeting Web-Ex	www.dimdim.com www.twitter.com www.voicethread.com www.gotomeeting .com www.webex.com	
Social Networking/ Sharing Sites Used to network with business professionals who may help you find employment, chat with and make friends, keep in touch, and post the latest news and photos	Facebook Twitter LinkedIn Google+	www.facebook.com www.twitter.com www.linkedin.com www.plus.google.com	
Photo/Video Building and Viewing Used to create and/ or view videos and share them with friends or colleagues	Jing YouTube Hulu Flickr Camtasia	www.techsmith.com/ jing www.youtube.com www.hulu.com www.flickr.com www.techsmith.com/ camtasia	

Description	Program	Website	How Could You Use These Programs to Help with a Class or Assignment?
Commonly Used Search/Research Engines Used to research topics of interest that may have been assigned to you by your professor; it is wise to use a variety of these sites instead of relying on just one	Google Dogpile Yahoo Ask Lycos Wikipedia Bing Alta Vista	www.google.com www.dogpile.com www.yahoo.com www.ask.com www.lycos.com www.wikipedia.com www.bing.com www.altavista.com	
Tools to Help You Learn to Use New Technology Offer easy-to-use video tutorials to help you use some of the technologies that may be required of you in the classroom	YouTube eHow Butterscotch	www.youtube.com www.ehow.com www.butterscotch.com	
Document Sharing Tools Allow you to share your word processing documents with others for additions, comments, and editing	Wiki Google Docs WorkZone WorkShare	www.pbworks.com www.docs.google.com www.workzone.com www.workshare.com	
Digital Note-Taking Systems Allow you to take notes online	MyNote Yahoo Notes Notefish Note IT Ubernote Springnote	www.mynote.com www.widgets.yahoo.com www.notefish.com www.noteit.com www.ubernote.com www.springnote.com	

Figure 4.3   **The Techno-Pedia**

Bookmarks	These allow you to tag popular sites so that you can easily access that site again, usually with one click.
Cookie	This term refers to data that is sent to your computer by a company's computer to monitor your actions while on their site. Cookies remember your login and password information and track what you viewed or purchased the last time you visited that site.
"dot.com"	**.com** is the most common ending for Internet addresses. However, there are many Internet endings. The following will help you direct your internet searches: ■ .com: Used to search **com**mercial, for-profit businesses ■ .edu: Used to search **edu**cational institutions, colleges, universities

(continued)

Figure 4.3   The Techno-Pedia (*Continued*)

	■ .net: Used by Inter**net** service providers ■ .gov: Used to search documents within the U.S. **gov**ernment ■ .org: Used to search non-profit **org**anizations ■ .mil: Used to search information from the U.S. **mil**itary ■ .us: Used to search any organization in specific countries such as (.us) **U**nited **S**tates, (.uk) **U**nited **K**ingdom (England), (.fr) **Fr**ance, (.se) **Sw**eden, or (.de) Germany (**De**utschland)
Hacker	A modern-day bank robber. This is a person who electronically breaks into your computer and steals your private and sensitive information, often to use for illegal purposes.
HDTV/HDV	**H**igh **d**efinition **t**elevision or **h**igh **d**efinition **v**ideo. They are high quality, crisp, visually appealing TV or video recordings.
Phishing	A scheme by hackers to acquire your private information, such as passwords, login codes, and credit card information, by using "real" company logos in their correspondence. They trick you into updating your information for a company or site you trust, when in actuality, you are directly providing the hacker your information. To avoid phishing schemes, do not click on suspicious links within e-mails, do not provide personal information in any format, and call the company to answer questions asked in the correspondence.
PDF	**P**ortable **d**ocument **f**ormat. This format was created by Adobe as a document-sharing format that is independent of software programs and applications, such as Word and PowerPoint.
Podcasts	Combines the terms iPod and broadcast into a single word. It is a video or audio file you can access on your smart phone, tablet, or other media device.
Malware	A catchphrase for "*Malicious Software,*" or viruses. Malware are programs that are unknowingly placed on your computer to cause technological harm. Common types of malware are ***Trojan horses, worms, and spyware*** that delete files or directory information and cause your computer to function improperly. To avoid them, do not open files from unknown sites and keep your spyware and virus programs up-to-date.
Right Click	Refers to clicking on the right side of your mouse to reveal additional menus and pop-ups. A mouse is automatically set to the Left Click for common tasks.
RTF	**R**ich **t**ext **f**ormat. RTF was developed by Microsoft as a document file format to make files easier to open in most formats and programs on most computers.
URL	**U**niversal **R**etrieval **L**anguage. The URL is the Internet address that you type into your search bar, such as www.yahoo.com, www.youtube.com, or www.pearsonhighered.com.
Web 2.0	Web 2.0 is the new age of the Internet. Web 1.0 was created as a one-sided, "you search it, we define it" tool, while Web 2.0 is more interactive, with social media (Facebook, Twitter, etc.), blogs, document sharing, videos, and interactive searches.

USEFUL INTERNET SITES AND SEARCHES

How Can You Find Specific Information?

Often, you may need to find specific information. Perhaps you need to find a map of a specific country for your business management course, or you need to know if a book is in print, or find the population of Iowa. The information in Figure 4.4 can help you save a great deal of time.

Figure 4.4 Information Searches Made Easy

If You Need to Know . . .	Search These Addresses
How to locate a **place** or view a **map**	www.earth.google.com www.about.com www.mapquest.com
Find out if a **book is in print** Search **contents** and **entire scanned books**	www.amazon.com www.bookfinder.com www.bowker.com www.books.google.com www.openlibrary.org www.gutenberg.org
U.S. and state-by-state **population, economic, and workforce data**	www.census.gov
Information on famous people (**biographies**)	www.loc.gov (Library of Congress) www.who2.com www.biography.com
Unbiased information and comparisons on world **religions**	www.patheos.com
Federal or state **legislation**	www.thomas.loc.gov www.house.gov www.whpgs.org/f.htm
Magazine and newspaper **articles**	www.newslink.org www.infotrac.net www.ehow.com
Information about a **specific country**	www.infoplease.com www.countryreports.org
Information about **careers**	www.bls.gov www.careeroverview.com www.occupationalinfo.org
Simple, dynamic, and effective instructional **videos on math, algebra, calculus, biology, chemistry, government, history, art history, finance, business,** and more	www.khanacademy.org

Remember, it is always best to view a number of resources (online and in print) to ensure the accuracy and validity of your information.

OR! AND! NOT!

How Can These Simple Words Save Hours of Research Time?

As a first-year student, throughout your college career, and often into the world of work, you will be asked to research and write papers, prepare speeches, and develop projects based on data and facts. Learning to correctly and efficiently use the Internet and research methodology now can save you much time as you move through your studies and into your profession. Consider the following method using Boolean logic.

If you are trying to broaden or narrow your search on a specific topic, three simple words—"OR," "AND," and "NOT"—when typed into your search engine, can save you time online. Using *Boolean logic* ("Boolean Searching on the Internet," 2012) helps direct your search more effectively. This method will reduce the number of articles found, but more importantly, it will combine the topics for you to make your search easier. For example, if you were writing a paper or speech on Rosa Parks and the Civil Rights Movement and typed "Rosa Parks" into Google, you will get over 10 million hits. If you type "Civil Rights Movement" into Google, you will get over 8 million hits, for a **total of over 18 million hits**. However, if you type in "Rosa Parks **AND** The Civil Rights Movement", you will narrow your search to a total of approximately 187,000 hits that contain the two topics together in your search. This is still many more articles than any human can digest, but it does cut your search and combines the topics together for you. See Figure 4.5 for an example of an **AND** search.

If you want to search *only* for Rosa Parks and *not* the Civil Rights Movement, you would type "Rosa Parks **NOT** The Civil Rights Movement" into your search engine. This will limit your research to topics *only* on Rosa Parks and not on the Civil Rights Movement. See Figure 4.6 for an example of a **NOT** search.

To search for websites with synonymous terms on both topics, you would type "Rosa Parks **OR** The Civil Rights Movement" into your search engine.

If you want to get the results for an *exact* topic, put **quotation marks** around the word(s), for example, "Civil Rights Movement." The search engine will now search those exact words only. This can be helpful when you are looking for ideas, rather than exact titles, such as the "death of Rosa Parks." This search will only show articles on her death and obituary.

Figure 4.5 A Boolean Logic "AND" Search

Search Item	Results
Rosa Parks	>10 million
The Civil Rights Movement	>8 million
Rosa Parks **AND** The Civil Rights Movement	~187,000

Figure 4.6 A Boolean Logic "NOT" Search

Search Item	Results
Rosa Parks	>10 million
The Civil Rights Movement	>8 million
Rosa Parks **NOT** The Civil Rights Movement	~841,000

Figure 4.7 A "Quotation" Search

Search Item	Results
Rosa Parks	>10 million
Death of Rosa Parks	>3 million
"Death of Rosa Parks"	~63,500

Successful Decisions
AN ACTIVITY FOR CRITICAL REFLECTION

Anita is returning to school after a 30-year absence. When she was in high school, the latest piece of technology was the IBM electric typewriter and a copy machine. She took typing in high school, but it has been years since she used the skill. She can still type, but does so very slowly.

Upon registering for classes, Anita discovered that two of her instructors require her to access the course material from the learning management system, and one instructor requires all students to work in online groups. She is terrified. She has used a computer, but only sparingly. She has a negative attitude about learning Facebook or Twitter, and sees no point in using this technology for class. She does not have a computer at home, and she does not know if she can catch up with the skills she needs to be successful at her institution.

What suggestions would you make to Anita to help her adjust to the world of technology, social media, and online classes?

1. _____

2. _____

3. _____

SOCIAL MEDIA FOR EDUCATIONAL PURPOSES

Can Facebook Be Used for More Than Updating Your Photos?

Most educational institutions and businesses are using social networking sites in numerous ways to interact with students and customers. They use these sites to send messages, offer advice, and deliver positive advertising. Most everyone is now using some type of social media for "non-academic" purposes. As a first-year college student, we highly recommend that you familiarize yourself with as many social networking sites as possible, and become an expert on at least one of them, because you may be required to use one or more of them in your classes to gather data, do opinion polling, communicate with team members, or ask professors questions. Once you have mastered the skills needed to navigate the site, list your expertise on your resume. Regardless of what field you enter today, most employers will be looking for social media experts to help them develop, expand, and connect with their customer base. Information regarding a few of the most popular and widely used social media is discussed below.

Facebook is one of the most widely used and rapidly growing social media applications in existence. It is used to connect and communicate across social and business lines. Companies are using Facebook to promote their products, announce new products, interact with customers, track their customers' buying habits, and recruit and retain employees. "The fastest growing demographic of Facebook users is those twenty-five years and older" (Kabani, 2010). According to Kabani, Facebook is like a coffee shop—it is a great place to strike up a conversation. Research shows that many people use Facebook to share their personal information and identity. In college, you may be asked to use Facebook to connect with study groups or even communicate with your professors. Class and college announcements may be posted on Facebook pages. You can access Facebook and start your own page at www.facebook.com.

LinkedIn is considered the professionals' site and is described by Kabani (2010) as a "buttoned-down office-networking event. If Facebook is happy hour, LinkedIn is all business, suit and tie." This is a site that should be treated as strictly business, and is certainly not the place to post unflattering pictures or information that might be

How can social media help you with your current field of study?

damaging to you if a potential or current employer happened to see it. This site usually attracts well-educated people who tend to be more affluent. LinkedIn is a great place to post your resume, since the people frequenting this site might be searching for good employees. You can post recommendations from references (with their permission, of course) or positive letters from professors or peers. If someone posts a recommendation for you, you will get a message giving you an opportunity to accept or reject the recommendation's posting. As a first-year student, you may discover that LinkedIn can be important to you as you begin to develop a network of people in your field, search for summer or full-time employment, or begin a portfolio project. Some professors now require the use of LinkedIn as the format for the professional portfolio.

Twitter falls in the category of microblog. A microblog is a brief message (no more than 140 characters long) that typically uses abbreviations or Internet acronyms such OMG (Oh My God) or LOL (laugh out loud) in order to pack more information into a message. Some people are constantly sending "tweets," (messages) telling their friends every move they make. As a professional, you need to leave this behavior behind and learn how to use Twitter to deliver time-sensitive information, to inform your group about a special event, educational opportunity, or upcoming meeting. Twitter is an excellent way to grab online visibility, but this visibility can be positive or negative depending on your tweets. As a first-year student, you may be asked to use Twitter to quickly summarize an entire chapter, comment on a professor's or peer's statement, or even to work within a group.

Collaborative Communication Programs

Today, so many students and employees work in **virtual teams** (people who work together but are not physically located in the same place), and they find collaborative communication programs to be very helpful and effective. While there are several available, we are going to discuss two of the most popular: Wikis and Google Docs.

A **Wiki** is a web page that can be viewed and modified by anybody with a web browser, the Wiki URL, and access to the Internet—it could be called a web page with an edit button. This means that any visitor to the wiki can change its content if they desire, and it enables people to collaborate with others online easily. Wikis can be surprisingly robust and open-ended, and can make a good collaborative group site. They can be password protected, if desired. Participants can add information to a wiki or edit what someone else has written. You may be asked to use a Wiki in one of your classes to collaborate on a group paper or project.

Google Docs is a great tool for virtual teams because it is absolutely free and it enables you to create documents, spreadsheets, presentations, forms, drawings, etc. while working from anywhere around the world simply by accessing the Internet. Some people refer to it as an online alternative to the Microsoft Office package, which, of course, is not free. You can share documents, presentations, forms, spreadsheets, etc., with anyone you want from within Google Docs itself without manually finding a file and attaching it as an email. It is very easy to download documents to your hard drive if you want to save a document on your computer. Google Docs may be required as you get into more advanced classes where data, research, and opinions are shared with others.

Another great collaborative program is *Skype*, a program for working, communicating, and celebrating together although you may be miles apart from each other. This program can be used between two people (or more) and is a great way to hold a "face-to-face" conference when two people need to participate. More than two people can join the meeting on Skype, but at that point you lose video capability and have only audio capability unless you subscribe to Skype's monthly fee. You can hold meetings, have a work session, or just visit with friends. The great thing about Skype is that the basic program is free and can be downloaded to your computer or smartphone from the Internet. For a small fee, you can communicate internationally with friends and virtual team members. You may even find that your professor holds office hours on Skype. This is not an uncommon occurrence in today's educational setting, as it saves time, gives immediate access during prescribed times, and allows a face-to-face meeting with your professor.

MAXIMIZING THE USE OF TECHNOLOGY

How Can Tech Tools Help with Your Classes?

Regardless of the class, you are probably going to be required to use some type of technology. From research to editing to communication, the use of technology in today's college classroom is almost inescapable. Consider the classes found in the "Core of Classes" (Figure 4.8) for many colleges. List at least two ways that technology could help you in each of these classes. One example is given to you in each category.

Figure 4.8   **How Can Technology Help**

Core Class	Describe Two Ways Technology Can Help You Be Successful
English	**Example:** Research the proper use of a semicolon. 1. 2.
Hard sciences (biology, chemistry, physics)	**Example:** Watch the virtual dissection of a pig for your Biology class. 1. 2.
International language (Arabic, Spanish, French, Russian)	**Example:** Initiate a Twitter "conversation" with someone from Russia and ask him/her to converse with you in his/her native language for practice. 1. 2.
Fine arts (art, music, theatre)	**Example:** Watch a video snip of a Broadway play or dance concert. 1. 2.
Social sciences (psychology, sociology, anthropology)	**Example:** Research the population trends in Africa, plot them on a map, and distinguish what those trends mean. 1. 2.
Computer/information science	**Example:** Research how to create an Excel spreadsheet. 1. 2.
Mathematics	**Example:** Watch a YouTube video on how to divide fractions and then practice what you have learned. 1. 2.
One class in **your major** field of study	1. 2.

Level 2 Understand

PRIVACY AND SECURITY ISSUES

Did You Know You're a Published Author?

Congratulations! *You're an author*—that is, if you have ever sent a tweet. As of 2010, the Library of Congress has archived **every** tweet *ever sent* since Twitter's inception in 2006. If you have ever sent a tweet—good or bad, nice or naughty, serious or silly—you are a part of the Library of Congress. This is just *one* of the many aspects of privacy on the web. Privacy issues can be monumental obstacles to you now and later in your life. Therefore, it is important that you guard your privacy and watch your online activities. What you post online now in a silly, romantic moment can come back later to cost you that dream job. Be careful what you post online, as nothing on the Internet is private. In a world of Wikileaks, hackers, and savvy researchers, *your* words and photos are *public* words and photos.

To protect yourself and your online information as much as possible, consider the following tips and suggestions.

> "Treat your password like your toothbrush. Don't let anybody else use it, and get a new one every six months."
> —Clifford Stoll

Ten Ways to Protect Your Assets

- Create a strong, uncommon password for your accounts. Try to use a combination of at least eight letters, numbers, and symbols such as RO#99@SH.

- Do not share your passwords with anyone—not roommates, not family members, not even your best friends. Relationships change, and you may later regret providing this information.

- Do not use common events such as your birthday, anniversary, or child's birth as your password.

- Be careful when you post your photo. Even if you post your photo on your personal Facebook page, it can be found by a simple web search.

- Use only secure websites for any type of financial transaction. Look for the security seals on the website, such as Verisign, Comodo, and GeoTrust. Try to *never* use your debit card online. If you must purchase from an online site, use credit cards or the payment site PayPal (www.paypal.com).

- Learn how to use online security features and privacy settings. These are offered for your safety and for the protection of your information.

- Don't tell your Facebook or online friends that you will not be home. This invites break-ins and burglary at your home. It is best to post vacation photos when you return home, not while you are traveling.

- Install and run your security and spyware protections at least twice per week.

- Turn off or delete cookies from your computer.

- Be very wary of anyone asking for personal information to "update our records." It is probably a phishing scheme.

- Teach your children not to provide private information or to go onto unknown sites and chatrooms.

What is the most important thing you can do to avoid identity theft?

RIDIN' HIGH ON THE INFORMATION SUPER HIGHWAY

What Are the Rules of the Road?

Yes, there are rules for proper etiquette in an online class, when texting, IMing, tweeting, or simply conversing with friends. By knowing and applying these simple guidelines, you will be taken more seriously and so will your correspondence. Consider using the following "rules of the road" when sending e-communications.

- Never, ever send an e-mail, IM, tweet, or any other type of e-communication that you would not want anyone else to read. *E-communication is not private,* especially when done from a computer at work. Information is available on the web for a long, long time.

- Avoid language that may come across as angry, mean, insulting, or strong. People can't see your face online and may not know you're "kidding." If you use ALL CAPS, this may come across as angry.

- Use the twenty-four hour rule when responding to a piece of correspondence. Do not respond in anger or fear. Once the "send" button has been pressed, you can't take it back. Use restraint, re-read the correspondence, and once you have "cooled off," make your decision about what to write.

- Read your e-mails before you send them. Check for errors in grammar, content, and fact.

- Text language (LOL, OMG, BFF, :-(, BTW, FYI) is fine when texting or IMing with your friends, but not for e-mails or class projects/papers. Use text language sparingly.

- If possible, let someone read your e-correspondence for accuracy and clarity. If the other person can't understand it, you need to re-write it.

- When texting, IMing, and e-mailing, consider other people's time and how many pieces of e-correspondence they may get in one day.

- Don't forward e-correspondence that you do not have permission to forward.

- Treat people online with the same courtesy, politeness, and respect you would give them in a face-to-face situation.

- Don't use language you would not want your grandmother to read.

- Don't forward e-mail hoaxes, urban legends, or chain letters, as people find them annoying and you may also be forwarding a virus. Anything promising ten million dollars from an overseas account is a scam, and Bill Gates is *not* going to give you any of his money for e-mailing your friends—even if your friend's doctor's best friend's mother's lawyer checked it out!

- If you receive an e-mail along with 15 or 20 other people, respond *only* to the person who sent the e-mail unless otherwise advised. Don't hit "reply all."

- Online e-communications, especially e-mails, *should* contain proper opening and closing salutations, not just content that begins and ends.

By adhering to these online "rules of the road," you will soon find that your online correspondence is more effective.

DID YOU *Know?*

APOLO OHNO was born to a Japanese father and a Caucasian American mother who divorced when he was an infant. Apolo was raised by his father in Seattle, and he has had practically no contact with his mother or his half-brother. Because his father worked long hours as a hair stylist, he carefully found activities for Apolo to engage in so he would not become a latchkey child. Apolo became involved in competitive swimming and quad speed skating at age 6, and later was instructed in inline speed skating. Ohno's days were spent practicing swimming, going to school, and attending long skating practices every afternoon. He became a national inline speed skating champion.

At the age of 14, Apolo became the youngest U.S. National Champion in short track racing, and remained the champion from 2001–2009. In December 1999, he became the first American and the youngest skater to win a World Cup event. In 2001, he was the first American to win a World Cup overall title, which he recaptured in 2003 and 2005. Apolo was named U.S. Speedskating's Athlete of the Year for 2003. He has worked as a motivational speaker and started his own philanthropic foundation. Because he believes in healthy eating habits, Apolo started his own business marketing nutritional supplements called 8 Zone. In 2007, he won the competition on *Dancing With the Stars*. He is working on a cookbook with top Seattle chefs that will promote healthier food choices.

ON THE GO AND GOING ONLINE— WHERE IT ALL COMES TOGETHER

How Do You Succeed in Distance Education Courses?

Distance learning classes can be great for students who may live far from campus, have transportation issues, work full-time, or have families and small children. These courses are scheduled with flexible hours and few, if any, class meetings. Most online classes allow you to work at your own pace, but most still have stringent deadlines for assignment submission.

Do not let anyone try to tell you that these courses are easier than regular classroom offerings; they are not. Distance learning courses are usually more difficult for the average student because you must be highly self-disciplined and be an independent worker. Some colleges reserve distance-learning courses for students with GPAs of 3.0 or higher. You need to be a self-starter and highly motivated to complete and do well in these courses. Take the assessment in Figure 4.9 to determine if an online class is right for you.

Figure 4.9 Distance Education Readiness Assessment

Please answer each question truthfully to determine your readiness for online learning.

1. Do you own your own computer?	Yes	No
2. Is your computer relatively new (enough memory, flash drive slots, graphics card, wireless internet, etc.)?	Yes	No
3. Can you type (not just text or "hunt and peck," but type)?	Yes	No
4. Are you comfortable using a computer and web technology such as an LMS, Skype, and document sharing?	Yes	No
5. Do you have the technical requirements for online learning? (Internet access, Internet browser, Adobe, Word or compatible program, PowerPoint, Excel, etc.)	Yes	No
6. Are you highly organized?	Yes	No
7. Do you manage your time well?	Yes	No
8. Are you highly motivated, a self-starter?	Yes	No
9. If you work full or part time, do you feel you have at least 6–8 hours per week to spend working with each of your online classes?	Yes	No
10. If you have family issues that require a great deal of your time, do you have family support?	Yes	No
11. Do you have "down time" to spend working on your online classes?	Yes	No
12. Can you get to campus if necessary?	Yes	No
13. Do you feel comfortable chatting online with unknown persons?	Yes	No
14. Do you think you can "relate" to others in an online relationship?	Yes	No
15. Do you consider yourself a good online reader with high-level comprehension skills?	Yes	No
16. Can you concentrate on your work even with online distractions (e-mail, friends, etc.)?	Yes	No
17. Do you feel comfortable calling your instructors during their office hours if you need to do so?	Yes	No
18. Do you think you will be able to take notes during an online chat or class session?	Yes	No
19. Can you use an online note-taking system?	Yes	No
20. Are you excited about taking an online class?	Yes	No

If you answered "no" to more than three of these questions, you should reconsider taking an online class at this time. To prepare for future classes, you may also want to spend time researching and becoming more familiar with the questions that you marked "no". You can also speak with your advisor or professor about your possibility for success in his or her course. Your campus probably offers an online orientation from which you might benefit.

© Robert M. Sherfield, Ph.D.

If you decide to take an online class, consider the following advice:

- If at all possible, review the course material before you register. This may help you in making the decision to enroll. Often, professors' syllabi are accessible online.

- Begin before the beginning! If at all possible, obtain the distance learning materials (or at least the text) before the semester begins. Getting ahead gives you more confidence.

- Know if your class is totally online or a hybrid course—it makes a huge difference.

- Make an appointment to meet the instructor as soon as possible. Some institutions will schedule a meeting for you. If it is not possible to meet, at least phone the professor and introduce yourself.

- Log in on a daily basis, even if nothing is due. Important messages may be posted.

- **Quickly learn** the required technology and software programs to be successful and make sure you have access to these programs.

- Develop a schedule for completing each assignment and stick to it! Don't let time steal away from you—this is the biggest problem with online classes.

- Keep a copy of all work mailed, e-mailed, or delivered to the instructor.

- Always mail, e-mail, or deliver your assignment on time—early if possible.

- Take full advantage of any online orientation, training sessions, tutoring, and advisement.

- Participate in class, in chats, and in your groups (if you are assigned a group).

- If you have computer failure, have a back-up plan.

- Alert your instructor immediately if you have family, computer, or personal problems that would prevent you from completing an assignment on time—after the due date is too late.

- Work ahead if possible.

- Find out where to go or whom to call on campus should you encounter technical problems with the learning platform or getting online.

- **Never** be afraid to knock on your instructor's digital office door. Many instructors hold office hours online and welcome your comments and questions.

PRACTICING INFORMATION LITERACY IN THE AGE OF TECHNOLOGY

Why Is It Important to Know How to Sort Through and Evaluate Information?

Anyone, yes, **anyone,** can post information on the Internet. Much of the information online is not screened for accuracy, judged on truth, or critiqued for its worth. Often, much of what you find online may not even indicate an author's name. Some of it will be accurate and valuable, while other pieces will be full of half-truths, downright lies, and false claims. Some information will be legitimate and helpful, and some will be nothing more than a false advertisement to con you into buying something. Some will be unbiased and impartial, and some will be slanted and unbalanced by the person or company who posted it. Therefore, it is up to you to learn how to determine the worth, value, and accuracy of the information you find online.

Information literacy (IL) includes the skills a person needs to determine what information is needed, where to find it, how much of it you need for a specific topic, how to analyze and organize it to create your "product," and, finally, how to properly cite it. The procedure is that simple and that complex. *Information literacy* impacts all aspects of your college career and will later play a major

"More information, by overwhelming and distracting the brain, can make it harder to tap into just the core information you need."

—Eric Kessler

role in your success in the workplace. You will use information literacy when you write a paper, read an article and evaluate it, listen to presenters and determine if you believe what they are saying, and when preparing and making your own presentations. Information literacy is the cornerstone of an educated mind.

If you master the processes of information literacy in the digital age, you will gain more control over what you are learning and how you can apply it. You will become more adept at distinguishing facts from untruths while selecting points that support your topic or research problem. Regardless of your major, you cannot escape the need to locate, analyze, apply, and present information in a compelling and logical manner. You will also become a more savvy consumer because you can make informed decisions about shopping, voting, investing, purchasing a home or car, choosing your major, and a host of other important life decisions.

THE INFORMATION LITERACY PROCESS

Can You Hit the Bulls Eye with Darts?

Becoming information literate does not just happen by opening a book or logging onto Google. True IL begins by understanding the process of research. This section will help you identify and remember the steps in using IL skills. Using the **DARTS System for Information Literacy** (Figure 4.10), you can easily remember the steps, use them often, and benefit from their practicality.

D = Determine the Information You Need by Narrowing Your Topic

Research begins by asking a question. Suppose that you have been assigned a paper or speech and the topic is up to you. You decided that you want to write or speak on Rosa Parks. You begin the research and type Rosa Parks into Google. You get over 10 million hits. This is just a few too many articles to read by Monday. However, if you begin with a question in mind, you can narrow your topic and determine what information you need early on.

Figure 4.10 **The D.A.R.T.S. Information Literacy System**

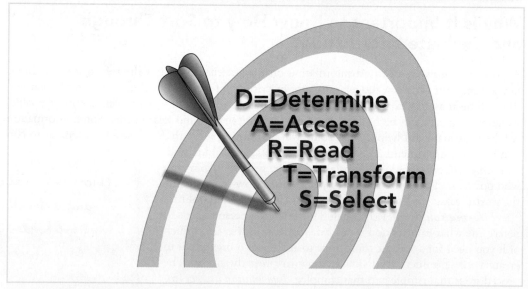

D=Determine
A=Access
R=Read
T=Transform
S=Select

© Robert Sherfield and Patricia Moody

After some thought, you decide that your research question will be, *"What was Rosa Park's philosophy on Civil Rights?"* If you search this topic, you get over 465,000 hits. Still far too many, but over nine million fewer hits than before, *and,* you have a direction to begin your paper. So, the first step in becoming a more information literate student is to **identify and narrow your topic** and **determine what information is needed on this topic**. You will also need to determine what **type** of information you need and want to use in your project. Do you want facts, opinions, eye-witness reports, interviews, debates, and/or arguments? Each may provide you with different types of information.

Cyber research can be an amazing tool in your educational pursuit. However, when you are faced with over 9 million articles on one topic, it can also become overwhelming. **Information overload** can have negative effects on the learning process. Angelika Dimoka, director of The Center for Neural Decision Making at Temple University, suggests that with the vast amounts of information we face in an online search, "the brain's emotion region runs as wild as toddlers on a sugar high" (Begley, 2011). We begin to make stupid mistakes and bad decisions. Our frustration and anxiety levels also soar. Too much information can lead to **information paralysis**. This basically means that you have so much information that you don't know what to do with it so you do nothing.

> *"The booming science of decision making has shown that more information can lead to objectively poorer choices, and to choices that people come to regret."*
> — A. Dimoka

The new field of decision-making research also suggests that when people are faced with too much information and too many decisions, we tend to make no decision at all. When the amount of information coming at us is coupled with the *speed* at which it comes, this can lead to devastating results. According to Sharon Begley, in her article, "I Can't Think" (2011), when faced with too much information, "we sacrifice accuracy and thoughtfulness to the false god of immediacy." We tend to make quick, bad decisions, rather than slower, well-reasoned ones. It is for these reasons that step one in the **DARTS Information Literacy System** is imperative. When determining what information is needed on your narrowed topic, you should also make sure that you do the following:

- understand your instructor's guidelines for the project
- understand your intended audience
- determine the availability of reliable resources and how many are required by your instructor
- develop a timeline to complete your project.

A = Access the Information from a Variety of Sources

After you have made your topic decision and narrowed your research question, you will want to begin the process of accessing valuable, reliable, credible information. While Wikipedia and Google are valuable tools, it is also important to use a variety of sources, such as journals, scholarly books, newspapers, and maybe even interviews to gather the information needed.

You may be asking, *"Is the Library Still Important in the Digital Age?"* Yes! The answer is an absolute yes! Many people think of a library as a place that is quiet as a tomb with a crabby old librarian presiding over it who is prepared to pounce on you if you ask a question or touch one of her precious books. Fortunately, that stereotype went the way of the horse and buggy, and today, libraries are literally the hub of a college campus. Your library is the key used to unlock the secrets to your education and help you become more information literate by accessing a variety of sources. Although the Internet is an amazing tool, serious research requires you to use the library and its tools, including print books, maps, charts, government data, periodicals, and your librarian. It may be fun and easy to use Google, Dogpile, or Wikipedia, but you will also need to hone your library research skills and critical thinking abilities.

> *"The library is the hospital of the mind."*
> — M. Tullins

Some of the things that your librarian can assist you with include helping you discover, understand, search, and use the online catalog; narrow your digital search to get to the information you need; search other libraries for information and sources not available on your campus; discover, use, and evaluate databases for almost every subject area; and make use of interlibrary loan tools. They can also help you understand your own library's online data search systems.

Becoming information literate requires you to seek and use a variety of sources, however, you must also determine how much is enough. You don't want to overwhelm yourself. When searching for your resources, keep the following tips in mind:

- Understand that information comes in a variety of media, including government documents, maps, videos, books, scholarly journals, online databases, and YouTube interviews, just to name a few.
- As you begin to put your information together to create your project, determine what information is missing and where you might locate it. You will also need to determine if you have too much information on a particular aspect of your topic.
- Manage your information carefully so that you know exactly where you found it. This will allow you to access the information later if needed, and allow you to provide proper citations once your project is complete

Now it is your turn. Consider that you have been asked to write a paper on *"how to deal with illegal questions asked during a job interview."* First, develop a brief thesis for your paper, and then find at least three online resources to help you write this paper. Wikipedia is a great tool, but, for this exercise, ***do not*** use it.

Level 5 Evaluate

Thesis: _____

_____

Source #1: _____

Citation: _____

Why is this source suitable, valid, and reliable? _____

_____

_____

Source #2: _____

Citation: _____

Why is this source suitable, valid, and reliable? _____

_____

_____

Source #3: _____

Citation: _____

Why is this source suitable, valid, and reliable? _____

_____

_____

_____

R = Read and Evaluate the Information for Accuracy and Credibility

You have chosen your topic, narrowed it into a workable thesis, and found a variety of sources that you can use for your project. Let's say that you have found three Internet articles, one book, one YouTube video, and one journal article. It is now time to read or watch your material in great detail and evaluate the information to determine if it is valid, accurate, and credible. Basically, you are working to discover if your sources present facts correctly and if the information is up-to-date, logical, fair, unbiased, and useable. By using the ***Credibility Checklist*** in Figure 4.11. you will have a better understanding of the quality of your information.

Figure 4.11 Credibility Checklist

Are the information and author credible, valid, accurate, and reliable?	■ Who is the author and what are his/her credentials, educational background, past writings, or experience? ■ What edition is the source? Second, third, or higher editions suggest that the source has been updated to reflect changes and new knowledge. ■ Who is the publisher? If the source is published by a university press, it is likely to be a scholarly publication. ■ Does the information appear to be valid and well researched, or does it just gloss over the material? Is it supported by evidence?
Is the article fact or opinion, popular or scholarly?	■ What is the title of the source? This will help you determine if the source is popular, sensational, or scholarly, and indicates the level of complexity. Popular journals are resources such as *Time, Newsweek, Vogue, Ebony,* and *Reader's Digest.* They seldom cite their sources. Sensational resources are often inflammatory and written on an elementary level. They usually have flashy headlines, and they cater to popular superstitions. Examples are *The Globe, The National Enquirer,* and *The Star.* ■ Is the source factually objective, is it opinionated, or is it propaganda? Objective sources look at all angles and report on each one honestly. ■ Are sources documented with footnotes or links? In scholarly works, the credibility of most writings is proven through the footnote or endnote documentation.
Is it up-to-date and timely?	■ When was the source published? If it is a web page, the date is usually found on the last page or the home page. Is the source current or out of date for your topic? ■ Look for the date that the article was last updated. Is the page dated? Is it current enough for your research or is it stale and outdated?
Does it have depth?	■ What is the intended audience of your source? Is the information too simple, too advanced, or too technical for your audience?
Is it logical?	■ Could the article be parody, humorous, or satire? ■ Ask yourself, "Why was this page put on the web?"
Is it fair?	■ Does the article present both sides of the argument? Is it balanced? ■ Was the article written by a neutral source on the topic?
Are the sources of the information cited? Does the author provide a bibliography?	■ Does the writer of the book, article, or web site cite sources? If not, what does this mean to the credibility of the information?

Source: Adapted from Ormondroyd, Engle, and Cosgrave (2001) and UC-Berkeley (2005).

T = Transform the Information to Create Your Project

Now that you have found your information and evaluated its credibility and usefulness, it is time to actually *use* what you have found. It is time to transform these facts, figures, interviews, charts, graphs, and opinions into your project. You will need to determine what type of organizational pattern best suits your information (this may have been included in your instructor's

What services are available to help you with your technology needs?

guidelines). Organizing the body of your paper or speech can be done using one of several proven methods.

Spatial organization is when you arrange information or items according to their direction or location.

Example: If you were describing the mall in Washington, DC, you could begin with the Lincoln Memorial and then move on to the reflecting pond, the World War II Monument, the Washington Monument, and the Smithsonian.

Cause–effect organization is when you arrange your information in the cause-and-effect order. You would discuss the causes of a problem and then explore its effects.

Example: If you were speaking about high blood pressure, you would first examine the causes of high blood pressure, such as diet, hereditary factors, and weight, and then move on to the effects, such as heart attack and stroke.

Chronological organization is presenting information in the order in which it happened. Speeches that deal with historical facts and how-to speeches often use chronological organization.

Example: If you were writing a paper on the history of automobiles in America since 1950, you would begin with the 50s, then move to the 60s, 70s, 80s, and 90s.

Problem-solving organization is often used in persuasive papers. Usually, you are trying to get your reader to accept your proposal. You first begin by pointing out the major problem(s), and then move on to revealing the solutions, and the advantages of the solutions.

Example: If you were writing about crime on college campuses, you would begin by informing the reader or listener about the problems, the crime statistics, and the personal toll on students. You would then propose solutions and tell how the solutions would help all students.

Topical/categorical organization is when you group information into subdivisions or cluster information into categories. Some information naturally falls into specific categories, such as the different types of palm trees or the types of rollerblades available.

Example: If you were writing a paper on taxes in the United States, you might categorize your information into local taxes, state taxes, federal taxes, luxury taxes, "sin" taxes, and special taxes.

Compare/contrast organization is when you present your information in a fashion that shows its similarities to and differences from other information.

Example: You may be writing a paper that compares the health care system in the United States to that of England or Canada.

Importance/priority organization allows you to arrange information from the most important issue to the least, or the least important to the most important. You can also arrange your information from the top priority to the lowest priority, or vice versa.

Example: If you were writing a paper to inform readers and listeners about buying diamonds, you might arrange your information so that you speak first about the most important aspects of diamond buying—clarity, color, and cut—and later about less important factors.

S = Select the Appropriate Documentation Style

You're not finished yet. Now, you must let your readers or listeners know where you located your information. This is called citation or documentation of your sources. You will need to document and cite all statistics, quotes, and excerpts from works that you referenced. This not only saves you the cost of plagiarism, but it gives you credibility with the reader. The most common means of doing this is by quoting within the paper and then compiling a reference or bibliography sheet at the end. If you have questions about what to document, consider the following by Kirszner and Mandell (1995):

The following must be cited if used:

- *Any* copyrighted information (music, poems, literary works, films, photographs, videos, artwork, advertisements, plays, computer programs, or audio files, just to name a few). Most of these works require that you seek permission to use them and many require that you pay royalty to the author or his/her heirs.
- Direct quotations
- Opinions, judgments, and insights of others that you summarize or paraphrase
- Information that is not widely known
- Information that is open to dispute
- Information that is not commonly accepted
- Tables, charts, graphs, and statistics taken from a source

There are several acceptable ways to document your research. The three most widely used research resources are the **MLA** (Modern Language Association), the **APA** (American Psychological Association), and the **CMS** (Chicago Manual of Style). All three styles can be explained by your librarian, through the MLA, APA, or CMS style guides, and/or by searching online.

Correct APA Style for the Citation of a Web Page

Sherfield, R., & Moody, P. (2013). How to document an article found on the web. Retrieved March 25, 2013, from http://www.sherfieldmoodydocuments.com.

Correct MLA Style for the Citation of a Web Page

Sherfield, Robert, and Patricia Moody. (2013). "How to Document an Article Found on the Web." 20 Dec. 2012. 25 Mar. 2013. http://www.sherfieldmoodydocuments.com.

Correct CMS Style for the Citation of a Web Page

Sherfield, Robert, and Patricia Moody. (2013). "How to Document an Article Found on the Web." Accessed March 25, 2013. http://www.sherfieldmoodydocuments.com.

By using the *DARTS System of Information Literacy,* you can rest assured that you are approaching the mountains of information in a more organized and reasonable fashion. These simple steps can mean the difference between information overload and information mastered.

USING INFORMATION LITERACY TO DEVELOP A RESEARCH PROJECT

Do Research, Organizing Notes, Outlining, and Citations Really Matter?

Writing a research project is not at the top of every college student's list of favorite things to do! In fact, it stands right up there with a final exam in advanced biochemistry. Keep in mind you are in good company, since completing a research project is a requirement at most colleges, so it is important to start now and learn how to do it right. And yes, research, organizing notes, outlining, and citing your sources **do** matter.

from ORDINARY to *Extraordinary*

Luke Bryan *Country Music Singer/Songwriter*
2010 Top New Solo Vocalist, Academy of Country Music Awards

Basically, I'm a country boy who grew up in the very small town of Leesburg, Georgia. During high school, I worked on my dad's farm and in his peanut and fertilizer businesses. I played sports and loved everything about the outdoors. Because I loved country music, my mother often urged me to belt out George Strait songs over and over while she drove me into town to shop. When I was 14, my parents bought me an Alvarez guitar. By age 15, my father would take me down to a nearby club, Skinner's, where I shared guitar licks and lead vocals with other local country singers.

At age 16, two local songwriters who'd enjoyed some success providing tunes for Nashville artists invited me to join their twice-a-week writing sessions at a local church. By that time, I was leading my own band, playing at Skinner's and various community events.

Encouraged by everyone who heard me play, I planned to move to Nashville after high school graduation. Supported by my family, I was loading my car for the move when tragedy struck. My older brother, Chris, one of my biggest supporters and one of my best friends, was killed in an auto accident the

day I was to leave town. This was a devastating blow to me that still impacts me today. All I wanted to do was be close to my family, so my plans for Nashville were put on hold.

I continued to devote myself to my music, finding escape and emotional release in my songs. I poured my feelings into my songwriting, and, after enrolling at Georgia Southern University, my band and I performed nearly every weekend on campus or at nearby clubs or parties. I eventually recorded an album of 10 songs, nine of which I wrote. I played throughout my college career and was able to pay my way through Georgia Southern University playing and singing country music.

After I graduated from college, I went back home to work for my Dad. I did this for a year and a half, but my heart just wasn't in it. By then, I had begun to realize that I was way too passionate about country music to turn it loose without going for it. One day my father took me for a drive. "Look, your heart is in your music," my father told me. "It's what you were meant to do. You either quit this job and move to Nashville, or I'm going to fire you." With the encouragement of my family, I headed for Nashville. My dad agreed to help support me for a

First, it is advisable to take this assignment one step at a time. Think of the process as going up a ladder. You start at the bottom rung and work your way to the top. If you have worked hard, allotted yourself enough time, avoided cutting corners, given critical thought to your processes, and sought help from qualified people along the way, your paper is going to be a good one when you reach the top of the ladder. As a writer, you will need to divide your paper into small, manageable tasks with several goals in mind—the quality of your research, the excellence of your writing, and the date on which the project is due. Writing a solid research project of which you can be proud is not a task for a weekend or an overnighter. Consider using the **DARTS System of Information Literacy** (found earlier in this chapter) as you develop your research project. A detailed action plan is explained in Figure 4.12.

year to see if I could make it in the country music business. He said, "You will always wonder if you could have made it, so you need to go try." Within two months I had signed a recording contract. I will always be grateful to my parents for their support and encouragement.

Like most new artists, I struggled in the beginning, but I tried to keep a level head and to plug myself into a positive community of singers and performers. I can tell you for sure that who you hang out with has a great impact on who you become. I advise you to surround yourself with people in your field who seem to be moving and shaking. I watched lots of my friends succeed, and this made me feel that I could make it, too. It's easy to get in with the wrong crowd in college or after you graduate, so I highly recommend that you associate with a good group of people who are trying to make something of themselves. My fellow writers and performers had a major impact on my life.

One of the biggest days in my life was signing a contract with Capitol Records. When they offered me a contract, all I could think about is "I've got to call Mama and Daddy." All my dreams and wishes came together right there in that room.

I spent many long hours preparing to tour and sing in front of big crowds. Becoming a recording artist encompasses many hours of hard work, but it has paid off. Capitol Records released my debut album in 2006. Now, I am living my dream! I have a tour bus and I have been fortunate enough to open for some of the greats in the business like Kenny Chesney. I am very happy when my wife and children travel with me.

> One of the biggest days of my life was signing a contract with Capitol Records. All my dreams and wishes came together right there in that room.

I can't say that it's been easy breaking into a competitive field. I've worked very hard for many years, but it's all been worth it because I am beginning to see success. I've written several songs that have been well received, including "Good Directions," which climbed to number one and was recorded by Billy Currington. My "Country Man" song, which I recorded, made top ten. Another big hit for me was "All My Friends Say." I recently released, "We Rode in Trucks" and "Do I." I wrote "Do I" with Lady Antebellum, a trio of popular, well-known country music stars. We were all thrilled when "Do I" went to the top of the charts and stayed there several weeks. Our record company, Capitol Records, gave us a Number One party in Nashville. One of my latest songs, "Country Girl," has enjoyed amazing success. Being nominated as Male Vocalist of the Year is a great honor and dream come true.

The best advice I can give you is to follow your dreams; do what you love; trust your instincts. Don't get trapped into doing something you don't love and look forward to every day.

EXTRAORDINARY REFLECTION

Luke mentions that he was encouraged to go after his dream by his family and friends. He also states how important it is to surround yourself with people who are on the move and believe in their dreams. Who supports you and your dreams? How have your family and friends helped you reach your goals thus far?

Figure 4.12 The DARTS Guide to Developing a Research Project

D = Determine the Information You Need by Narrowing Your Topic

Your professor will most likely give you the details and guidelines for the research project. You may not have a great deal of control over the *type* of project on which you will be working, however, the *topic* is usually up to you. Before you begin your project, take some time and review the guidelines as set by your professor, and then consider the purpose of your project, the topic, and the information needed. Consider the following:

■ Why am I writing this? What is the purpose of this project? Who is the audience?

■ Exactly what does the assignment require that I accomplish?

(continued)

Figure 4.12 The DARTS Guide to Developing a Research Project (*continued*)

- What are my overall topic and my specific thesis statement?
- Have I narrowed my topic enough to adequately cover it in the allotted space and time?
- Can I find valid, credible resources?

A = Access the Information from a Variety of Sources

Now that you have selected and narrowed your topic and developed your thesis statement, you are ready to begin accumulating information to support your project. As you begin to consider resources, you will want to investigate and explore a variety of sources, going beyond Wikipedia, as some professors do not allow this resource. Other research sources might include:

- Personal interviews with experts on your topic
- Electronic and print indexes
- Books, journals, and periodicals on the subject
- Newspapers, such as *The New York Times, Chicago Sun Times,* and *Atlanta Constitution*
- Reference materials, such as encyclopedias, dictionaries, directories, atlases, almanacs and yearbooks, books of quotations, and bibliographical directories
- Government documents
- The Internet (Yahoo!, Infoseek, Dogpile, or Google, for example)

R = Read and Evaluate the Information for Accuracy and Credibility

As a researcher, you should know the validity of the sources and research that you plan to use in your project. The credibility of your sources can mean the difference between having a valid argument or having unsubstantiated claims and opinions. You may begin your research project by asking for research advice from your professor or librarian. You may also want to ask and answer the following questions as you conduct your research. Does your research come from a reliable, respected source? Is your research related to the argument or point you are making? Is the person you are quoting highly respected and reputable in the field? Is the data skewed or biased by an organization with special interest? Consider the following questions:

- Who is the author and what are his or her credentials, training, past writings, and experience?
- When was the source published? Is it still valid and up-to-date?
- Who is the publisher? Was the information published by a reputable online or textual publisher?
- From where is your research coming? Are your sources from scholarly works, such as *The New England Journal of Medicine* or *The Journal of Ultrasound in Medicine*; a popular source, such as *Time, Newsweek, Vanity Fair,* or *Ebony*; or a sensational source, such as *The Globe, The National Enquirer,* and *The Star*? The last category should be avoided in research projects.
- Is the information too simple, too advanced, or too technical for your audience?
- Are sources documented with footnotes or links? In scholarly works, the credibility of most writings is proven through the footnote or endnote documentation.

T = Transform the Information to Create Your Project

Now that you have gathered enough information from a variety of resources, what is the most effective way to present your findings and ideas? As you probably know, every good paper or speech will have an introduction, body, and conclusion. They can best be developed when creating an outline from your research notes. To begin, think about the organizational pattern that best suits your project. Consider one of the organization patterns discussed in this chapter: *spatial, cause-effect, chronological, problem-solving, topical/categorical, compare/contrast,* and *importance/priority*. Using one of these patterns will help you develop a well-organized project.

You will need to take your research and organize your notes for your project so that they are logical and cover the required areas. Review the following basic outline:

I. Introduction
   A. Thesis statement
   B. Overview of the paper

   II. Issue One
     A. Discuss the issue
     B. Why is the issue relevant?
     C. Research to support your claims
  III. Issue Two
     A. Where and why does this issue exist?
     B. Who is involved?
     C. Research to support your claims
  IV. Issue Three
     A. What are possible solutions to this issue?
     B. How can they be implemented?
     C. Your plan for implementation
     D. Research to support your claims
  V. Conclusion
     A. Restate your thesis
     B. Provide a brief overview of your findings
     C. Conclude with a powerful, memorable statement, facts, and data

S = Select the Appropriate Documentation Style

When writing your paper, and certainly once it has been written, you should take careful precautions to document all research and information that is not your own. You will need to document and cite all statistics, quotes, and excerpts from works that you referenced. The most common means of doing this is by quoting within the paper and then compiling a reference or bibliography sheet or endnotes. Be careful to document all references as you write because it can become very difficult to go back and try to find them later. We recommend that you review the rules of citation and your institution's definition of plagiarism. You will need to cite:

- Direct quotations and excerpts
- Findings of others that you summarize or paraphrase
- Information that is not widely known or may be open to dispute
- Tables, charts, graphs, and statistics taken from a source

The Writer's Final Checklist

As you complete your project, take the time to make sure that you have not missed any small or logistical items that could cost you points. Read your work carefully and consider the following checklist:

_____ My paper is the right length, not too long or too short.

_____ My thesis statement is concise and clear.

_____ I have presented my topic in a comprehensive, convincing manner.

_____ My major points are presented in a logical, organized sequence.

_____ I began my project in an engaging and compelling way by telling a story or creating a vivid, visual illustration.

_____ I have considered ethical standards, sharing only what I know and can prove to be true.

_____ I have been very careful not to use someone else's intellectual property as my own.

_____ I have used the style manual recommended by my professor and followed it carefully.

_____ I have checked carefully to be sure I followed all instructions assigned by the professor.

_____ I have double-checked my references and citations to be sure I reported them accurately.

_____ I have used several types of sources—books, articles, newspapers, online sources, journals, and interviews.

_____ I have checked the validity of my sources.

_____ I have included quotations and ideas from relevant, credible sources.

_____ I have chosen and used a logical organizational pattern to present my findings.

_____ I have ended my project powerfully, compelling the reader to remember the main points.

_____ I have taken the time to revise my paper several times, working to improve it each time.

_____ I have proofed my paper several times and made corrections, not relying solely on a spell or grammar checker.

_____ I have used campus resources, such as the writing center or tutorial services, to review my project.

_____ I am going to submit my project on time, with pride and a sense of accomplishment, knowing that I did my very best work.

REFLECTIONS ON TECHNOLOGY, RESEARCH, AND INFORMATION LITERACY

Technology is an amazing part of our lives. It is also a wicked, double-edged sword. It can bring us joy and give us heartache. It can make some tasks in life easier, and can frustrate us to no end with others. It can help us complete tasks more quickly, but, when it fails, it can slow us down, and in some cases bring us to a complete stop. It can allow us to have continual communication, but it can also remove us from personal, face-to-face interaction. It can help us learn new information, and it can sometimes freeze our brains solid.

The most effective advice we can give you when dealing with new and ever-changing technology is this: Take *one new program* or application at a time and learn it well, practice it, and discover its strengths and limitations. After you have learned this program, move on to another program to continue your growth. If you are new to computers and technology in education, resist the urge to learn every step of every tool at the same time. Master what you must know to be successful and then move on to what you want to know. Build on your strengths and let your challenges be your goals for the future.

As you work toward improving your technology, research, and information literacy skills, consider the following:

- Work hard to learn the technology tools that will help you be successful in your classes.
- Manage your time online carefully and do your work before you play and socialize.
- Learn the terms of technology to help you grow in this field of study.
- Learn to use effective search engines, tools, and bookmarking to help save time.
- Use the DARTS System of Information Literacy to guide your research.
- Guard your online privacy like you would guard your personal bank account.
- Practice proper netiquette when online.
- Take your online classes as seriously as you take your face-to-face classes.

BUILDING YOUR INFORMATION LITERACY SKILLS

Utilizes Levels 4 and 5 of the Taxonomy (See Bloom's Taxonomy at the front of this text)

Directions: Find a website that provides in-depth information or an online article about a *major national event within the last month*. Using the information from the article and/or website, complete the following *Information Literacy Checklist and Worksheet*. Justify your answers.

Event? _____

Why is this event important? _____

Name of website or online article _____

URL address of website or article _____

Publisher or affiliation _____

Publication date_____

Author _____

After reading the website or article, use other sources (books, journals, or other online sites) to compare/contrast your findings and to justify your responses.

Question	Your Response	Justify Your Response
Is the author's name indicated?	Yes No	Name?
Is the author of the source credible? Reliable? How do you know?	Yes No	Why?
Is the source from an individual's web page, an organization, a government agency, a for-profit agency, an international source, a military site, or an educational institution?	Type:	How do you know?
Is this site easy to navigate, read, and use?	Yes No	Why?
Does the author provide contact information or can you find the contact information online?	Yes No	Contact information:
Is this source masked as an advertisement?	Yes No	Justify:
Does this source require that you have or purchase special software to view portions of the material?	Yes No	What is required? How much does it cost?
Did the source provide enough information to begin a project on this person? Does it offer an in-depth look at the topic?	Yes No	List three important facts you gained from this source:
Is the information accurate?	Yes No	Justify:
Does the article have a date on it?	Yes No	Date of publication:
Is the information current?	Yes No	Justify:
Is the information objective and fair?	Yes No	Justify:
Is the article an opinion piece or a factual piece?	Opinion Fact	Justify:
Does the article provide both sides to the event?	Yes No	Justify:
Does the article provide live links within the piece?	Yes No	List the URL of one link:
Does the author provide footnotes and references for his/her research?	Yes No	List one references used to write this piece:

Based on your readings and investigations of this article or site, summarize your findings into a 250–300 word essay. Be certain to use the author's name, facts, dates, references, and new information learned about the event.

_____

_____

_____

SQ3R MASTERY STUDY SHEET

EXAMPLE QUESTION (FROM PAGE 76) Why is it important to know the different types of technology used in education?	**ANSWER:**
EXAMPLE QUESTION (FROM PAGE 87) What is information literacy?	**ANSWER:**
AUTHOR QUESTION (FROM PAGE 73) How can you manage your time online more effectively?	**ANSWER:**
AUTHOR QUESTION (FROM PAGE 76) What is a learning management system?	**ANSWER:**
AUTHOR QUESTION (FROM PAGE 86) List and briefly discuss three tips for succeeding in an online class.	**ANSWER:**
AUTHOR QUESTION (FROM PAGE 89) What is information paralysis?	**ANSWER:**
AUTHOR QUESTION (FROM PAGE 90) How can you evaluate an online research source?	**ANSWER:**
YOUR QUESTION (FROM PAGE ____)	**ANSWER:**
YOUR QUESTION (FROM PAGE ____)	**ANSWER:**
YOUR QUESTION (FROM PAGE ____)	**ANSWER:**
YOUR QUESTION (FROM PAGE ____)	**ANSWER:**
YOUR QUESTION (FROM PAGE ____)	**ANSWER:**

Finally, after answering these questions, recite this chapter's major points in your mind. Consider the following general questions to help you master this material.

- What is it about?
- What does it mean?
- What is the most important thing you learned? Why?
- What are the key points to remember?

chapter five

THINK

BUILDING CRITICAL THINKING, EMOTIONAL INTELLIGENCE, AND PROBLEM SOLVING SKILLS

"Many people think they are thinking when they are merely rearranging their prejudices." —William James

THINK

Why read this chapter?

Because you'll learn...

- To use critical and creative-thinking skills to enhance your life
- The steps in the critical-thinking process
- To tolerate uncertainty

Because you'll be able to...

- Distinguish the difference between logical and false arguments
- Identify, narrow, and solve problems
- Apply the skills of healthy emotional intelligence

Scan and QUESTION

Take a few moments, **scan this chapter** and on page 126, write **five of your own questions** that you think will be important to your mastery of this material. You will also find five questions listed from your authors.

Example:

☑ **Why is emotional intelligence important to critical thinking?** (from page 106)

☑ **What are false arguments?** (from page 118)

MyStudentSuccessLab

MyStudentSuccessLab is an online solution designed to help you acquire and develop (or hone) the skills you need to succeed. You will have access to peer-led video presentations and develop core skills through interactive exercises and projects.

Name: Erin Phillips
Institution: Graduate! The University of South Carolina
Major: Retail Management

"Who knew that you could study abroad in London and hold an internship? Who knew that you could give back to the community and learn about the importance of investing in others? I found these answers at the University of South Carolina. I found that learning about subjects that interested me only made me want to learn more." These are the words of Erin Phillips, a recent graduate of the University of South Carolina. During her time as a student, Erin realized that learning not only occurs from her professors inside the classroom, but with travel to other countries, experiences in the community, and from the other students. Erin took advantage of the opportunities that were presented to her. She states, "I became more focused on my future goals professionally and learned ways to achieve them by studying hard and being involved in various groups."

One of the top skills that employers look for in their new employees is critical thinking. Erin acknowledges her newfound understanding that the ability to think critically is a key component of any professional field today. "Critical thinking is essential in any workplace and any job

description. It is important to have an objective mind and to be open for honest feedback. I think that many of the group projects in my college classes taught me how to fine-tune my critical thinking skills and how to collaborate with others in a productive fashion." Employers now expect new hires to have the ability to seek global understanding in today's world. Erin capitalized on an opportunity that most colleges and universities create for their students: to study abroad! I vividly recall the day that Erin approached me about writing a letter of recommendation for her to apply for a study abroad experience in London, England. I knew that she would be fine, and that it would be a tremendous growth opportunity for her personally. "Studying abroad was the best experience in my four years of college. Not only did I learn so much, but I saw so much. I had the opportunity to experience different cultures and observe how people in other countries live. I had the opportunity to see how international businesses operate first hand. I would encourage anyone who has the opportunity to study abroad to do it—you won't regret it."

For all of my students, I am confident that they will leave the university with the professional knowledge needed to ensure civic responsibility. Erin really embraced social problems facing our community during her service-learning classes. She admits that it "opened my eyes to the reality of the hardships that face the local community. Oftentimes in college we tend to get so wrapped up in sporting events, friends, trips, school, and

An interview conducted and written by Collin Crick, Director of Recruitment, The University of South Carolina

other things that we forget about the world around us. College opened my eyes to the needs of the community and the realization that every little bit helps."

Erin graduated in May 2011 with a BS in Retail Management (Fashion Merchandising) and a minor in Advertising/Public Relations. She currently works as an Advertising and Marketing Specialist in Corporate Marketing at U.S. Bank in Cincinnati, OH.

"I see education as a privilege and an opportunity to attain success. I decided to attend the University of South Carolina because of the wonderful education, faculty, and unique learning opportunities that are presented to each student. The university, specifically the College of Hospitality, Retail, and Sport Management, fosters a great learning community that is truly involved beyond the campus lines."

THINK about it

1. Erin mentions her internship in London, England. How could traveling and studying in a different part of the country or internationally help you in your career?

2. Erin became involved in several groups while at USC. What groups could you join to enhance your college experience and help you with your future plans?

THE IMPORTANCE OF CRITICAL THINKING

When Will You Ever Use It?

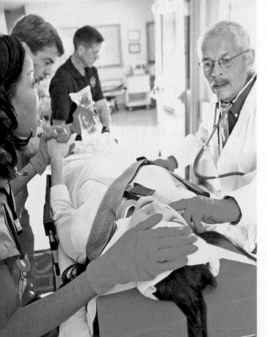

Can you think of a professional career in which critical thinking will not be required?

Have you ever made a decision that turned out to be a mistake? Have you ever said to yourself, *"If only I could go back and …"*? Have you ever regretted actions you took toward a person or situation? Have you ever planned a paper or speech that was flawless? Have you ever had to make a hard, painful decision that turned out to be "the best decision of your life?" If the answer to any of these questions is yes, you might be able to trace the consequences back to your ***thought process*** at the time of the decision. Let's face it, sometimes good and bad things just happen out of luck or circumstance. More often than not, however, many events in our lives are driven by the thought processes involved when we made the initial decisions and chose to act on those decisions.

Critical thinking can serve us in many areas as students and citizens in a free society. As a student, ***critical thinking can help you***:

- focus on relevant issues/problems and avoid wasting time on trivia
- gather relevant, accurate information regarding finances, goals, decision making, relationships, civic responsibility, and environmental issues, to name a few
- understand and remember facts and organize thoughts logically
- look more deeply at problems, analyze their causes, and solve them more accurately
- develop appropriate and meaningful study plans and manage your priorities
- assist in your problem-solving skills
- help you control your emotions so that you can make rational judgments and become more open-minded
- produce new knowledge through research and analysis
- help you determine the accuracy of printed and spoken words
- assist you in detecting bias and determining the relevance of arguments and persuasion

AN EIGHT-POINT PLAN FOR CRITICAL THINKING

Can You Really Make Critical Thinking Work for You in Everyday Life?

Does critical thinking really matter? Seriously? Can it do anything to improve the quality of your life? Can it help with your finances? Can it help solve relationship problems? The answer is yes. Critical thinking has daily, practical uses, from making sound financial decisions, to improving personal relationships, to helping you become a better student, to helping you make a good deal on purchasing a car. You can improve your critical-thinking skills by watching your emotional reactions, using solid research and facts to build your positions and thoughts, and practicing open-mindedness.

Conversely, can the lack of critical-thinking skills cause real problems? The answer, once again, is yes. Poor critical-thinking skills can impair your judgment, lead you to make rash decisions, and even cause you to let your emotions rule (and sometimes ruin) your life. Critical thinking can be hampered by a number of factors, including closed-mindedness, unflappable opinions based on rumor instead of facts, cultural and/or religious bias, lack of accurate information, faulty arguments, and negativity.

As you begin to build and expand your critical-thinking skills, consider the steps in Figure 5.1.

Figure 5.1 **The Eight Steps in Critical Thinking**

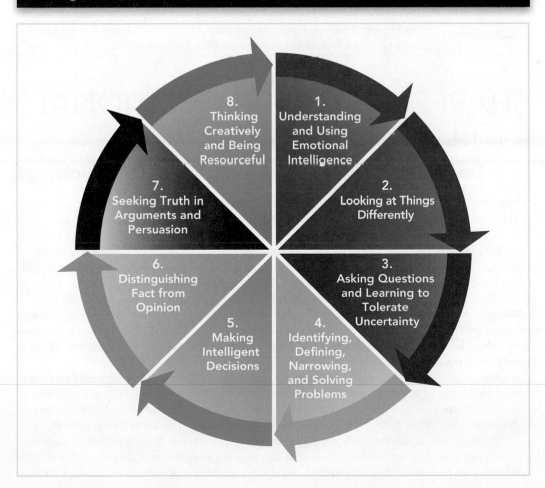

1. Understanding and Using Emotional Intelligence
2. Looking at Things Differently
3. Asking Questions and Learning to Tolerate Uncertainty
4. Identifying, Defining, Narrowing, and Solving Problems
5. Making Intelligent Decisions
6. Distinguishing Fact from Opinion
7. Seeking Truth in Arguments and Persuasion
8. Thinking Creatively and Being Resourceful

Step One: Understanding and Using Emotional Intelligence (EI)

Emotions play a vital role in our lives. They help us feel compassion, help others, reach out in times of need, and relate to others. On the other hand, emotions can cause some problems in your critical thinking process. You do not—and should not—have to eliminate emotions from your thoughts, but it is crucial that you know when your emotions are clouding an issue and causing you to act and speak before thinking.

Consider the following topics:

- Should drugs and prostitution be totally legalized in the United States?
- Can the theories of evolution and creationism coexist?
- Should illegal aliens be given amnesty and made U.S. citizens?
- Should terminally ill patients have the right to assisted suicide?
- Should prayer be allowed in public schools?

As you read these topics, did you immediately form an opinion? Did old arguments surface? Did you feel your emotions coming into play as you thought about the questions? If you had an immediate answer, it is likely that you allowed some past judgments, opinions, and emotions to enter the decision-making process, unless you have just done a comprehensive, unbiased study of one of these issues. If you had to discuss these issues in class or with your friends and had to defend your position, how would you react? Do you think you would get angry? Would you find yourself groping for words? Would you find it hard to explain why you held the opinion that you voiced? If so, these are warning signs that you are allowing your emotions to drive your decisions. If you allow your emotions to run rampant and fail to use research, logic, and evidence, you may not be able to examine the issues critically or have a logical discussion regarding the statements.

> *"Simply stated, people who are emotionally intelligent harness emotions and work with them to improve problem solving and boost creativity."*
>
> —Snyder and Lopez

SHARPENING YOUR EMOTIONAL INTELLIGENCE SKILLS

How Does EI Affect Critical Thinking and Problem Solving?

If you have ever heard the old saying, "think before you act," you were actually being told to use *emotional intelligence*. Everyone knows that **IQ** (Intelligence Quotient) is important to success in college, work, and life, but many experts also believe that **EI** is just as important to being successful. EI helps people cope with the social and emotional demands in daily life. "Emotional intelligence is the single most influencing variable in personal achievement, career success, leadership, and life satisfaction" (Nelson and Low, 2003). "The data that exist suggest it can be *as powerful*, and at times *more powerful*, than IQ" (Goleman, 2006).

Exactly what is EI? EI includes all the skills and knowledge necessary for building strong, effective relationships through managing and understanding emotions. *It is knowing how you and others understand and managing feelings and emotions in a rational manner that is good for both parties.*

Our emotions originate in the brain. If you have EI skills, your *thinking mind* and *emotional mind* should function together, making it more likely that you will craft sound, rational decisions. In other words, you will **think** before you **act.** When these two minds do not operate in harmony, you might make highly emotional decisions that can be viewed as irrational.

The amygdala, discussed in Figure 5.2, remembers frustrations, fears, hurt feelings, and anger from our past. The tension from these past experiences causes the amygdala to go into default behavior—we *feel* and act before we *think*—and this can create a potentially explosive situation.

If you had a bad experience several years ago and are placed in a similar situation, the amygdala will remember and trigger emotions that cause the body to respond. These feelings often cause people to bypass critical thinking (the logical brain) and to respond with angry words or actions (the emotional brain). For example:

- They get angry—*you* get angry
- They curse you—*you* curse them
- They use physical violence—*you* use physical violence

However, if you remain calm and levelheaded, you will begin to see that the other person usually begins to calm down, too. They follow your emotional lead, positively or negatively, and if you're calm and rational, anger and violence become out of place for most people.

Because emotional intelligence skills and knowledge are so important to your success in all areas of your life, you are encouraged to read extensively about this subject and to design your own personal plan for dealing with emotional concerns. Consider the tips in Figure 5.3 for managing emotions on a daily basis.

Figure 5.2 The Amygdala

Don't let this word or concept frighten you. If you have never heard of the amygdala (pronounced ah-MIG-da-la), you're not alone. Most people have not. But this term and concept are important for you to be able to understand the overall aspects of EI. The amygdala is an innate, prehistoric part of the brain's emotional reaction system. It can cause us to go into default behavior based on what we remember from a similar experience. Do I use **fight or flight?** Basically, the amygdala is there to protect us when we become afraid or emotionally upset. When influenced by the amygdala, everything becomes **about us**. We become more judgmental. We don't stop to think about differences or the other person's feelings or the relationship. The amygdala can trigger an emotional response **before** the brain has had time to understand what is happening, and this situation causes us to have problems with others.

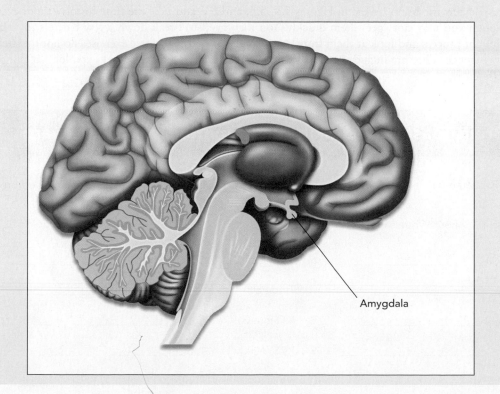

Amygdala

Figure 5.3 Guidelines for Emotional Management at School, Work, and Beyond

- Face each day with an "I feel great, nothing is going to ruin my day" attitude.
- Hear all sides of an argument before you say anything, make a decision, or take an action.
- Practice a win-win philosophy at all times and work tirelessly to make it happen.
- Avoid letting your personal feelings about a person dictate your decisions.
- Never, never, never lose control—verbally or physically.
- Avoid negative stereotyping and typecasting people into negative categories.
- Never look at or judge someone through someone else's eyes or experiences.
- Learn to keep a tight rein on any emotional "hotspots" such as anger, rage, and jealousy.
- Strive to treat people so well that you can always put your head on your pillow and sleep well, knowing that you have not been underhanded, rude, or unfair.

Step Two: Looking at Things Differently

Critical thinking involves looking at something you may have seen many times and examining it from many different angles and perspectives. It involves going beyond the obvious, beyond "easy," to seek new understanding and rare solutions. It encourages you to dig deeper than you have before, to get below the surface, to struggle, experiment, and expand. It asks you to look at something from an entirely different view so that you might develop new insights and understand more about the problem, situation, question, or solution. Critical thinking involves looking at *common issues* with uncommon eyes; *known problems* with new skepticism; *everyday conflicts* with probing curiosity; and *daily challenges* with greater attention to details.

Review the brain teasers in Figures 5.4, 5.5, and 5.6 and take the time to solve them even though you may not "get" them quickly. You may need to break down a few barriers in your thought process and look at them from a new angle. Remember, these exercises do not measure intelligence. They are included to prod your thought process along and help you look at things differently.

Figure 5.4 Brain Teaser 1—Looking at Common Terms Backward

Consider the following clues. Two examples are given to help you get started. Answer the following ten teasers based on the clues.

Example: 4 W on a C   Four Wheels on a Car   13 O C   Thirteen Original Colonies

1. SW and the 7D _____
2. I H a D by MLK _____
3. 2 Ps in a P _____
4. HDD (TMRUTC) _____
5. 3 S to a T _____

6. 100 P in a D _____
7. T no PLH _____
8. 4 Q in a G _____
9. I a SWAA _____
10. 50 S in t U _____

Figure 5.5   **Brain Teaser 2—The Penny**

Pretend that all life on Earth has ended and all traces of civilization are gone. There are no buildings, no people, no animals, no plants—nothing is left but dirt and one penny. Someone from another planet who knows our language comes to Earth and finds the penny. List all of the things that could be inferred about our civilization based on this one small penny. You should find at least 10.

1. _____

2. _____

3. _____

4. _____

5. _____

6. _____

7. _____

8. _____

9. _____

10. _____

How did you do? Was it hard to look at the situation backward or to look for clues within a series of letters and numbers? Most of us are not used to that. But part of critical thinking is trying to find ***clues or patterns***. Perhaps the easiest brain teaser was question 2 in Figure 5.4. Most people know MLK as Martin Luther King, Jr. When you figure that part out, the name of his most popular speech, *I Have a Dream*, becomes easier. Often, when trying to solve problems or dealing with unknowns, things become easier when you can find a clue or a pattern and build from what you already know.

Examine the brain teaser in Figure 5.6. This teaser is included to help you look at an issue beyond what is actually given to you and consider what is not given. Once again, you are given a basic clue, but you must go beyond what is given. You must look at the nine dots, but you must not let them confine you. You can't let the nine dots control your thoughts—you must move beyond what is given; beyond what you actually see. When you do this, the answer will come to you.

Figure 5.6   **Brain Teaser 3— Seeing What Is Not Given**

Look at the design below. You will find nine dots. Your mission is to connect all nine dots with four straight lines without removing your pencil or pen from the paper. Do not retrace your lines.

As you continue to look at common things differently and think beyond the obvious, examine the penny in Figure 5.5.

Drawing inferences often takes the ability to look at things differently and take something very common and examine it like you have never examined it before. Just as you looked at the penny, you learned new things about it by studying it with different eyes. Think about how you might solve a common problem that you face every day simply by looking at the problem with different eyes.

While these activities may seem somewhat trivial, they are provided to help you begin to think about and consider information from different angles. This is a major step in becoming a critical thinker: looking beyond the obvious, thinking outside the box—literally, examining details, and exploring possibilities. Basically, looking beyond what is given to you.

Step Three: Asking Questions and Learning to Tolerate Uncertainty

You've asked questions all of your life. As a child, you asked your parents, "What's that?" a million times. You probably asked them, "Why do I have to do this?" In later years, you've asked questions of your friends, teachers, strangers, store clerks, and significant others.

> "It is not possible to become a good thinker and be a poor questioner. Thinking is not driven by answers, but, rather, by questions."
>
> —Paul and Elder

Questioning is not new to you, but it may be a new technique to you for exploring, developing, and honing your critical-thinking skills. Curiosity may have killed the cat, but it was a smart cat when it died! Your curiosity is one of the most important traits you possess. It helps you grow and learn, and sometimes it may cause you to be uncomfortable. That's OK. This section is provided to assist you in learning how to ask questions to promote knowledge, solve problems, foster strong relationships, and critically analyze difficult situations. It is also included to help you understand the value of knowing how to tolerate uncertainty and avoid jumping to faulty conclusions because uncertainty "got the better of you." It is important to know that, sometimes, **the question is more important than the answer**—especially a faulty answer.

Types of Questions

Basically, there are three types of questions according to Paul and Elder (2006):

Questions of Fact—Require answers based in facts and evidence and have a correct or incorrect answer.

Example: What is the freezing point of water?

Questions of Preference—Require answers that state a subjective preference and do not necessarily have a correct or incorrect response.

Example: What is your favorite color?

Questions of Judgment—Require answers based on your judgment drawn from logic and evidence and can have more than one defensible answer.

Example: Should *Roe v Wade* be overturned?

Asking questions helps us gain insight where we may have limited knowledge. Answering properly posed questions can also help us expand our knowledge base. For example, if you were assigned to write a paper or present a speech on the topic of "creationism versus evolution," what five questions would you definitely want that paper or speech to answer when you were finished? Take some time to think about the issue. Write down at least five questions that you consider essential to understanding the topic of creationism versus evolution.

My five questions are:

1. _____

2. _____

3. _____

4. _____

5. _____

Learning to ask probing questions can help you in everyday situations by challenging you to look beyond the obvious and critically examine everyday situations. Examine the car advertisement in Figure 5.7. The car dealership has provided some information, but it is not enough to make a smart, rational decision. What other questions would you ask the dealer to make sure that you are getting a good deal?

Figure 5.7   Auto Ad

What questions would you need to ask the dealer to ensure that you are getting a "good" deal?

1. _____

2. _____

3. _____

4. _____

5. _____

TOLERATING UNCERTAINTY

Are You 100 Percent Sure That You're Sure?

Asking questions that can be answered is vitally important to critical thinking, but so is learning to tolerate uncertainty and learning to ask questions that may not have an **immediate answer**. Uncertainty causes you to keep going, to not get lazy or give up. If we thought we knew the answers to everything, we would still be beating rocks together to make fire, and we would still be walking everywhere instead of driving or flying. Uncertainty causes humanity to move forward and create new knowledge, to try new things, to consider the impossible. Uncertainty also breeds creative thinking.

Think about all of the uncertainty that can arise your daily life:

"Can I be certain *my spouse/partner will not leave me?"* No.

"Can I be certain that I will remain healthy?" No.

"Can I be certain my children will turn out as good, caring, loving adults?" No.

DID YOU *Know?*

CESAR CHAVEZ, was born in 1927, near Yuma, Arizona. He was raised during the Great Depression in unspeakable poverty. His parents owned a small store, but lost everything during the depression. The entire family became migrant workers just to survive. He spent his youth working in the fields of Arizona and California. From first to eight grade (when he left school), he attended over 30 schools. Often his family did not have even the basic necessities of water and toilets to survive. They faced not only poverty, but extreme prejudice and injustice.

Later, Chavez joined the Navy. Upon his return, seeing the many problems faced by migrant families, he vowed to try to solve the problems and find a way to make life better for his family and the families living in such poverty. He founded the United Farm Workers, which was responsible for increasing public awareness of the plight of the migrant workers in America. He is considered to be one of the greatest civil rights activists in American history.

"Can I be certain what happens to me after I die?" No.

"Can I be certain the plane won't crash or someone won't crash into my car?" No.

"Can I be certain that this will not embarrass me or someone else?" No.

"Can I be certain that my investments will grow and I can retire comfortably?" No.

The inability to tolerate uncertainty can cause stress and anxiety. Sometimes, we just have to "let go" and accept that we do not know the answers. We can work hard to try to find the answers and/or direct our actions so that the answers will be favorable to us, but ultimately, many things in this universe require our tolerance of uncertainty. Sometimes, the best we can hope for is to keep asking questions and seeking truth.

Think of the good things that initially unanswered questions and uncertainty brought to humanity in many fields of study.

"Can we send someone to the moon and return them safely?"

"Can we transplant a human heart and have that person live and prosper afterwards?"

"Can we establish a new country with a new constitution and have it work?"

"Can we design and build a skyscraper that is over 140 stories high and have it remain safe?"

"Can we create an automobile that will get over 50 miles per gallon of fuel?"

"Can we help reduce global warming and its effects on the polar ice caps?"

All of these uncertainties have contributed to the development of new knowledge, new skills, new jobs, new outlooks, and new ways of living. Therefore, it is important to remember that in your quest for answers, sometimes uncertainty can be the most important thing you discover.

Step Four: Identifying, Defining, Narrowing, and Solving Problems

What would your life be like if you had no problems? Most people do not like to face or deal with problems, but the critical thinker knows that problems exist every day and that they must be faced and helpfully solved. Some of our problems are larger and more difficult than others, but we all face problems from time to time. You may have transportation problems. You may have financial problems. You may have childcare problems. You may have academic problems or interpersonal problems. Many people don't know how to solve problems at school, home, or work. They simply let the problem go unaddressed until it is too late to reach an amiable solution. There are many ways to address and solve problems. In this section, we will discuss how to *identify and narrow* the problem, *research and develop* alternatives, *evaluate* the alternatives, and *solve* the problem.

Not every problem has a solution. That can be a hard pill for many people to swallow, but it is a raw truth and a part of the uncertainty we just discussed. Many problems have solutions, but the solution may not be what you wanted. It is imperative to remember the words of Mary Hatwood Futrell, President of the National Education Association. She states that "finding the right answer is important, of course. But more important is developing the ability to see that many problems have *multiple solutions,* that getting from X to Y demands basic skills and mental agility, imagination, persistence, patience" (2007). Consider the problem-solving model in Figure 5.8.

Figure 5.8 Steps in the Problem-Solving Process

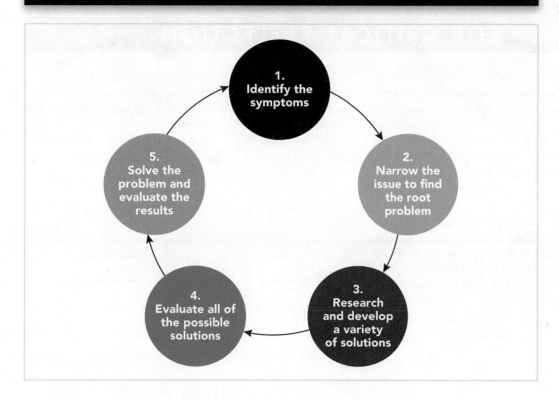

Identify the Symptoms

Symptoms and ***problems*** are not the same thing. Symptoms are *part* of the problem, but may not be the problem itself. Think of a problem like you think of your health. For example, you may have aches in your joints, experience cold chills, and have a severe headache. Those seem like problems, but in actuality, they are really symptoms of something larger—perhaps the flu or an infection. You can treat the headache with medicine, and soothe your joint pain with ointment, but until you get at the *root* of the problem, these symptoms will come back. Problems are much the same way. If you don't move beyond symptoms, the problem may seem to be solved, but shortly, it will reappear, usually worse than before. Therefore, it is imperative that you identify the symptoms of the ***greater problem*** before you begin solving anything.

Narrow the Symptoms to Find the Root Problem

Often, problems keep coming up because we did not deal with the ***real problem***, the root problem, but, rather, we dealt with a symptom. Getting to the heart of a problem is hard work that requires a great deal of thought, research, and patience. Begin by putting your symptoms in writing, perhaps on notecards so that you can lay them out and see them all at once. When doing this, be sure to jot down all of the major and minor symptoms, such as:

- What are the daily challenges that keep coming up?
- Who is involved?

"When I'm getting ready to reason with a man, I spend one-third of my time thinking about myself and what I am going to say—and two-thirds thinking about him and what he is going to say."

—Abraham Lincoln

Successful Decisions

AN ACTIVITY FOR CRITICAL REFLECTION

Carson's class was assigned an activity asking them to determine whom they would like to meet if they could meet anyone, and which questions they would like to ask them. Some of the class members thought it was a stupid assignment, and Carson was not so sure that she wanted to spend any time on this "weird" activity either. That evening, she began to think about the question seriously. "Who has been important to the world?" she thought. "Who had done something powerful and extraordinary? Who has been awful and caused needless pain?"

She decided that if she could ask anyone anything, she would choose Hitler. She decided that she would ask him these questions: (1) If you had to do it all over again, would you? (2) From where did your hatred come? (3) Why did you have everyone killed who could have revealed your own past? (4) You did not look like the master race you chose to promote. Why did you choose to promote it? (5) Why did you become such a coward in the end and kill yourself?

This interesting project led Carson to use World War II, Hitler, and the German Occupation as the basis for her presentation in speech class. She did not just brush off what seemed to be a "crazy" assignment.

In your own words, what three suggestions would you give to a classmate who thinks an assignment is crazy or a waste of time? Be specific.

1. _____
   _____

2. _____
   _____

3. _____
   _____

- How are the symptoms hindering your overall goals?
- Who or what is responsible for creating these symptoms?
- Are the symptoms internal (self-inflicted) or external (inflicted by others)?
- What obstacles are these symptoms creating?
- Are the symptoms part of one major problem or several problems?

Research and Develop a Variety of Solutions

It is a mistake to try to solve a problem when you don't have enough information to do so. It may be that you need to conduct interviews, research what others have done who face similar issues, read current data and reports, or even explore historical documents. Paul and Elder (2006) suggest that the type of information you need is determined by the type of problem you have and the question(s) you are trying to answer. "If you have a historical question, you need *historical information*. If you have a biological question, you need *biological information*. If you have an ethical question, you must identify at least one relevant *ethical principle*." Therefore, part of the problem solving process is to gather your facts—the correct facts—before you try to reach a resolution.

Evaluate and Analyze All Possible Solutions

After you have gathered your research (through formal methods and/or brainstorming), you must now evaluate your solutions to determine which would work best and why. After careful study and deliberation, without emotional interference, analyze the solutions you came up with and determine if they are appropriate or inappropriate. To analyze, create Columns A and B. Write the possible *solutions in Column A*, and an evaluative *comment in Column B.*

EXAMPLE.   (Using the problem "I don't have enough time to study due to my job"):

A (Possible Solutions)	B (Comments)
Quit the job.	Very hard to do; I need the money for tuition and car.
Cut my hours at work.	Will ask my boss if this is a possibility.
Find a new job.	Hard to do because of the job market—but will look into it.
Get a student loan.	Visit financial aid office tomorrow and fill out the FASFA.
Quit school.	No—it is my only chance for a promotion and to get a better job later on.

With your comments in Column B, you can now begin to eliminate some of the alternatives that are inappropriate at this time.

Solve the Problem and Evaluate the Results

Now that you have a few strong possible solutions, you have some work to do. You will need to talk to your boss, go to the financial aid office, and possibly begin to search for a new job with flexible hours. Basically, you are creating a *plan* to bring this solution to life. After you have researched each possible solution further, you will be able to make a decision based on solid information and facts. You will be able to figure out which solution is the best option for you.

Your Turn

Using the diagram in Figure 5.9, work through the following situation and determine the steps that could be taken to solve this problem.

Your best friend, Nathan, has just come to you with a problem. He tells you that his parents are really coming down hard on him because he is going to college. It is a strange problem. They believe that Nathan should be working full time, and that he is just wasting his time and money, since he did not do well in high school. They have threatened to take away his car and kick him out of the house if he does not find a full-time job. Nathan is doing well and does not want to leave college. He has a goal of becoming an architect and knows that he has talent in this area. He is making A's and B's in all of his classes. This does not matter to his parents. They do not value education and see it as a luxury.

Step Five: Making Intelligent Decisions

You make decisions every day. These decisions may be small, such as, "What am I going to have for lunch?" or large decisions, such as, "Should I change jobs in this economy?" There are many factors that influence our decisions, including our past experiences, our tolerance for risk, our comfort level, our desire to change, and our relationships with others. To further complicate the issue of decision making, we are faced with immediacy. In today's information-centered world, we seldom have time to sit back and digest all of the facts and angles before we're required to make life-altering decisions. Because of the pace at which decision making is required in today's business world, we sometimes add two and two together and get five (MindTools, 2011).

Decision making is such an important tool when it comes to being effective in the workplace and enhancing your leadership skills. When faced with a difficult decision, we've all asked the age-old question, "How do I know if I'm making the right decision?" With so many factors tugging at us, including people in our lives, past experiences, and our amygdala (the emotional brain), it is difficult to know if the decision we're making is a wise one. Our emotional brain tries to play tricks on us. It wants us to make decisions based on our emotions and not our intellect. Then, you have your reasoning brain telling you to make the decision based on logic, reasoning, and facts and leave your heart out of it. It's enough to drive you crazy, or worse yet, to drive you to making a poor decision or no decision at all.

In his book, *How We Decide* (2010), Jonah Leher speaks of "***The Sin of Certainty***." This is a situation when our strong desire to *believe we're right* flies in the face of the evidence that

Figure 5.9 Solutions in Bloom Diagram

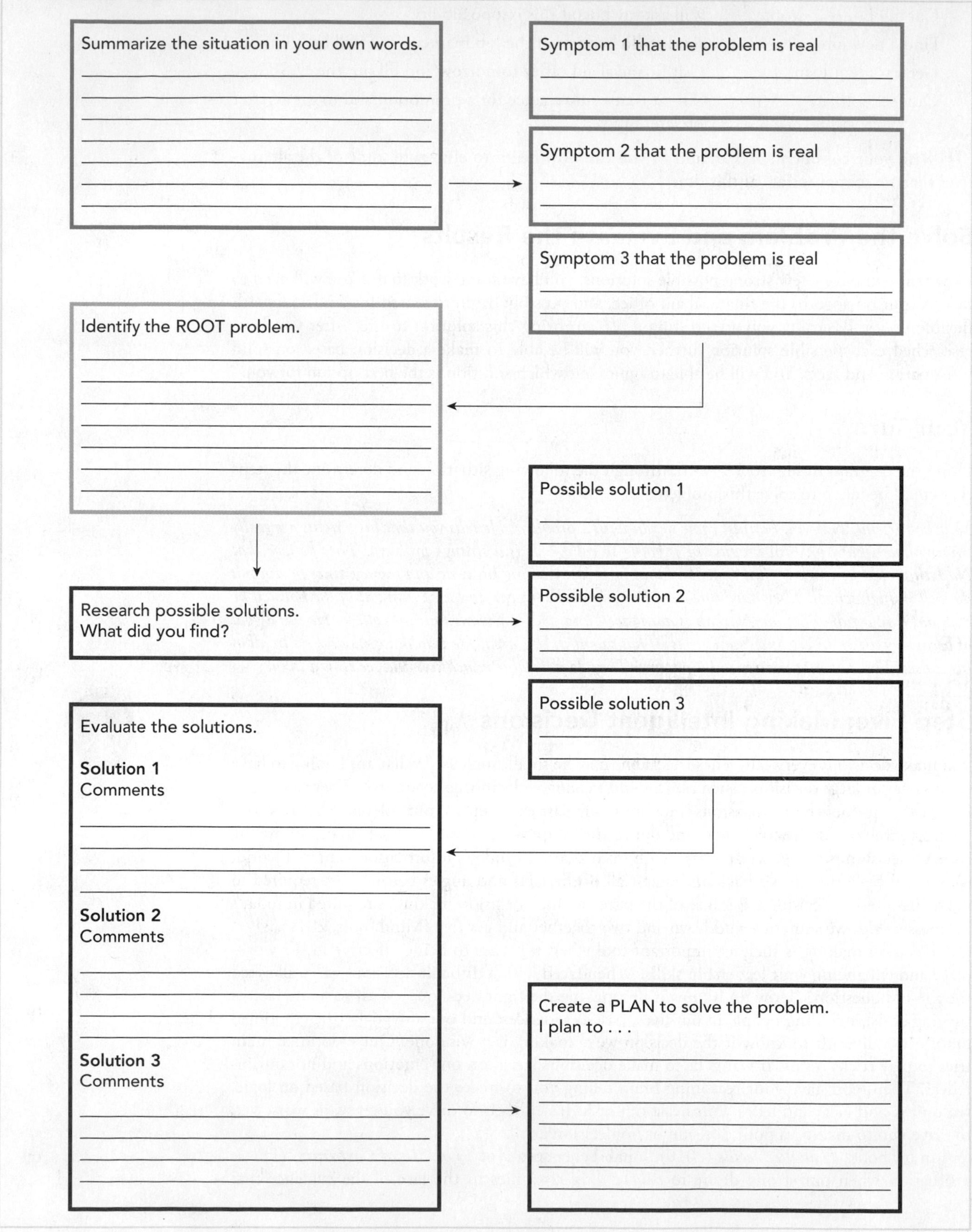

Summarize the situation in your own words.

_____
_____
_____
_____
_____
_____

Symptom 1 that the problem is real

_____
_____

Symptom 2 that the problem is real

_____
_____

Symptom 3 that the problem is real

_____
_____

Identify the ROOT problem.

_____
_____
_____
_____
_____
_____

Possible solution 1

_____
_____

Possible solution 2

_____
_____

Possible solution 3

_____
_____

Research possible solutions.
What did you find?

Evaluate the solutions.

Solution 1
Comments

_____
_____
_____

Solution 2
Comments

_____
_____
_____
_____

Solution 3
Comments

_____
_____
_____
_____

Create a PLAN to solve the problem.
I plan to . . .

_____
_____
_____
_____
_____

clearly states otherwise. It is a neurological condition where we convince ourselves that our actions are just, fair, and based in fact, when in actuality, we have simply told ourselves the lie so many times that we believe the incorrect assumptions. We have given our brain so many facts and figures that it begins to "cherry pick" only what is needed to make the decision *we want* to make, not the decision *we need* to make based on evidence and logical reasoning. He states that our brains are very complex, and sometimes the best decisions are going to come from our head, and sometimes the best decisions are going to come from our heart. We have to know when to use both—either separately or together.

One of the most effective ways to make a decision is to use a numerical scale to actually assign a "score" to each choice. This works as follows:

- **Create an Element column.** This column lists the aspects of the decision that are important to you, such as pay, potential for growth, joy of work, etc.
- **Create a Rating of Importance column.** This column gives each element a rating that you assign based on how important this element is to you. Using a scale of 1 to 10, you will decide if pay is very important (an 8, 9, or 10), or if it is not very important (a 1, 2, or 3).
- **Create a Choice #1 column.** This column will list the numerical calculations for your first choice. You will decide on its importance and then multiple that number by your importance rating.
- **Create a Choice #2 column.** This column will list the numerical calculations for your second choice. You will decide on its importance and then multiple that number by your importance rating.

Once you have created your columns (see Figure 5.10), you will work through your decisions using your head and your heart.

Figure 5.10   Decision-Making Chart

The following example shows a decision-making chart between two job offers for Samantha. The Elements column lists the items that are most important to Samantha in selecting a new job.

Elements The things I value in a career	My Rating of Importance 1–10	Choice #1 Job at Mercy Hospital	Choice #2 Job at Grace Hospital
Distance to work from home	8	Rating = 5 $8 \times 5 = 40$	Rating = 2 $2 \times 8 = 16$
Pay	10	Rating = 9 $10 \times 9 = 90$	Rating = 7 $10 \times 7 = 70$
Benefits	9	Rating = 2 $9 \times 2 = 18$	Rating = 7 $9 \times 7 = 63$
Potential for growth	5	Rating = 5 $5 \times 5 = 25$	Rating = 5 $5 \times 5 = 25$
Upgraded facility	7	Rating = 6 $7 \times 6 = 42$	Rating = 4 $7 \times 4 = 28$
		TOTAL SCORE = 215	TOTAL SCORE = 202

A numerical score may not be the ultimate in decision making, but at least you have taken the time to think about what is important to you, what is offered within the choices, and how it ranks in importance to you. By using this system, you are calling on your head and your heart to make decisions that could impact your life for a very long time.

Step Six: Distinguishing Fact from Opinion

An important aspect of critical thinking is the ability to distinguish fact from opinion. ***In most mediums—TV, radio, newspapers, magazines, and the Internet—opinions surface more often than facts.*** *Reread the previous sentence.* This is an example of an opinion cloaked as a fact. There is no research supporting this opinion. It sounds as if it could be true, but without evidence and proof, it is just an opinion.

> *"Everyone is entitled to their own opinion, but not their own facts."*
>
> —Senator Daniel Patrick Moynihan

A fact is something that can be ***proven***, something that can be ***objectively verified***. An opinion is a statement that is held to be true, but one that has no objective proof. *Statements that cannot be proved should always be treated as opinion.* Statements that offer valid proof and verification from credible, reliable sources can be treated as factual.

Learning to distinguish fact from opinion can be a paramount step in building your critical-thinking skills at work, with family, and especially when analyzing media.

Step Seven: Seeking Truth in Arguments and Persuasion

Whether or not you realize it, arguments and persuasive efforts are around you daily—hourly, for that matter. They are in newspaper and TV ads, editorials, news commentaries, talk shows, TV magazine shows, political statements, and religious services. They pop up every time you go online. It seems at times that almost everyone is trying to persuade us through arguments or advice. This section is included to assist you in recognizing faulty arguments and implausible or deceptive persuasion.

First, let's start with a list of terms used to describe faulty arguments and deceptive persuasion. As you read through the list, try to identify situations in which you have heard arguments that fit these descriptions.

Terminology for Fallacious (False) Arguments

Ad baculum	Ad baculum is an argument that tries to persuade based on force. Threats of alienation, disapproval, or even violence may accompany this type of argument.
Ad hominem	Ad hominem is when someone initiates a personal attack on a person rather than listening to and rationally debating his or her ideas. This is also referred to as slander.
Ad populum	An ad populum argument is based on the opinions of the majority of people. It assumes that because the majority says X is right, then Y is not. It uses little logic.
Ad verecundiam	This argument uses quotes and phrases from people in authority or popular people to support one's own views.
Bandwagon	The bandwagon approach tries to convince you to do something just because everyone else is doing it. It is also referred to as "peer pressure."
Scare tactic	A scare tactic is used as a desperate measure to put fear in your life. If you don't do X, then Y is going to happen to you.
Straw argument	The straw argument attacks the opponent's argument to make one's own argument stronger. It does not necessarily make argument A stronger; it simply discounts argument B.
Appeal to tradition	This argument looks only at the past and suggests that we have always done it "this way" and we should continue to do it "this way."

Plain folks	This type of persuasion is used to make you feel that the people making the argument are just like you. Usually, they are not; they are only using this appeal to connect with your sense of space and time.
Patriotism	This form of persuasion asks you to ignore reason and logic and support what is right for state A or city B or nation C.
Glittering generalities	This type of persuasion or argumentation is an appeal to generalities (Bosak, 1976). It suggests that a person or candidate or professional is for all the "right" things: justice, low taxes, no inflation, rebates, full employment, low crime, free tuition, progress, privacy, and truth.

Identifying Fallacious Arguments

Below, you will find statements intended to persuade you or argue for a cause. Beside each statement, identify which type of faulty persuasion is used.

AB	Ad baculum	SA	Straw argument	AH	Ad hominem
AT	Appeal to tradition	AP	Ad populum	PF	Plain folks
AV	Ad verecundiam	PM	Patriotism	BW	Bandwagon
ST	Scare tactic	GG	Glittering generalities		

_____ **1.** *This country has never faltered in the face of adversity. Our strong, united military has seen us through many troubled times, and it will see us through our current situation. This is your country; support your military.*

_____ **2.** *If I am elected to office, I will personally lobby for lower taxes, a new comprehensive crime bill, a $2500 tax cut on every new home, and better education, and I will personally work to lower the unemployment rate.*

_____ **3.** *This is the best college in the region. All of your friends will be attending this fall. You don't want to be left out; you should join us, too.*

_____ **4.** *If you really listen to Governor Wise's proposal on health care, you will see that there is no way that we can have a national system. You will not be able to select your doctor, you will not be able to go to the hospital of your choice, and you will not be able to get immediate attention. His proposal is not as comprehensive as our proposal.*

_____ **5.** *My father went to Honors College, I went to Honors College, and you will go to Honors College. It is the way things have been for the people in this family. There is no need to break with tradition now.*

_____ **6.** *The witness's testimony is useless. He is an alcoholic; he is dishonest and corrupt. To make matters worse, he was a member of the Extremist Party.*

_____ **7.** *The gentleman on the witness stand is your neighbor, he is your friend, he is just like you. Sure, he may have more money and drive a Mercedes, but his heart never left the Elm community.*

_____ **8.** *John F. Kennedy once said, "Ask not what your country can do for you; ask what you can do for your country." This is the time to act, my fellow citizens. You can give $200 to our cause and you will be fulfilling the wish of President Kennedy.*

_____ **9.** *Out of the 7000 people polled, 72 percent believed that there is life beyond our planet. Therefore, there must be life beyond Earth.*

from ORDINARY to *Extraordinary*

Dino J. Gonzalez, M.D. Board-Certified Internal Medicine and AAHIVM Certified HIV Specialist Internal Medical Associates, Las Vegas, NV

Can one person make a difference in your life? Can one person change the course of your destiny? The answer is yes! Most definitely, yes! The person who altered the course of my future was my third-grade teacher, Mrs. Allison. She was a strong African American lady who pushed us to do our best and would not let us fail. She was hard and demanded the best from us, but she was fair and an awesome teacher. She made us bring a toothbrush from home so that we could brush our teeth after lunch. She corrected our grammar and let us know that "street English" would not fly in her classroom. She even made us do Jazzercise after lunch to teach us how to take care of our bodies. I was lucky to be under her tutelage again in the fifth grade.

Why was she so dynamic? Why did she mean so much to my life? Well, I had always been a good student in school, earning mostly A's. However, my home life was another story.

I was born in 1970 in a HUD housing project in Las Vegas, Nevada, in the gang-infested 28th Street area. My mother, two brothers, and I lived in poverty. By the time I was three, my mother was bedridden and on disability due to chronic obstructive pulmonary disease, caused by a three-pack-a-day smoking habit. We were on welfare, food stamps, and the free lunch program.

As it turned out, my father never married my mother or helped support us because he was already married to another woman with children of their own. My mother did not know this until after my birth. So basically, we were on our own. Often, I felt alone in my community because I looked different. My father was Hispanic, but my mother was a blond, light-skinned Norwegian. I was not brown. I was not white. I felt like I did not have a real place in my community or in school. Mrs. Allison helped change all of that.

_____ **10.** *Without this new medication, you will die.*

_____ **11.** *I don't care what anyone says. If you don't come around to our way of thinking, you'd better start watching your back.*

> "There is nothing so powerful as truth, and often, nothing so strange."
> —Daniel Webster

As you develop your critical-thinking skills, you will begin to recognize the illogical nature of many thoughts, the falsehoods of many statements, the deception in some advertisements, and the irrational fears used to persuade. You will also begin to understand the depths to which you should delve to achieve objectivity, the thought and care that should be given to your own decisions and statements, and the methods by which you can build logical, truthful arguments.

Step Eight: Thinking Creatively and Being Resourceful

Creative thinking is a major and important aspect of critical thinking in that you are producing something that is uniquely yours—introducing something to the world that is new, innovative, and useful. Creative thinking does not mean that you have to be an artist, a musician,

Because of Mrs. Allison and a few close friends, I began to see the positive aspect of school and getting an education. I managed to stay away from the heavy gang influence that had engulfed my brothers. By the time I began high school, one of my brothers was already in prison because of drugs and gang activity. Because of Mrs. Allison's influence, I began to surround myself with people who were positive and worked hard. I wanted to be around people who *wanted something*—who had a more visionary view of the world than I had.

> I was born in a HUD housing project in the gang-infested area of Las Vegas, Nevada.

The harder I worked and studied, the better I did. I excelled in junior high and high school, and by the time I graduated, I did so with honors. I became the first person in my family to attend college. I was offered four scholarships, and they paid for everything, even giving me some spare money to live on. I had been working anywhere from 20 to 30 hours per week since I was fourteen years old, but I continued to work full-time while attending college.

I had always loved science and the study of the human body, so I decided to major in chemistry and education. I began to develop a keen interest in infectious diseases and viruses. By the time I was a junior in college, I had decided to become a doctor, so I dropped my education major and focused on biology. After graduation, I applied to medical school and was accepted into the University of Nevada School of Medicine. I completed my studies, did a three-year residency, and decided to open my own practice. I became board certified in internal medicine as an HIV specialist. Six years later, my practice is hugely successful and I enjoy days filled with helping people maintain or regain their health. My dream of doing something real and helping others is now an everyday occurrence in my life.

My advice to you as a first-year college student is this: You have the power to make your dreams come true. You *can* change your life if you truly know what you want and do the work that comes with making dreams come true. Surround yourself with upbeat, positive, smart, giving, open-minded people from whom you can learn and grow. Mrs. Allison was my inspiration. Yours is out there, too.

EXTRAORDINARY REFLECTION

Dr. Gonzalez talks about his teacher, Mrs. Allison, and how she challenged him and changed his life. What teacher(s) can you think of who have dramatically altered the course of your life?

or a writer. Creative thinking means that you have examined a situation and developed a new way of explaining information, delivering a product, or using an item. It can be as simple as discovering that you can use a small rolling suitcase to carry your books around campus instead of the traditional backpack. Creative thinking means that you have opened your mind to possibilities!

Creative thinking is really about being resourceful, and in today's times, resourcefulness is a powerful tool. Resourcefulness is an *internal* quality, not an *external* gift. If you have ever seen the TV series, "*Survivor*" or "*Man versus Wild,*" you know that it takes a strong person to eat a slug just carved out of a tree trunk. It takes internal will to drink water with so many bacteria that flies die when they drink it. Yes, both shows are somewhat staged, but they show the basics of creativity, intelligence, imagination, and *resourcefulness*.

Think of internal resourcefulness as **renewable thinking energy**. When you have to draw on your wits, creativity, and determination, these qualities multiply. The more you are required by circumstance to use them, the stronger and more plentiful they become. Conversely, if you've always been able to buy anything you want or all that you need is provided to you by an external force, your internal resourcefulness begins to wither and die like uneaten fruit on the winter vine. You are not forced to use the whole of yourself. Your energy fades. Your harvest dies.

If you had to use your creativity to survive in the wild, could you do it?

Your inner resourcefulness and creativity also make you more secure and offer more protection from outside forces. When you know how to make ends meet, you can always do it. When you know how to pay the rent on limited income, you can always do it. When you know how to cut firewood to heat your home, you can always do it. When you know how to navigate the public transportation system in your town, you can always do it—even when the time comes when you don't have to do it anymore, you could if you had to. The more you know and the more inner strength and resourcefulness you have, the safer you are against the unknown. The more confidence you possess, the greater the likelihood that you can survive anything at any time. The more resourceful you are, the more you understand that this one quality will help you rebuild all that may have been lost. When the world *has* been handed to you on a silver platter, you cannot be ready for what the world *can* hand you.

To begin the creative process, consider the items in Figure 5.11. These are some of the characteristics creative thinkers have in common.

Using your imaginative and innovative juices, think about how you would *creatively* solve this problem. Write down at least five possibilities. Come on, make it count!

The Problem

Jennifer is a first-year student who does not have enough money to pay her tuition, buy her books, purchase food, and purchase a few outfits and shoes to wear to class and her work-study job on campus.

What should she do? Should she pay her tuition and purchase her books, or pay her tuition and buy new clothes and shoes to wear to class and work? What creative, resourceful ideas (solutions) can you give Jennifer?

My creative solutions:

1. _____

2. _____

3. _____

4. _____

5. _____

Level 6 Create

Figure 5.11 Characteristics of Creative Thinking

Compassion	Creative thinkers have a zest for life and genuinely care for the spirit of others.	Example: More than 40 years ago, community members who wanted to feed the elderly created Meals on Wheels, now a national organization feeding the elderly.
Courage	Creative thinkers are unafraid to try new things, to implement new thoughts and actions.	Example: An NBC executive moves the *Today Show* out of a closed studio onto the streets of New York, creating the number one morning news show in America.
Truth	Creative thinkers search for the true meaning of things.	Example: The astronomer and scientist Copernicus sought to prove that Earth was *not* the center of the universe—an unpopular (albeit true) view at the time.

Dreams	Creative thinkers allow themselves time to dream and ponder the unknown. They can see what is possible, not just what is actual.	Example: John F. Kennedy dreamed that space exploration was possible. His dream became reality.
Risk taking	Creative thinkers take positive risks every day. They are not afraid to go against popular opinion.	Example: Barack Obama took a risk and ran for president of the United States. He became one of only a few African Americans to ever run for the office, and the only African American to be nominated by his party. In November 2008, he because the first African American president of the United States.
Innovation	Creative thinkers find new ways to do old things.	Example: Instead of continuing to fill the earth with waste, such as aluminum, plastic, metal, and old cars, means were developed to recycle these materials for future productive use.
Competition	Creative thinkers strive to be better, to think bolder thoughts, to do what is good, and to be the best at any task.	Example: A textbook writer updates the publication every three years to include new and revised information so the product remains competitive and informative.
Individuality	Creative thinkers are not carbon copies of other people. They strive to be true to themselves.	Example: A young man decides to take tap dancing instead of playing baseball. He excels and wins a fine arts dancing scholarship to college.
Curiosity	Creative thinkers are interested in all things; they want to know much about many things.	Example: A 65-year-old retired college professor goes back to college to learn more about music appreciation and computer programming to expand her possibilities.
Perseverance	Creative thinkers do not give up. They stick to a project to its logical and reasonable end.	Example: Dr. Martin Luther King, Jr., did not give up on his dream in the face of adversity, danger, and death threats.

CHANGING IDEAS to Reality

REFLECTIONS ON CRITICAL AND CREATIVE THINKING

Critical thinking, emotional intelligence, and information literacy require a great deal of commitment on your part. They may not be easy for everyone at first, but with practice, dedication, and an understanding of the immense need of all three, everyone can think more critically and logically, evaluate information sources, and use emotional intelligence to his or her best advantage.

Critical thinking and emotional intelligence can affect the way you live your life, from relationships to purchasing a new car, from solving family problems to investing money, from taking the appropriate classes for graduation to getting a promotion at work. Both are vitally important to your growth and education.

As you continue on in the semester and work toward personal and professional motivation and change, consider the following ideas:

- Use only *credible* and *reliable* sources.
- Learn to distinguish *fact* from *opinion*.
- Be *flexible* in your thinking and *avoid* generalizations.
- Use emotional intelligence and *restraint*.
- Avoid *stereotyping* and prejudging and strive for *objectivity* in your thinking.
- *Reserve* judgment until you have looked at every side.
- Do *not* assume—do the research and *ask* questions.
- Work hard to distinguish *symptoms from problems*.

Critical thinking is truly the hallmark of an educated person. It is a hallmark of character and integrity, and a hallmark of successful students. Let it be yours.

Knowledge in Bloom

EVALUATING THE VALIDITY, CREDIBILITY, AND PURPOSE OF AN ARTICLE

Utilizes Levels 3 and 4 of the Taxonomy (See Bloom's Taxonomy at the front of this text)

Explanation: Thousands of articles are written every day for magazines, newspapers, online journals, and other print media. Depending on the article or where it is published, it can have a slant. You may have heard this called bias (as in liberal or conservative bias). One of journalism's purposes should be to objectively present the facts of what has happened with an incident or the facts of what is being discussed. Bias should not enter the argument unless it is an editorial.

Process: For this activity, you are to find an article (not an editorial) in a mainstream newspaper or magazine (*USA Today, Newsweek, Time, New York Times, The Washington Post, The National Review*, etc.), read the article, and determine if the article has bias, unsubstantiated opinions, or weak research.

To assist you in this project, you will find a list of questions below to help you evaluate and assess your article.

Name of the article: _____

Writer of the article: _____

His/her affiliation: _____

Publication in which the article was found: _____

Date of publication: _____

Before you read this article, based on the title and subject matter, what five questions do you want to be able to answer once you have read the article?

1. _____

2. _____

3. _____

4. _____

5. _____

After reading the article, what is the author's main reason for writing it? _____

_____

_____

_____

What is the most important fact(s) or information in the article? _____

_____

_____

_____

By writing this article, what is the author implying? _____
_____
_____
_____

By writing this article, what is the author proving? _____
_____
_____
_____

In writing this article, what assumptions were made? _____
_____
_____
_____

What sources does the writer cite to prove his/her point? _____
_____
_____
_____

Is the article fairly presented? In other words, does the author examine both sides of the issue or just one side?
Justify your answer. _____
_____
_____

Do you believe and trust the article? Why or why not? Justify your answer. _____
_____
_____
_____

If this article is accurate (or inaccurate depending on your judgment), what are the implications for society? _____
_____
_____
_____

Answer the five question you wrote earlier in this exercise.

1. _____
2. _____
3. _____
4. _____
5. _____

List one way that you can use the information in this article to enhance your creativity and/or resourcefulness. _____
_____

(This project is adapted, in part, from the work of Paul & Elder, 2006.)

SQ3R MASTERY STUDY SHEET

EXAMPLE QUESTION (FROM PAGE 106) Why is Emotional Intelligence important to critical thinking?	**ANSWER:**
EXAMPLE QUESTION (FROM PAGE 118) What are false arguments?	**ANSWER:**
AUTHOR QUESTION (FROM PAGE 106) What is the relationship between the amygdala and emotional restraint?	**ANSWER:**
AUTHOR QUESTION (FROM PAGE 110) Why is asking questions so important in critical thinking?	**ANSWER:**
AUTHOR QUESTION (FROM PAGE 113) What is the difference between a symptom and a problem?	**ANSWER:**
AUTHOR QUESTION (FROM PAGE 118) Define fact and opinion and give an example of each.	**ANSWER:**
AUTHOR QUESTION (FROM PAGE 118) Define ad hominem and find an example of this in a recent newspaper or magazine.	**ANSWER:**
YOUR QUESTION (FROM PAGE ____)	**ANSWER:**
YOUR QUESTION (FROM PAGE ____)	**ANSWER:**
YOUR QUESTION (FROM PAGE ____)	**ANSWER:**
YOUR QUESTION (FROM PAGE ____)	**ANSWER:**
YOUR QUESTION (FROM PAGE ____)	**ANSWER:**

Finally, after answering these questions, recite this chapter's major points in your mind. Consider the following general questions to help you master this material.

- What is it about?
- What does it mean?
- What is the most important thing you learned? Why?
- What are the key points to remember?

ANSWERS TO TEASERS

Brain Teaser #1, Looking at Common Terms Backward

1. Snow White and the Seven Dwarfs
2. *I Have a Dream* by Martin Luther King, Jr.
3. Two peas in a pod
4. Hickory dickory dock, the mouse ran up the clock
5. Three sides to a triangle
6. One hundred pennies in a dollar
7. There's no place like home
8. Four quarts in a gallon
9. *It's a Small World After All*
10. Fifty state in the union

Brain Teaser #2, The Penny
Your answers might include:

- We had more than one language
- We knew geometry
- We had a calendar system
- We honored people
- We knew metallurgy
- We had a numeric system
- We knew architecture
- We were united
- We valued liberty
- They could infer our physical attributes

Brain Teaser #3, Thinking Beyond What Is Given to You

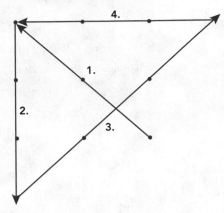

chapter six

PRIORITIZE

PLANNING YOUR TIME AND REDUCING STRESS

"If you want to make good use of your time, you've got to know what's most important and then give it all you've got." —Lee Iacocca

Scan
and QUESTION

Take a few moments, **scan this chapter** and on page 153, write **five of your own questions** that you think will be important to your mastery of this material.

Example:

- ☑ **How can I simplify my life and get more done?** (from page 136)
- ☑ **What are the three procrastination types?** (from page 139)

Why
read this chapter?

Because you'll learn...

- The relationship between priority management, your value system, and self-discipline
- How you spend your time and how to develop a "to do" list based on your findings
- How to deal with the major stressors in your life

Because you'll be able to...

- Simplify your life
- Avoid distractions and interruptions in your daily life
- Beat procrastination and get more done

MyStudentSuccessLab

MyStudentSuccessLab is an online solution designed to help you acquire and develop (or hone) the skills you need to succeed. You will have access to peer-led video presentations and develop core skills through interactive exercises and projects.

Name: Alencia Anderson

Institution: Graduate! Delgado Community College, New Orleans, LA

Major: Sociology and Criminal Justice

She was 27 years old with a baby and a 7 year old, working a job in retail, when she decided to go back to school. She knew she was supposed to go to college, but had let life get in the way of her dreams. She said, "I was working, paying bills, but ends were not meeting, and I knew I had to do something different so I decided to go back to school. Delgado Community College is where my life began. Change just happened, overnight my entire life just changed," Alencia said.

Alencia caught my attention because she seemed to hang onto every word that was being said. She was a young, professionally-dressed woman who seemed older than the fresh out of high school student. During the semester I related my story of returning to school at the age of 35 after a divorce. We had a lot in common and had many discussions regarding her future. "I didn't know for certain if I wanted to go on to a four year college. I thought I wanted to major in English. After talking with Ms. Deffendall, I did transfer to a four year college after completing my basics and majored in sociology. I now

An interview conducted and written by Melanie Deffendall, Director of the Women's Center, and Coordinator of College Success, Delgado Community College, New Orleans, LA

have a Master's Degree in Criminal Justice and will begin law school in the fall at Southern University."

"It all began at Delgado. I was a first-generation college student, first to graduate from high school, and the first to enter college—the first in my family on both sides—now the first to hold a degree, two degrees. I asked myself if I was smart enough to go to college. Your words spoke to me, to my life, you cared and I felt that. When I think about community college, I think that is where my self-esteem developed. It gave me the confidence to believe that the goals I had thought about and wrote down could be achieved. It opened doors for me even before I graduated. I am so grateful for community college, for this community college," Alencia stated.

Alencia's confidence grew and so did her abilities. Students need to believe they can achieve. Her success is my success, because that is why I teach at a community college—to change lives. She still has her textbook and remarks that, "Knowledge is power. I just believe that before you can do something, you have to have knowledge. This is where the knowledge began. I thought I knew a great deal, but there was so much more I needed to know. This is where the knowledge started, where the doors opened. Not just walking through one door, but so many more doors; so many more opportunities that I didn't even know existed. Until you go to college and learn what is available, you have no idea what you can become. This was a great start. College changed my life."

THINK
a b o u t *it*

1. Alencia had several home and family issues that could have prevented her from attending college. However, she determined that her best bet for the future was to secure her education. What obstacles will you need to overcome to make your dream of a college degree a reality?

2. How has college helped you develop your self-esteem and personal passion? What have you learned about careers since you began your college experience?

TIME—YOU HAVE ALL THERE IS

Can You Take Control of Your Life and Make the Most of Your Time?

You can definitely say four things about time: *It is fair. It does not discriminate. It treats everyone the same. Everyone has all there is.* No person has any more or less hours in a day than the next person. The good news is that by learning how to manage our priorities more effectively, we don't need to slow time down or stop it. We can learn how to get things done and have more time for joy and fun.

So, how do you spend your time? Some people are very productive while others scramble to find a few moments to enjoy life and have quality relationships. According to priority management and personal productivity expert Donald Wetmore (2008), "The average working person spends less than two minutes per day in *meaningful* communication with their spouse or significant other and less than 30 seconds per day in *meaningful* communication with their children." Think about that for a moment—*thirty seconds*. If you think that is amazing, consider the following list. As strange as it may seem, these features are taken from the Bureau of Labor Statistics of the U.S. Department of Census Time Use Survey (2011). During your *working years* (ages 20–65, a 45-year span) you spend an average of:

- 16 years sleeping
- 2.3 years eating
- 3.1 years doing housework
- 6 years watching TV
- 1.3 years on the telephone

This totals *28.7 years of your working life* doing things that you may not even consider in your priority-management plan. What happens to the remaining 16.3 years? Well, you will spend *14 of those years working*, which leaves you with 2.3 years, or only 20,000 hours, during your working life to embrace joy, spend time with your family, educate yourself, travel, and experience a host of other life-fulfilling activities. Dismal? Scary? It does not have to be. By learning how to manage your priorities, harness your energy and passion, and take control of your day-to-day activities, 2.3 years can be a long, exciting, productive time.

Why is it that some people seem to get so much more done than other people? They appear to always be calm and collected and have it together. You are probably aware of others who are always late with assignments, never finish their projects on time, rarely seem to have time to study, and appear to have no concrete goals for their lives. Sometimes, we get the idea that the first group accomplishes more because they have more time or because they don't have to work or they don't have children or they are smarter or have more help. Actually, some of these reasons may be true, but in reality, many of them have learned how to overcome and beat procrastination, tie their value system to their priority management plan, and use their personal energy and passion to accomplish more.

Do the figures regarding how we spend our time surprise you? Where do you think most of your "free" time goes?

"I can't do any more than I am doing right now," you may say to yourself. But is that really true? One of the keys to managing your priorities is to consider your values. You tend to put more passion, energy, and time toward what you value, enjoy, and love. Do you value your family? If so, you make time for them. Do you value your friends? If so, you make time for them. Now you have to ask yourself, **how much do I value my education**? How important is it that I succeed in college and get my degree? If you place this as a high value for your life and your future, you will find that you make more time for your studies, your classes, and your projects. **We spend time on what we value!**

PRIORITY MANAGEMENT AND SELF-DISCIPLINE

> *"Self-discipline is teaching ourselves to do the things necessary to reach our goals without becoming sidetracked by bad habits."*
>
> —Denis Waitley

Do You Have What It Takes to "Git 'er Done?"

Priority management is actually about managing you! It is about taking control and assuming responsibility for the time you are given on this Earth. The sooner you understand and take control of how you use your time, the quicker you will be on your way to becoming successful in college and many other activities. Learning to manage your priorities is a lesson that you will use throughout your studies, and beyond. Actually, **you can't control time**, but you can control yourself and your priorities. Priority management is basically self-discipline—and self-discipline involves self-motivation. Priority management is paying attention to how you are spending your most valuable resource, and then devising a plan to use it more effectively. This is one of the goals of this chapter.

The word discipline comes from the Latin word meaning, *"to teach."* Therefore, **self-discipline** is really about "teaching ourselves" (Waitley, 1997). Consider the chart in Figure 6.1 regarding self-discipline. **Self-discipline is really about four things**: m**aking choices, making changes, employing your willpower, and taking responsibility.**

Once you have made the **choice** to engage in your education, stop procrastinating, and manage your time more effectively, you have to make the **changes** in your thoughts and behaviors to bring those choices to fruition. Then, you have to **accept responsibility** for your actions and take control of your life. You will have to call upon your **inner strength, or willpower**—and you **do** have willpower, it may just be hidden or forgotten, but you do have it. You have the ability to empower yourself to get things done. No one can do this for you. You are responsible for your life, your actions, and your willpower. Self-discipline and willpower help you move in the direction of your dreams. Even in the face of fear, anxiety, stress, defeat, and darkness, self-discipline will help you find your way.

Willpower and self-discipline are all about **re-training your mind** to do what *you* want it to do and not what *it* wants to do. It is about eliminating the negative self-talk that so often derails us and causes us to procrastinate and get stressed out. By re-training your mind and resisting the urge to simply "obey" your subconscious, you are basically re-training your life. Consider the following situations:

- You come home from three classes and you are tired and weary. Your subconscious mind tells you to sit down, put your feet up, and watch TV for a while. You have to tell your mind, *"No! I am going to take a short walk around the block to get my adrenalin flowing and then I'm going to read my chapter for homework."*

- You look at your desk or study space and you see all of the books and papers you have gathered for your research paper and your subconscious mind tells you to just ignore it for a while—there's still time to get it done! You have to tell your mind, *"Absolutely not! I'm going to get those articles organized and make an outline of my paper before I do anything else today. Period."*

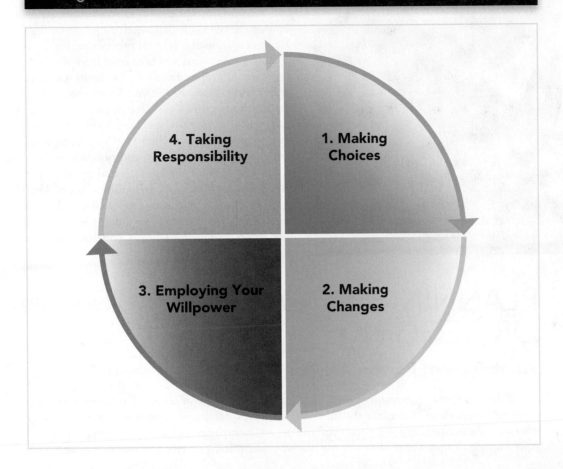

Figure 6.1 Components of Self-Discipline

- You come home and you are tired and hungry and your mind tells you to eat that candy bar or donut. You have to tell your mind, "**No way!** *I am going to have an apple instead. It is better for me and my memory to avoid sugar right now.*"

By re-training your mind and paying attention to your subconscious, you can re-train yourself to develop the self-discipline and willpower to get things done and avoid the stress caused by procrastination. Willpower gives you strength to stay on track and avoid the guilt associated with putting things off or not doing them at all. Guilt turns to frustration and frustration turns to anger, and before you know it, your negative self-talk and subconscious mind have "won" and nothing gets done. You **do** have the power to change this.

> "*Begin doing what you want to do now. We are not living in eternity. We have only this moment, sparkling like a star in our hand and melting like a snowflake.*"
>
> —Marie B. Ray

I'LL DO IT WHEN I HAVE A LITTLE FREE TIME

Is Time Really Free?

What is *"free time"* and when does it happen? We've all used that expression at one time or another; "*I'll do that when I get a little more free time,*" or "*I'm going to wait until I find a little more time.*" Can time be found? Is time free? Do we ever have a moment to call our own? The answer

How can becoming a more organized person help you manage your priorities more effectively?

is "maybe," but free time has to be created by you and it can only be created by getting the things done that must be completed for your success.

Free time is *not* time that you simply create by putting off work that needs to be done. Free time is *not* time that is spent procrastinating. Free time is *not* time that you take away from your duties, chores, studies, family, and obligations. That is **borrowed time**, and if you know the rules of good behavior, you know that anything you borrow, you must repay. Free time *is* time that you reward yourself with when you have completed your studies, tasks, chores, and obligations. Free time *is* time that you have created by planning ahead and avoiding procrastination. One of your goals in managing your time more effectively is to create more free time in your life for joy. Joy will not come to you, however, if you have projects looming over your head.

PLANNING, DOODLING, OR BEGGING

What Type of Person Are You Anyway?

We all have different personality types, but did you know we also have different priority management personalities? Consider the list in Figure 6.2 explaining the different negative priority management personalities. Respond "yes" or "no" to the types you think most resemble you and your lifestyle. Then, out to the side, explain why you think this type represents you and your

Figure 6.2 Priority Management Types

Type	Explanation	Do you have any of these tendencies?	What actions make you like this type of person?	What can you do to begin eliminating this type of behavior?
The Circler	Doing the same things over and over again and again and hoping for a different result; basically, going around in circles.	YES NO		
The Doodler	Not paying attention to details; doing things that do not really matter to the completion of your project.	YES NO		
The Squanderer	Wasting too much time trying to "get ready" to study or work and never really getting anything done; then it is too late to do a good job.	YES NO		

Type	Explanation	Do you have any of these tendencies?	What actions make you like this type of person?	What can you do to begin eliminating this type of behavior?
The Beggar	Expecting time to "stop" for you after you've wasted time doing nothing or going in circles. Then, becoming frustrated when you don't have enough time.	YES NO		
The Planner	Planning out your project so carefully and meticulously that by the time you have everything you think you need, there is no time to really do the project.	YES NO		
The Hun	Waiting too late to plan or get things done and then stomping on anyone or anything to get the project done with no regard for others' feelings, time, or relationships.	YES NO		
The Passivist	Convincing yourself that you'll never get it all done and that there is no use to try anyway.	YES NO		

daily thoughts on time. Then, in the last column, list at least one strategy that you can begin to implement to overcome this type of negative priority management style.

ABSOLUTELY NO... WELL, MAYBE

Do You Know How to Say No?

"No, I'm sorry, I can't do that," is perhaps one of the most difficult phrases you must learn to say when it comes to effective priority management. *"Jeez, I should have never agreed to do this in the first place,"* is perhaps one of the most common phrases used when you don't know how to say "No." If you continually say "Yes" to everyone and every project, then quickly, you have no time left for yourself, your family, your friends, and your projects. Many of us are taught from an early age that "No" is a bad word and that we should always try to avoid saying it to others. However, we are not taught that never saying "No" can cause us undue stress and feelings of guilt and frustration, and can throw our time-management plans into disarray. Now that you have so much going on from so many different projects, saying "No" needs to become a part of your everyday vocabulary.

Do you think saying "No" is rude, or necessary?

> *"Time is the most valuable and most perishable of our possessions."*
> —John Randolph

Steps to Learning to Say No—It's as Simple as Not Saying Yes

- Think before you answer out loud with an insincere or untrue "Yes."
- Make sure you understand exactly what is being asked of you and what the project involves before you give a "Yes" or "No" answer.
- Review your schedule to see if you really have the time to do a quality job. (If you have to have an answer immediately, it is "No." If you can wait a few days for me to finish project X, and review my schedule, the answer may be "Yes.")
- Learn the difference between assertiveness (politely declining) and rudeness (have you lost your mind?).
- Say "No" at the right times (to the wrong things) so that you can say "Yes" at the appropriate times (to the right things).
- Learn how to put yourself and your future first (for a change). By doing this, you can say "Yes" more often later on.
- Inform others of your priority-management schedule so that they will have a better understanding of why you say "No."
- If you must say "Yes" to an unwanted project (something at work, for example), try to negotiate a deadline that works for everyone—you first!
- Keep your "No" short. If you have to offer an explanation, be brief so that you don't talk yourself into doing something you can't do and to avoid giving false hope to the other person.
- If you feel you simply have to say "Yes," try to trade off with the other person and ask him or her to do something on your list.
- Put a time limit on your "Yes." For example, you might agree to help someone but you could say, "I can give you thirty minutes and then I have to leave."

Your Turn

Level 3 Apply

You are taking four classes and the reading and homework are mounting day-by-day. Your family needs you, your friends think you've abandoned them, and you want to continue to do a good job at work. Your schedule is tight and you have things planned down to the hour in order to be able to get it all done well. Suddenly, you are asked to help with a project for disadvantaged children that seems very worthy and timely. You know that your schedule is full, but your conscience begins to gnaw at you and you really do want to help.

Applying the tips from the list above, predict how you might be able to address this situation.

_____

_____

_____

BEGINNING YOUR DAY WITH PEACE

Can You Start Your Day as a Blank Page and Simplify Your Life?

Imagine a day with nothing to do! That may be difficult, if not impossible for you to imagine right now. But as an exercise in building your own day from scratch and simplifying your life, think about having a day where *you* build your schedule and where you do not have to be constrained by activities and projects that others have thrust upon you. Think about a day where you are in charge. Crazy? Impossible? Outrageous? Maybe not as much as you think.

12 WAYS TO SIMPLIFY YOUR LIFE

- Know what you value and work hard to eliminate activities that are not in conjunction with your core value system. This can be whittled down to one statement: ***"Identify what is important to you. Eliminate everything else."***
- Get away from technology for a few hours a day. Turn off your computer, cell phone, tablet, and other devices that can take time away from what you value.
- Learn to delegate to others. You may say to yourself, "My family does not know how to use the washing machine." Guess what? When all of their underwear is dirty, they'll learn how to use it. Don't enable others to avoid activities that complicate your life.
- Make a list of everything you are doing. Prioritize this list into what you enjoy doing and what fits into your value system. If you can only feasibly do three or four of these activities per day, draw a line after number four and eliminate the rest of the list.
- Do what is essential for the well being of you and your family and eliminate everything else.
- Don't waste time saving money. Spend money to save time. In other words, don't drive across town to save three cents per gallon on fuel or ten cents on a gallon of milk. Pay the extra money and have more time to do what you like.
- Clean your home of clutter and mess. Work from cleanliness. De-clutter and organize. Make sure everything has a place.
- Donate everything you don't need or use to charity. Simplifying your life may also mean simplifying your closets, drawers, cabinets, and garage.
- Go through your home or apartment and eliminate everything that does not bring you joy or have sentimental value. If you don't love it, ditch it.
- Clean up the files on your computer. Erase everything that you don't need or want so that you can find material more easily. If you have not used the file in a month, put it on a flash drive for later use.
- Live in the moment. Yes, it is important to plan for the future, but if you ignore "the moment," your future will not be as bright.
- Spend a few moments each morning and afternoon reflecting on all of the abundance in your life. Learn to give thanks and learn to do nothing. (Get More Done, 2008; Zen Habits, 2008)

In Figure 6.3, compile a list that can help you simplify your life in each category. Add *only* those things to the list that you can actually do on a daily basis.

Figure 6.3 **Simplify Your Life**

Level 6 Create

Two things I can do to simplify my life at home	
Two things I can do to simplify my life at work	
Two things I can do to simplify my life at school	
Two things I can do to simplify my life with my children	
Two things I can do to simplify my life with my spouse/partner/loved one	
Two things I can do to simplify my economics (financial matters)	

Successful Decisions
AN ACTIVITY FOR CRITICAL REFLECTION

Darius is a single father of two young daughters. He and his wife divorced several years ago and he was granted custody of Alice and Marianne. Shortly after the divorce, Darius was laid off from his job as a construction foreman. He had been making a very good living, but now it was hard to make ends meet. He could not find another job that paid well enough to support the three of them.

Therefore, he decided to go back to school to pursue his dream of becoming a draftsman. His classes, along with his new part-time job, demanded much of his time. He found that he was spending much less time with his daughters than he had in the past—and he did not like this at all.

His daughters were cast in the school play and the performance was scheduled for Friday night, the same night as one of his drafting classes. He knew that he had a conflict on

his hands. He knew that class was very important, but so was supporting his daughters. In your own words, what would you suggest that Darius do at this point? List at least three things that he could do to handle this situation, manage his time to meet all of his obligations, and maintain his sanity.

1. _____

    _____

2. _____

    _____

3. _____

    _____

THE DREADED "P" WORD

Why Is Procrastination So Easy to Do and How Can You Beat It Once and for All?

It's not just you! Almost everyone procrastinates, and then we worry and tell ourselves, "I'll never do it again if I can just get through this one project." But then someone comes along with a great idea for fun, and off we go. Or there is a great movie on TV, the kids want to play a game of ball, and you go to the refrigerator for a snack, and before you know it, you reward yourself with *free* time before you have done your work.

The truth is simple: We tend to avoid the hard jobs in favor of the easy ones. Even many of the list makers fool themselves. They mark off a long list of easy tasks while the big ones still loom in front of them. Many of us put off unpleasant tasks until our back is against the wall. So why do we procrastinate when we all know how unpleasant the results can be? Why aren't we disciplined and organized and controlled so we can reap the rewards that come from being prepared?

> *"If you have to eat two frogs, eat the ugliest one first."*
>
> —Brian Tracy

The biggest problem with procrastination, even beyond not getting the job, task, or paper completed, *is doing it poorly,* and then suffering the stress caused by putting it off or turning in a sub-par project. By putting the project off, you have cheated yourself out of the time needed to bring your best to the table and, most likely, you are going to hand over a project, with your name on it, that is not even close to your potential. And to top it off, more stress is created by this vicious cycle of, "I'll do it tomorrow—or this weekend."

What has procrastination cost you? This is perhaps one of the most important questions that you can ask and answer with regard to managing your time more effectively. Did it cost you a good grade? Did it cost you money? Did it cost you your reputation? Did it cost you your dignity? Did it cost you your ability to do your best? ***Procrastination is not free.*** Every time you do it, it costs you something. You need to determine what it is worth.

In order to beat procrastination, you will also need to consider what *type* of procrastinator you are. Each type requires a different strategy and different energy to overcome, but make no

Figure 6.4 Procrastinator Types

Chronic Procrastinator	You procrastinate all of the time in most aspects of your life including social situations, financial affairs, career decisions, personal responsibilities, and academic projects. Usually, you do not meet any deadlines if you complete the project at all. It is going to take a great deal of thought, planning, and energy to overcome this type of procrastination.
Moderate Procrastinator	You procrastinate much of the time. You usually get things done, but it is not your best work and you create a great deal of stress in your own life. It is going to take a fair amount of planning and energy to overcome this type of procrastination. With some planning, your projects could be much more effective and you could eliminate much stress and guilt.
Occasional Procrastinator	You occasionally put things off. You do not do this often, but when you do, you feel guilty and rush to get the project completed. Sometimes you turn in work that is not your best. You are good at planning most things, but you do need to concentrate on sticking to your plan and not letting unscheduled events obstruct your success.

doubt about it, success requires overcoming all degrees and types of procrastination. Which are you? Consider Figure 6.4.

Take a moment and complete the time management assessment in Figure 6.5. Be honest and truthful with your responses. The results of your score are located after the assessment.

Procrastination is quite simply a bad habit formed after many years of practice. There are reasons, however, that cause us to keep doing this to ourselves. Often, we let our negative self-talk cause us to procrastinate. We allow our negative attitude to override what we know is best for us. An attitude adjustment may be just the thing you need to overcome and beat the trap of procrastination. Consider the following list of negative statements. On the right-hand side, re-write the statement to become a positive, procrastination-beating statement.

NEGATIVE STATEMENT	**POSITIVE STATEMENT**
I'll do it at 9:30 when this TV show is over.	_____
I'm tired.	_____
I can't concentrate.	_____
This is too hard.	_____
This is boring.	_____
I don't know why anyone would ask me to do this crazy stuff.	_____

Learning to apply this type of positive thinking can help you beat the procrastination trap and manage your time and life more effectively.

Figure 6.5 Priority Management Assessment

Answer the following questions with the following scale:

1 = Not at all   2 = Rarely   3 = Sometimes   4 = Often   5 = Very often

1. I prioritize my tasks every day and work from my priority list.	1 2 3 4 5
2. I work hard to complete tasks on time and not put them off until the last minute.	1 2 3 4 5
3. I take time to plan and schedule the next day's activities the night before.	1 2 3 4 5
4. I make time during my daily schedule to study and get my projects completed so that I can have more quality time at home.	1 2 3 4 5
5. I study and get my work done before I take fun breaks.	1 2 3 4 5
6. I analyze my assignments to determine which ones are going to take the most time and then work on them first and most often.	1 2 3 4 5
7. I have analyzed my daily activities and determined where I actually spend my time.	1 2 3 4 5
8. I know how to say "No," and do so frequently.	1 2 3 4 5
9. I know how to avoid distractions and how to work through unexpected interruptions.	1 2 3 4 5
10. I do not let "fear of the unknown" keep me from working on a project.	1 2 3 4 5
11. I know how to overcome apathy and boredom toward a project.	1 2 3 4 5
12. I know how to fight and overcome my own laziness.	1 2 3 4 5
13. I know how to re-frame a project that may not interest me so that I can see the benefits from it and learn from it.	1 2 3 4 5
14. I know how to break down a major, complex, or overwhelming task to get it done in pieces and then put it all together.	1 2 3 4 5
15. I build time into my schedule on a daily or weekly basis to deal with "unexpected" interruptions or distractions.	1 2 3 4 5

YOUR TOTAL SCORE: _____

RESULTS:

60–75   You manage your priorities well and you know how to build a schedule to get things done. Your productivity is high. You don't let procrastination rule your life.

45–59   You are good at doing some things on time, but you tend to procrastinate too much. Learning how to build and work from a priority list may help you manage your priorities more effectively.

30–44   You need to work hard to change your priority management skills and learn how to set realistic goals. Procrastination is probably a major issue for you, causing you much stress and worry. Working from a priority list can help you greatly.

29–below   Your priority management skills are very weak, and without change and improvement, your success plan could be in jeopardy. You could benefit from learning to set realistic goals, work from a priority list, and re-frame your thought process toward tasks.

GETTING THE MOST OUT OF THIS MOMENT

What Are the Causes of and Cures for Procrastination?

Below, you will find a list of the ten most common causes of procrastination and some simple, do-able, everyday strategies that you can employ to overcome each cause. We have provided three strategies for each cause. Add at least two of your own strategies to overcome each type of procrastination.

- **Superhuman expectations and trying to be a perfectionist**
  - Allow yourself **more time than you think you need** to complete a project
  - Realize that no one, including you, is (or ever will be) perfect. Perfection does not exist.
  - **Allow enough time to do your very best** and let that be that. If you plan and allow time for excellence, you can't do more.

  _____

  _____

- **Fear of not knowing how to do the task**
  - **Ask for clarification** from whomever asked you to do the project.
  - **Read** as much as you can about the task at hand and **ask for help.**
  - Break up big tasks into **small ones.**

  _____

  _____

- **Lack of motivation and the inability to find internal motivation**
  - **Re-frame your attitude** to find the good and beneficial in any task.
  - Consider how this task will help you **reach your overall goals and dreams.**
  - Take time to do the **things you love,** creating a healthy balance in your life.

  _____

  _____

- **Fear of failing or fear of the task being too hard**
  - Start the project with **positive, optimistic thoughts.**
  - **Face your fears**—look them straight in the face and make a decision to defeat them.
  - **Visualize your successful completion** of the project

  _____

  _____

- **No real plan or goal for getting the task done**
  - Set reasonable, concrete goals that you can reach in about **20–25 minutes.**
  - **Draw up an action plan** the night before you begin the project.
  - Look at completing the project in terms of your **long-range goals** and your overall life plan.

  _____

  _____

  _____

Is there a difference between laziness, procrastination, and resting?

- **Considering the task too unpleasant or uninteresting**
  - **Realize** that most tasks are not as unpleasant as we've made them out to be.
  - **Do the hardest tasks first** and save the easiest for last.
  - Schedule tasks that you consider unpleasant to be done **during your peak hours.**

    _____

    _____

- **Distractions and/or lack of focus**
  - **Ask for help** from your professors, advisor, counselor, or other professionals.
  - Start on the difficult, **most boring tasks first.**
  - Weed out your personal belongings and living space. Organization helps you manage your time and **get to work**.

    _____

    _____

- **Choosing "fun" before responsibility**
  - Actually **reward yourself** when you have accomplished an important body of work.
  - **Don't get involved** in too many organizations, accept too many commitments, or overextend yourself so that you can concentrate on what needs to be done.
  - **Consider the consequences** of not doing what you're responsible for doing.

    _____

    _____

EVALUATING HOW YOU SPEND YOUR TIME

Where Does Your Time Go?

So how do you find out where your time goes? The same way that you find out where your money goes—you track it. Every 15 minutes for one week, you will record exactly how you spent that time. This exercise may seem a little tedious at first, but if you will complete the process over a period of a week, you will have a much better concept of where your time is being used. Yes, that's right—for a week, you need to keep a written record of how much time you spend sleeping, studying, eating, working, getting to class and back, cooking, caring for children, watching television, doing yard work, going to movies, attending athletic events, hanging out, doing laundry, whatever.

Create a time chart in your notebook, phone, or tablet and take it with you and keep track of your activities during the day. To make things simple, round off tasks to 15-minute intervals. For example, if you start walking to the cafeteria at 7:08, you might want to mark off the time block that begins with 7:00. If you finish eating and return to your home at 7:49, you can mark off the next two blocks. You will also want to note the activity so you can evaluate how you spent your time later. Study the example that is provided for you in Figure 6.6.

Remember to take your chart with you and record how you are spending your time during the day. As you progress through the week, try to improve the use of your time. When you finish this exercise, review how you spent your time.

Figure 6.6 How Do You Really Spend Your Time?

7:00	get up & shower	7:00				12:15	
		7:15				12:30	
		7:30		Walked to Union		12:45	
	Breakfast	7:45	1:00	Ate lunch		1:00	
8:00		8:00				1:15	
		8:15				1:30	
	Read paper	8:30		Talked w/ Joe		1:45	
	Walked to class	8:45	2:00			2:00	
9:00	English 101	9:00		Went to book		2:15	
		9:15		store		2:30	
		9:30		Walked to		2:45	
		9:45	3:00	my room		3:00	
10:00		10:00		Called Ron		3:15	
		10:15				3:30	
		10:30				3:45	
	Walked to class	10:45	4:00	Watched		4:00	
11:00	History 210	11:00		TV		4:15	
		11:15				4:30	
		11:30		Walked to		4:45	
		11:45	5:00	library		5:00	
12:00		12:00				5:15	

FOCUSING ON AND ELIMINATING DISTRACTIONS AND INTERRUPTIONS

When Is Enough Really Enough?

If you were diligent and kept an accurate account of all of your time, your evaluation will probably reveal that much of your time is spent dealing with distractions, getting sidetracked, and handling interruptions. These three things account for much of the time wasted within a 24-hour period. In Figure 6.7, you will find a list of some of the most common distractions faced by college students. Consider how you might deal with these distractions in an effective, assertive manner.

PLANNING AND PREPARING

Is There a Secret to Priority Management?

In the past, you may have said to yourself, "*I don't have time to plan.*" "*I don't like to be fenced in and tied to a rigid schedule.*" "*I have so many duties that planning never works.*" Scheduling does not have to be a tedious chore or something you dread. Scheduling can be your lifeline to more free time. After all, if *you* build your own schedule, it is yours! As much as you are able, build your schedule the way you want and need it.

Figure 6.7 Common Distractions

Common Distractions	My Plan to Overcome These Distractions
Friends/family dropping by unexpectedly	
Technology (playing on YouTube, Facebook, iTunes, Google, etc.)	
Constant phone calls that do not pertain to anything in particular or of importance	
Not setting aside any time during the day to deal with "the unexpected"	
Friends/family demanding things of you because they do not understand your schedule or commitments	
Not blocking private time in your daily schedule	
Being unorganized and spending hours upon hours piddling and calling it "work"	
Playing with your children or pets before your tasks are complete (and not scheduling time to be with them in the first place)	
Saying "Yes" when you need to say "No"	
Other distractions you face…	

To manage your priorities successfully, you need to spend some time planning. To plan successfully, you need a calendar that has at least a week-at-a-glance or month-at-a-glance section, as well as sections for daily notes and appointments. If you have not bought a calendar, you can download one from the Internet or create one using Word or another computer programs.

Planning and Organizing for School

Each evening, you should take a few minutes (and literally, that is all it will take) and sit in a quiet place and make a list of all that needs to be done tomorrow. Successful priority management comes from **planning the *night before*!** Let's say your list includes:

Research speech project	Exercise
Study for finance test on Friday	Buy birthday card for mom
Read Chapter 13 for chemistry	Wash the car
Meet with chemistry study group	Take shirts to dry cleaner
English class at 8:00 am	Buy groceries

Mgt. class at 10:00 am   Call Janice about weekend

Work from 2:00–6:00 pm

Now, you have created a list of tasks that you will face tomorrow. Next, separate this list into three categories:

Must Do	**Need to Do**	**Would Like to Do**
Read Chapter 13 for chemistry	Research speech project	Wash the car
Study for finance test on Friday	Buy birthday card for mom	Call Janice about weekend
Exercise	Shirts to cleaner	
English class at 8:00 am	Buy groceries	
Mgt. class at 10:00 am		
Meet with chemistry study group		
Work from 2:00–6:00 pm		

Don't get too excited yet. Your priority-management plan is **not finished**. The most important part is still ahead of you. Now, you will need to rank the items in order of their importance. You will put a 1 by the most important tasks, a 2 by the next most important tasks, and so on, in each category.

Must Do	**Need to Do**	**Would Like to Do**
1 Read Chapter 13 for chemistry	1 Research speech project	2 Wash the car
2 Study for finance test on Friday	2 Buy birthday card for mom	1 Call Janice about weekend
3 Exercise	3 Shirts to cleaner	
1 English class at 8:00 am	2 Buy groceries	
1 Mgt. class at 10:00 am		
2 Meet with chemistry study group		
1 Work from 2:00–6:00 pm		

You have now created a *plan* to actually get these tasks done! Not only have you created your list, but now you have divided them into important categories, ranked them, and you have made a written commitment to these tasks.

Now, take these tasks and schedule them into your daily calendar. You would schedule category 1 first (MUST DO), category 2 next (NEED TO DO), and category 3 (WOULD LIKE TO DO) last. Remember, *never* keep more than one calendar. Always carry your calendar with you, and always schedule your tasks immediately so that you won't forget them.

STRESS? I DON'T HAVE ENOUGH TIME FOR STRESS!

Do You Feel Like You're Going to Explode?

The word *stress* is derived from the Latin word **strictus,** meaning "to draw tight." Stress is your body's response to people and events in your life; it is the mental and physical wear and tear on your body as a result of everyday

DID YOU *Know?*

TINA TURNER, born and raised Anna Mae Bullock in Nutbush, Tennessee, was abandoned by her migrant worker parents. She was raised by her grandmother and worked in the cotton fields as a child. She endured a rough and very abusive marriage. She was repeatedly beaten and raped by her husband, Ike. During their divorce hearings, she had to defend the right to even keep her name. She went on to record many number one hits, such as "Private Dancer" and "What's Love Got to Do with It?" She has won seven Grammy awards, has a star on the Hollywood Walk of Fame, is listed in the Rock and Roll Hall of Fame, and a motion picture was made about her life starring Angela Bassett.

from ORDINARY to *Extraordinary*

*Chef Odette Smith-Ransome, Hospitality Instructor,
The Art Institute of Pittsburgh, Pittsburgh, PA*

At the age of 15, I found myself constantly in conflict with my mother, until one day I stood before her as she held a gun to my head. It was at that moment I knew I had to leave my parent's home, not just for my emotional well-being, but for my actual life and survival. My father was a good man, but he did not understand the entire situation with my mother's alcohol and diet pill addiction, and he could do little to smooth out the situation with my mother and me. To complicate matters even more, my brother had just returned home from fighting in Vietnam and everyone was trying to adjust. It was a horrible time in the house where my ancestors had lived for over 100 years. So, I packed my clothes, dropped out of the tenth grade, and ran away over 1000 miles to Charleston, South Carolina.

My first job was as a waitress. I worked in that job for over three years, realizing more every day that I was not using my talents, and that without an education, I was doomed to work for minimum wage for the rest of my life. During this time, I had met a friend in Charleston who was in the Navy. When he was released, he offered to take me back to Pittsburgh. I agreed, and upon my return, I went to work in the kitchen of a family-owned restaurant. They began to take an interest in me and made me feel proud of my work. I decided to get my GED and then determine what road to take that would allow me to use my culinary talents and help others at the same time.

I began my Associate's degree, which required that students complete an apprenticeship. We worked 40 hours per week, Monday through Thursday, under the direction of a

life and all that you have to accomplish. Stress is inevitable, and it is not in itself bad. It is your response to stress that determines whether it is good stress (**eustress**) or bad stress (**distress**). The same event can provoke eustress or distress, depending on the person experiencing the event; just as "one person's trash is another's treasure" so one person's eustress may be another person's distress.

The primary difference between eustress and distress is in your body's response. It is impossible to exist in a totally stress-free environment; in fact, some stress is important to your health and well being. Good stress can help you become more motivated and even more productive. It helps your energy level, too. It is only when stress gets out of hand that your body becomes distressed. Some physical signs of distress are:

Headaches	Muscular tension and pain	Fatigue
Coughs	Diarrhea	Mental disorders
Dry mouth	Hypertension and chest pain	Insomnia
Impotence	Heartburn and indigestion	Suicidal tendencies
Twitching/trembling	Abdominal pain	Apprehension
Jitters	Diminished performance	Decreased coping ability

If you begin to experience any of these reactions for an extended period of time, you know that your body and mind are probably suffering from undue stress, anxiety, and pressure. This can lead to a very unhealthy situation. You may even require medical attention for hypertension. Test your stress by completing the assessment in Figure 6.8.

master chef, and we were in class eight hours a day on Friday. My apprenticeship was at the Hyatt Regency in Pittsburgh. In order to obtain my degree, I had to pass the apprenticeship, all of the classes, and a bank of tests that proved my proficiency in a variety of areas. If I failed one part of the test, I could not get my degree. Proudly, I passed every test, every class, and my apprenticeship.

My first professional job came to me upon the recommendation of a friend. I interviewed for and was hired to become the private chef for the chancellor of the University of Pittsburgh. I loved the job and it afforded me the opportunity to get my bachelor's degree. So, I juggled a full-time job, a two-year-old child, and a full load of classes. As I neared the end of my degree, I was offered a fellowship at the University of Pittsburgh that trained people how to teach students with special needs. I graduated cum laude and began teaching and working with people who had cerebral palsy at Connelley Academy. I loved the work and that position solidified my desire to work with adults.

From there I taught at the Good Will Training Center, and later at the Pittsburgh Job Corps, where my culinary

> *I packed my clothes, dropped out of the tenth grade, and ran away over 1000 miles to Charleston, South Carolina.*

team won a major, national competition. Today, I am an instructor at The Art Institute of Pittsburgh, helping others reach their dreams of working in the hospitality industry. In 2005, I was named *Culinary Educator of the Year* by the American Culinary Federation. I try to let my life and my struggles serve as a light for students who have faced adversity and may have felt that their past was going to determine their future. My advice to my students, and to you is this: *never* let anyone tell you that you can't do it, that you're not able to do it, that you don't have the means to do it, or that you'll never succeed. **You** set your own course in life, and you determine the direction of your future.

EXTRAORDINARY REFLECTION

Chef Smith-Ransome had to literally leave her family to protect her life. Think about your family situation at the moment. Are they supportive of your efforts? Do they offer you support? Are they working with you to help you achieve your goals? If so, how does this make you stronger? If not, how do you plan to address this situation?

I DON'T THINK I FEEL SO WELL

What Is the Relationship between Poor Priority Management, Monumental Stress, and Your Health?

Most stress does not "just happen" to us. We allow it to happen by not planning our day or week. We allow our "to-do" list to get out of hand (or we do not create a to-do list), and before we know it, our lives are out of control because of all of the activities we are required to accomplish or because of the things we agreed to by saying "Yes." Because of poor planning and procrastination, we become anxious and nervous about not getting it all done. By planning, prioritizing, and developing an action strategy, we can actually lower our stress level and improve our general, overall health and our memory.

Medical research has shown that exposure to stress over a long period of time can be damaging to your body. Many of the physical and mental symptoms of stress are mentioned on page 146, but stress can also have an effect on your **memory.** When you are stressed, your brain releases **cortisol,** which has effects on the neurons in your brain. Over time, cortisol can be toxic and can damage parts of the hippocampus, the part of the brain that deals with memory and learning. Therefore, learning to control stress through managing your time more effectively can be a key to better memory. The amygdala, or emotional part of the brain, is also affected negatively by prolonged stress, causing you to say and do things you regret later.

Figure 6.8 Test Your Stress

Take the following stress assessment to determine the level of distress you are currently experiencing in your life. Check the items that reflect your behavior at home, work, or school, or in a social setting.

☐   1.   Your stomach tightens when you think about your schoolwork and all that you have to do.

☐   2.   You are not able to sleep at night.

☐   3.   You race from place to place trying to get everything done that is required of you.

☐   4.   Small things make you angry.

☐   5.   At the end of the day, you are frustrated that you did not accomplish all that you needed to do.

☐   6.   You get tired throughout the day.

☐   7.   You need some type of drug, alcohol, or tobacco to get through the day.

☐   8.   You often find it hard to be around people.

☐   9.   You don't take care of yourself physically or mentally.

☐   10.   You tend to keep everything inside.

☐   11.   You overreact.

☐   12.   You fail to find the humor in many situations others see as funny.

☐   13.   You do not eat properly.

☐   14.   Everything upsets you.

☐   15.   You are impatient and get angry when you have to wait for things.

☐   16.   You don't trust others.

☐   17.   You feel that most people move too slowly for you.

☐   18.   You feel guilty when you take time for yourself or your friends.

☐   19.   You interrupt people so that you can tell them your side of the story.

☐   20.   You experience memory loss.

Total Number of Check Marks

0–5   = Low, manageable stress

6–10 = Moderate stress

11+   = High stress, could cause medical or emotional problems

Other physical symptoms include *exhaustion,* where one part of the body weakens and shifts its responsibility to another part and causes complete failure of key organ functions. *Chronic muscle pain* and malfunction are also affected by unchecked stress. "Chronically tense muscles also result in numerous stress-related disorders including headaches, backaches, spasms of the esophagus and colon (causing diarrhea and constipation), posture problems, asthma, tightness in the throat and chest cavity, some eye problems, lockjaw, muscle tears and pulls, and perhaps rheumatoid arthritis" (Girdano, Dusek, & Everly, 2009).

As you can see from this medical research, stress is not something that you can just ignore and hope it will go away. It is not something that is overblown and insignificant. It is a real, bona fide condition that can cause many physical and mental problems, from simple exhaustion to death. By learning how to recognize the signs of stress, identifying what causes you to be "stressed out," and by effectively dealing with your stress, you can actually control many of the negative physical and emotional side effects caused by prolonged stress. Examine Figure 6.9.

Figure 6.9 **Three Types of Major Stressors in Life**

Cause	What You Can Do to Reduce Stress
SITUATIONAL	
Change in physical environment	• If at all possible, change your residence or physical environment to better suit your needs. • If you can't change it, talk to the people involved and explain your feelings.
Change in social environment	• Work hard to meet new friends who support you and upon whom you can rely in times of need. • Get involved in some type of school activity. • Enroll in classes with friends and find a campus support group.
Daily hassles	• Try to keep things in perspective and work to reduce the things that you allow to stress you out. • Allow time in your schedule for unexpected events. • Find a quiet place to relax and study.
Poor priority management	• Work out a priority management plan that allows time to complete your projects, while allowing time for rest and joy, too. • Create "to-do" lists.
Conflicts at work, home, and school	• Read about conflict management (Chapter 3 in this text) and realize that conflict can be managed. • Avoid "hot" topics, such as religion or politics, if you feel this causes you to engage in conflicts. • Be assertive, not aggressive or rude.
People	• Try to avoid people who stress you out. • Put people into perspective and realize that we're all different with different needs, wants, and desires. • Realize that everyone is not going to be like you.
Relationships	• Work hard to develop healthy, positive relationships. • Move away from toxic, unhealthy relationships and people who bring you down. • Understand that you can *never* change the way another person feels, acts, or thinks.
Death of a loved one	• Try to focus on the good times you shared and what they meant to your life. • Remember that death is as much a part of life as living. • Talk about the person with your friends and family—share your memories. • Consider what the deceased person would have wanted you to do.
Financial Problems	• Cut back on your spending. • Seek the help of a financial planner. • Determine why your financial planning or spending patterns are causing you problems. • Apply for financial assistance.

(continued)

Figure 6.9 Three Types of Major Stressors in Life (continued)

Cause	What You Can Do to Reduce Stress
PSYCHOLOGICAL	
Unrealistic expectations	• Surround yourself with positive people and work hard to set realistic goals with doable timelines and results. • Expect and anticipate less.
Homesickness	• Surround yourself with people who support you. • Call or visit home as often as you can until you get more comfortable. • Meet new friends on campus through organizations and clubs.
Fear	• Talk to professors, counselors, family, and friends about your fears. Put them into perspective. • Visualize success and not failure. • Do one thing every day that scares you to expand your comfort zone.
Anxiety over your future and what is going to happen	• Put things into perspective and work hard to plan and prepare, but accept that life is about constant change. • Talk to a counselor or advisor about your future plans and develop a strategy to meet your goals. • Don't try to control the uncontrollable. • Try to see the big picture and how "the puzzle" is going to come together.
Anxiety over your past	• Work hard to overcome past challenges and remember that your past does not have to dictate your future. • Learn to forgive. • Focus on your future and what you really want to accomplish.
BIOLOGICAL	
Insomnia	• Watch your caffeine intake. • Avoid naps. • Do not exercise two hours prior to your normal bedtime. • Complete all of your activities before going to bed (studying, watching TV, e-mailing, texting, etc.)—your bed is for sleeping.
Anxiety	• Laugh more. Share a joke. • Enjoy your friends and family. • Practice breathing exercises. • Talk it out with friends. • Learn to say "No" and then do it. • Turn off the TV if the news makes you anxious or nervous.
Weight loss/gain	• Develop an exercise and healthy eating plan. • Meet with a nutrition specialist on campus or in the community. • Join a health-related club or group.
Reduced physical activity	• Increase your daily activity. • If possible, walk to class instead of drive. • Take the stairs instead of the elevator.
Sexual difficulties/ dysfunction	• Seek medical help in case something is physically wrong. • Determine if your actions are in contradiction with your value system.

REFLECTIONS ON PRIORITY AND STRESS MANAGEMENT

Managing your time and reducing your levels of stress are two skills that you will need for the rest of your life. By learning to avoid procrastinating and taking the time to enhance the quality of your life, you are actually increasing your staying power as a college student. Further, as you enter the world of work, both of these skills will be necessary for your success. Technological advances, fewer people doing more work, and pressure to perform at unprecedented levels can put your life in a tailspin, but with the ability to plan your time and reduce your own stress level, you are making a contribution to your own success.

REDUCING STRESS IN YOUR EVERYDAY LIFE

Utilizes levels 4, 5, and 6 of the Taxonomy. (See Bloom's Taxonomy at the front of this text)

Take a moment and examine your academic and personal life right now. You probably have many things going on and may feel as if you're torn in many directions.

If you had to list the one major stressor in your life at this moment, what would it be? Be specific and explain this situation in detail.

_____

_____

_____

_____

_____

Why is this stressor a major cause of stress in your life?

_____

_____

_____

_____

What does this stressor do to your priority management plan?

_____

_____

_____

_____

_____

Are there other people or things contributing to this stressor? In other words, is someone or something making the matter worse? If so, who or what?

_____

_____

_____

_____

_____

A *narrative statement* is a statement that "paints a verbal picture" of how your life is going to look once a goal is reached. Reflect for a moment and then write a paragraph predicting how your life would change if this major source of stress was gone from your life. Be realistic and optimistic. How would alleviating this stressor help your priority-management plan?

_____

_____

_____

_____

_____

As you know, accomplishing anything requires action. Now that you have a picture of how your life would look if this stress was gone, develop a plan from beginning to end to eliminate this stressor from your life.

Step 1: _____

_____

Step 2: _____

_____

Step 3: _____

_____

Step 4: _____

_____

Step 5: _____

_____

SQ3R MASTERY STUDY SHEET

EXAMPLE QUESTION (FROM PAGE 136) How can I simplify my life and get more done?	**ANSWER:**
EXAMPLE QUESTION (FROM PAGE 139) What are the three procrastination types?	**ANSWER:**
AUTHOR QUESTION (FROM PAGE 132) What is self-discipline and how is it related to priority management?	**ANSWER:**
AUTHOR QUESTION (FROM PAGE 135) What are the benefits of learning how to say "No"?	**ANSWER:**
AUTHOR QUESTION (FROM PAGE 140) What are three "cures" for procrastination?	**ANSWER:**
AUTHOR QUESTION (FROM PAGE 146) How does good stress differ from bad stress?	**ANSWER:**
AUTHOR QUESTION (FROM PAGE 146) What are some of the physical and mental symptoms of stress?	**ANSWER:**
YOUR QUESTION (FROM PAGE _____)	**ANSWER:**
YOUR QUESTION (FROM PAGE _____)	**ANSWER:**
YOUR QUESTION (FROM PAGE _____)	**ANSWER:**
YOUR QUESTION (FROM PAGE _____)	**ANSWER:**
YOUR QUESTION (FROM PAGE _____)	**ANSWER:**

Finally, after answering these questions, recite this chapter's major points in your mind. Consider the following general questions to help you master this material.

- What was it about?
- What does it mean?
- What is the most important thing you learned? Why?
- What are the key points to remember?

chapter seven
LEARN

DISCOVERING YOUR LEARNING STYLE, DOMINANT INTELLIGENCE, AND PERSONALITY TYPE

"We are led to truth by our weaknesses as well as our strengths." —Parker Palmer

LEARN

Scan and QUESTION

Take a few moments, **scan this chapter** and on page 178, write **five questions** that you think will be important to your mastery of this material. In addition to the two questions below, you will also find five questions from your authors.

Example:

☑ **What is the difference between a learning style and a learning strategy?** (from page 169)

☑ **What is the definition of tactile learning, and how do you use it?** (from page 169)

MyStudentSuccessLab

MyStudentSuccessLab is an online solution designed to help you acquire and develop (or hone) the skills you need to succeed. You will have access to peer-led video presentations and develop core skills through interactive exercises and projects.

Why read this chapter?

Because you'll learn...

- Several historical theories about how we learn
- The steps in learning something new
- To use your learning style, dominant intelligence, and personality type to increase your learning power

Because you'll be able to...

- Create a study plan based on your learning style and dominant intelligence
- Use your personality type to improve studying, learning, and career development
- Develop a Personal Life Profile based on your strengths, challenges, and interests

Name: Diana Daugherty
Institution: Graduate! West Virginia University
Major: Speech Pathology and Audiology

When Diana tells people that she went to college for eight years, their initial reaction is "You must be crazy!" However, after receiving both her Bachelor's and Doctoral degrees from WVU, she states, "I would have to strongly disagree." College was always discussed in Diana's family. "From the time I was little, my parents stressed the importance of a college education."

Diana grew up in north central West Virginia. She loved being a West Virginian and knew she wanted to be a Mountaineer long before she was old enough to apply for college. "Paying for college was always a major concern for my parents and me," she said. "Thankfully, during my senior year of high school, WV started the Promise Scholarship Program. The scholarship allowed me to attend college and set my sights on much more."

When Diana started school at WVU, she, like many first-year students, chose a major, only to find out after a few classes that it was not the right fit for her. She remembers, "I was frantic. I sat down with the undergraduate handbook and began to flip through the pages. Then it hit me, I needed to choose a field that would allow me to help

the people in my community." Her grandfather, who was always an inspiration to her, was a WV coalminer for 44 years. During this time he developed a hearing loss. Diana remembers that growing up, "we had to talk a little louder to papaw if we wanted him to hear us. I always wished that there was something I could do to make things easier for him." As she skimmed the WVU handbook, she came across the field of audiology—the study of hearing and balance—and she knew this would be her career. "It was my chance to help my papaw and other people like him," she remembers.

Thankfully, WVU offered an undergraduate degree in speech pathology and audiology, and a graduate degree in audiology. The close-knit feel of the program helped to provide Diana with the resources she needed to complete both degrees. Setting and keeping the goals she set for herself, along with the support of her family and the WVU faculty, made her time at WVU successful.

"College forced me to make many tough choices along the way. Whose opinions did I value most? Was it more important to go hang out with friends or stay in and study? Initially, I did not always make the right choice. However, I knew that I wanted to be successful and had to make those tough choices to do so." Throughout her college years, she made friends and grew apart from others. She passed some tests and did not do so well on others. She remembers that all of those

An interview conducted and written by Robin Jones, Director of First-Year Seminar, and Rhonda Black, Program Coordinator, West Virginia University, Morgantown, WV

experiences, good and bad, helped to show her what she wanted and needed to reach her goals.

In addition to Diana's undergraduate scholarship, she was lucky enough to have been awarded a graduate assistantship while in her doctoral program. The assistantship allowed her to work with first-year students and share her experiences from her undergraduate years. "Some of my students still contact me to let me know

their progress. Several of them are completing their graduate degrees as well. This brings me a great deal of joy and pride. Without my college education, this would have never been possible." Diana is now employed at Stonewall Jackson Memorial Hospital as a full-time clinical audiologist. She happily accepted this job as it allows her the opportunity to work in the community in which she grew up.

THINK about it

1. When Diana began her studies at WVU, she quickly realized that she had chosen the wrong major. Are you still satisfied with your career choice? If not, what do you plan to do about it?

2. Diana chose her career path based on wanting to help others in her community. What has led you to your career choice? If you have not made a career choice yet, what experiences have you had that may help you make this decision?

WE HOPE YOU LEARNED YOUR LESSON!

What Is This Thing Called Learning, Anyway?

In its purest and simplest form, learning is a ***cognitive mental action*** where new information is acquired or where you learn to use old information in a new way. Learning can be ***conscious*** and/or ***unconscious***. Do you remember the very day you learned how to walk or talk? Probably not. This learning was more of an unconscious nature. However, you probably do remember studying about the fifty states or subtraction or reading an Edgar Allen Poe poem for the first time. This learning was more conscious in nature. Learning can also be ***formal*** (schooling) or ***informal*** ("street knowledge"). Learning can happen in many ways, such as through play, trial and error, mistakes, successes, repetition, environmental conditioning, parental discipline, social interactions, media, observation, and, yes, through formal study methods.

Learning is what you do ***for*** yourself; it is not done ***to*** you. Try as they might, parents may discipline you time and time and time again, but until *you* learn the lesson trying to be taught, it will *not* be learned. Teachers can preach and talk until they are blue in the face about the thirteen original colonies, but until you learn them and commit them to memory, they will *not* be learned. That is what this chapter is all about—helping you discover how you learn and why you learn, and assisting you in finding the best way to learn so that you can *do* the learning for yourself on a more effective level.

Have you encountered people with learning styles different from yours? How are they different?

> *"Many things in life cannot be transmitted well by words, concepts, or books. Colors that we see cannot be described to a person born blind. Only a swimmer knows how swimming feels; the non-swimmer can get only the faintest idea of it with all the words and books in the world. And so it goes. Perhaps it is better to say that all of life must first be known experientially. There is no substitute for experience, none at all."*
>
> *—Abraham H. Maslow*

What Do the Experts Say?

The question still begs, ***How do we really learn?*** By studying a textbook? By reading a newspaper? By looking at pictures? By interviewing someone about a topic? By watching a movie? By trying something to see if it works? Yes, but the process is much more complex than this. Study Figure 7.1 and consider what some of the leading experts throughout history have said about how we learn.

Figure 7.1 Learning Through the Ages

As you can see from these historical experts in the fields of learning, educational psychology, and philosophy, there are many theories on just *how* we learn best. Perhaps the most important thing to take from these examples is tied into Jean Piaget's theory of ***holistic learning***—as individuals with diverse and varied needs, backgrounds, and experiences, we require a variety of stimuli to help us learn and we all learn differently at different stages in our lives from a variety of things.

Socrates	
	Around 300 BC, the great Greek philosopher **Socrates** introduced his theory of learning. He believed that we learn by asking questions. This is called the ***Socratic Method***.

Plato	
	Socrates' student **Plato** expanded on this theory and believed that we learn best by dialogue, or the ***Dialectic Method,*** which involves "the searcher" beginning a conversation on a topic and having a dialogue with "an expert." He believed that through this back-and-forth conversation, knowledge could be acquired.

Lao-Tse	
	In the Fifth Century BC, the Chinese philosopher **Lao-Tse** wrote, *"If you tell me, I will listen. If you show me, I will see. But if you let me experience, I will learn."* He was one of the first to proclaim that ***active, involved learning*** was a viable form of acquiring information.

Kung Fu-tse (Confucius)

Confucius first introduced the **case study,** which included telling stories or parables and then having people discuss the issues in the case to learn and acquire knowledge.

John Locke

In 1690, the English philosopher **John Locke** introduced the theory of "the blank slate." He believed that all humans were born with empty minds and that we learn information about the world through what our senses bring to us (**sensory learning**). He believed that learning was like a pyramid—we learn the basics and then build on those simple principles until we can master complex ideas.

Jean Jacques Rousseau

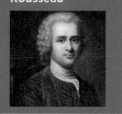

In the 1760s, French philosopher **Jean Jacques Rousseau** expanded on a theory that suggested that people learn best by *experiencing* rather than by *listening*. In other words, we learn best by doing something rather than being told how someone else did it. He was the first to thoroughly introduce individual **learning styles,** believing that learning should be natural to us and follow our basic instincts and feelings.

J. B. Watson

In the early 1900s, American psychologist **J..B. Watson** developed the theory of **behaviorism,** believing that we learn best by conditioning or training. His theory was based on that of Pavlov (and his dog), and held the tenant that we act and learn in certain ways because we have been conditioned or trained to do so. If a dog (or a person) is fed when a bell is rung, the dog (or the person) quickly learns to ring the bell when it **wants** to be fed.

Jean Piaget

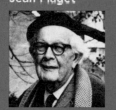

In the mid 1900s, Swiss psychologist **Jean Piaget** introduced the groundbreaking theory of **holistic learning**. This theory is widely held today as one of the most important breakthroughs in educational psychology. He believed that we learn best by experiencing a wide variety of stimuli, including reading, listening, experimenting, exploring, and questioning.

Benjamin Bloom

In 1956, **Benjamin Bloom** introduced his taxonomy (modeled and discussed at the start of this text, throughout all chapters, and at the end of this chapter). Bloom believed in a **mastery approach** to learning. This theory suggests that we learn simple information and then transform that information into more complex ideas, solutions, and creations. His was an idea of learning how to process and actually **use information** in a meaningful way.

from ORDINARY to Extraordinary

H.P. Rama CEO, JHM Hotels, Greenville, SC

I have led a life filled with a great variety of experiences, trials, challenges, and triumphs. Born in Africa, I was sent to India to live with my grandparents and to go to school when I was just five years old. I lived away from my parents, whom I missed greatly, in a little farming village in India, where I finished school and ultimately earned an undergraduate degree. I knew I wanted to come to America and pursue the American dream, so at the age of 21, I left India and arrived in this country with only $2 in my pocket.

I had to get a job quickly, so I took the first job offered to me as a dishwasher, which I quit in just four hours. My next job was as a waiter at a Howard Johnson's restaurant in Manhattan. While I worked as a waiter to support myself, I attended Xavier University to pursue my MBA. My life was primarily one of work and sacrifice, as I worked hard to pay my expenses

and to graduate with this degree I prize so much. While working at Howard Johnson's, I paid attention to everything that happened around me because I had no intentions of remaining a waiter all my life. I was absorbing knowledge of the hotel and restaurant business, which I would put to use later. At the time, I had no intentions of becoming a hotelier. My goal was to go into banking. I always say that I became an accidental hotelier, but this field has served me well and offered me many opportunities. I was pursuing the American dream, and that was all that mattered. I considered myself fortunate to have this great opportunity to be in America, to be going to school, and to have a job that supported me.

After receiving my MBA from Xavier, I worked as a staff accountant for 14 months. In 1973, I had an opportunity to buy my first hotel in Pomona, California. My brother and I bought

GIVE YOUR BRAIN A WORKOUT

Can I Really Learn All This Stuff?

> "The mind is not a vessel to be filled, but rather a fire to be kindled."
> —Plutarch

Yes! Yes! Yes! You can learn! Think about all that you have already learned in your lifetime. You learned how to eat, walk, talk, play, make decisions, dress yourself, have a conversation, tie your shoes, make your bed, ride a bicycle, play a sport, drive a car, protect yourself, make associations based on observations, use a cell phone, play a video game, ask questions, and countless other simple and highly complex skills. There is *proof* that you **can learn** because you **have learned** in the past. The old excuse of *"I can't learn this stuff"* is simply hogwash! You have the capacity to know more, do more, experience more, and acquire more knowledge. Your brain is a natural learning machine, just as your heart is a natural pumping machine. It is in our nature to learn every single day. You just have to understand how this process works in order to make the most of your brain's natural learning power. And you have to **devote the time necessary to learn** the basics of something new and then build on that knowledge base. Time and effort are very important aspects of the learning process.

the hotel, and we had only two other employees. We worked 24/7, and lived behind the office. There was no job that we did not do. But we were chasing the dream, and we were off and running with no idea of how many opportunities we would have.

Then I moved east, still focused on achieving the American dream, and bought a 36-room hotel in Buffalo, Tennessee. My wife and I did everything—front desk, night duty, all the maintenance. We both worked very hard, long hours. In 1977, we moved to Greenville, SC, and bought a foreclosed property from a bank. In 1983, I bought four Howard Johnson hotels—just 13 years after working for HJ as a waiter. Over the years, my brothers and I have owned and developed 78 hotels, and still own 38 today.

We developed a five-star hotel in India in 1990, and today we are expanding and adding other hotels. We are most proud of the fact that we are developing a mixed-use development in India that will include a hospitality college campus, a retail and entertainment campus, a hospital campus, and luxury accommodations. We are using our knowledge learned in this wonderful country to continue the dream in India.

In 1999, I was named Chairman of the American Motel and Hotel Lodging Association, which was a significant

> *At the age of 21, I left India and arrived in this country with $2 in my pocket.*

honor for me. Because I wanted to give back to this field that has done so much for me, I donated $1 million for scholarships for hospitality students. In 1989, I was the founding member of the Asian American Hotel Owners Association. Today, I serve on several advisory boards for hospitality programs, and am an Executive Ambassador for Cornell University, a role in which I speak to graduate students about my experiences.

My advice to students today is this: Anything is possible if you have the vision, pay the price, work hard, and take risks. I have been very blessed, but I have also worked very hard. And I am living proof that the American dream is alive and well.

EXTRAORDINARY REFLECTION

Mr. Rama worked his way up the ladder and became Chairman of the American Motel and Hotel Lodging Association, a major organization. What top honors do you hope to achieve in your own career? Why? How would they change your life?

You also have to give your brain a "workout" to make sure it stays in shape. Just as your body needs exercise and activities to stay in shape, your brain does, too. When you "work out" your brain and use it to learn new material, your brain releases a chemical called **cypin** (*sigh-pin*). Cypin is found throughout the body, but in the brain, it helps build new branches, like a tree sprouting new growth. In a nutshell, when you exercise your brain, your brain rewards you with new learning patterns and new learning receptors. This is sometimes referred to as **neuroplasticity,** or the brain's ability to change with new knowledge.

THE LEARNING PROCESS

What Are the Steps to Active, Authentic Learning?

"Human beings have an innate learning process, which includes a motivation to learn" (Smilkstein, 2003). You may be saying to yourself, *"If I have a natural, innate ability to learn, then why is chemistry so difficult for me*

to master? Why is English such a crazy language with so many rules that I don't understand?" The answer could rest in the notion that you are going *against* your natural, neurological learning pattern, that you are being taught, or trying to learn by yourself, in a way that is unnatural to you, and your brain simply is having trouble adapting to this unnatural process.

If you learn best by doing and touching, **you need to do and touch**. If you learn best by listening and questioning, you need to **listen and question**. If you learn best by reading and studying in a quiet place, you need to **find a quiet place to read and study**. Basically, you must figure out your natural inclination for learning and build on it. You will also need to understand that learning takes time, and people need different amounts of time to master material. Janet may learn Concept X in a few hours, but it may take William three days of constant practice to learn the same concept. One thing is true: The more *involved* you are with the information you are trying to learn, the more you retain.

In the chart in Figure 7.2, we have tried to simplify thousands of years of educational study on the topic of learning. Basically, learning something new can happen in the six steps shown.

$Figure$ 7.2 The Learning Process

1. Motivation to learn the material is the first step in the learning process. You have to possess the internal motivation and passion to want to learn what is being presented or what you are studying. You must also be motivated enough to devote the time to learning something new. Deep, purposeful learning does not happen in an instant; it takes work, patience, and yes, motivation.

2. Understand the material through ambitious curiosity, keen observations, purposeful questioning, intense studying, eager determination, robust effort, and time devoted to task. You must be able to answer such questions as: Who is involved? What happened? When did it happen? Where did it happen? How did it happen? How could it have happened? What does it all mean? Why is it important? What is the relationship between *x* and *y*? You should be able to describe it, discuss it, give examples, put the information into your own words, and tell others about it clearly.

3. Internalize the material by asking, How can this information affect my life, my career, my studies, and my future? Why does this information matter? How can I control my emotions regarding the value of this information? If I think this information is useless, how can I change this perception?

4. Apply the material by asking, How can I use this information to improve? How can I use this information to work with others, to develop new ideas, or to build meaningful conclusions? Can I demonstrate it? Can I share this information with or teach this information to others intelligently? Is it possible to practice what I have learned?

5. Evaluate the material by determining the value of what you just learned. Ask yourself, Do I trust my research and sources? Have I consulted others about their findings and knowledge? What did they learn? What can I learn from them? Have I asked for feedback? Can I debate this information with others?

6. Use the material to grow and change. Ask yourself, How could I take this information (or the process of learning this information) and change my life, attitudes, or emotions? How could this information help me grow? What can I create out of this new information? How can I expand on this knowledge to learn more?

UNDERSTANDING YOUR STRENGTHS

What Are the Advantages of Discovering and Polishing Your Talents?

On the next few pages, you will have the opportunity to complete three inventories: one to identify your **learning style,** one to identify your **personality type,** and one to identify your **dominant intelligence**. At the end of the chapter, you will have the opportunity to pull all of this information together to help you understand your learning patterns and to formulate a learning plan for the future.

These assessments are in no way intended to "label you." They are not a measure of how smart you are. They do not measure your worth or your capacities as a student or citizen. The three assessments are included so that you might gain a better understanding of your dominant intelligence, identify your learning style, and discover your strongest personality type—and how to use them all to your best advantage.

There are no right or wrong answers, and there is no one, best way to learn. We hope that by the end of this chapter, you will have experienced a "Wow!" or an "Ah-ha!" moment as you explore and discover new and exciting components of your education. We also hope that by the end of this chapter, you will have the skills needed to more effectively use your dominant traits and improve your less dominant characteristics.

UNDERSTANDING MULTIPLE INTELLIGENCES

Why Is It Important to Discover New Ways of Looking at Yourself?

In 1983, Howard Gardner, a Harvard University professor, developed a theory called Multiple Intelligences. In his book, *Frames of Mind* (1983), he outlines seven intelligences that he feels everyone possesses: visual/spatial, verbal/linguistic, musical/rhythm, logic/math, body/kinesthetic, interpersonal, and intrapersonal. In 1996, he added an eighth intelligence, naturalistic (Owen, 1997). For more information about the intelligences, see Figure 7.4.

In short, if you have ever done things that came easily for you, you are probably drawing on one of your well-developed intelligences. On the other hand, if you have tried to do things that are very difficult to master or understand, you may be dealing with material that calls on one of your less-developed intelligences. If playing the piano by ear comes easily to you, your musical/rhythm intelligence may be very strong. If you have trouble writing an English paper, your verbal/linguistic intelligence may not be as well developed. This does not mean that you will never be able to write a paper; it simply means that this is not your dominant intelligence and you may need to spend more time on this activity.

Take the Multiple Intelligences Survey in Figure 7.3. In Figure 7.4, you will find each intelligence described and some helpful tips to assist you in creating a study environment and study habits using the eight intelligences. Read each category because you may need to improve your less-dominant intelligence in some of the classes you take. This list can help you build on your strengths and develop your less-dominant areas.

Figure 7.3 The MIS—Multiple Intelligences Survey

Directions: Read each statement carefully and thoroughly. After reading the statement, rate your response using the scale below. There are no right or wrong answers. This is not a timed survey. The MIS is based, in part, on *Frames of Mind* by Howard Gardner (1983).

3 = Often Applies   2 = Sometimes Applies   1 = Never or Almost Never Applies

_____ 1. When someone gives me directions, I have to visualize them in my mind in order to understand them.

_____ 2. I enjoy crossword puzzles and word games like Scrabble.

_____ 3. I enjoy dancing and can keep up with the beat of music.

_____ 4. I have little or no trouble conceptualizing information or facts.

_____ 5. I like to repair things that are broken, such as toasters, small engines, bicycles, and cars.

_____ 6. I enjoy leadership activities on campus and in the community.

_____ 7. I have the ability to get others to listen to me.

_____ 8. I enjoy working with nature, animals, and plants.

_____ 9. I know where everything is in my home, such as supplies, gloves, flashlights, camera, and CDs.

_____ 10. I am a good speller.

_____ 11. I often sing or hum to myself in the shower or car, or while walking or just sitting.

_____ 12. I am a very logical, orderly thinker.

_____ 13. I use a lot of gestures when I talk to people.

_____ 14. I can recognize and empathize with people's attitudes and emotions.

_____ 15. I prefer to study alone.

_____ 16. I can name many different things in the environment, such as clouds, rocks, and plant types.

_____ 17. I like to draw pictures, graphs, or charts to better understand information.

_____ 18. I have a good memory for names and dates.

_____ 19. When I hear music, I "get into it" by moving, humming, tapping, or even singing.

_____ 20. I learn better by asking a lot of questions.

_____ 21. I enjoy playing competitive sports.

_____ 22. I communicate very well with other people.

_____ 23. I know what I want and I set goals to accomplish it.

_____ 24. I have some interest in herbal remedies and natural medicine.

_____ 25. I enjoy working puzzles or mazes.

_____ 26. I am a good storyteller.

_____ 27. I can easily remember the words and melodies of songs.

_____ 28. I enjoy solving problems in math and chemistry and working with computer programming problems.

_____ 29. I usually touch people or pat them on the back when I talk to them.

_____ 30. I understand my family and friends better than most other people do.

_____ 31. I don't always talk about my accomplishments with others.

_____ 32. I would rather work outside around nature than inside around people and equipment.

_____ 33. I enjoy and learn more when seeing movies, slides, or videos in class.

_____ 34. I am a very good listener and I enjoy listening to others' stories.

_____ 35. I need to study with music.

_____ 36. I enjoy games like Clue, Battleship, chess, and Rubik's Cube.

_____ 37. I enjoy physical activities, such as bicycling, jogging, dancing, snowboarding, skateboarding, or swimming.

_____ 38. I am good at solving people's problems and conflicts.

_____ 39. I have to have time alone to think about new information in order to remember it.

_____ 40. I enjoy sorting and organizing information, objects, and collectibles.

Refer to your score on each individual question. Place that score beside the appropriate question number below. Then, tally each line across and put the final number at the side.

Score					Total Across	Code
1 _____	9 _____	17 _____	25 _____	33 _____	_____	Visual/Spatial
2 _____	10 _____	18 _____	26 _____	34 _____	_____	Verbal/Linguistic
3 _____	11 _____	19 _____	27 _____	35 _____	_____	Musical/Rhythm
4 _____	12 _____	20 _____	28 _____	36 _____	_____	Logic/Math
5 _____	13 _____	21 _____	29 _____	37 _____	_____	Body/Kinesthetic
6 _____	14 _____	22 _____	30 _____	38 _____	_____	Interpersonal
7 _____	15 _____	23 _____	31 _____	39 _____	_____	Intrapersonal
8 _____	16 _____	24 _____	32 _____	40 _____	_____	Naturalistic

MIS Tally

Look at the scores on the MIS. What are your top three scores? Write them in the space below.

Top Score _____ Code _____

Second Score _____ Code _____

Third Score _____ Code _____

This tally can help you understand where some of your strengths may be. Again, this is not a measure of your worth or capacities, nor is it an indicator of your future successes. Refer to the text to better understand multiple intelligences.

© Robert M. Sherfield, Ph.D.

UNDERSTANDING LEARNING STYLES THEORY

Why Is It Important to Know How I Learn?

A learning style is "the way in which each learner begins to concentrate on, process, and retain new and difficult information" (Dunn, 2000). There is a difference between a **_learning style_** and a **_learning strategy_**. A learning **_style_** is innate and involves your five senses. It is how you best process information that comes to you. A learning **_strategy_** is how you might choose to learn or study, such as by using notecards, flip charts, color slides, or cooperative learning groups. Learning strategies also involve where you study (at a desk, in bed, in the library, in a quiet place, with music, etc.), how long you study, and what techniques you use to help you study (mnemonics, cooperative learning teams, or SQ3R).

If you learn best by **_seeing information_**, you have a more dominant **_visual learning style_**. If you learn best by **_hearing_** information, you have a more dominant **_auditory learning style_**. If you learn best by **_touching or doing_**, you have a more dominant **_tactile learning style_**. You may also hear the tactile learning style referred to as kinesthetic, or hands-on.

Some of the most successful students master information and techniques by using all three styles. If you were learning how to skateboard, you might learn best by _hearing_ someone talk about the different styles or techniques. Others might learn best by _watching a video_ where someone demonstrates the techniques. Still others would learn best by actually getting on the board and _trying it_. Those who engage all of their senses gain the most.

Figure 7.4 Understanding and Using the Eight Intelligences

VISUAL/SPATIAL— PICTURE SMART

Thinks in pictures; knows where things are in the house; loves to create images and work with graphs, charts, pictures, and maps.

- Use visuals in your notes such as timelines, charts, graphs, and geometric shapes.
- Work to create a mental or visual picture of the information at hand.
- Use colored markers to make associations or to group items together.
- Use mapping or webbing so that your main points are easily recognized.
- Re-type your notes on the computer; consider using a spreadsheet.
- Draw pictures in the margins to illustrate the main points when taking notes.
- Visualize the information in your mind.

VERBAL/LINGUISTIC— WORD SMART

Communicates well through language, likes to write, is good at spelling, great at telling stories, loves to read books.

- Establish study groups so that you will have the opportunity to talk about the information.
- Using the information you studied, create a story or a skit.
- Read as much information about related areas as possible.
- Outline chapters in your own words as you read them.
- Summarize and recite your notes aloud.

MUSICAL/RHYTHMIC— MUSIC SMART

Loves to sing, hum, and whistle; comprehends music; responds to music immediately; performs music.

- Listen to music while studying (if it does not distract you).
- Write a song, jingle, or rap about the chapter or information.
- Take short breaks from studying to listen to music, especially classical music.
- Commit the information being studied to the music from your favorite song.

LOGICAL/MATHEMATICAL— NUMBER SMART

Can easily conceptualize and reason, uses logic, has good problem-solving skills, enjoys math and science.

- Strive to make logical connections between subjects.
- Apply facts to real-life situations—don't just memorize them.
- Think of problems in society and how this information could solve those problems as you study the information.
- Organize the material in a logical sequence.
- Create analyzing charts. Draw a line down the center of the page, put the information at hand in the left column and analyze, discuss, relate, and synthesize it in the right column.
- Allow yourself some time to reflect after studying.

BODY/KINESTHETIC— BODY SMART

Learns through body sensation, moves around a lot, enjoys work involving the hands, is graced with some athletic ability.

- Don't confine your study area to a desk or chair; move around, explore, go outside.
- Act out the information.
- Study in a group of people and change groups often.
- Create and use charts, posters, flash cards, and chalkboards to study.
- When appropriate or possible, build models using the information studied.
- Verbalize the information to others.
- Create and use games such as chess, Monopoly, Twister, or Clue when studying.
- Trace words as you study them.
- Use repetition to learn facts; write them many times.
- Make study sheets.

INTERPERSONAL— PEOPLE SMART

Loves to communicate with other people, possesses great leadership skills, has lots of friends, is involved in extracurricular activities.

- Study in groups.
- Share the information with other people.
- Teach the information to others.
- Interview outside sources to learn more about the material at hand.
- Have a debate with others about the information.
- Participate in online chats and discussions groups.

INTRAPERSONAL— SELF SMART

Has a deep awareness of own feelings, is very reflective, requires time to be alone, does not get involved with group activities.

- Study in a quiet area.
- Study by youself.
- Allow time for reflection and meditation about the subject matter.
- Study in short time blocks and then spend some time absorbing the information.
- Work at your own pace.
- Although you may not contribute much to chats and discussions, read them carefully and reflect on what others are saying.

NATURALISTIC— ENVIRONMENT SMART

Has interest in the environment and in nature; can easily recognize plants, animals, rocks, and cloud formations; may like hiking, camping, and fishing.

- Study outside whenever possible.
- Categorize information.
- Relate the information to the effect on the environment whenever possible.
- When given the opportunity to choose your own topics or research projects, choose something related to nature.
- Collect your own study data and resources.
- Organize and label your information.
- Keep separate notebooks on individual topics so that you can add new information to each topic as it becomes available to you.

After taking the LEAD Assessment (Figure 7.5) and reading more about learning styles in Figure 7.6 list at least three concrete strategies that you can employ to enhance your learning strategies for each of the three areas in Figure 7.6.

Figure 7.5 The LEAD—Learning Evaluation and Assessment Directory

Directions: Read each statement carefully and thoroughly. After reading the statement, rate your response using the scale below. There are no right or wrong answers. This is not a timed survey. The LEAD is based, in part, on research conducted by Rita Dunn (1993).

3 = Often Applies   2 = Sometimes Applies   1 = Never or Almost Never Applies

_____ 1. I remember information better if I write it down or draw a picture of it.

_____ 2. I remember things better when I hear them instead of just reading or seeing them.

_____ 3. When I get something that has to be assembled, I just start doing it. I don't read the directions.

_____ 4. If I am taking a test, I can "see" the page of the text or lecture notes where the answer is located.

_____ 5. I would rather the professor explain a graph, chart, or diagram than just show it to me.

_____ 6. When learning new things, I want to "do it" rather than hear about it.

_____ 7. I would rather the instructor write the information on the board or overhead instead of just lecturing.

_____ 8. I would rather listen to a book on tape than read it.

_____ 9. I enjoy making things, putting things together, and working with my hands.

_____ 10. I am able to quickly conceptualize and visualize information.

_____ 11. I learn best by hearing words.

_____ 12. I have been called hyperactive by my parents, spouse, partner, or professor.

_____ 13. I have no trouble reading maps, charts, or diagrams.

_____ 14. I can usually pick up on small sounds like bells, crickets, or frogs, or distant sounds like train whistles.

_____ 15. I use my hands and gesture a lot when I speak to others.

Refer to your score on each individual question. Place that score beside the appropriate question number below. Then, tally each line at the side.

Score					Total Across	Code
1 _____	4 _____	7 _____	10 _____	13 _____	_____	Visual
2 _____	5 _____	8 _____	11 _____	14 _____	_____	Auditory
3 _____	6 _____	9 _____	12 _____	15 _____	_____	Tactile

Lead Score

Look at the scores on the LEAD. What is your top score?

Top Score _____

Code _____

Figure 7.6 Learning Styles

Learning Style

In the space below, use the information from the LEAD and the information on learning styles to create a study plan for each learning style.

VISUAL—EYE SMART

Thinks in pictures. Enjoys visual instructions, demonstrations, and descriptions; would rather read a text than listen to a lecture; avid note-taker; needs visual references; enjoys using charts, graphs, and pictures.

I can use my visual learning style to enhance learning by . . .

1. _____
   _____
2. _____
   _____
3. _____
   _____

AUDITORY—EAR SMART

Prefers verbal instructions; would rather listen than read; often tapes lectures and listens to them in the car or at home; recites information out loud; enjoys talking, discussing issues, and verbal stimuli; talks out problems.

I can use my auditory learning style to enhance learning by . . .

1. _____
   _____
2. _____
   _____
3. _____
   _____

TACTILE—ACTION SMART

Prefers hands-on approaches to learning; likes to take notes and uses a great deal of scratch paper; learns best by doing something, by touching it, or manipulating it; learns best while moving or while in action; often does not concentrate well when sitting still and reading.

I can use my tactile learning style to enhance learning by . . .

1. _____
   _____
2. _____
   _____
3. _____
   _____

WANTED: A VISUAL LEARNER WITH TACTILE SKILLS

Do You Know the Differences Between Your Primary Learning Style and Your Dominant Intelligence?

As discussed earlier, a ***learning style*** and a ***learning strategy*** are different. A learning style and a ***dominant intelligence*** are also quite different. When you read over the descriptions of the Multiple Intelligences theory and learning styles, you probably noticed several common elements.

Successful Decisions

AN ACTIVITY FOR CRITICAL REFLECTION

Kristin knew that her most powerful learning style was visual. She knew that she had always learned best when she could "see" the information in pictures, charts, graphs, PowerPoint presentations, videos, or other powerful visuals. Kristin also knew that when she was able to get involved with the information, she seemed to retain it better. She did not know what this was called, but later learned that she was also a tactile or "hands-on" learner.

When she discovered that different people have different ways of learning and instructors have different ways of teaching, things began to make more sense to her. She wondered why she had done poorly in classes that were all lecture, like her history class. This semester, she was becoming increasingly worried about her literature class. It, too, was all lecture—information about poems, plays, and sonnets. She decided to go to the Tutoring Center to find out what she could do to retain the information more effectively. Her tutor showed her how to make the terms and ideas more "visual" by drawing pictures beside each one, using colors in her notes, creating small storyboards, and creating a visual image of what was being discussed.

In your own words, what would you suggest that a classmate do if he/she was having trouble understanding, interpreting, or remembering information from a drawing class where there was very little discussion or lecture and he/she is a very strong auditory learner? List at least three things that could be done to strengthen his/her less-dominant intelligence, learning style, and/or personality type. Think about what services are offered on your campus and what people might be of assistance.

1. _____
   _____

2. _____
   _____

3. _____
   _____

Both theories deal with the visual, auditory, and tactile (or kinesthetic). While there are similarities among the two theories, the differences are great and important.

Simply stated, you can have a visual learning style and yet **not have** visual/spatial as your dominant intelligence. *"How can this be possible?"* you may be asking. It may be that you **learn best** by watching someone paint a picture—watching their brush strokes, their method of mixing paints, and their spatial layout (this is your dominant *visual learning style*). However, you may not be as engaged or as talented at actually painting as the person you watched. Your painting may lack feeling, depth, and expression. You may find it hard to paint anything that is not copied from something else. You can't visualize a landscape in your mind because your visual/spatial intelligence is not very strong. In other words, you are not an innate artist at heart. This is an example of how your ***visual learning style*** can be a strong way for you to learn, but your visual/spatial intelligence may not be your dominant intelligence.

In your own words, compare and contrast *your* primary learning style with your dominant intelligence. Give one example.

Level 2 Understand

_____
_____
_____
_____
_____
_____

UNDERSTANDING PERSONALITY TYPE

Are You ENFJ, ISTP, or ENTJ, and Why Does It Matter?

In 1921, Swiss psychologist Carl Jung (1875–1961) published his work, *Psychological Types*. In his book, Jung suggested that human behavior is not random. He felt that behavior follows patterns, and these patterns are caused by differences in the way people use their minds. In 1942, Isabel Briggs-Myers, and her mother, Katharine Briggs, began to put Jung's theory into practice. They developed the Myers-Briggs Type Indicator, which after more than 50 years of research and refinement, has become the most widely used instrument for identifying and studying personality.

Personality typing can "help us discover what best motivates and energizes each of us as individuals" (Tieger & Barron-Tieger, 2007). The questions on the Personality Assessment Profile (PAP) in Figure 7.7 can help you discover whether you are an **E** or **I** (**E**xtroverted or **I**ntroverted),

---

Figure 7.7   **Take the PAP—Personality Assessment Profile**

Directions: Read each statement carefully and thoroughly. After reading the statement, rate your response using the scale below. There are no right or wrong answers. This is not a timed survey. The PAP is based, in part, on the Myers-Briggs Type Indicator (MBTI) by Katharine Briggs and Isabel Briggs-Myers 1962

3 = Often Applies 2 = Sometimes Applies 1 = Never or Almost Never Applies

_____ 1a. I am a very talkative person.

_____ 1b. I am a more reflective person than a verbal person.

_____ 2a. I am a very factual and literal person.

_____ 2b. I look to the future and I can see possibilities.

_____ 3a. I value truth and justice over tact and emotion.

_____ 3b. I find it easy to empathize with other people.

_____ 4a. I am very ordered and efficient.

_____ 4b. I enjoy having freedom from control.

_____ 5a. I am a very friendly and social person.

_____ 5b. I enjoy listening to others more than talking.

_____ 6a. I enjoy being around and working with people who have a great deal of common sense.

_____ 6b. I enjoy being around and working with people who are dreamers and have a great deal of imagination.

_____ 7a. One of my motivating forces is to do a job very well.

_____ 7b. I like to be recognized. I am motivated by my accomplishments and awards.

_____ 8a. I like to plan out my day before I go to bed.

_____ 8b. When I get up on a non-school or non-work day, I just like to let the day "plan itself."

_____ 9a. I like to express my feelings and thoughts.

_____ 9b. I enjoy a great deal of tranquility and quiet time to myself.

_____ 10a. I am a very pragmatic and realistic person.

_____ 10b. I like to create new ideas, methods, or ways of doing things.

_____ 11a. I make decisions with my brain.

_____ 11b. I make decisions with my heart.

(Continued)

Figure 7.7 Take the PAP—Personality Assessment Profile (*Continued*)

_____12a. I am a very disciplined and orderly person.

_____12b. I don't make a lot of plans.

_____13a. I like to work with a group of people.

_____13b. I would rather work independently.

_____14a. I learn best if I can see it, touch it, smell it, taste it, or hear it.

_____14b. I learn best by relying on my gut feelings or intuition.

_____15a. I am quick to criticize others.

_____15b. I compliment others very easily and quickly.

_____16a. My life is systematic and organized.

_____16b. I don't really pay attention to deadlines.

_____17a. I can be myself when I am around others.

_____17b. I can be myself when I am alone.

_____18a. I live in the here and now, in the present.

_____18b. I live in the future, planning and dreaming.

_____19a. I think that if someone breaks the rules, the person should be punished.

_____19b. I think that if someone breaks the rules, we should look at the person who broke the rules, examine the rules, and look at the situation at hand before a decision is made.

_____20a. I do my work, then I play.

_____20b. I play, then do my work.

Refer to your score on each individual question. Place that score beside the appropriate question number below. Then, tally each line at the side.

Score					Total Across	Code
1a _____	5a _____	9a _____	13a _____	17a _____	_____	E—Extroverted
1b _____	5b _____	9b _____	13b _____	17b _____	_____	I—Introverted
2a _____	6a _____	10a _____	14a _____	18a _____	_____	S—Sensing
2b _____	6b _____	10b _____	14b _____	18b _____	_____	N—iNtuitive
3a _____	7a _____	11a _____	15a _____	19a _____	_____	T—Thinking
3b _____	7b _____	11b _____	15b _____	19b _____	_____	F—Feeling
4a _____	8a _____	12a _____	16a _____	20a _____	_____	J—Judging
4b _____	8b _____	12b _____	16b _____	20b _____	_____	P—Perceiving

PAP Scores

Look at the scores on your PAP. Is your score higher in the E or I line? Is your score higher in the S or N line? Is your score higher in the T or F line? Is your score higher in the J or P line? Write the code to the side of each section below.

Is your higher score	E or I	Code _____
Is your higher score	S or N	Code _____
Is your higher score	T or F	Code _____
Is your higher score	J or P	Code _____

S or **N** (**S**ensing or i**N**tuitive), **T** or **F** (**T**hinking or **F**eeling), and **J** or **P** (**J**udging or **P**erceiving). When all of the combinations of E/I, S/N, T/F, and J/P are combined, there are 16 personality types. Everyone will fit into **one** of the following categories:

ISTJ	ISFJ	INFJ	INTJ
ISTP	ISFP	INFP	INTP
ESTP	ESFP	ENFP	ENTP
ESTJ	ESFJ	ENFJ	ENTJ

Let's take a look at the four major categories of typing. Notice that the higher your score in one area, the stronger your personality type is for that area. For instance, if you scored 15 on the E (extroversion) questions, this means that you are a strong extrovert. If you scored 15 on the I (introversion) questions, this means that you are a strong introvert. However, if you scored 7 on the E questions and 8 on the I questions, your score indicates that you possess almost the same amount of extroverted and introverted qualities. The same is true for every category on the PAP.

E Versus I (Extroverted/Introverted)

This category deals with the way we *interact with others and the world around us; how we draw our energy.*

Extroverts prefer to live in the outside world, drawing their strength from other people. They are outgoing and love interaction. They usually make decisions with others in mind. They enjoy being the center of attention. There are usually few secrets about extroverts.

Introverts draw their strength from the inner world. They need to spend time alone to think and ponder. They are usually quiet and reflective. They usually make decisions by themselves. They do not like being the center of attention. They are private.

S Versus N (Sensing/iNtuitive)

This category deals with the way we *learn and deal with information.*

Sensing types gather information through their five senses. They have a hard time believing something if it cannot be seen, touched, smelled, tasted, or heard. They like concrete facts and details. They do not rely on intuition or gut feelings. They usually have a great deal of common sense.

Intuitive types are not very detail-oriented. They can see possibilities, and they rely on their gut feelings. Usually, they are very innovative people. They tend to live in the future and often get bored once they have mastered a task.

T Versus F (Thinking/Feeling)

This category deals with the way we *make decisions.*

Thinkers are very logical people. They do not make decisions based on feelings or emotions. They are analytical and sometimes do not take others' values into consideration when making decisions. They can easily identify the flaws of others. They can sometimes be seen as insensitive and lacking compassion.

Feelers make decisions based on what they feel is right and just. They like to have harmony, and they value others' opinions and feelings. They are usually very tactful people who like to please others. They are very warm people.

J Versus P (Judging/Perceiving)

This category deals with the way we *live and our overall lifestyle.*

Judgers are very orderly people. They must have a great deal of structure in their lives. They are good at setting goals and sticking to their goals. They are the type of people who would seldom, if ever, play before their work was completed.

Perceivers are just the opposite. They are less structured and more spontaneous. They do not like timelines. Unlike the judger, they will play before their work is done. They will take every chance to delay a decision or judgment. Sometimes, they can become involved in too many things at one time.

After you have studied the chart in Figure 7.8 and other information in the chapter regarding your personality type, you can make some decisions about your study habits and even your career choices. For instance, if you scored very strong in the extroversion section, it may not serve you well to pursue a career where you would be forced to work alone. It would probably be unwise to try to spend all of your time studying alone. If you are a strong extrovert, you would want to work and study with other people.

Figure 7.8 A Closer Look at Your Personality Type

ISTJ—The Dutiful (7–10% of America)	ISFJ—The Nurturer (7–10% of America)	INFJ—The Protector (2–3% of America)	INTJ—The Scientist (2–3% of America)
Have great power of concentration; very serious; dependable; logical and realistic; take responsibility for their own actions; not easily distracted	Hard workers; detail-oriented; considerate of others' feelings; friendly and warm to others; very conscientious; down-to-earth and like to be around the same	Enjoy an atmosphere where all get along; do what is needed of them; strong beliefs and principles; enjoy helping others achieve their goals	Very independent; enjoy challenges; inventors; can be skeptical; perfectionists; believe in their own work, sometimes to a fault
Possible Careers:	**Possible Careers:**	**Possible Careers:**	**Possible Careers:**
Accountant, Purchasing Agent, Real Estate Agent, IRS Agent, Corrections Officer, Investment Counselor, Law Researcher, Technical Writer, Judge, Mechanic	Dentist, Physician, Biologist, Surgical Technician, Teacher, Speech Pathologist, Historian, Clerical, Bookkeeper, Electrician, Retail Owner, Counselor	Career Counselor, Psychologist, Teacher, Social Worker, Clergy, Artist, Novelist, Filmmaker, Health Care Provider, Human Resource Manager, Coach, Crisis Manager, Mediator	Economist, Financial Planner, Banker, Budget Analyst, Scientist, Astronomer, Network Specialist, Computer Programmer, Engineer, Curriculum Designer, Coroner, Pathologist, Attorney, Manager
ISTP—The Mechanic (4–7% of America)	ISFP—The Artist (5–7% of America)	INFP—The Idealist (3–4% of America)	INTP—The Thinker (3–4% of America)
Very reserved; good at making things clear to others; interested in how and why things work; like to work with their hands; can sometimes be misunderstood as idle	Very sensitive and modest; adapt easily to change; respectful of others' feelings and values; take criticism personally; don't enjoy leadership roles	Work well alone; must know others well to interact; faithful to others and their jobs; excellent at communication; open-minded; dreamers; tend to do too much	Extremely logical; very analytical; good at planning; love to learn; excellent problem solvers; don't enjoy needless conversation; hard to understand at times
Possible Careers:	**Possible Careers:**	**Possible Careers:**	**Possible Careers:**
Police Officer, Intelligence Officer, Firefighter, Athletic Coach, Engineer, Technical Trainer, Logistics Manager, EMT, Surgical Technician, Banker, Office Manager, Carpenter, Landscape Architect	Artist, Chef, Musician, Nurse, Medical Assistant, Surgeon, Botanist, Zoologist, Science Teacher, Travel Agent, Game Warden, Coach, Bookkeeper, Clerical Worker, Insurance Examiner	Entertainer, Artist, Editor, Musician, Professor, Researcher, Counselor, Consultant, Clergy, Dietitian, Massage Therapist, Human Resources Manager, Events Manager, Corporate Leader	Software Designer, Programmer, Systems Analyst, Network Administrator, Surgeon, Veterinarian, Lawyer, Economist, Architect, Physicist, Mathematician, College Professor, Writer, Agent, Producer

ESTP—The Doer (6–8% of America)	ESFP—The Performer (8–10% of America)	ENFP—The Inspirer (6–7% of America)	ENTP—The Visionary (4–6% of America)
Usually very happy; don't let trivial things upset them; very good memories; very good at working with things and taking them apart	Very good at sports and active exercises; good common sense; easygoing; good at communication; can be impulsive; do not enjoy working alone; have fun and enjoy living and life	Creative and industrious; can easily find success in activities and projects that interest them; good at motivating others; organized; do not like routine	Great problem solvers; love to argue either side; can do almost anything; good at speaking/motivating; love challenges; very creative; do not like routine; overconfident
Possible Careers:	**Possible Careers:**	**Possible Careers:**	**Possible Careers:**
Police Officer, Firefighter, Detective, Military, Investigator, Paramedic, Banker, Investor, Promoter, Carpenter, Chef, Real Estate Broker, Retail Sales, Insurance Claims Adjuster	Nurse, Social Worker, Physician Assistant, Nutritionist, Therapist, Photographer, Musician, Film Producer, Social Events Coordinator, News Anchor, Fund Raiser, Host, Retail Sales	Journalist, Writer, Actor, Newscaster, Artist, Director, Public Relations, Teacher, Clergy, Psychologist, Guidance Counselor, Trainer, Project Manager, Human Resources Manager	Entrepreneur, Manager, Agent, Journalist, Attorney, Urban Planner, Analyst, Creative Director, Public Relations, Marketing, Broadcaster, Network Solutions, Politician, Detective
ESTJ—The Guardian (12–15% of America)	ESFJ—The Caregiver (11–14% of America)	ENFJ—The Giver (3–5% of America)	ENTJ—The Executive (3–5% of America)
"Take charge" people; like to get things done; focus on results; very good at organizing; good at seeing what will not work; responsible; realistic	Enjoy many friendly relationships; popular; love to help others; do not take criticism very well; need praise; need to work with people; organized; talkative; active	Very concerned about others' feelings; respect others; good leaders; usually popular; good at public speaking; can make decisions too quickly; trust easily	Excellent leaders; speak very well; hard-working; may be workaholics; may not give enough praise; like to learn; great planners; enjoy helping others reach their goals
Possible Careers:	**Possible Careers:**	**Possible Careers:**	**Possible Careers:**
Insurance Agent, Military, Security, Coach, Credit Analyst, Project Manager, Auditor, General Contractor, Paralegal, Stockbroker, Executive, Information Officer, Lawyer, Controller, Accounts Manager	Medical Assistant, Physician, Nurse, Teacher, Coach, Principal, Social Worker, Counselor, Clergy, Court Reporter, Office Manager, Loan Officer, Public Relations, Customer Service, Caterer, Office Manager	Journalist, Entertainer, TV Producer, Politician, Counselor, Clergy, Psychologist, Teacher, Social Worker, Health Care Provider, Customer Service Manager	Executive, Senior Manager, Administrator, Consultant, Editor, Producer, Financial Planner, Stockbroker, Program Designer, Attorney, Psychologist, Engineer, Network Administrator

Adapted from Tieger and Baron-Tieger, 2007, and The Personality Type Portraits at www.personalitypage.com

REFLECTIONS ON LEARNING HOW TO LEARN

Unlike an IQ test, learning styles, Multiple Intelligences theory, and personality type assessments do not pretend to determine if you are "smart" or not. These assessments simply allow you to look more closely at how you learn, what innate strengths you possess, and what your dominant intelligence may be.

Discovering your learning style can greatly enhance your classroom performance. For example, finally understanding that your learning style is visual and that your professor's teaching style is totally verbal (oral) can answer many questions about why you may have performed poorly in the past in a strictly lecture class. Now that you have discovered that you are a feeling-extrovert, you can better understand why you love associating with others and learn a great deal by working in groups. And now that you have discovered that your primary intelligence is logical/mathematical, you know why math and science are easier for you than history or literature.

Possessing this knowledge and developing the tools to make your learning style, dominate intelligence, and personality type work for you, not against you, will be paramount to your success. As you continue to use your learning style, dominant intelligence, and personality type to enhance learning, consider the following:

- Get involved in a *variety* of learning and social situations.
- Use your less-dominant areas more often to *strengthen* them.
- *Read more* about personality typing and learning styles.
- *Surround yourself* with people who learn differently from you
- Try *different ways* of learning and studying.
- Remember that inventories *do not* measure your worth.

By understanding how you process information, learning can become an entirely new and exciting venture for you. Good luck to you on this new journey.

Knowledge in Bloom

CREATING YOUR PERSONAL LIFE PROFILE

Utilizes levels 4 and 5 on the Taxonomy (See Bloom's Taxonomy at the front of this text)

Throughout this chapter, you have discovered three things about the way you learn best: your dominant intelligence, your learning style, and your personality type. Write them down in the space below:

My **dominant intelligence** is _____

My **primary learning style** is _____

My **strongest personality type** is _____

Now that you see them all together, think of them as a puzzle and "connect the dots." In other words, put them all together and what do they look like? What do they mean? How do they affect your studies, your relationships, your communication skills, and your career choices?

Example: If Mike's dominant intelligence is **interpersonal,** his learning style is **verbal,** and his personality type is **ENFJ,** *connecting the dots* may suggest that he is the type of person who loves to be around other people, that he is an extravert who learns best by listening to other people or explaining how something is done. He is a person who would probably speak out in class, be more of a leader than a follower, and someone who would start a study group if one did not exist because he is outgoing, organized, and very much a goal setter. Mike is the type of person who values relationships and listens to what others

are saying. He is a person who shares and does not mind taking the time to explain things to others. He could easily become a good friend.

Some of the challenges Mike could encounter might involve taking a class where discussions are rare, having to sit and never share ideas or views, or having a professor who is not very organized and skips around. He would not deal very well with peers who are disrespectful and did not pull their own weight in the study group. He might also have a hard time with group members or classmates who are very quiet and prefer to observe rather than become involved. He would have trouble being around people who have no goals and direction in life. He might also run into some trouble because he is a very social person and loves to be around others in social settings. He may over-commit himself to groups and clubs, and, on occasion, he may socialize more than study.

As you can see, by connecting the dots, Mike's **Personal Life Profile** tells us a great deal about his strengths and challenges. It also gives him an understanding of how to approach many different situations, capitalize on his strengths, and work to improve his weaker areas.

Now, it is your turn. Take your time and refer back to the chapter for any information you may need. Examine your assessments and create your own profile in the four areas listed below. Discuss your strengths and challenges for each area.

THE PERSONAL LIFE PROFILE OF _____

Academic Strengths: I found that I . . .

_____

_____

_____

Academic Challenges: I found that I . . .

_____

_____

_____

Communication Strengths: I found that I . . .

_____

_____

_____

Communication Challenges: I found that I . . .

_____

_____

_____

Relationship Strengths: I found that I . . .

_____

_____

_____

Relationship Challenges: I found that I . . .

_____

_____

_____

Career Strengths: I found that I . . .

_____

_____

_____

Career Challenges: I found that I . . .

_____

_____

_____

Looking at all of this together, write an extensive paragraph about what all of this means about you. Include thoughts on your learning style, your personality, your study habits, your communication skills, and your overall success strategy.

_____

_____

_____

SQ3R MASTERY STUDY SHEET

EXAMPLE QUESTION (FROM PAGE 169) What is the difference between a learning style and a learning strategy?	**ANSWER:**
EXAMPLE QUESTION (FROM PAGE 169) What is the definition of tactile learning, and how do you use it?	**ANSWER:**
AUTHOR QUESTION (FROM PAGE 158) Discuss at least three theories of learning from the historical figures discussed.	**ANSWER:**
AUTHOR QUESTION (FROM PAGE 163) Who is Howard Gardner, and why is his work important?	**ANSWER:**
AUTHOR QUESTION (FROM PAGE 169) Explain the difference between your learning style and your dominant intelligence.	**ANSWER:**
AUTHOR QUESTION (FROM PAGE 169) What is the difference between a visual learning style and visual intelligence?	**ANSWER:**
AUTHOR QUESTION (FROM PAGE 171) How can your personality type affect your career aspirations?	**ANSWER:**
YOUR QUESTION (FROM PAGE ____)	**ANSWER:**
YOUR QUESTION (FROM PAGE ____)	**ANSWER:**
YOUR QUESTION (FROM PAGE ____)	**ANSWER:**
YOUR QUESTION (FROM PAGE ____)	**ANSWER:**
YOUR QUESTION (FROM PAGE ____)	**ANSWER:**

Finally, after answering these questions, recite this chapter's major points in your mind. Consider the following general questions to help you master this material.

- What is it about?
- What does it mean?
- What is the most important thing you learned? Why?
- What are the key points to remember?

chapter eight

READ

BUILDING SUCCESSFUL READING STRATEGIES FOR PRINT AND ONLINE MATERIAL

"The difference between the right word and the almost right word is the difference between lightning and the lightning bug." —Mark Twain

READ

Why read this chapter?

Because you'll learn...

- How to determine your reading speed and become an active reader
- How to avoid visual fixation to increase reading speed
- How to read in pieces to enhance your comprehension

Because you'll be able to...

- Calculate and use your reading speed to manage your study time more effectively
- Develop a reading and study plan using the SQ3R method to your best advantage
- Appraise and judge reading passages, sections, and chapters

Scan and QUESTION

Take a few moments, **scan this chapter** and on page 201, write **five of your own questions** that you think will be important to your mastery of this material. You will also find five questions listed from your authors.

Example:

- ☑ **Describe the process of fixation.** (from page 186)
- ☑ **Why is comprehension more important than speed?** (from page 186)

MyStudentSuccessLab

MyStudentSuccessLab is an online solution designed to help you acquire and develop (or hone) the skills you need to succeed. You will have access to peer-led video presentations and develop core skills through interactive exercises and projects.

How
COLLEGE CHANGED MY LIFE

Name: Patricia Walls
Institution: Graduate! The College of Southern Nevada and The University of Nevada–Las Vegas, Las Vegas, NV
Major: Secondary Education

*N*early twenty-five years ago, during my first year at Eastern Washington University, one of my professors told a group of us first-time graduate teaching assistants that one day we would meet a student who would possess greater writing and critical thinking skills than we did. We should not fear this student, but rather use the experience to learn *from* the student. "This student will offer you new truths yet to discover." I am certain that I encountered students who were better writers than I very early on in my career, but never had I been so struck by a student's natural ability to write, think, and communicate as I was when I met Patricia (Pat) Walls at the College of Southern Nevada (CSN). Perhaps even more surprising than Pat's innate writer's ability was her genuine modesty about it.

CSN is an institution proud to educate those students returning to education after years spent in the work- and/or parent-force. Pat, born in Atlanta, Georgia, in 1950, was one of those students. She had already navigated her roles of wife and mother of five when she decided to pursue higher education in the summer of 2000. Pat decided to follow a new dream and study education at CSN.

An interview conducted and written by T. D. Eliopulos, Professor, The College of Southern Nevada

Pat and I met when she enrolled in my Composition One course. After reading her first essay, I knew I had found the student whom my professor had predicted all those years earlier. Assignment after assignment, Pat wrote with insightful intellect and rhetorical command. Her eye for description, her humor, and her precise language were those of the already published writer, not those of an uncertain community college student. But much to my amazement, uncertain she was. During one of our first conversations, Pat shared with me her apprehension: "I'm worried someone's going to tap me on the shoulder and tell me to go home." At that time, Pat actually believed she did not belong in college. For years she had possessed such an inflated idea of what the college experience was that she had convinced herself she was not "worthy" of it. Luckily, after a semester or two, she realized that she did belong in college. Pat recalled, "After a few semesters at CSN, I realized that I was wrong in placing education on a pedestal, that it was something that was achievable."

After spending two years at CSN, where she earned her AA in education, she transferred to the University of Nevada–Las Vegas, where in 2006 she received her degree in secondary education along with a TESOL certificate. Removed from her college and university experiences, she can now distinguish the differences between the college and university environments. According to Pat, CSN is "a very positive learning community," whereas UNLV "is a place of greater ambition, a place to jump-start a career." She added that the college experience gives students the opportunity to engage in the "learning process" and toughens them through experiences and challenges. Her experience has allowed her to pass along her knowledge to her own students. Pat states, "It is not the smartest student who succeeds, but those who stay the course, those who do not allow the many forms of discouragement to impede their learning process and shake them loose."

Seven years into her own professional career, Pat teaches three courses of English Language Learners and two courses of sophomore English at Rancho High School in Las Vegas, Nevada, benefiting the lives of nearly 125 students each year. Clearly, Pat Walls continues to instill the learning and life processes, and fortunately for the Clark County School District, she is gifting her students with a desire to engage in the same activity that she once thought above her. I am certain that learning *from* her has been among the most satisfying moments of my professional career.

THINK about *it*

1. Pat states that she was afraid that someone was going to tap her on the shoulder and tell her to go home. What has been your greatest fear since beginning your studies? How have you dealt with this fear?

2. Pat suggests that it is not the "smartest students" who persist, but those who do not let discouragement impede their learning. What steps do you plan to take to turn your discouraging moments into learning experiences?

DISCOVERING YOUR READING STYLE

Are You Active or Passive?

Active reading is really nothing more than a mind-set. It is the attitude you have as you begin the reading process. For the next few days, try approaching your reading assignments with a positive, open-minded approach and notice the difference in your own satisfaction, understanding, and overall comprehension. Instead of saying things like, "I hate reading" or "This stuff is worthless," reframe your self-talk into statements such as, "I'm going to learn from this" and "I think I can apply this to my life now." See Figure 8.1 to determine your reading style.

Figure 8.1 **Discovering Your Reading Style**

Take a few moments and circle TRUE or FALSE for each of the statements below to determine if you are more of an active or a passive reader.

1. I enjoy reading for pleasure.	TRUE	FALSE
2. College textbooks have little connection to my real life.	TRUE	FALSE
3. I look for the deeper meaning in words and phrases.	TRUE	FALSE

4. I seldom visualize what I am reading.	TRUE	FALSE
5. I look up words that I do not understand.	TRUE	FALSE
6. I read only what I have to read, and that is a stretch for me.	TRUE	FALSE
7. I stop reading to ponder what something means.	TRUE	FALSE
8. I never take notes when reading.	TRUE	FALSE
9. Reading brings me great joy.	TRUE	FALSE
10. My mind wanders constantly when I read.	TRUE	FALSE
11. I make time for reading even when I am not required to read.	TRUE	FALSE
12. Words are just words—they add no real meaning to my life or work.	TRUE	FALSE
13. I get excited about reading something new because I know I will learn something new and useful.	TRUE	FALSE
14. When reading, I just want to get it over with.	TRUE	FALSE
15. I usually have no trouble concentrating when reading.	TRUE	FALSE
16. I never look up words; I just read on.	TRUE	FALSE

Total of even-numbered TRUE responses _____

Total of odd-numbered TRUE responses _____

If you answered TRUE to more even numbers, you tend to be a more passive reader.
If you answered TRUE to more odd numbers, you tend to be a more active reader.

I FEEL THE NEED . . . THE NEED FOR SPEED!

Do You Know Your Personal Reading Rate?

You've heard the advertisements: "Breeze through a novel on your lunch hour," "Read an entire computer instruction book over dinner," or "Read *The New York Times* in 10 minutes." Sure, there are people who have an incredible gift for speed reading and a photographic memory, but those people are not the norm.

In the activity in Figure 8.2, you will find a passage on binge drinking. Read the section at your normal pace. Use a stopwatch or a watch with a second hand to accurately record your time, and then calculate your rate and comprehension level using the scales provided.

This section is included to give you some idea about how long it will take to read a chapter so that you can *plan your reading time* more effectively. There is an average of 450 words on a college textbook page. If you read at 150 words per minute, each page may take you an average of 3 minutes to read.

This is a **raw number** for just reading. It *does not* allow for marking, highlighting, taking notes, looking up unfamiliar words, reflecting, or comprehension. When these necessary skills are coupled with basic reading, they can sometimes triple the amount of reading time required. So, that page that you estimated would take you 3 minutes to read may actually take you 9 to 10 minutes. This matters greatly when you have a 40-page chapter to read for homework.

Have you ever timed yourself to determine how long it takes you to read a complete chapter?

Figure 8.2 Calculating Your Reading Rate

Start time _____ : _____ : _____
          Hour   Min.   Sec.

BINGE DRINKING

Binge drinking is classified as having more than five drinks at one time. Many people say, "I only drink once a week." However, if that one drinking spell includes drink after drink after drink, it can be extremely detrimental to your liver, your memory, your digestive system, and your overall health.

Most college students report that they do not mean to binge drink, but it is caused by the situation, such as a ballgame, party, campus event, or special occasion. Researchers at Michigan State University found that only 5 percent of students surveyed say they party to "get drunk" (Warner, 2002).

In their breakthrough work, *Dying to Drink*, Harvard researcher Henry Wechsler and science writer Bernice Wuethrich explore the problem of binge drinking. They suggest that "two out of every five college students regularly binge drink, resulting in approximately 1,400 student deaths, a distressing number of assaults and rapes, a shameful amount of vandalism, and countless cases of academic suicide" (Wechsler & Wuethrich, 2002).

It is a situation reminiscent of the old saying, "letting the fox guard the henhouse." After a few drinks, it is hard to "self-police," meaning that you may not be able to control your actions once the drinking starts.

Perhaps the greatest tragedy of drug and alcohol abuse is the residual damage of pregnancy, sexually transmitted diseases, traffic fatalities, verbal/physical abuse, and accidental death. You know that drugs and alcohol lower your resistance and can cause you to do things that you would not normally do, such as drive drunk or have unprotected sex. Surveys and research results suggest that students who participate in heavy episodic (HE) or binge drinking are more likely to participate in unprotected sex with multiple sex partners. One survey found that 61 percent of men who binge drink participated in unprotected sex, as compared to 23 percent of men who do not binge drink. The survey also found that 48 percent of women who binge drink participated in unprotected sex, as compared to only 8 percent of women who do not binge drink (Cooper, 2002).

These staggering statistics suggest one thing: alcohol consumption can cause people to act in ways in which they may never have acted without alcohol—and those actions can result in personal damage from which recovery may be impossible. (386 words)

Finishing time _____ : _____ : _____
          Hour   Min.   Sec.

Reading time in seconds = _____
Words per minute (use the following chart) = _____

Example: If you read this passage in 2 minutes and 38 seconds, your reading time in seconds would be 158. Using the Rate Calculator Chart, your reading rate would be about 146 words per minute.

Rate Calculator for "Binge Drinking" Passage	
Time in Seconds	Words per Minute
40	581
50	464
60 (1 minute)	387
120 (2 minutes)	194
130	179
140	165
150	155
160	145
170	137
180 (3 minutes)	129
190	122
200	116
210	110
220	106
230	101

Test Your Comprehension Skills

Answer the following questions with T (true) or F (false) without looking back over the material.

_____ 1. Binge drinking has resulted in the deaths of students.

_____ 2. Men who binge drink have unprotected sex more often than men who do not binge drink.

_____ 3. Women who binge drink have unprotected sex no more often than women who do not binge drink.

_____ 4. "Self-policing" means that you are able to look out for yourself.

_____ 5. Binge drinking is classified as having more than three drinks at one time.

Each question is worth 20%. Comprehension = _____ %

Example: If you answered two correctly, your comprehension rate would be 40% (2 × 20%). If you answered four correctly, your comprehension rate would be 80% (4 × 20%).

Test Your Comprehension Skills Answers: 1 = T, 2 = T, 3 = F, 4 = F, 5 = F.

YOU DON'T HAVE TO BE A LOGODAEDALIAN TO ENJOY WORDS

Can a Powerful Vocabulary Really Be Developed?

Thankfully, it is not every day you run across words like logodaedalian. (A _logodaedalian_ is a person who has a great passion for unique, sly, and clever words and phrases.) Perhaps the best way to develop a dynamic vocabulary is through reading. By reading, you come across words that you may have never seen before. You are exposed to aspects of language that you may not have experienced in your family, neighborhood, or geographic location.

Of course, the words with which you are unfamiliar in a passage, section, or chapter will not become a part of your vocabulary unless you **stop** and look them up. Looking up unfamiliar words is the way to begin building a masterful vocabulary.

Tips to Develop a Strong Vocabulary

- Look up words that you do not know (download a free dictionary on your smartphone or tablet).
- Read often and read a variety of material, including difficult material.
- Ask for clarifications in class and online.
- Try to remember the word in its usage, whether in a phrase, sentence, or explanation.
- Keep a running list of words you do not know (put them in the memo section of your smartphone).
- Make connections through rhyming the new word with familiar words.
- Draw a picture of the word's definition on a index card.
- Work crossword puzzles and word games such as Scrabble.

LEARNING TO READ FASTER AND SMARTER

Can You Improve Speed and Comprehension?

As you begin to practice reading for comprehension, review the following tips to help you read the material more quickly and understand it more clearly. Whenever you are faced with having to choose between *comprehension* or *speed,* choose comprehension! The following two tips will help as you begin to master reading college-level material:

1. Learn to Concentrate

Both speed and comprehension require deep, ***mindful concentration***. Neither can be achieved without it. In order to comprehend information, your body needs to be ready to concentrate. You need sleep, rest, and proper nutrition. Most importantly, you need a quiet, peaceful place to concentrate on your reading. To increase your concentration and comprehension, consider the following:

- Reduce outside distractions, such as people talking, rooms that are too hot or cold, cell phones ringing, etc.
- Reduce internal distractions, such as fatigue, self-talk, daydreaming, hunger, and emotions that cause you to think of other things.
- Set a goal for reading a certain amount of material in an allotted time. This goal can help you focus.
- Take a short break every 20 minutes. Don't get distracted and do something else; come back to your reading in 3–5 minutes.
- Take notes as you read. This helps reading become an active process.
- When reading online material, don't become distracted by other technology, e-mails, Facebook posts, Tweets, posts, etc.

2. Overcome Fixation

Overcoming fixation is another important step in learning to read for speed and comprehension. Fixation is when your eyes stop on a single word to read it. Your eyes stop for only a fraction of a second, but those fractions add up over the course of a section or chapter. Your mind sees the words something like this:

Nutrition   is   important   to   good   health.

As you read this, you probably had six fixations because the words are spaced out. However, if they were not spaced, many people would still have six fixations. To increase your speed, try to see two or more words with one fixation; this will cut your reading time nearly in half. Try to see the sentence like this:

Nutrition is important   to good health.

Smith (2007) states: "research has shown that the average reader can see approximately 2.5 words per fixation." To reduce your fixation time for active reading, consider the following:

- Practice seeing two or more words with one fixation.
- As you practice, try to read in phrases like the example below:

Nutrition is important   to good health. Therefore,   you should work hard   to eat proper meals   every day.   By doing this you can maintain   good health

READING ONLINE MATERIAL

Do I Need a New Set of Reading Skills?

You may be asking, "Is reading online really different from reading the printed word?" The answer is yes, especially with today's online, interactive, multimedia environment. Not too long ago, college students purchased their books or reading packets from the college bookstore and read the printed word. Today, this is not necessarily the case. You may be required to download entire books or chapters, you will be assigned websites by your instructors, and you will sometimes decide to explore topics further through online research. Reading online requires an adjusted set of skills. You will still need to use the reading tips in this chapter, especially SQ3R, but you will also need to familiarize yourself with the strategies for successfully reading online (non-textual) material. Consider the tips offered in Figure 8.3.

DID YOU Know?

JAY LENO has always been a hard worker. Having mild dyslexia, he did not do very well in high school, getting mainly C's and D's. Jay, however, was determined to accomplish his goals, and despite his poor grades, he was resolute to attend Emerson College in Boston.

The admissions office decided that Jay was not a good candidate for the college and refused him admission. However, he had his heart set on attending Emerson so he sat outside the admission officers' office 12 hours a day, 5 days a week until he was accepted into the university.

He credits his dyslexia with helping him develop the drive and perseverance needed to succeed in comedy and in life in general. (*Source:* www.dyslexiaonline.com)

Figure 8.3   Tips for Reading Online Material

- Before you even open the site, plan some undisturbed time to survey, explore, and read the site. Make it a point to avoid distractions or multitasking, such as downloading songs on iTunes, reading your Facebook page, or checking e-mail. Devote this time to reading the material.

- Know why you are reading the online material. What is your objective?

- As you open the site, browse through (survey) it first to determine the length, view the main headings, and find out if you'll need to download plug-ins or any additional programs on your computer to access the material. Get a "feel" for the site and the material.

- Click on any menus or tabs to determine what additional information is available.

- Work to avoid eye strain. You can do this several ways:
  - Read in periods of 20 minutes. After 20 minutes, take a short break.
  - Increase the size of your view screen to make the site larger.
  - Copy the material, paste it into a word document, and enlarge the font so that you can read it more clearly.

- While reading, use *virtual sticky notes* to mark important material. You can download several free sticky notes programs by going online and searching "Free Online Sticky Notes."

- While reading, use an *online highlighter* to mark important material. To access an online highlighter, download one of the free online highlighting programs such as www.awesomehighlighter.com.

- While reading online, just as reading from printed material, take notes! This is one of the most important tools for memory and comprehension. As you read online material, take notes the traditional way or take *virtual online notes*. To do this, open a word processing program, reduce it into the bottom menu bar, and as you read, click on it and add notes to your online page. Double space between lines to make it easier to read during your review period. You can also download several free online note-taking systems by searching, "Free Online Note Taking Software."

- Use free *text-to-speech* programs to convert your online material to verbal material. If you're on the run, download any free text-to-speech program and then copy and paste the written work into the program. Next, download the file to your MP3 player or burn it to a CD. You now have "reading on the run."

Successful Decisions
AN ACTIVITY FOR CRITICAL REFLECTION

Whitney is 19 years old and just completed high school. She enrolled at Seymore Technical Institute with dreams of becoming a phlebotomist. She had done well in high school, but reading had never been her strongest talent.

She became increasingly worried when she began to review her texts for the first semester. The readings were much more difficult than she expected. Further, she was stunned at the amount of reading required by each instructor.

Realizing that reading *and* comprehending were going to play a major role in her academic success, Whitney began to set aside two hours per day devoted strictly to reading, taking notes, vocabulary building, and comprehension. She was doing better but was still struggling with her difficult texts and handouts.

Pretend that Whitney is a student at your institution. What services are available that you could recommend to her to help her improve her reading and comprehension skills?

1. _____

2. _____

What would you recommend that she do on a daily basis to improve her reading and comprehension?

1. _____

2. _____

FINDING THE MAIN IDEA

Can You Get to the Main Point?

In many books, each paragraph or section has a ***main idea***. You're familiar with this through your English class. It is usually called a topic sentence. The topic statement is what the paragraph or section is about. Identifying the main idea of a section can greatly aid your comprehension of the material. However, in many college texts, each paragraph will *not* have a main, topic sentence. Some paragraphs simply give further details of the previous paragraph. You may have to find the main idea by reading an entire section of a chapter from heading to heading.

For practice, read the following paragraph and determine the main idea, the point.

Do you remember where you were and what you were doing when you first heard about Barack Obama's election as the first African American president of the United States? Chances are good that you remember some of the details surrounding what you were doing when you heard this historic news. Experts report that most people will remember exactly where they were and what they were doing when a major event occurs. Depending on your age, you or your parents probably remember where you were when you heard about the attacks on the World Trade Center. Many people who were alive when John Kennedy was assassinated remember vividly where they were, even though this event happened over fifty years ago. Events of this magnitude appear to be seared into our memories.

Circle the one option below that best describes the main idea.

1. The election of Barack Obama

2. The assassination of John Kennedy

3. The fact that we tend to remember what we were doing when events of great magnitude happen

When reading, do you stop after each paragraph and think about the meaning?

Which did you choose? Statement one, although mentioned in the first sentence of the paragraph, has very little to do with the paragraph's intended message. It is simply a prompt. Statement two is closer, but it is too vague and does not adequately address the fact that we remember what we were doing during a tragic event. Statement three is the correct topic for this paragraph.

Finding the topic sentence or main idea in a paragraph, section, or chapter is not hard, but it does take concentration and a degree of analytical skill. If you approach each paragraph or section as a detective searching for clues, you will soon find out how easy and effortless it is to determine main points.

Read the following paragraph and identify the topic in your own words. Justify your answer. Then, identify the main idea of the paragraph. See if you can determine what the authors really want you to know. Finally, develop (predict) one test question for this paragraph. You *will not* have to do this for every paragraph you read in college. As you become a stronger reader, you will do this type of analysis after each heading or chapter section. But for now, as you work on building your skills as a reader, take the time to learn how to fully analyze a small portion of a chapter.

> *The origin of emotion is the brain. You might say that there are two minds—one that thinks (the thinking mind) and one that feels (the emotional mind). Think of thoughts and emotions as two different mechanisms for knowing and making sense of the world. The two minds are not adversarial or physically separate; rather, they operate interactively to construct your mental life. Passion (the heart) dominates reason (the mind) when feelings are intense.*

—*Emotional Intelligence,* Nelson & Low, 2010

Level 4 Analyze

Vocabulary Builder

Define the following:

mechanism _____

adversarial _____

dominate _____

The **topic** of this paragraph is _____

_____

_____

_____

Who or what is the paragraph about (the **main idea**)?

_____

_____

_____

What does the author of the paragraph really want you **to know**?

_____

_____

_____

_____

Develop one **test question** from this paragraph using Bloom's Taxonomy test prompts found inside the front cover of this text. Example: What is Fixation? How is reading comprehension related to academic success?

_____

_____

_____

_____

SQ3R TO THE RESCUE

How Can You Do It Right the First Time?

There are as many ways to approach a chapter in a textbook as there are students who read textbooks. Most would agree that there is no "right" or "wrong" way to begin the process. However, many would agree that there are a few ways of approaching a chapter that are more effective than others. One such approach is SQ3R.

The most basic and often-used reading and studying system is the SQ3R method, developed by Francis P. Robinson in 1941. This simple, yet effective, system has proved to be a successful study tool for millions of students. SQ3R involves five steps: Scan, Question, Read, Recite, and Review. The most important thing to remember about SQ3R is that it should be used on a daily basis, not as a method for cramming. See Figure 8.4.

Scan

The first step of SQ3R is to **scan,** or pre-read, an assigned chapter. Every chapter in this text begins with this feature, Scan and Question. This is a part of SQ3R. You begin by reading the title of the chapter, the headings, and each sub-heading. Look carefully at the chapter objectives, vocabulary, timelines, graphs, charts, pictures, and drawings included in each chapter. If there is a chapter summary, read it. Scanning also includes reading the first and last sentence in each paragraph. Scanning is not a substitute for reading a chapter. Reading is discussed later. Before going any further, scan the next chapter of this text paying attention to the chapter title, heading, subheadings, charts, graphs, photos, callouts, and features.

Question

The second step is to **question**. There are five common questions you should ask yourself when you are reading a chapter: Who? When? What? Where? and Why? As you scan and read your chapter, turn the information into questions and see if you can answer them. If you do not know the answers to the questions, you should find them as you read along. You have been doing this for each chapter thus far.

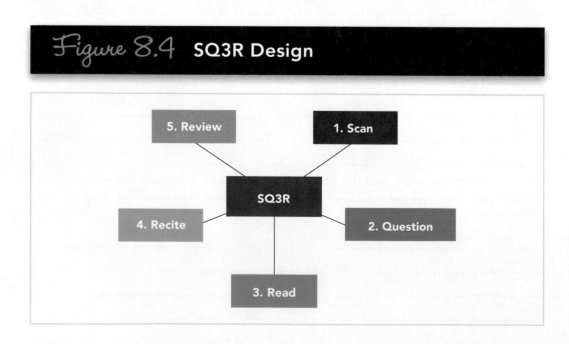

Figure 8.4 **SQ3R Design**

Another way to approach the chapter is to turn the major headings of each section into questions (see an example in Figure 8.5). When you get to the end of the section, having carefully read the material, taken notes, and highlighted important information, answer the questions that you posed at the beginning of the section.

After you scan the chapter and develop some questions to be answered from the chapter, the next step is to read the chapter. Remember, scanning is not reading. There is no substitute for reading in your success plan. Read slowly and carefully. The SQ3R method requires a substantial amount of time, but if you take each step slowly and completely, you will be amazed at how much you can learn and how much your grades will improve.

Read through each section. It is best not to jump around or move ahead if you do not understand the previous section. Paragraphs are usually built on each other, so you need to understand the first before you can move on to the next. You may have to read a chapter or section more than once, especially if the information is new, technical, or difficult.

Take notes, highlight, and make marginal notes in your textbook as you read along. You own your textbook and should personalize it as you would your lecture notes. Highlight areas that you feel are important, underline words and phrases that you did not understand or that you feel are important, and jot down notes in the margins. Refer to the Begin section of this book in the front matter to see how a text page should look after reading and using SQ3R.

> "There are worse crimes than burning books. One of them is not reading them."
>
> —Joseph Brodsky

As you begin to read your chapter, mark the text, and take notes, keep the following in mind:

- Read the entire paragraph before you mark anything.
- Identify the topic or thesis statement of each paragraph and highlight it.
- Highlight key phrases.
- Don't highlight too much; the text will lose its significance (see Figure 8.6).
- Use two different color highlighters—one for "important information" and one for "very interesting information."
- Stop and look up words that you do not know or understand and define them in the margins.

Figure 8.5   Forming Questions from Headings

Example: If you were describing the mall in Washington, D.C., you could begin with the Lincoln Memorial and then move on to the reflecting pond, the Washington Monument, and the Smithsonian.

Cause-Effect Organization is when you arrange your information in the cause-and-effect order. You would discuss the causes of a problem and then explore its effects.

Example: If you were speaking about high blood pressure, you would first examine the causes of high blood pressure such as diet, hereditary factors, and weight and then move on to the effects such as heart attack and stroke.

→ What is cause and effect?
Why is it important?

Chronological Organization is presenting information in the order in which it happened. Speeches that deal with historical facts and how-to speeches often use chronological organization.

Example: If you were giving a speech or writing a paper on the history of automobiles in the United States since 1950, you would begin with the 50s, move to the 60s, 70s, 80s, and 90s. If you were giving a how-to speech on refinishing a table, you would begin with the first process of stripping the old paint or varnish and move forward to the last step of applying a new coat of paint or varnish.

→ What is chronological organization?
When do I use chronological order?
Why?

> Order and simplification are the first steps toward mastery.
>
> —THOMAS MANN

While reading, you will want to take notes that are more elaborate than your highlighting or marginal notes. Taking notes while reading the text will assist you in studying the material and committing it to memory. **This is a major part of *actively learning*.** There are several effective methods of taking notes while reading (see Figure 8.7). They include:

Charts	Outlines	Flashcards
Mind maps	Timelines	Summaries
Key words		

Figure 8.6   The "Down Low" on Highlighting

D: Determine the Information You Need by Narrowing Your Topic

Research begins by asking a question. Suppose that you have been assigned a paper or speech and you decide to write or speak on Rosa Parks. You begin the research and type *Rosa Parks* into Google. You get 3,520,000 hits. This is just a few too many articles to read by Monday. However, if you begin with a question in mind, you can narrow your topic and determine what information you need early on.

After some thought, you decide that your research question will be "What was Rosa Parks's role in the civil rights movement?" If you Google this topic, you get 251,000 hits. Still far too many, but 3,269,000 fewer hits than before, and you have a direction to begin your paper. So, the first steps in becoming a more information literate student are to *identify and narrow your topic* and *determine what information is needed on this topic*. You will also need to determine what type of information you need and want to use in your project. Do you want facts, opinions, eyewitness reports, interviews, debates, and/or arguments? Each may provide you with different types of information.

> "The booming science of decision making has shown that more information can lead to objectively poorer choices, and to choices that people come to regret."
> —A. Dimoka

Cyber research can be an amazing tool in your educational pursuit. However, when you are faced with 3,520,000 articles on one topic, it can also become overwhelming. *Information overload* can have negative effects on the learning process. Angelika Dimoka, director of the Center for Neural Decision Making at Temple University, suggests that with the vast amounts of information we face in an online search, "the brain's emotion region runs as wild as toddlers on a sugar high" (Begley, 2011). We begin to make stupid mistakes and bad decisions. Our frustration and anxiety levels also soar. Too much information can lead to *information paralysis*. This basically means that you have so much information that you don't know what to do with it—so you do nothing.

The new field of decision-making research also suggests that when we are faced with too much information and too many decisions, we tend to make no decision at all. When the amount of information coming at us is coupled with the speed at which it comes, this can lead to devastating results. According to Sharon Begley in her article "I Can't Think" (2011), when faced with too much information, "we sacrifice accuracy and thoughtfulness to the false god of immediacy." We tend to make quick, bad decisions rather than slower, well-reasoned ones. It is for these reasons that step one in the D.A.R.T.S. System is imperative. When determining what information is needed on your narrowed topic, you should also make sure that you do the following:

- Understand your instructor's guidelines for the project.
- Understand your intended audience.
- Determine the availability of reliable resources and how many are required by your instructor.
- Develop a timeline to complete your project.

A: Access the Information from a Variety of Sources

After you have made your topic decision and narrowed your research question, you will want to begin the process of accessing valuable, reliable, credible information. While Wikipedia and Google are valuable tools, it is also important to use a variety of sources such as journals, scholarly books, newspapers, and maybe even interviews to gather the information needed.

You may be asking, "Is the library still important in the digital age?" Yes! The answer is an absolute yes! Many people think of libraries as quiet, tomb-like places presided over by a crabby old woman prepared to pounce on you if you ask a question or touch one of her precious books. Fortunately, that stereotype went the way of the horse and buggy. Today, libraries

As you read through a chapter in your textbook, you may find that you have to use a variety of these techniques to capture information. Try them for one week. Although taking notes while reading a chapter thoroughly is time consuming, you will be amazed at how much you remember and how much you are able to contribute in class or online notes after using these techniques. SQ3R works!

Figure 8.7   Sample Note-Taking Methods

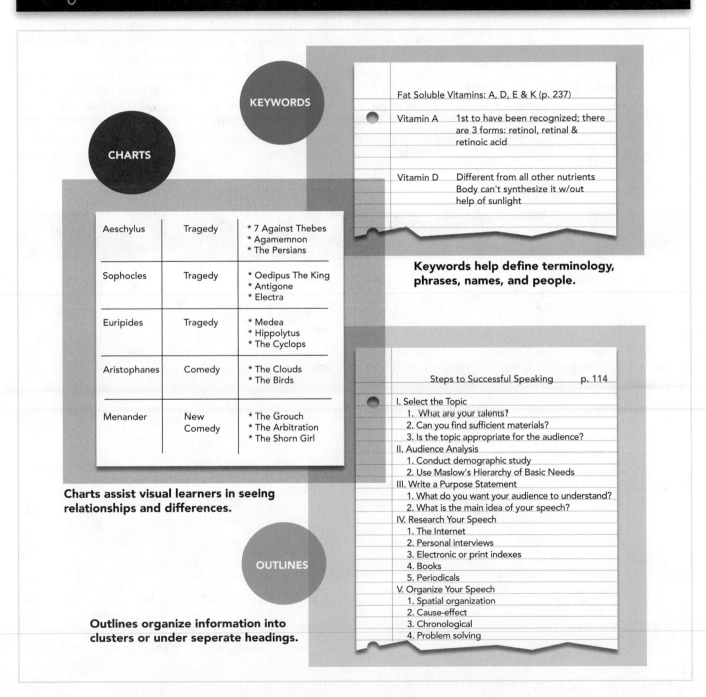

KEYWORDS

Fat Soluble Vitamins: A, D, E & K (p. 237)

Vitamin A   1st to have been recognized; there are 3 forms: retinol, retinal & retinoic acid

Vitamin D   Different from all other nutrients Body can't synthesize it w/out help of sunlight

Keywords help define terminology, phrases, names, and people.

CHARTS

Aeschylus	Tragedy	* 7 Against Thebes * Agamemnon * The Persians
Sophocles	Tragedy	* Oedipus The King * Antigone * Electra
Euripides	Tragedy	* Medea * Hippolytus * The Cyclops
Aristophanes	Comedy	* The Clouds * The Birds
Menander	New Comedy	* The Grouch * The Arbitration * The Shorn Girl

Charts assist visual learners in seeing relationships and differences.

OUTLINES

Steps to Successful Speaking   p. 114

I. Select the Topic
  1. What are your talents?
  2. Can you find sufficient materials?
  3. Is the topic appropriate for the audience?
II. Audience Analysis
  1. Conduct demographic study
  2. Use Maslow's Hierarchy of Basic Needs
III. Write a Purpose Statement
  1. What do you want your audience to understand?
  2. What is the main idea of your speech?
IV. Research Your Speech
  1. The Internet
  2. Personal interviews
  3. Electronic or print indexes
  4. Books
  5. Periodicals
V. Organize Your Speech
  1. Spatial organization
  2. Cause-effect
  3. Chronological
  4. Problem solving

Outlines organize information into clusters or under seperate headings.

IT'S NOT OVER UNTIL IT'S OVER

What Is Reading Piece-by-Piece and How Can It Help?

If you are reading material that is completely **new to you**—*difficult to understand* yet important to remember—you may have to disregard paragraphs and paraphrase sections of a paragraph. This can be done with simple "tick marks" in your reading. This can be one of *the* most effective reading tools you will ever learn how to use.

When you get to a point where you have "read enough" and your mind begins to wander, or the information becomes difficult, put a tick mark at that point (see Figure 8.8). Continue reading until you get to another section, putting tick marks in the places where you feel you have read a complete thought. You will not want to read an entire chapter at one time, simply sections, main heading to main heading. After you understand the section, move on to the next, and then the next until the chapter is complete.

When you get to the end of the paragraph or section, reread the first section that you marked off. Out to the side, paraphrase that section. Then go to the next section. Look at the right-hand side of Figure 8.8—there you will find the paraphrased sections.

Few techniques will assist your comprehension and retention more than this one because it requires you to be actively involved in the reading

> "The person who does not read good books has no advantage over those who can't read."
>
> —Mark Twain

Figure 8.8   Tick Mark Reading

A Brief History of Crime in America
(from F. Schmalleger, *Criminal Justice: A Brief Introduction*, 6th Edition. Prentice Hall, 2006.)

1 What we call criminal activity has undoubtedly been with us since the dawn of history, and crime control has long been a primary concern of politicians and government leaders world-wide./ 2 Still, the American experience with crime during the last half century has been especially influential in shaping the criminal justice system of today./

3 In this country, crime waves have come and gone, including an 1850–1880 crime epidemic, which was apparently related to social upheaval caused by large-scale immigration, and the spurt of widespread organized criminal activity associated with the Prohibition years of the early twentieth century./ 4 Following World War II, however, American crime rates remained relatively stable until the 1960s./

5 The 1960s and 1970s saw a burgeoning concern for the rights of ethnic and racial minorities, women, the physically and mentally challenged, and many other groups. The civil rights movement of the period emphasized the equality of opportunity and respect for individuals, regardless of race, color, creed, or personal attributes./ 6 As new laws were passed and suits filed, court involvement in the movement grew. Soon, a plethora of hard-won individual rights and prerogatives, based on the U.S. Constitution, the Bill of Rights, and the new federal and state legislation, were recognized and guaranteed. By the 1980s, the civil rights movement had profoundly affected all areas of social life—from education throughout employment to the activities of the criminal justice system./

1) Criminal activity has been around since the beginning of time and has been a concern to politicians and leaders.

2) Crime in Am. has greatly shaped our criminal justice system in the past 50 years.

3) Crime in Am. has come in waves including the 1850–1880 epidemic due to immigration and a later one due to Prohibition.

4) After WWII, crime in Am. remained stable until the 60s.

5) During the 60s and 70s, Am. saw the rise of individual rights regardless of race, creed, or attributes.

6) Due to laws based on the US Constitution the C.R. Movement profoundly impacted all aspects of life in Am. including the C.J. system.

from ORDINARY to *Extraordinary*

Sylvia Eberhardt, Fashion Model, Abercrombie and Fitch,
Hollister Magazine, and Other Top Agencies
Honor Graduate, Fairfax High School, Fairfax, VA
Honor Student, Howard University, Washington, DC

If you read my resume and look at my professional credits, you might think I had it made, that the world had been handed to me on a silver platter and that I never wanted for anything. Nothing could be further from the truth. Although I am an honor student at Howard University and a fashion model, having worked with some of the top stores and magazines in the nation, my beginnings were anything but easy and beautiful.

I was born into a crack-infested, gang-ridden, one bedroom house in inner city Washington, DC. I was raised a few doors down from a major crack house where I saw junkies, prostitutes, and pimps on a daily basis. It was simply a way of life. Poverty surrounded me and my two siblings at every turn. Unemployment was rampant and the streets were filled with trash and used needles. I slept in a bunk bed where nightly I could hear drug deals being made outside my window. The iron bars on the windows were the only thing that separated me from the ugliness of the world outside my home.

My mother died just before I entered high school and I was raised from that point on by my father. I was constantly teased and tormented growing up because I was so thin. My peers nicknamed me Anna (short for anorexic). What they did not know was that I suffered (and continue to suffer) from Crohn's disease, a life-threatening disability. Crohn's is an autoimmune disease affecting the gastrointestinal system causing rashes, severe abdominal pain, arthritis, vomiting, and weight loss.

How did I survive? How did I become an honors graduate at one of the top high schools in the nation? How did I become a fashion model at the age of fifteen? I am blessed to have an amazing, supportive father who taught me that you never have to let your past or present dictate your future. He believed and taught me that no matter how humble one's beginnings, no matter where you were born or the circumstances of your life, the test of a person's character is knowing that he/she holds his/her destiny in his/her own hands.

He taught me that I had to take responsibility for my own life. I had to be my own savior. Further, he taught my siblings and me that, "you may live in the ghetto, but the ghetto does not have to live in you." He always told us that you do not have to think and act poor simply because you live in a lower-class neighborhood. He also taught us that in order to enjoy the finer things in life, you first have to experience hard times. He would say to us, "you have to ride in an old, ragged car before you can appreciate a Mercedes." His attitude helped guide and change my life.

After we moved to Virginia, I began working hard and taking college-level classes at Northern Virginia Community College while still in high school. My dream is to become a heart surgeon. I knew from the very beginning that I would have to study hard and give up many things I enjoyed doing. It paid off, however. By the end of my senior year in high school, I had over 30 college credits in math, science, anatomy, microbiology, calculus, and physiology with a 4.0 grade point average. I won a full scholarship to Howard University and finished my first semester with a 3.92 GPA.

> *My father taught me, "you may live in the ghetto, but the ghetto does not have to live in you."*

I write all of this to you to say, "Your life is what you make of it. You can let your past and present dictate and ruin your future, or you can get over it, work hard, believe in yourself, push yourself, and work toward your dreams." I wish you so much good luck and good fortune in your future.

EXTRAORDINARY REFLECTION

Sylvia mentioned that her father would say to her, "in order to enjoy the finer things in life, you first have to experience hard times. You have to ride in an old, ragged car before you can appreciate a Mercedes." How do you plan to use your past experiences, positive or negative, to bring about positive change in your future?

process. You are reading, paraphrasing, clarifying, and looking up words you do not know. This process is essential if your reading comprehension is not at the college level.

Recite

Recitation is simple, but crucial. Skipping this step may result in less than full mastery of the chapter. Once you have read a section using one or more of the techniques from above, ask yourself this simple question: *"What was that all about?"* Find a classmate, sit down together, and ask questions of each other. Discuss with each other the main points of the chapter. Try to explain the information to each other without looking at your notes. If you are at home, sit back in your chair, recite the information, and determine what it means. If you have trouble explaining the information to your friend or reciting it to yourself, you probably did not understand the section and you should go back and re-read it. If you can tell your classmate and yourself exactly what you just read and what it means, you are ready to move on to the next section of the chapter.

Another way to practice reciting is to use the materials you produced as you read the chapter. Hopefully, you took notes, highlighted passages, underlined phrases, and paraphrased sections. From these, you can create flashcards, outlines, mind maps, timelines, and key word notecards. Using these materials is another way to "recite" the material.

Review

After you have read the chapter, immediately go back and read it again. **"What?! I just read it!"** Yes, you did. And the best way to determine whether you have mastered the information is to once again survey the chapter; review marginal notes, highlighted areas, and vocabulary words; and determine whether you can answer the questions you posed the during the Question step of SQ3R. This step will help you store and retain this information in long-term memory.

CHANGING IDEAS to Reality

REFLECTIONS ON READING AND COMPREHENSION

SQ3R can be a lifesaver when it comes to understanding material that is overwhelming. It is an efficient, comprehensive, and *doable* practice that can dramatically assist you in your reading efforts. It may take more time than your old method, but you will begin to see the results almost immediately. Seriously considering and practicing the strategies outlined in this chapter will help increase your comprehension level, and it will also increase your ability to recall the information when you need it later on.

It has been suggested that if you can effectively read, write, and speak the English language, there is nothing that you can't accomplish. The power of knowledge is monumental in your quest to become a productive and active citizen. Effective reading skills will help you acquire that knowledge.

As you continue to work to become an active, engaged learner, consider the following tips for reading comprehension and retention:

- Approach the text, chapter, or article with an *open mind.*
- *Free your mind* to focus on your reading.
- Underline and look up words you do not *understand.*
- Write down your *vocabulary words* and review them often.
- Use *SQ3R* to increase and test your comprehension.
- If you're having trouble, *get a tutor* to help you.
- Understand that *the more you read,* the better reader you will become.

Knowledge
in Bloom

READING FOR COMPREHENSION

Utilizes Levels 1, 2, 3, 4, 5, and 6 of the Taxonomy (See Bloom's Taxonomy at the front of this text)

Directions: Read the following story carefully, looking up words that you do not understand, highlighting phrases that you think are important, and paraphrasing in the spaces provided. When reading the story, use the SQ3R method. We've done paragraph #1 for you as an example.

THE LIFE AND DEATH OF HARVEY MILK

Read this section, identify unfamiliar words, highlight important words and phrases	Look up words that need to be defined	Paraphrase the main idea in your own words
More <u>perplexing</u> things have happened, but a Twinkie caused the death of Harvey Milk. That's right. In 1978, defense lawyers, using the "Twinkie Defense," explained an <u>inexplicable</u> murder away. This was the first mainstream trial to use the, "I am not responsible for my actions" defense.	Unfamiliar words and definitions: _Perplexing_ = confusing or puzzling _Inexplicable_ = not easily explained, unreasonable	Paraphrase the main idea of this paragraph: _In 1978, defense lawyers used a new strategy called "the Twinkie Defense" to explain why someone murdered Harvey Milk._
Harvey Milk was the first openly gay man elected to a significant office in America. In 1977, Milk was elected as a member of the San Francisco Board of Supervisors. This was quite arduous at this point in American history when most people, including many psychologists and religious leaders, still classified homosexuality as deviant and a mental illness.	Unfamiliar words and definitions:	Paraphrase the main idea of this paragraph:
Harvey Milk is to the Gay Rights Movement what Medgar Evers and Martin Luther King, Jr. were to the Civil Rights Movement. Before Evers and King, little was happening with the CRM, and before Milk, little was happening with the GRM. He changed the face of California politics and paved the way for countless other gays and lesbians to enter the world of politics.	Unfamiliar words and definitions:	Paraphrase the main idea of this paragraph:

	Unfamiliar words and definitions:	Paraphrase the main idea of this paragraph:
Dan White, a staunch anti-gay advocate, served on the board with Milk. They were constantly at odds with each other and often engaged in verbal confrontations.	Unfamiliar words and definitions:	Paraphrase the main idea of this paragraph:
White had been a policeman and a fireman in San Francisco before running for office. While running for office, he vowed to restore "family values" to the city government. He vowed to "rid San Francisco of radicals, social deviants, and incorrigibles."	Unfamiliar words and definitions:	Paraphrase the main idea of this paragraph:
Dan White was one of the most conservative members of the board, and many proposals brought to the board by Milk and the mayor of San Francisco, George Moscone, were defeated because of the heavily conservative vote led by White.	Unfamiliar words and definitions:	Paraphrase the main idea of this paragraph:
At that time, the Board of Supervisors was made up of eleven members; six of them, including Dan White, were conservative and had the power to defeat most, if not all, of the liberal measures brought before the board. This did not fare well with Harvey Milk and the other liberal members of the board.	Unfamiliar words and definitions:	Paraphrase the main idea of this paragraph:
Because the job offered diminutive wages, Dan White soon realized that he could not support his family on $9,800 per year, and he submitted his resignation to Mayor Moscone. This did not set well with the people who elected him. They urged him to reconsider and when he tried to rescind his resignation, Mayor Moscone refused. This decision was made, in part, because Harvey Milk convinced Moscone to deny his reinstatement.	Unfamiliar words and definitions:	Paraphrase the main idea of this paragraph:

In a fit of wrath over the decision, Dan White entered the San Francisco City Hall on the morning of November 27, 1978, through a basement window. He went to Mayor Moscone's office and shot him in the chest, and as he lay dying, shot him again in the head.	Unfamiliar words and definitions:	Paraphrase the main idea of this paragraph:
He then walked calmly down the hall and asked to see Harvey Milk. Once inside the office, he slew Milk with two bullets to the brain. He then left City Hall, called his wife, spoke with her in person at St. Mary's Cathedral, and then turned himself in.	Unfamiliar words and definitions:	Paraphrase the main idea of this paragraph:
It is reported that policemen representing the city of San Francisco shouted, cheered, and applauded when news of the murders reached the police department.	Unfamiliar words and definitions:	Paraphrase the main idea of this paragraph:
Dan White's defense lawyers used a "diminished capacity" defense, suggesting that he was led to his actions by too much sugar from junk food. The lawyers convinced a jury that he was not himself and his senses were off-kilter. This became known as the "Twinkie Defense."	Unfamiliar words and definitions:	Paraphrase the main idea of this paragraph:
Dan White was convicted of second-degree manslaughter and was sentenced to only seven years for two premeditated murders. After serving only five years, he was released. The "Twinkie Defense" had worked.	Unfamiliar words and definitions:	Paraphrase the main idea of this paragraph:

In 1985, after being released from Soledad Prison, Dan White walked into his garage, took a rubber hose, connected it to his car's exhaust, and killed himself with carbon monoxide poisoning. He was 39 years old. His tomb reads, "*Daniel J. White (1946–October 21, 1985), Sgt. U S. Army, Vietnam. Cause of death: Suicide.*"	Unfamiliar words and definitions:	Paraphrase the main idea of this paragraph:

In 100 words or fewer, thoroughly summarize this entire article. Be certain to include dates, names, places, and circumstances. Pretend that you have to explain this entire story to someone who has never heard the facts. This exercise will help you become more adept at the *essential cornerstone* skill of *knowledge*.

_____
_____
_____
_____
_____
_____
_____
_____
_____
_____
_____
_____
_____
_____
_____
_____
_____
_____
_____
_____

Find three web sites where you can learn more about this story. List them here.

_____
_____
_____
_____
_____
_____
_____

Sources: "He Got Away with Murder" at www.findagrave.com; "The Pioneer Harvey Milk" at www.time.com; "Remembering Harvey Milk" at www.lambda.net.

SQ3R MASTERY STUDY SHEET

EXAMPLE QUESTION(FROM PAGE 186) Describe the process of fixation.	**ANSWER:**
EXAMPLE QUESTION (FROM PAGE 186) Why is comprehension more important than speed?	**ANSWER:**
AUTHOR QUESTION (FROM PAGE 181) Differentiate between passive and active reading.	**ANSWER:**
AUTHOR QUESTION (FROM PAGE 187) Discuss three strategies for reading online material.	**ANSWER:**
AUTHOR QUESTION (FROM PAGE 193) What are some of the effective ways of taking notes while reading?	**ANSWER:**
AUTHOR QUESTION (FROM PAGE 194) How can you use tick marks to help you improve your reading ability?	**ANSWER:**
AUTHOR QUESTION (FROM PAGE 196) Why is recitation an important part of reading comprehension?	**ANSWER:**
YOUR QUESTION (FROM PAGE ____)	**ANSWER:**
YOUR QUESTION (FROM PAGE ____)	**ANSWER:**
YOUR QUESTION (FROM PAGE ____)	**ANSWER:**
YOUR QUESTION (FROM PAGE ____)	**ANSWER:**
YOUR QUESTION (FROM PAGE ____)	**ANSWER:**

Finally, after answering these questions, recite this chapter's major points in your mind. Consider the following general questions to help you master this material.

- What is it about?
- What does it mean?
- What is the most important thing you learned? Why?
- What are the key points to remember?

chapter nine

RECORD

CULTIVATING YOUR LISTENING SKILLS AND DEVELOPING A NOTE-TAKING SYSTEM THAT WORKS FOR YOU

"To listen well is as powerful a means of communication as to talk well." — Chinese Proverb

RECORD

Scan and QUESTION

Take a few moments, **scan this chapter** and on page 224, write **five questions** that you think will be important to your mastery of this material. In addition to the two questions below, you will also find five questions from your authors.

Example:

☑ **What are the four components of the character for the Chinese verb, "to listen?"** (from page 207)

☑ **Why is it important to identify key words during a lecture?** (from page 211)

Why read this chapter?

Because you'll learn...

- The difference between listening and hearing
- How to overcome the obstacles to listening
- The importance of note-taking

Because you'll be able to...

- Use the L-STAR note-taking system
- Apply the outline, Cornell, and mapping note-taking systems
- Determine which note-taking style works best for certain classes

MyStudentSuccessLab

MyStudentSuccessLab is an online solution designed to help you acquire and develop (or hone) the skills you need to succeed. You will have access to peer-led video presentations and develop core skills through interactive exercises and projects.

Name: Patricia G. Moody, Ph.D.

Institution: Georgia Southern University and The University of South Carolina

Major: Business and Educational Administration

I am the daughter of a peanut farmer and a housewife, and a first-generation college student who grew up in rural South Georgia. My mother graduated from high school, but my father only had a fifth-grade education. My father was the oldest of five children and had to quit school and go to work when his father died of influenza. He often said, "I am a farmer because I can't be anything else." My parents worked extremely hard to provide a good life for my brothers and me, to purchase their farmland, and to send us all to college.

Because they were undereducated and understood the importance of education, they not only encouraged my brothers and me to do well in school, they expected it. My father often told us, "Get yourself a good education!" We were expected to excel in academics and athletics, and we all did. My parents also expected us to have a good work ethic and to be good people with high personal standards. We were never to even think about giving up or ending up in second place! Most likely, my father's lessons were aimed directly at my two brothers, but I was listening, too, and I hung on every word.

Ironically, when I graduated from high school as the salutatorian of my class, star of the basketball team, president of the Senior class, and a member of the debate team, I was offered no academic or athletic scholarships because those awards went primarily to young men. It never occurred to me or other women to question this at the time, because "that was just the way it was."

Nevertheless, I knew I wanted to go to college because I loved learning. My older brother had gone to college, so he paved the way for me. I wanted more even though I had no idea what "more" was.

I had no idea what college was all about when my parents dropped me off at Georgia Southern University that Sunday afternoon, about five hours from my home. I didn't know how to register, how to choose a major, what a major was, or what three credit hours meant. This was a new world for me, and I was frightened of all the changes I was facing. Classes were much harder than high school, and I was no longer a star at anything, so I struggled with everything. I only knew a few people, and I was very homesick. Botany was the hardest course I had ever taken—still is—but I managed to pass. Because I "dug in," worked hard, and graduated from college, many wonderful opportunities came my way.

High school teachers, college professors, and the overall college experience changed my life. I often wonder what I might have done with my life if I had chosen not to go to college; most likely I would have stayed in South Georgia. Although this is a wonderful part of the country, had I not left and gone to college, I would have never had the great opportunities because of the doors education opened for me.

After teaching in high school for seven years, I moved with my family to Columbia, South Carolina, where my husband worked with General Motors. On a whim, I decided to enroll in two courses at the University of South Carolina to renew my certificate. I was offered a graduate assistantship to supervise student teachers, and then I was offered an instructor's position. After earning two Masters degrees, I pursued a Ph.D. and upon graduation, I was fortunate to have the opportunity of being placed in a tenure track. Over the next few years, I became a tenured professor, a department chair, and, ultimately, Dean of my college at the University of South Carolina.

The advice I offer anyone today is this: "Many doors will open for you if you get a good education and work hard and pay the price—but you have to walk through the door; in other words, you have to take risks." I have been richly blessed because I heeded my father's advice: "Get yourself a good education!" I am grateful for the opportunities and struggles that came my way through the college experience. Because I have a good education, I have been able to travel all over the country speaking to over 100,000 people; I have authored and co-authored over 30 books; and from China to Africa to Ireland to Switzerland, I have traveled all over the world. So I say to you, as my father said to me, "Get yourself a good education!" College will change your world!

1. Patricia refers to the high expectations her parents had for her and her brothers. How do you think this influenced her accomplishments? Who has high expectations for you? What if you were the only one who had high expectations for yourself?

2. Patricia had many doors opened to her—the opportunity to teach in college, to speak in over 40 states, and to travel all over the world. What opportunities do you expect college to offer you?

THE IMPORTANCE OF LISTENING

Why Does Listening Really Matter in Classes and Relationships?

Listening is a survival skill. Period! It is that simple! *"I know listening is important,"* you might say, but few ever think of the paramount significance listening has on our everyday lives. It is necessary for:

- establishing and improving relationships
- personal growth
- showing respect to others
- professional rapport
- showing empathy and compassion
- learning new information
- understanding others' opinions and views
- basic survival
- entertainment
- health

How can becoming a critical listener help you in and out of the classroom?

How much time do you think you spend listening every day? Research suggests that we spend almost 70 percent of our waking time communicating, and **53 percent of that time is spent in listening situations** (Adler, Rosenfeld, and Proctor, 2009). Effective listening skills can mean the difference between success or failure, A's or F's, relationships or loneliness, and in some cases and careers, life or death.

For students, good listening skills are critical. Over the next four years, you will be given a lot of information through lectures. Cultivating and improving your active listening skills will help you to understand the material, take accurate notes, participate in class discussions, communicate with your peers more effectively, and become more actively engaged in your learning process.

I THINK I HEARD YOU LISTENING

Is There Really a Difference Between Listening and Hearing?

No doubt you've been in a communication situation where a misunderstanding took place. Either you hear something incorrectly or someone hears you incorrectly *or* it could be that someone hears your message but misinterprets it. These communication blunders arise because we tend to view listening (and communication in general) as an automatic response, when in fact it is not.

Listening is a learned, voluntary activity. You must choose to do it. It is a skill, just as driving a car, painting a picture, or playing the piano. Becoming an active listener requires practice, time, mistakes, guidance, and active participation.

Hearing, however, is not learned; it is automatic and involuntary. If you are within range of a sound you will probably hear it, although you may not be listening to it. Hearing a sound does not guarantee that you know what it is, or from where it came. Listening actively, though, means making a conscious effort to focus on the sound you heard and to determine what it is.

> *"You cannot truly listen to anyone and do anything else at the same time."*
> —M. Scott Peck

LISTENING DEFINED

According to Ronald Adler (Adler et al., 2010), the drawing of the Chinese verb "to listen" (Figure 9.1) provides a comprehensive and practical definition of listening.

To the Chinese, listening involves the *ears,* the *eyes,* your *undivided attention,* and the *heart.* Do you make it a habit to listen with more than your ears? The Chinese view listening as a whole-body experience. People from Western cultures seem to have lost the ability to involve their whole body in the listening process. We tend to use only our ears, and sometimes we don't even use them very well.

At its core, listening is "the ability to hear, understand, analyze, respect, and appropriately respond to the meaning of another person's spoken and nonverbal messages" (Daly & Engleberg, 2006). Although this definition involves the word "hear," listening goes far beyond just the physical ability to catch sound waves.

The first step in listening *is* hearing, but true listening involves one's full attention and the ability to filter out distractions, emotional barriers, cultural differences, and religious biases. Listening means that you are making a conscious decision to understand and show reverence for the other person's communication efforts.

Listening needs to be personalized and internalized. To understand listening as a whole-body experience, we can define it on three levels:

1. Listening with a **purpose**
2. Listening **objectively**
3. Listening **constructively**

Successful Decisions
AN ACTIVITY FOR CRITICAL REFLECTION

Jennifer greatly disliked her biology instructor. She could not put her finger on just *why* she disliked her, but she just knew that Dr. Lipmon rubbed her the wrong way. This had been the case since the first day of class.

Other students seemed to like her and were able to carry on conversations with her, but not Jennifer. "Why?" she thought. "Why do I dislike her so much? She's not a bad teacher," she reasoned, "but I just can't stand to listen to her."

Jennifer decided to sit back for the next week and really try to figure out what the main problem was. As she sat in class and listened, she figured it out. She finally put her finger on the problem: she and Dr. Lipmon had completely different views on many things, including evolution and a woman's reproductive rights.

Every time Dr. Lipmon made a statement contrary to Jennifer's core beliefs, she cringed. She "shut down" and refused to listen any further. She transferred her dislike of Dr. Lipmon's lectures and opinions onto her as a person. She knew this was affecting her grade and her knowledge base in class, but did not know how to manage or change the situation.

In your own words, what would you suggest that Jennifer do at this point? Pretend that she is enrolled at your institution. List at least five things that she could do to ensure her success. Think about what services are offered and what people might be of assistance to her.

1. _____
2. _____
3. _____
4. _____
5. _____

Figure 9.1 Chinese Verb "To Listen"

Listening with a purpose suggests a need to recognize different types of listening situations—for example, class, worship, entertainment, and relationships. People do not listen the same way in every situation.

Listening objectively means listening with an open mind. You will give yourself few greater gifts than the gift of knowing how to listen without bias and prejudice. This is perhaps the most difficult aspect of listening. If you have been cut off in mid-conversation or mid-sentence by someone who disagreed with you, or if someone has left the room while you were giving your opinion of a situation, you have had the experience of talking to people who do not know how to listen objectively.

Listening constructively means listening with the attitude of asking "How can this be helpful to my life, my education, my career, or my finances?" This type of listening involves evaluating the information you are hearing and determining whether it has meaning to your life. Sound easy? It is more difficult than it sounds because, again, we all tend to shut out information that we do not view as immediately helpful or useful. To listen constructively, you need to know how to listen and store information for later.

FOUR LISTENING STYLES DEFINED

What Is Your Orientation?

According to Steven McCornack (2007), interpersonal communication expert, author, and educator, there are *four different listening styles*: action-oriented, time-oriented, people-oriented, and content-oriented. Study Figure 9.2 to determine which best describes you as a listener.

Figure 9.2 **Four Listening Styles**

Action-Oriented Listeners:

- want to get their messages quickly and to-the-point
- do not like fluff and grow impatient when they perceive people to be "wasting their time"
- become frustrated when information is not orderly
- are quick to dismiss people who "ramble" and falter when they speak

Time-Oriented Listeners:

- want their information in brief, concise meetings
- are consumed with how much time is taken to convey a message
- set time limits for listening (and communicating in general)
- will ask people to "move the message along" if they feel it is taking too long

People-Oriented Listeners:

- are in contrast to time- and action-oriented listeners
- view listening as a chance to connect with other people
- enjoy listening to people so that relationships can be built
- become emotionally involved with the person communicating

Content-Oriented Listeners:

- enjoy an intellectual challenge
- like to listen to technical information, facts, and evidence
- enjoy complex information that must be deciphered and filtered
- carefully evaluate information and facts before forming an opinion
- enjoy asking questions

Which style best describes you? _____

What are the "pros" of being this type of listener? _____

_____

_____

_____

Level 1 Remember

What are the "cons" of being this type of listener? _____

_____

_____

_____

LISTENING CAN BE SO HARD

Can the Obstacles to Listening Be Overcome?

Several major obstacles stand in the way of becoming an effective listener. To begin building active listening skills, you first have to remove some barriers.

Obstacle One: Prejudging

Prejudging means that you automatically shut out what is being said, and it is one of the biggest obstacles to active listening. You may prejudge because you don't like or agree with the information or the person communicating. You may also have prejudging problems because of your environment, culture, social status, or attitude.

Do You Prejudge Information or Its Source?

Answer yes or no to the following questions:

1. I tune out when something is boring.	Yes	No
2. I tune out when I do not agree with the information.	Yes	No
3. I argue mentally with the speaker about information.	Yes	No
4. I do not listen to people I do not like.	Yes	No
5. I make decisions about information before I understand all of its implications or consequences.	Yes	No

If you answered yes to two or more of these questions, you tend to prejudge in a listening situation.

Tips for Overcoming Prejudging

- Listen for information that may be valuable to you as a student. Some material may not be pleasant to hear but may be useful to you later on.
- Listen to the message, not the messenger. If you do not like the speaker, try to go beyond personality and listen to what is being said, without regard to the person saying it.

Conversely, you may like the speaker so much that you automatically accept the material or answers without listening objectively to what is being said.

- Try to remove cultural, racial, gender, social, and environmental barriers. Just because a person is different from you or holds a different point of view does not make that person wrong; and just because a person is like you and holds a similar point of view does not make that person right. Sometimes, you have to cross cultural and environmental barriers to learn new material and see with brighter eyes

Obstacle Two: Talking

Not even the best listener in the world can listen while he or she is talking. The next time you are in a conversation with a friend, try speaking while your friend is speaking—then see if you know what your friend said. To become an effective listener, you need to learn the power of silence. Silence gives you the opportunity to think about what is being said before you respond. The first rule of listening is: stop talking. The second rule of listening is: stop talking. And you guessed it—the third rule of listening is: stop talking.

Are You a Talker Rather Than a Listener?

Answer yes or no to the following questions:

1. I often interrupt the speaker so that I can say what I want.		Yes	No
2. I am thinking of my next statement while others are talking.		Yes	No
3. My mind wanders when others talk.		Yes	No
4. I answer my own questions.		Yes	No
5. I answer questions that are asked of other people.		Yes	No

If you answered yes to two or more questions, you tend to talk too much in a listening situation

Tips for Overcoming the Urge to Talk Too Much

- Avoid interrupting the speaker. Force yourself to be silent at parties, family gatherings, and friendly get-togethers. You should not be unsociable, but force yourself to be silent for 10 minutes. You'll be surprised at what you hear. You may also be surprised how hard it is to do this. Test yourself.
- Ask someone a question and then allow that person to answer the question.
- Too often we ask questions and answer them ourselves. Force yourself to wait until the person has formulated a response. If you ask questions and wait for answers, you will force yourself to listen.
- Concentrate on what is being said at the moment, not what you want to say next.

Obstacle Three: Becoming Too Emotional

Emotions can form a strong barrier to active listening. Worries, problems, fears, and anger can keep you from listening to the greatest advantage. Have you ever sat in a lecture, and before you knew what was happening your mind was a million miles away because you were angry or worried about something? If you have, you know what it's like to bring your emotions to the table.

Do You Bring Your Emotions to the Listening Situation?

Answer yes or no to the following questions:

1. I get angry before I hear the whole story.	Yes	No
2. I look for underlying or hidden messages in information.	Yes	No
3. Sometimes, I begin listening on a negative note.	Yes	No
4. I base my opinions of information on what others are saying or doing.	Yes	No
5. I readily accept information as correct from people whom I like or respect.	Yes	No

If you answered yes to two or more of these questions, you tend to bring your emotions to a listening situation.

Tips for Overcoming Emotions

- Know how you feel before you begin the listening experience. Take stock of your emotions and feelings ahead of time.
- Focus on the message; determine how to use the information.
- Create a positive image about the message you are hearing.
- Avoid overreacting and jumping to conclusions.

LISTENING FOR KEY WORDS, PHRASES, AND HINTS

Do Professors Really Offer Test Clues in Their Lectures?

Learning how to listen for key words, phrases, and hints can help you become an active listener and an effective note-taker. For example, if your English instructor begins a lecture saying, "There are 10 basic elements to writing poetry," jot down the number 10 under the heading "Poetry" or number your notebook page 1 through 10, leaving space for notes. If at the end of class you listed six elements to writing poetry, you know that you missed a part of the lecture. At this point, you need to ask the instructor some questions.

Here are some key phrases and words to listen for:

in addition to	another way	above all
most important	such as	specifically
you'll see this again	therefore	finally
for example	to illustrate	as stated earlier
in contrast	in comparison	nevertheless
the characteristics of	the main issue is	moreover
on the other hand	as a result of	because

Do you find it easy or hard to pick up the clues a professor gives in class that may indicate important test information?

THE INTERNATIONALLY famous performer **Lady Gaga** states that she was very studious and disciplined when attending a private, all-girls, Roman Catholic school, The Convent of the Sacred Heart. Gaga was the daughter of a hard-working, lower-class family. She described herself as "insecure" and shares that she was made fun of by her classmates. She said she never fit in and felt that she was a freak. Even then singing topped her list of important things in her life.

Gaga loved music from an early age, writing her first song at age 13. She had lead roles in high school productions. After high school, she attended a musical theatre conservatory at New York University's Tisch School of the Arts. She withdrew from school during her second semester to focus on her musical career. Her father agreed to pay her rent for one year if she agreed to re-enroll at Tisch if she was not successfully established in her career. She struggled to pay her bills and buy groceries.

Gaga was signed to Def Jam in September 2006 only to be dropped by the label after three months. She was devastated and returned to her family's home, where she began experimenting with go-go dancing and burlesque outfits, as well as experimenting with drugs, to her family's dismay. She later moved away from drugs, still concentrating on her music. In 2009, *Just Dance*, her lead single on a new album hit the international charts. Her song, *Poker Face*, followed and earned her Best Dance Recording at the 52nd Grammy Awards. Since then, Gaga has become an internationally famous performer and recording artist who is known for her bizarre outfits and great talent.

Picking up on *transition words* such as these will help you filter out less important information and thus listen more carefully to what is most important. There are other indicators of important information, too. You will want to listen carefully when the instructor:

- Writes something on the board
- Uses a PowerPoint presentation
- Uses computer-aided graphics
- Speaks in a louder tone or changes vocal patterns
- Uses gestures more than usual
- Uses any visual aids

TAKING EFFECTIVE NOTES

Is It Just a Big, Crazy Chore?

Go to class, listen, and write it down. Read a text and take notes. Watch a film and write down a summary of what you saw. Is it really that important? Actually, knowing how to take useful, accurate notes can dramatically improve your life as a student. If you are an effective listener and note-taker, you have two of the most valuable skills any student could ever use. There are several reasons why it is important to take notes:

- You become an active part of the listening process.
- You create a history of your course content when you take notes.
- You have written criteria to follow when studying.
- You create a visual aid for your material.
- Studying becomes much easier.
- You retain information at a greater rate than non-note-takers.
- Effective note-takers average higher grades than non-note-takers (Kiewra & Fletcher, 1984).

TIPS FOR EFFECTIVE NOTE-TAKING

Can You Write It Right?

You have already learned several skills you will need to take notes, such as cultivating your active listening skills, overcoming obstacles to effective listening, and familiarizing yourself with key phrases used by instructors. Next, prepare yourself mentally and physically to take effective notes that are going to be helpful to you. Consider the following ideas as you think about expanding your note-taking abilities.

- **Physically and mentally attend class**. This refers to in the classroom and online instruction. This may sound like stating the obvious, but it is surprising how many students feel they do not need to do anything to learn.
- **Come to class prepared**. Scan, read, and use your textbook to establish a basic understanding of the material before coming to class It is always easier to take notes when

you have a preliminary understanding of what is being said. Coming to class prepared also means bringing the proper materials for taking notes: lab manuals, pens, a notebook, highlighter, computer, or tablet.

- **Bring your textbook** to class. Although many students think they do not need to bring their textbooks to class if they have read the homework, you will find that many instructors repeatedly refer to the text while lecturing. The instructor may ask you to highlight, underline, or refer to the text in class, and following along in the text as the instructor lectures may also help you organize your notes.

- **Ask questions** and participate in class. Two of the most critical actions you can perform in class are to ask questions and to participate in the class discussion. If you do not understand a concept or theory, ask questions. Don't leave class without understanding what has happened and assume you'll pick it up on your own.

How can good listening and effective note taking skills help you learn and retain material?

YOU'LL BE SEEING STARS

What Is The L-STAR System and How Can It Be Used?

One of the most effective ways to take notes begins with the **L-STAR system,** outlined in Figure 9.3.

This five-step system will enable you to compile complete, accurate, and visual notes for future reference. Along with improving your note-taking skills, using this system will enhance your ability to participate in class, help other students, study more effectively, and perform well on exams and quizzes.

L—Listening

One of the best ways to become an effective note-taker is to become an active listener. A concrete step you can take toward becoming an active listener in class is to sit near the front of the room, where you can hear the instructor and see the board and overheads. Choose a spot that

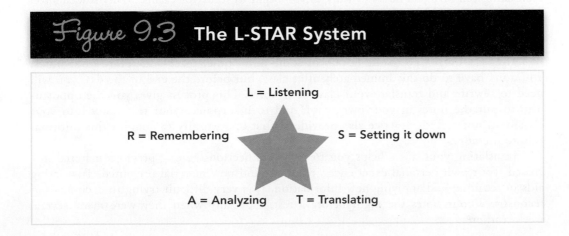

Figure 9.3 **The L-STAR System**

L = Listening

R = Remembering   S = Setting it down

A = Analyzing   T = Translating

allows you to see the instructor's mouth and facial expressions. If you see that the instructor's face has become animated or expressive, you can bet that you are hearing important information. Write it down. If you sit in the back of the room, you may miss out on these important clues. If you are listening to an instructor who is online, be certain to take notes, jot down questions for later, and participate as often as allowed.

S—Setting It Down

The actual writing of notes can be a difficult task. Some instructors are organized in their delivery of information; others are not. Some stick to an easy-to-follow outline and others ramble around, making it more difficult to follow them and take notes. Your listening skills, once again, are going to play an important role in determining what needs to be written down. In most cases, you will not have time to take notes verbatim. Some instructors talk very fast. You will have to be selective about the information you choose to set down. One of the best ways to keep up with the information being presented is to develop a shorthand system of your own. Many of the symbols you use will be universal, but you may use some symbols, pictures, and markings that are uniquely your own. Some of the more common symbols are:

w/	with	w/o	without
=	equals	≠	does not equal
<	less than	>	greater than
%	percentage	#	number
&	and	∧	increase
+	plus or addition	–	minus or subtraction
*	important	etc.	and so on
e.g.	for example	vs	against or as compared to
esp	especially	"	quote
?	question	…	and so on

These symbols can save you valuable time when taking notes. Because you will use them frequently, it might be a good idea to memorize them.

T—Translating

Translating can save you hours of work as you begin to study for exams. Many students feel that this step is not important, or too time-consuming, and leave it out. Don't. Often, students take notes so quickly that they make mistakes or use abbreviations that they may not be able to decipher later.

After each class, go to the library or some other quiet place and review your notes. You don't have to do this immediately after class, but before the end of the day, you will need to rewrite and translate your classroom notes. This process gives you the opportunity to put the notes in your own words and to incorporate your text notes into your classroom notes. This practice also provides a first opportunity to commit this information to memory.

Translating your notes helps you to make connections among previous material discussed, your own personal experiences, readings, and new material presented. Translating aids in recalling and applying new information. It is very difficult trying to decipher and reconstruct your notes the night before a test, especially when they were made several weeks earlier.

A—Analyzing

This step takes place while you translate your notes from class. When you analyze your notes, you are asking two basic questions: (1) What does this mean? and (2) Why is it important? If you can answer these two questions about your material, you have almost mastered the information. Though some instructors will want you to spit back the exact same information you were given, others will ask you for a more detailed understanding and a synthesis of the material. When you are translating your notes, begin to answer these two questions using your notes, textbook, supplemental materials, and information gathered from outside research. Once again, this process is not simple or quick, but testing your understanding of the material is important. Remember that many lectures are built on past lectures. If you do not understand what happened in class on September 17, you may not be able to understand what happens on September 19. Analyzing your notes while translating them will give you a more complete understanding of the material. Asking questions using Blooms Taxonomy can greatly assist you, too.

R—Remembering

Once you have listened to the lecture, set your notes on paper, and translated and analyzed the material, it is time to study, or remember, the information. Some effective ways to remember information include creating a visual picture, speaking the notes out loud, using mnemonic devices, and finding a study partner.

THREE COMMON NOTE-TAKING SYSTEMS

Why Doesn't Everyone Listen and Take Notes the Same Way?

There are three common note-taking systems: (1) the **outline** technique; (2) the **Cornell,** or split-page technique (also called the T system); and (3) the **mapping** technique.

THE OUTLINE TECHNIQUE

Is It As Simple As A, B, C—1, 2, 3?

The outline system uses a series of major headings and multiple subheadings formatted in hierarchical order (see Figure 9.4). The outline technique is one of the most commonly used note-taking systems, yet it is also one of the most misused systems. It can be difficult to outline notes in class, especially if your instructor does not follow an outline while lecturing.

When using the outline system, it is best to get all the information from the lecture, and then to combine your lecture notes and text notes to create an outline afterward. Most instructors would advise against using the outline system of note-taking in class, although you may be able to use a modified version. The most important thing to remember is not to get bogged down in a system during class; what is critical is getting the ideas down on paper. You can always go back after class and rearrange your notes as needed.

If you are going to use a modified or informal outline while taking notes in class, you may want to consider grouping information together under a heading as a means of outlining. It is easier to remember information that is logically grouped than to remember information that is scattered across several pages. If your study skills lecture is on listening, you might outline your notes using the headings "The Process of Listening" and "Definitions of Listening."

After you have rewritten your notes using class lecture information and material from your textbook, your notes may look like those in Figure 9.4.

Figure 9.4   The Outline Technique

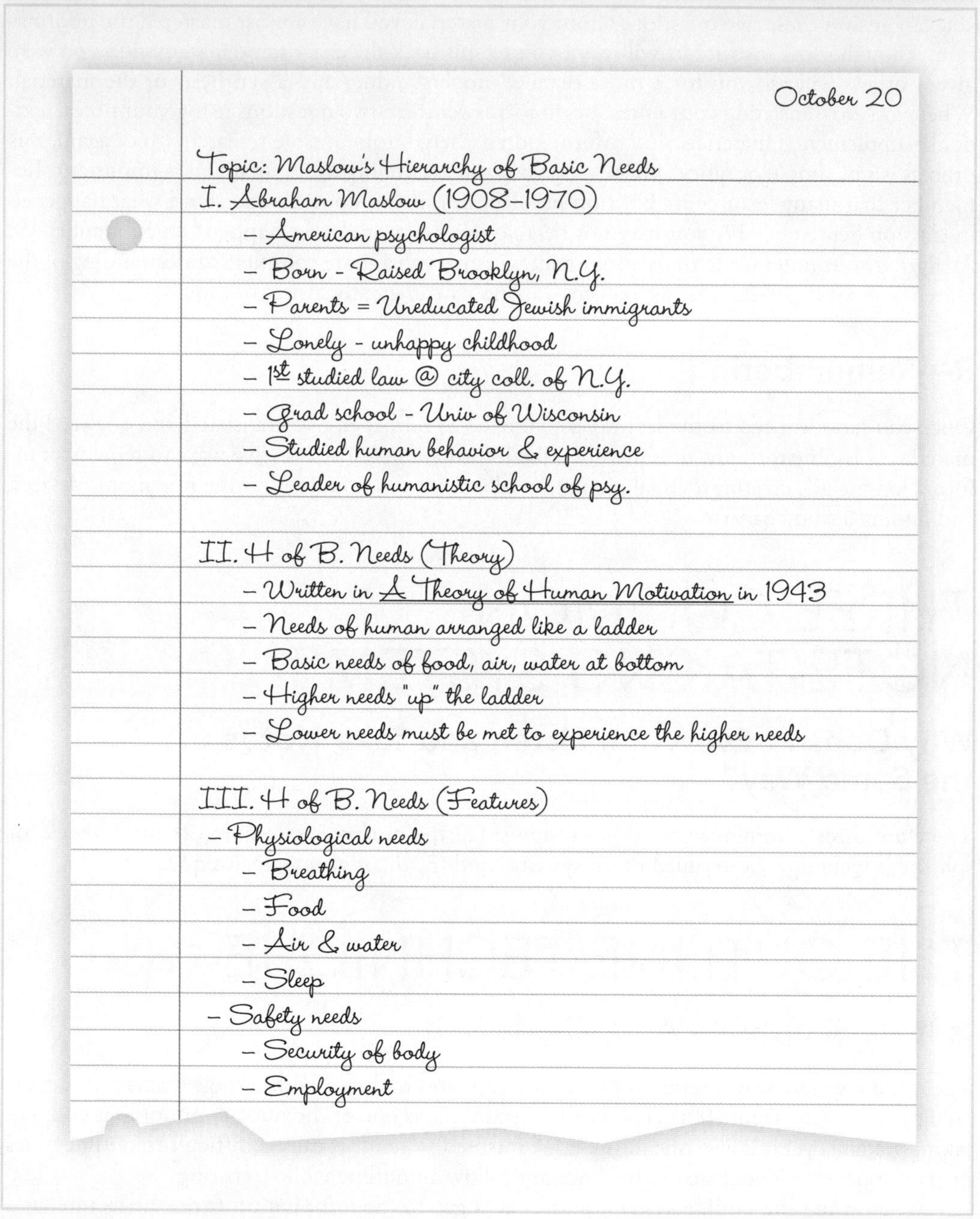

October 20

Topic: Maslow's Hierarchy of Basic Needs
I. Abraham Maslow (1908–1970)
   - American psychologist
   - Born - Raised Brooklyn, N.Y.
   - Parents = Uneducated Jewish immigrants
   - Lonely - unhappy childhood
   - 1st studied law @ city coll. of N.Y.
   - Grad school - Univ of Wisconsin
   - Studied human behavior & experience
   - Leader of humanistic school of psy.

II. H of B. Needs (Theory)
   - Written in A Theory of Human Motivation in 1943
   - Needs of human arranged like a ladder
   - Basic needs of food, air, water at bottom
   - Higher needs "up" the ladder
   - Lower needs must be met to experience the higher needs

III. H of B. Needs (Features)
   - Physiological needs
      - Breathing
      - Food
      - Air & water
      - Sleep
   - Safety needs
      - Security of body
      - Employment

THE CORNELL SYSTEM

Is It A Split Decision?

The basic principle of the Cornell system, developed by Dr. Walter Pauk of Cornell University, is to split the page of your notebook into two columns. Column A is to be used for major headings or questions and section B is to be used for actual notes from the class, text, or online readings. See Figure 9.5 for an example of the Cornell note-taking system.

Figure 9.5   Outline Using a Cornell Frame

October 30

Topic: Maslow's Hierarchy of Basic Needs

What is the theory of basic needs ?	I. Published in 1943 in
	– "A Theory of human motivation"
	– Study of human motivation
	– Observation of innate curiosity
	– Studied exemplary people
	II. Needs arranged like ladder
	– Basic needs at the bottom
	– Basic needs = deficiency needs
	– Highest need = aesthetic need
What are the Steps in the Hierarchy ?	I. Physiological needs
	– Breathing
	– Food, water
	– Sex
	– Sleep
	II. Safety needs
	– Security of body
	– Security of employment
	– Resources of
	– Family
	– Health
	III. Love - Belonging needs
	– Friendships
	– Family
	– Sexual intimacy

To implement your note-taking system, you will want to choose the technique that is most comfortable and beneficial for you. You might use mapping (Figure 9.6, discussed later), mapping on a Cornell frame (Figure 9.7), or outlining on a Cornell frame (Figure 9.5).

THE MAPPING SYSTEM

Are You Going Around in Circles?

If you are a visual learner, the mapping system may be especially useful for you. The mapping system of note-taking generates a picture of information (see Figure 9.6). The mapping system creates a map, or web, of information that allows you to see the relationships among facts or ideas. A mapping system using a Cornell frame might look something like the notes in Figure 9.7.

Your note-taking system *must work for you.* Do not use a system because your friends use it or because you feel that you should use it. Experiment with each system or a combination to determine what is best for you.

Work hard to keep your notes organized, dated, and neat. Notes that cannot be read are no good to you or to anyone else.

Figure 9.6 **The Mapping System**

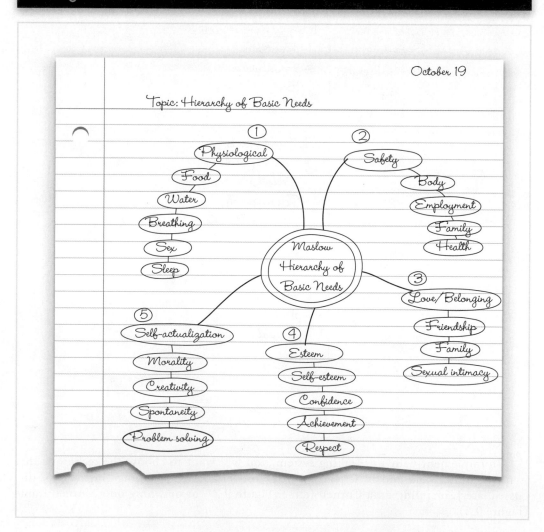

Figure 9.7 The Mapping System in a Cornell Frame

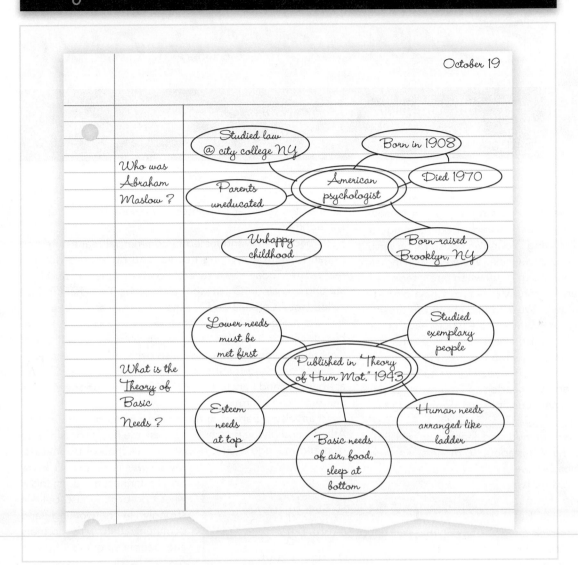

TMI! TMI! (TOO MUCH INFORMATION)

What Do I Do if I Get Lost While Taking Notes During the Lecture?

Have you ever been in a classroom trying to take notes and the instructor is speaking so rapidly that you cannot possibly get all of the information? Just when you think you're caught up, you realize that he or she has made an important statement and you missed it. What do you do? How can you handle, or avoid, this difficult note-taking situation? Here are several hints:

- Raise your hand and ask the instructor to repeat the information.
- Ask your instructor to slow down.

from ORDINARY to Extraordinary

Vivian Wong *Founder, Global Trading Consortium, Greenville, SC*

In the early 1960s, I was a very young woman and a new wife when my husband began talking about coming to America. We dreamed of living in our own house with a yard, rather than a flat as we did in China. We were working as front desk clerks in a Hong Kong hotel when fate intervened in the person of Robert Wilson, who was in China marketing his Barbeque King grills. We told him about our dream, and he decided to help us. Many people would have never followed through, but Mr. Wilson gave us $100 and told us to get photos made and to acquire passports. He promised to work on a visa for us. It took a year for us to finally be granted a trainee visa, and we headed to Greenville, SC, to work for Mr. Wilson, leaving our little girl behind with her grandparents.

In South Carolina we trained and learned to sell Barbeque King grills in China. After about 10 months, we were very homesick for China, so we went home. We realized after we got back to Hong Kong that our hearts were really in America, because now we were homesick for Greenville. Without even realizing it, Greenville and America had become our home. Mr. Wilson brought us back, and this time, we brought our little girl.

In 1967, we were blessed with twin girls, and in 1968, we were given a permanent visa and granted U.S. citizenship. I often say, "We spent the first twenty years in America simply trying to earn a meager living and put food on the table." We began to look around to try to figure out what kind of edge we had that we could use to start our own business in Greenville, because we didn't want to work for other people the rest of our lives. In 1970, with Mr. Wilson as a partner, we opened our first business, a Chinese restaurant, but before we opened, my husband spent two years in Washington, DC, training for restaurant ownership. We opened other restaurants in 1975, 1976, and 1988. By then, I could put food on the table, and I wanted to do something other than sell eggrolls.

I became very interested in commercial real estate and began to learn everything I could, and I branched out into real estate. Today I own several hotels in America, and I am starting a chain in China with my brother. This chain will be called Hotel Carolina and is aimed at business travelers. We found a niche that had not been tapped—a clean, reasonable, three-star hotel for business travelers who can't afford five-star accommodations. We also own and operate a large business park and foreign trade zone in Greenville, SC. We are partners and franchisees of the Medicine Shoppe, China's first American pharmacy.

I am also a partner in three banks located in Greenville, Atlanta, and Myrtle Beach. People ask me how I know how to own and manage such a disparate collection of businesses. My answer is simple, "I know how to connect the dots; this is what I do best." I also believe strongly in networking and communicating with partners and people who know how to get things done. I have partners all over the world in a great variety of businesses. I have developed the vision, action plans, and good teams to make things happen. I take nothing for granted!

We have been very blessed to live in America and now to open businesses in our native land. In this wonderful country, we have succeeded beyond our wildest dreams! So can you!

> We spent the first twenty years in America simply trying to earn a meager living and put food on the table.

EXTRAORDINARY REFLECTION

Mrs. Wong mentions how important it is to establish relationships, communicate, and network with other people. How can communication, networking, and strong relationships help you in your chosen field?

- If he or she will do neither, leave a blank space with a question mark at the side margin You can get this information after class from your instructor, a classmate, the text, or your study buddy. This can be a difficult task to master. The key is to focus on the information at hand. Focus on what is being said at the exact moment. Don't give up!

- Meet with your instructor immediately after class or at the earliest time convenient for both of you.

- Form a note-taking group that meets after each class. This serves two purposes: (1) you can discuss and review the lecture, and (2) you will be able to get any notes you missed from one of your note-taking buddies.

- Never lean over and ask questions of another student during the lecture. This will cause them to lose the information as well, and it will probably annoy your peers and the instructor also.

- Rehearse your note-taking skills at home by taking notes from TV news magazines like Dateline or 60 Minutes or channels like the History Channel.

- Ask the instructor's permission to use a recording device during the lecture. Do not record a lecture without permission. We suggest that you try to use other avenues, such as the ones listed above, instead of taping your notes. It is a time-consuming task to listen to the lecture for a second time. However, if this system works for you, use it.

REFLECTIONS ON LISTENING AND NOTE TAKING

Yes, listening is a learned skill, but it is more than that. It is a gift that you give to yourself. It is a gift that promotes knowledge, understanding, stronger relationships, and open-mindedness. Good listening skills can help you manage conflict, avoid misunderstandings, and establish trusting relationships. Perhaps most importantly at this point in your life, listening can help you become a more successful student. Once you learn how to listen with your whole body and mind, you will begin to see how your notes, your grades, your attitude, your relationships, and your learning processes changes.

LISTENING WITH AN OPEN MIND

Utilizes levels 4 and 5 of the Taxonomy (see Bloom's Taxonomy at the front of this text)

Explanation: Seldom (if ever) would you pop in a CD, click your iPod, or tune your radio to a station that you strongly disliked. It just does not seem like a good use of time and it is not something that you would probably enjoy on a daily basis. However, for this exercise, we are going to ask that you do precisely what we've described above and then apply what you've experienced and learned to answer several questions.

Process: Over the course of the next few days, find a song from your *least favorite* genre. If you are a huge fan of R&B,

then move away from that genre and choose something from a genre of which you are not particularly fond. You might choose an old country song or a song from rap or bluegrass. If you enjoy listening to "easy love songs," try something different, such as metal or swing. The only stipulation is that the **song must have lyrics.**

You will have to listen to the song several times to answer the questions below. **However,** it is important to read the questions below *before* you listen to the song—particularly question #2. The key to this exercise is to practice listening with an open mind, listening for content, and listening to words when barriers are in the way (the barrier would be the actual music, itself).

1. What is the song's title and artist?

_____

_____

_____

_____

2. What emotional and mental response did you have to the music the first time you listened to it? Why do you think you had this response?

_____

_____

_____

_____

3. While listening to the song, what happened to your appreciation level? Did it increase or decrease? Why?

_____

_____

_____

_____

4. In your opinion, what was the message (theme) of the song?

_____

_____

_____

_____

5. What were you most surprised about with the song? The lyrics? The actual music? Your like or dislike of the song? The artist's voice? etc.

_____

_____

_____

_____

6. If you *had* to say that you gained or learned one positive thing from this song, what would it be?

_____

_____

_____

_____

7. From memory, list at least two statements, comments, or quotes from the song.

_____

_____

_____

_____

Now, consider how becoming a more effective listener can help you with each of the following.

By enhancing my listening skills, I can become more **open-minded** by

_____

_____

_____

_____

By enhancing my listening skills, I can become more **creative** by

_____

_____

_____

_____

By enhancing my listening skills, I can become more **knowledgeable** by

_____

_____

_____

_____

By enhancing my listening skills, I can increase my **resourcefulness** level by

_____

_____

_____

_____

SQ3R MASTERY STUDY SHEET

EXAMPLE QUESTION (FROM PAGE 207) What are the four components of the character for the Chinese verb, "to listen"?	**ANSWER:**
EXAMPLE QUESTION (FROM PAGE 211) Why is it important to identify key words during a lecture?	**ANSWER:**
AUTHOR QUESTION (FROM PAGE 207) What is objective listening?	**ANSWER:**
AUTHOR QUESTION (FROM PAGE 208) List and define the four listening styles.	**ANSWER:**
AUTHOR QUESTION (FROM PAGE 213) Discuss the five steps in the L-STAR note-taking system.	**ANSWER:**
AUTHOR QUESTION (FROM PAGE 214) Why is translating your notes important?	**ANSWER:**
AUTHOR QUESTION (FROM PAGE 218) When would be the best time to use the mapping system of note-taking? Justify your answer.	**ANSWER:**
YOUR QUESTION (FROM PAGE ____)	**ANSWER:**
YOUR QUESTION (FROM PAGE ____)	**ANSWER:**
YOUR QUESTION (FROM PAGE ____)	**ANSWER:**
YOUR QUESTION (FROM PAGE ____)	**ANSWER:**
YOUR QUESTION (FROM PAGE ____)	**ANSWER:**

Finally, after answering these questions, recite this chapter's major points in your mind. Consider the following general questions to help you master this material.

- What is it about?
- What does it mean?
- What is the most important thing you learned? Why?
- What are the key points to remember?

chapter ten

STUDY

DEVELOPING YOUR MEMORY, STUDY, AND TEST-TAKING SKILLS

"We can learn something new at any time we believe we can." —Virginia Satir

STUDY

Why read this chapter?

Because you'll learn...

- How to study more effectively
- To use memory tricks to retain information
- Tips for taking different types of assessments

Because you'll be able to...

- **Apply** memory techniques to your study efforts
- **Use** mnemonic devices to help with memory
- **Prepare** for and **take** tests with confidence

Scan and QUESTION

$\top$ ake a few moments, **scan this chapter** and on page 248, write **five of your own questions** that you think will be important to your mastery of this material. You will also find five questions listed from your authors.

Example:

☑ **Why are mnemonics important?** (from page 233)

☑ **Discuss three strategies for studying math.** (from page 238)

MyStudentSuccessLab

MyStudentSuccessLab is an online solution designed to help you acquire and develop (or hone) the skills you need to succeed. You will have access to peer-led video presentations and develop core skills through interactive exercises and projects.

Name: Kayla Stevens

Institution: Graduate! North Central Texas College, Gainesville, TX

Major: Elementary/Special Education

"Life has never been easy, and few people thought I would amount to much," Kayla begins. "My success story is not common—I beat all the odds. I made good grades all though elementary and middle school. I was in honor classes, and stayed on the honor roll. When I walked through the doors of junior high school, everything changed."

Kayla states that her friends, her environment, and her views on herself and the world changed. She began to make poor choices and started down a dark road. "At 15, I became pregnant, and staying in school was not an option for me. I dropped out of high school my sophomore year feeling ashamed and scared about what my future held." At 16, Kayla was a wife and mother. Although she didn't feel like it at the time, she now believes that having her first child was a blessing in disguise. She wanted so many things for her daughter and she wanted her daughter to do something great with her life. Kayla wanted to have all the opportunities she would need in order to be successful and provide for her child. Kayla says, "I couldn't fathom explaining to my

An interview conducted and written by Karen Morris, Chair of Teacher Education, North Central Texas College, Gainesville, TX.

daughter the importance of an education as a dropout. I didn't want to be a hypocrite, so I went back to school and received my GED. I wasn't sure what I would do with it, but I knew one day it would be important."

Kayla now has three daughters and has been married to her husband since she was 16. When they started their family, she and her husband decided that she would be a stay-at-home mom and raise the children until they started school. This allowed Kayla's husband to focus on his career. Together, they decided that once their youngest started school Kayla would begin her college studies. "I spent 12 years as a stay-at-home mom and loved every minute of it. I nurtured, taught, and guided my girls as they grew. I loved watching them learn new things, and found that I enjoyed teaching them. It was during those years that I discovered my passion for teaching."

As promised, Kayla started school when her youngest went to kindergarten. She knew it would be difficult, but she was not prepared for how life-changing going to college would be. She was not like many of the students at NCTC. She was older, married, and had children. But she looked upon this as an advantage. She was stable, responsible, and had her family to hold her accountable. "I had three daughters watching my every move. I had lectured the importance of doing well in school, and now it was time to lead by example. I did just that. I loved school and found that I was good at it. With the support of my family, advisors, and my mentor, Karen Morris, I knew I would have amazing success."

Kayla quickly learned that time management, organization, and personal effort are needed to succeed in college. She found that it took dedication, but she also realized that she could do it if she tried and stayed focused. "It wasn't easy stepping back into the classroom after so many years and after such a negative experience in school. Starting at North Central Texas College changed my life. It made my transition to Texas Woman's University and then on to the workplace manageable for me and my family. It also showed me that I am capable and able to achieve my goals. Because of the help and support of those around me, my hard work, and my

dedication to excellence, I earned my Associate's and Bachelor's degrees in teaching and am now living my dream of being a teacher."

It was also during Kayla's time at North Central Texas College that she realized her own love of learning and her desire to obtain more than a Bachelor's degree, so she began working toward a Master's of Education degree.

"Those who thought I wouldn't amount to much were wrong—including me. Even though I made some poor decisions, I made some good ones, too. By far, going back to school was the best decision I ever made and has changed my life. I would say never doubt your potential if you follow it up with hard work, focus, and passion."

THINK a b o u t *it*

1. Kayla states that she could not imagine explaining to her children the importance of education when she was a dropout. How important do you think obtaining your education is to those around you like your children, siblings, parents, or friends? Why?

2. Kayla found a mentor in Ms. Morris. Who do you think could be a mentor for you at your college? Why? What qualities do they possess that you admire and would like to emulate?

THE THREE TYPES OF MEMORY
Can Information Really be Stored and Easily Retrieved?

Psychologists have determined that there are three types of memory: **sensory** memory; **short-term, or working** memory; and **long-term** memory.

Sensory memory stores information gathered from the five senses: taste, touch, smell, hearing, and sight. Sensory memory is usually temporary, lasting about one to three seconds, unless you decide that the information is of ultimate importance to you and make an effort to transfer it to long-term memory.

Short-term, or working memory holds information for a short amount of time. Consider the following list of letters:

jmplngtoplntstsevng

Now, cover them with your hand and try to recite them.

It is almost impossible for the average person to do so. Why? Because your working memory bank can hold a limited amount of information, usually about five to nine separate new facts or pieces of information at once (Woolfolk, 2009). However, consider this exercise. If you break the letters down into smaller pieces and add *meaning* to them, you are more likely to retain them. Example:

jum   lng   to   plnts   ts   evng

This may still not mean very much to you, but you can probably remember at least the first three sets of information—jum lng to.

Now, if you were to say to yourself, this sentence means "Jump Long To Planets This Evening," you are much more likely to begin to remember this information. Just as your memory can "play tricks" on you, you can "play tricks" on your memory.

Although it is sometimes frustrating when we "misplace" information, it is also useful and necessary to our brain's survival that every piece of information that we hear and see is not in the forefront of our minds. If you tried to remember everything, you would not be able to function. As a student, you would never be able to remember all that your instructor said during a 50-minute lecture. You have to take steps to help you to remember important information. Taking notes, making associations, drawing pictures, and visualizing information are all techniques that can help you move information from your short-term memory to your long-term memory bank.

What study techniques have you used in the past to help you commit information to long-term memory?

Long-term memory stores a lot of information. It is almost like a hard drive on your computer. You have to make an effort to put something in your long-term memory, but with effort and memory techniques, such as rehearsal, practice, and mnemonic devices, you can store anything you want to remember there. Long-term memory consists of information that you have heard often, information that you use often, information that you might see often, and information that you have determined necessary and/or important to you. Just as you name a file on your computer, you name the files in your long-term memory. Sometimes, you have to wait a moment for the information to come to you. While you are waiting, your brain's CD-ROM is spinning; if the information you seek is in long-term memory, your brain will eventually find it if you stored it properly. You may have to assist your brain in locating the information by using mnemonics and other memory devices.

POWERFUL VISUALIZATION TECHNIQUES

How Can VCR3 Be Used to Increase Memory Power?

Countless pieces of information are stored in your long-term memory. Some of it is triggered by necessity, some may be triggered by the five senses, and some may be triggered by experiences. The best way to commit information to long-term memory and retrieve it when needed can be expressed by:

- **V**isualizing
- **C**oncentrating
- **R**elating
- **R**epeating
- **R**eviewing

Consider the following story:

As Katherine walked to her car after her evening class, she heard someone behind her. She turned to see two students holding hands walking about 20 feet behind her. She was relieved. This was the first night that she had walked to her car alone.

Do you find that studying at the library, at home, or somewhere else is most effective for you? Why?

Katherine pulled her book bag closer to her as she increased her pace along the dimly lit sidewalk between the Salk Biology Building and the Horn Center for the Arts. "I can't believe that Shana didn't call me," she thought to herself. "She knows I hate to walk to the parking lot alone."

As Katherine turned the corner onto Suddith Street, she heard someone else behind her. She turned but did not see anyone. As she continued to walk toward her car, she heard the sound again. Turning to see if anyone was there, she saw a shadow disappear into the grove of hedges along the sidewalk.

Startled and frightened, Katherine crossed the street to walk beneath the streetlights and sped up to get closer to a group of students about 30 feet in front of her. She turned once more to see if anyone was behind her. Thankfully, she did not see anyone.

By this time, she was very close to her car. The lighting was better and other students were around. She felt better, but vowed never again to leave class alone at night.

Visualizing information means that you try to create word pictures in your mind as you hear or read the information. If you are being told about a Revolutionary War battle in Camden, SC, try to see the soldiers and the battlefield, or try to paint a "mind picture" that will help you to remember the information. You may also want to create visual aids as you read or study information.

As you read Katherine's story, were you able to visualize her journey? Could you see her walking along the sidewalk? Did you see the two buildings? What did they look like? Could you see the darkness of her path? Could you see that shadow disappearing into the bushes? Could you see her increasing her pace to catch up to the other students? What was she wearing?

If you did this, then you are using your visual skills—your *mind's eye*. This is one of the most effective ways to commit information to long-term memory. See it, live it, feel it, and touch it as you read and study it, and it will become yours.

Concentrating on the information given will help you commit it to long-term memory. Don't let your mind wander. Stay focused. If you find yourself having trouble concentrating, take a small break (2–5 minutes) and then go back to work.

Relating the information to something that you already know or understand will assist you in filing or storing the information for easy retrieval. Relating the appearance of the African zebra to the American horse can help you remember what the zebra looks like. You may not know what the building in Katherine's story looked like, but try to see her in front of a building at your school. Creating these types of relationships increases memory retention of the material.

Repeating the information out loud to yourself or to a study partner facilitates its transfer to long-term memory. Some people have to hear information many times before they can commit it to long-term memory. Memory experts agree that repetition is one of the *strongest* tools to increase the retention of material.

Reviewing the information is another means of repetition. The more you see and use the information, the easier it will be to remember it when the time comes. As you review, try to remember the main points of the information.

Walter Pauk (2010), educator and inventor of the Cornell note-taking method, concluded from a research study that people reading a textbook chapter forgot 81 percent of what they had read after 28 days. With this in mind, it may be beneficial for you to review Katherine's story (and other material in your texts) on a regular basis. Reviewing is a method of repetition and of keeping information fresh.

Remembering Katherine

Without looking back, answer the following questions about Katherine. Use the power of your visualization and concentration to recall the information.

1. What was the name of the biology building?

_____

2. Did she see the shadow before or after she saw the two people behind her?

_____

3. What were the two people behind her doing?

_____

4. What was the name of the arts building?

_____

5. Why did she cross the street?

_____

6. How far ahead of her was the group of students?

_____

7. When she saw the group of students in front of her, how far was she from her car?

_____

8. What was Katherine's friend's name?

_____

Level 1 Remember

THE CAPABILITY OF YOUR MEMORY

What Is the Difference Between Memorizing and Owning?

Why don't you forget your name? Why don't you forget your address? The answer is that you _know_ that information. **_You own it_**. You didn't just "rent it." It belongs to you. You've used it often enough and repeated it often enough that it is highly unlikely that you will ever forget it. Conversely, why can't you remember the details of Erickson's Stages of Development or Maslow's Hierarchy of Basic Needs or Darwin's Theory of Evolution? Most likely because you memorized it and never "owned" it.

Knowing something means that you have made a personal commitment to make this information a part of your life. For example, if you needed to remember the name Stephen and his phone number, 925-6813, the likelihood of your remembering this depends on your _attitude._ Do you need to recall this information because he is in your study group and you might need to call him, or because he is the caregiver for your infant daughter while you are in class? How badly you need that name and number will determine the commitment level that you make to either _memorizing_ it (and maybe forgetting it) or _knowing_ it (and making it a part of your life).

In Figure 10.1 you will find two photos. Follow the directions above each photo.

> "The illiterate of the 21st century will not be those who cannot read and write, but those who cannot learn, unlearn, and relearn."
>
> —Alvin Toffler

Figure 10.1 **Seeing Clearly**

Consider this picture. Study it carefully.
Look at everything from left to right, top to bottom.

Now, notice the picture and pay close attention to the areas marked.

Notice the people on the trampoline

Notice the storage building

Notice
the color
of the
protective
padding

Notice
the green
foliage

Notice the utility meter

Now, cover both photos and answer the following questions:

1. How many people are on the trampoline? _____

2. What color is the protective padding on the edge? _____

3. What is the season of the year based on the foliage color? _____

4. What colors are used on the storage building? _____

5. Is there one utility meter or two? _____

6. How many children are in the air? _____

7. Are the children all male, female, or mixed? _____

8. How many people are wearing striped shirts? _____

9. What type of fence surrounds the house? _____

10. What colors are used on the house?_____

11. Is the house made of one material or more?_____

12. What color are the flowers on the bush? _____

"Not fair!" you may be saying right now. "We were not asked to look at the fence, colors on the house, or what people are wearing." Regardless, could you answer all of the questions without looking? The purpose of this exercise is to help you understand the real difference between casually looking at something and *really* looking at something. To truly know something, you have to go beyond what is on the surface—even looking beyond reading and studying what was asked of you. You have to look and examine more than you are told or more than what is pointed out to you. In order to own information, you have to be totally committed to examining every detail, every inch, and every angle of it. You will need to practice and master the technique of "going beyond."

USING MNEMONIC DEVICES

What Does a Greek Goddess Have to Do with My Memory?

The word *mnemonic* is derived from the Greek goddess of memory, **Mnemosyne** (pronounced ne-mo-ze-knee). She was considered one of the most important goddesses because it was believed that memory separated us from lower animal life forms. It was believed that memory was the very foundation of civilization (The Goddess Path, 2009). Memory was so very important because most of the transmission of human history depended on oral stories and parables committed only to memory, not on paper.

In modern times, **mnemonic devices** are memory tricks or techniques that assist you in putting information into your long-term memory and pulling it out when you need it. According to research into mnemonics and their effectiveness, it was found that mnemonics can help create a phenomenon known as the **bizarreness effect**. This effect causes us to remember information that is "bizarre" or unusual more rapidly than "normal," everyday facts. "The bizarreness effect occurs because unusual information and events trigger heightened levels of our attention and require us to work harder to make sense of them; thus we remember the information and its associated interaction better" (McCornack, 2007). The following types of mnemonic devices may help you with your long-term memory.

Jingles/Rhymes. You can make up rhymes, songs, poems, or sayings to assist you in remembering information; for example, "Columbus sailed the ocean blue in fourteen hundred and ninety-two."

Jingles and rhymes have a strong and lasting impact on our memory—especially when repetition is involved.

Sentences. You can make up sentences, such as "Some men can read backward fast," to help you remember information. Another example is "**P**lease **e**xcuse **my** **d**ear **A**unt **S**ally," which corresponds to the order of mathematical operations: **p**arentheses, **e**xponents, **m**ultiplication, **d**ivision, **a**ddition, and **s**ubtraction.

The Greek goddess of memory, Mnemosyne.

Other sentences used in academic areas include:

1. **M**y **V**ery **E**lderly **M**other **J**ust **S**aved **U**s **N**icely is a sentence mnemonic for the eight planets, in order from the sun: Mercury, Venus, Earth, Mars, Jupiter, Saturn, Uranus, Neptune.

Words. You can create words. For example, **Roy G. Biv** may help you to remember the colors of the rainbow: **r**ed, **o**range, **y**ellow, **g**reen, **b**lue, **i**ndigo, and **v**iolet.
Other word mnemonics include:

1. **HOMES** is a word for the Great Lakes in no particular order: **H**uron, **O**ntario, **M**ichigan, **E**rie, **S**uperior.

Story lines. If you find it easier to remember stories than raw information, you may want to process the information into a story that you can easily tell. Weave the data and facts into a creative story that can be easily retrieved from your long-term memory. This technique can be especially beneficial if your instructor gives essay exams, because the "story" that you remember can be what was actually told in class.

Acronyms. An acronym is a word that is formed from the first letters of other words. You may see reruns for the famed TV show *M*A*S*H*. This is an acronym for **m**obile **a**rmy **s**urgical **h**ospital. If you scuba dive, you know that *scuba* is an acronym for **s**elf-**c**ontained **u**nderwater **b**reathing **a**pparatus. Other common acronyms include:

- *NASA* (**N**ational **A**eronautic **S**pace **A**dministration)
- *NASCAR* (**N**ational **A**ssociation of **S**tock **C**ar **A**uto **R**acing)
- *NASDAQ* (**N**ational **A**ssociation of **S**ecurities **D**ealers **A**utomated **Q**uotation)
- *NATO* (**N**orth **A**tlantic **T**reaty **O**rganization)
- *BART* (**B**ay **A**rea **R**apid **T**ransit)

Pegging. The pegging system uses association, visualization, and attachment to aid in memory. With this system, you literally "attach" what you want to remember to something that is already familiar to you—the pegs that you create. This is a visual means to remember lists, sequences, and even categories of information.

Pretend that you are looking at a coat rack mounted on the wall with 10 pegs sticking out of it, as shown in Figure 10.2. Just as you would hang a hat or coat on the pegs of a rack, you can hang information there, too.

For the sake of explaining this technique more thoroughly, we have named 10 pegs for you with corresponding rhyming words. You, however, can name your pegs anything that would be easy for you to remember. Once you memorize these pegs, you can attach anything to them with visualization and imagination. The key to using the pegging mnemonic system is to name your pegs *once* and use those names each time you hook information to them. This way, they become second nature to you.

For our example, our 10 pegs are named:

1 = sun	2 = shoe	3 = bee	4 = shore	5 = alive
6 = sticks	7 = heaven	8 = gate	9 = line	10 = sin

Repeat these until you have memorized them.

To attach the information that you want to remember to the peg, you use visualization to attach a term or word to that peg. For example, if you wanted to remember a shopping list that included (1) ice cream, (2) rice, (3) Ajax, (4) milk, (5) water, and (6) cookies, this might be your visualization plan.

1–sun	You see ice cream melting in the **sun.**
2–shoe	You see a **shoe** being filled with rice.

3–bee	You see Ajax being sprinkled on a **bee.**
4–shore	You see milk instead of water rushing to the **shore** in waves.
5–alive	You see water keeping you **alive** on a deserted island.
6–sticks	You see cookies being offered to you on a **stick** (like a s'more).

Read over this list one more time and you'll be surprised at how easy it is to remember your shopping list. It becomes even easier when *you* name your pegs and *you* create the visualization. If you need more than 10 pegs, you can create as many as you need.

Suppose that we wanted to remember a list for "***personal and professional success***" (passion, motivation, knowledge, resourcefulness, creativity, adaptability, open-mindedness, communication, accountability, and vision). If your instructor suggests that you need to know this list, in order, for your midterm exam, use the pegging system to memorize it.

1–sun	I look at the ***sun*** on a beautiful day with ***passion***.
2–shoe	I walk in my ***shoes*** with ***motivation***.
3–bee	I see a ***bee*** flying around that seems to be very ***knowledgeable***.
4–shore	The ***shore*** washes many ***resources*** to the beach.
5–alive	My brain is ***alive*** because I use ***creativity***.
6–sticks	I see a ***stick*** bending into a half circle, making it very ***adaptable***.
7–heaven	Believing in ***heaven*** takes ***open-mindedness***.
8–gate	Many ***gates*** open for people who know how to ***communicate***.
9–line	If you walk a straight ***line,*** you will be ***accountable***.
10–sin	It is a ***sin*** to lack ***vision***.

Read over these one more time, then cover the list and you'll be amazed at how easy it is to repeat it. You will, of course, need to study each one to know what it means, but now you have the list memorized, in order.

Figure 10.2   **The Pegging System**

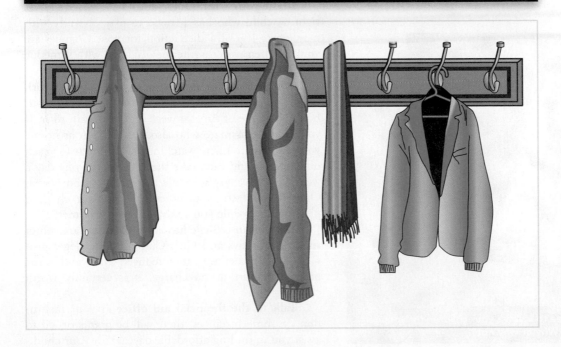

HAKUNA MATATA

How in the World Can I Study with Small Children in the House?

For many college students, finding a place or time to study is the hardest part of studying. Some students live at home with younger siblings; some students have children of their own. If you have young children in the home, you may find the following hints helpful when it comes time to study.

Study at school. Your schedule may have you running from work to school then directly to home. Try to squeeze in even as little as half an hour at school for studying, perhaps immediately before or after class. A half hour of uninterrupted study time can prove more valuable than five hours at home with constant interruptions.

Create crafts and hobbies. Your children need to be occupied while you study. It may help if you have crafts and hobbies available that they can do while you are involved with studying. Choose projects your children can do by themselves, without your help. Depending on their ages, children could make masks from paper plates, color, do pipe cleaner art or papier-mâché, use modeling clay or dough, or build a block city. Explain to your children that you are studying and that they can use this time to be creative; when everyone is finished, you'll share what you've done with each other. Give them little rewards for their work and for helping you have quiet time to study.

Study with your children. One of the best ways to instill the value of education in your children is to let them see you participating in your own education. Set aside one or two hours per night when you and your children study. You may be able to study in one place, or you may have separate study areas. If your children know that you are studying and you have explained to them how you value your education, you are killing two birds with one stone: you are able to study, and you are providing a positive role model as your children study with you and watch you.

Rent movies or let your children watch TV. Research has shown that viewing a limited amount of educational television, such as *Sesame Street, Reading Rainbow,* or *Barney and Friends,* can be beneficial for children. If you do not like what is on television, you might consider renting or purchasing age-appropriate educational videos for your children to keep them busy while you study, and it could help them learn as well.

Invite your children's friends over. What?! That's right. A child who has a friend to play or study with may create less of a distraction for you. Chances are your children would rather be occupied with someone their own age, and you will gain valuable study time.

Hire a sitter or exchange sitting services with another student. Arrange to have a sitter come to your house a couple of times a week if you can afford it. If you have a classmate who also has children at home, you might take turns watching the children for each other. You could each take the children for one day a week, or devise any schedule that suits you both best. Or you could study together, and let your children play together while you study, alternating homes.

Ask if your college has an on-site daycare center such as the Boys and Girls Club. Some colleges provide daycare facilities at a reduced cost, and some provide daycare at no charge. It is certainly worth checking out.

Talk to the financial aid office at your institution. In some instances, there will be grants or aid to assist you in finding affordable daycare for your child.

Do you think it is a good idea to involve your children (or younger siblings) in your education? Why or why not?

Studying at any time is hard work. It is even harder when you have to attend to a partner, children, family responsibilities, work, and a social life as well. You will have to be creative in order to complete your degree. You are going to have to do things and make sacrifices that you never thought possible. But if you explore the options, plan ahead, and ask questions of other students with children and with responsibilities outside the classroom, you can and will succeed.

STUDYING IN A CRUNCH

TOMORROW? What Do You Mean the Test Is Tomorrow?

Let's be straight up front. No study skills textbook will ever advise you to cram. It is simply a dangerous and often futile exercise in desperation. You will ***never read the words,*** "Don't waste your time studying, just **cram** the night before so you can party harder and longer!" Cramming is just the opposite of what this whole chapter is about—knowing versus memorizing. Cramming will not help you own the material; it may only help you memorize a few things for storage in short-term memory. You may spend several hours cramming, and shortly after the test, the information is gone, evaporated, vanished!

But, let's be straight about something else. We know that you may have obligations that take enormous hours from your week. This is simply a fact of life in the twenty-first century. So, there may be times when time runs out and the only option is to cram. If you find yourself in this spot, consider the following tips and suggestions for cramming. These probably won't get you an A, but they may help you with a few questions.

Depressurize. Just tell yourself up front what you are doing. Don't pretend that cramming is going to save you. Let yourself realize that you are memorizing material for short-term gain and that you won't be able to keep it all. With this admission, your stress will diminish.

Ditch the blame game. You know you're at fault, so accept that and move on. Sitting around bemoaning your fate will not help; it just takes up more of your valuable time. Just tell yourself, "I messed up this time; I won't let it happen again."

Know the score. When cramming, it is important to know what you're cramming for. If you're cramming for a multiple-choice test, you'll need different types of information than for an essay test. Know the type of test for which you are studying.

Read it quick. Think about H2 FLIB. This is a mnemonic for: read the headings, highlight the important words, read the first sentence of every paragraph, read the last sentence of every paragraph, read the indented and boxed material. This can help you get through the chapter when pinched for time.

Make connections. As you are reading, quickly determine if any of the information has a connection with something else you know. Is there a comparison or contrast? Is there a relationship of any kind? Is there a cause and effect in motion? Can you pinpoint an example to clarify the information? Is there a mnemonic that can help you with this information? These questions can help you with retention and long-term memory commitment.

Use your syllabus or study guide. If your instructor lists questions that you should know (mastery questions) in the syllabus, or if he/she gave you a study sheet, this is the place to start. Answer those questions. If you don't have either, look to see if the text gives study questions at the end of the chapter. Try to answer the questions using the text *and* your lecture notes.

DID YOU *Know?*

MICHAEL JORDAN was born in Brooklyn, NY, in 1963. During his sophomore year in high school, Michael tried out for his varsity basketball team. However, because he was only 5'11" he was considered too short to play and he was cut from the team. He was devastated, but this experience only increased his determination to make the team and excel.

The following summer, he grew 4 inches, and with this growth spurt and intense training, he not only made the team but averaged over 25 points per game during his last two years in high school.

Jordan then attended the University of North Carolina, where he was named ACC Freshman of the Year. In 1984, he was drafted into the NBA by the Chicago Bulls. He led the NBA in scoring for 10 seasons, he holds the top career and playoff scoring averages, and today he is considered by many to be *the* most accomplished basketball player ever to hit the court.

See it. Visualizing the information through mapping, diagrams, photos, drawings, and outlines can help you commit the information to short-term memory.

Check your notes. Did the professor indicate that certain things were important for the test?

Repeat! Repeat! Repeat! Repetition is the key to committing information to memory. After you read information from the text or lecture notes, repeat it time and time again. When you think you've got it, write it down, then repeat it again.

Choose wisely. If you're cramming, you can't do it all. Make wise choices about which material you plan to study. This can be driven by your study sheet, your lecture notes, or questions in your syllabus (if they are listed).

Information is going to leave you when you cram. Don't rely on it for the next test or the final. You will need to go back and re-learn (truly understand) the information you "crammed" to commit it to long-term memory. See Figure 10.3 for some specific tips for studying math and science.

Figure 10.3   **A Quick Reference Guide to Studying Math and Science**

Before Class

■ **Never** take a math or science course (or any course for that matter) for which you are not prepared. If you think you need, or test into, a basic, remedial, or transitional class, *take it*! Look at it as a chance to start over with new hope and knowledge.

■ **Understand** that most math and science classes build on previous knowledge. If you begin the class with a weak background, you must work very hard to learn missed information.

■ **Avoid** taking math or science classes during "short" terms if possible. The more time you spend with the material, the better, especially if math and/or science are not your strong suits.

■ **Know** your own learning style. If you're visual, use colors, charts, and photos. If you're auditory, practice your listening skills. If you're tactile, work to create situations where you can "act out" or touch the material.

■ **Prepare** yourself *before class* by reading the chapter. Even if you don't understand all of it, read through the material and write down questions about material you did not understand.

■ **Scan** all of the introductory and summation materials provided in the text or study guides.

■ **Join** a study group. If there is not one, start one. Cooperative learning teams can be lifesavers.

■ **Seek** tutorial assistance on campus from the first day. Go visit the tutoring center and get familiar with how it operates. Get to know the people who work there. Don't wait until you get behind to seek assistance.

During Class

■ **Come to** *every* class, study group, or lab.

■ **Control** your own anger and frustration. The past is the past and you can't change any part of it —but you can change *your* future. Learn to make your negative self-talk "be quiet!"

■ **Ask** questions. **Ask** questions. **Ask** questions. **Ask** questions…and be specific in your questioning. Don't just say, "I don't understand that." Ask detailed and specific questions, such as, "*I don't understand why f(x + h) doesn't equal f(x) + f(h).* Or, "*I don't understand the difference between 'algia' and 'dynia.' Why are two different words used for pain?*"

■ **Slow down** and read the material carefully.

■ **Find** the formulas and write them down on notecards.

■ **Write** down the explanatory remarks made by the instructor, such as:
  ■ How you get from one step to the next
  ■ How this problem differs from other problems
  ■ Why you need to use formula "x" instead of formula "y"
  ■ Were any steps combined— why or why not

- **Try** to learn from a *general to specific* end. That is, try to get a feeling of the overall goal of the material before you hone in on smaller problems.
- **Write** down any theorem, formula, or technique that the instructor puts on the board, overhead, or PowerPoint.
- **Leave** a space in your notes for any material you missed or did not understand. This will help you keep your notes organized when you go back after class and add the explanation.
- **Bring** Post-it notes, strips of paper, or bookmarks to class with you so that you can "tag" pages with important information and concepts. Use the tabs included with your text to help you mark important information.

After Class

- **Visit** your instructor's office (make an appointment to visit during office hours).
- **Fill** in the missing information in your notes by reviewing the text, going to your study group, or getting clarification from your instructor.
- **Practice** the problems in your text or study guide, and then practice them again, and again, and again until they become second nature. Much of math and science is learned by *doing* … so do … and then *do* again.
- **Apply** what you learned in class or lab. Find a way to make it "speak" to your life in a practical way.
- **Continually** review all of the theorems, formulas, concepts, and terms from each chapter so they become second nature to you.
- When taking practice tests, **pretend** that you are in an actual test and adhere to the timelines, rules, and policies of your instructor. This helps replicate the actual testing situation.

Before the Test

- **Ask** questions that will reduce your anxiety, such as:
  - What is the point value of each question?
  - How many questions will be on the test?
  - Will the questions be multiple choice, fill-in-the-blank, etc.?
  - What materials do I need to bring to class?
  - Will I be allowed to use a calculator or any other technology?
  - Is there a time limit on the test?
  - What is the overall grade value of the test?
- **Make** every effort to attend any study or review sessions offered by the instructor or peers

During Tests

- **Read** the directions carefully.
- **Quickly** glance over the test to determine the number of questions and the degree of difficulty as related to the time you have to complete the test.
- **Work** by the clock. If you have 60 minutes to take a test that has 120 questions, this means you have about 30 seconds per question.
- **Begin** by solving the problems that are easiest or most familiar to you.
- **Read** the questions on the test carefully and *more* than once, and don't jump to conclusions.
- **Determine** which formulas you will need to use.
- **Decide** how you want to solve the problem.
- **Check** your work by using multiple solving techniques. (If the problem is division, can it be re-checked with multiplication? This is called "opposite operations.")
- **Draw** pictures if you encounter word problems. Visualization is very important.
- **Show** all of your work, even if it is not required. This will help the instructor (and you) see what you did correctly and/or incorrectly.
- **Re-check** every answer if you have time.
- **Work** backward if at all possible. This may help answer the question and catch mistakes.

(continued)

Figure 10.3 A Quick Reference Guide to Studying Math and Science (*Continued*)

During Tests (*Continued*)

■ After you've completed the answer, **re-read** the question to determine if you did everything the question asked you do to.

■ **Never** erase your margin work or mistakes. This wastes time and you may erase something that you need (or worse, something that was correct).

After Tests

■ **Immediately** after the test, try to determine if the majority of test questions came from classroom notes, your textbook, your study guide, or your homework. This will help you prepare for the next test.

■ **Think** about the way you studied for this test and how you could improve your techniques for the next time. Consider the amount of time spent studying for this test.

■ Once the test is graded, **determine** what caused you to lose the most points: Simple errors? Applying incorrect formulas or theorems? Misunderstanding the questions asked? Intensified test anxiety? Poor study habits in general?

© Robert M. Sherfield, Ph.D.

USING STUDY GROUPS

How Can Working with Peers Enhance Learning?

There may be situations where you will need or want to study in a group. You may find a study group at your institution or your may establish a study group online through your learning management system discussion board, Skype, WebEx, Go to Meeting, or other electronic meeting site. Study groups can be extremely helpful because they give you the opportunity to listen to others, ask questions, share information, cover more ground, solve problems, brainstorm ideas, and develop a support system.

The following tips will help you when you establish or join a study group:

What techniques help reduce your anxiety and negative self-talk during quizzes and exams?

■ Limit the number of participants to 3–5 people and spend some time getting acquainted. Exchange contact information if you're comfortable doing so.

■ Each member should make a personal commitment to bring their best to the group each time you meet.

■ Members of the group should be able to get along with each other, take and give constructive criticism, and make a valued contribution.

■ Limit the group to those people who can meet at the specified times, dates, and locations.

■ Set rules so that all members know the objectives and goals of the study period.

■ Limit the study time to 2–3 hours—longer periods tend to be less productive.

■ All members of the group should be prepared to share and participate.

■ The study group should have a goal for each session.

■ Assignments should be made for the next study session so that everyone comes prepared and you can cover the material that needs to be learned.

- Select a leader so that you reach your goals during the meeting.
- Use the study group as a supplement to, not a replacement for, the class.

PREPARING FOR THE TEST

What Do You Need To Know Before the Test Begins?

Several classes before the test is scheduled, quiz **your instructor** about the specifics of the test. This information can help you study more effectively and eliminate the anxiety that comes with uncertainty. If you don't know if the test is going to be true–false, or essay, or both, it is much more difficult to study for. Some questions you need to ask are:

1. What types of questions will be on the test?
2. How many questions will be on the test?
3. Is there a time limit on the test?
4. Will there be any special instructions, such as use pen only or use a #2 pencil?
5. Is there a study sheet?
6. Will there be a review session?
7. What is the grade value of the test?
8. What chapters or sections will the test cover?

Asking these simple questions will help you know what type of test will be administered, how you should prepare for it, and what supplies you will need.

TEST-TAKING STRATEGIES AND HINTS FOR SUCCESS

What Do You Do When You Can't Remember the Answer?

Almost every test question will elicit one of three types of responses from you as the test taker:

- **Quick-time response**
- **Lag-time response**
- **No Response**

Your response is a *quick-time response* when you read a question and know the answer immediately. You may need to read only one key word in the test question to know the correct response. However, even if you have a quick-time response, always read the entire question before answering. The question may be worded in such a way that the correct response is not what you originally expected. By reading the entire question before answering, you can avoid losing points to a careless error.

You have a *lag-time response* when you read a question and the answer does not come to you immediately. You may have to read the question several times, or even move on to another question, before you think of the correct response. Information in another question will sometimes trigger the response you need. Don't get nervous if you have a lag-time response. Once you've begun to answer other questions, you usually begin to remember more, and the response may come to you. You do not have to answer questions in order on most tests.

No response is the least desirable situation when you are taking a test. You may read a question two or three times and still have no response. At this point, you should move on to

Successful Decisions

AN ACTIVITY FOR CRITICAL REFLECTION

After the second week of classes, Jose was devastated over his first test score. The instructor put the range of grades on the board and he was even more shocked to see that many people passed the test, and that his score was in the bottom 10 percent.

He began asking classmates if they did well or not and found some that had made A's, and others who had made D's. When he spoke with one classmate, Letty, she told him that he should just chill and take a "cheat sheet" to class. "The instructor never looks, man, and she left the classroom twice. She'll never know. That's how I got my A."

"Cheat," Jose thought, "I don't think I can do that." He knew that others had made better grades than he had over the years, but he also knew that he had never once cheated on an exam. Ever.

Jose went to the Tutoring Center and worked with a tutor on content and on how to take a test more effectively. On the next test, Jose scored a C. "It may not be the best grade in the class," he thought, "but it is all mine. I did it myself."

In your own words, what two suggestions would you give Jose to improve his grades without cheating:

1. _____

_____

2. _____

_____

another question to try to find some related information. When this happens, you have some options:

1. Leave this question until the very end of the test.
2. Make an intelligent guess.
3. Try to eliminate all unreasonable answers by association.
4. Watch for modifiers within the question.

Remember these important tips about the three types of responses:

1. Don't be overly anxious if your *response is quick*; read the entire question and be careful so that you don't make a mistake.
2. Don't get nervous if you have a *lag-time response*; the answer may come to you later, so just relax and move on.
3. Don't put down just anything if you have *no response*; take the remaining time and use intelligent guessing.

What Are Some Tips for Test Taking

Before you read about the strategies for answering these different types of questions, think about this: ***There is no substitute for studying!*** You can know all the tips, ways to reduce anxiety, mnemonics, and strategies on earth, but if you have not studied, they will be of little help to you.

Strategies for Matching Questions

Matching questions frequently involve knowledge of people, dates, places, or vocabulary. When answering matching questions, you should:

- Read the directions carefully.
- Read each column before you answer.

from ORDINARY to Extraordinary

Matthew L. Karres, Motivational Speaker/Team Leader, Weight Watchers International

"Fatso!" The word still rings in my ears 40 years after she yelled it. When I was four years old and in preschool, I rode a bus to school and I was the second person to be picked up. One student was already on the bus. When I climbed the steps and took my seat that first day, she yelled that word, "Fatso," and thus began the years of verbal and emotional abuse.

I had always been big for my age. I had to have a larger than "normal" desk from kindergarten onward. By my eighth birthday, I weighed about 120 pounds and stood 5'9" tall. By the time I was in the sixth grade, I was 6'2" tall and even heavier. So there I was, tall, overweight, shy, and introverted. In junior high school, we had to weigh in for gym class, and my class-mates would run over to see how much I weighed. The scale read 225 pounds. In the ninth grade, my weight had soared to 280 pounds and I wore a size 48 pants. This is when my mother took me to Overeaters Anonymous (OA).

In the time period between the ninth and tenth grades, I lost 100 pounds by going on a very restricted diet called "The Gray Sheet" from OA. By the time I began the tenth grade, I was thin, people noticed me for something other than my weight, and I looked good for the first time that I could remember. I was happy—or so I thought. My happiness was short-lived, as my weight soon began rising again.

For the next eight years, I began to gain massive amounts of weight, and the depression that followed was just as massive. My parents moved 3000 miles away, college was not going well for me, and I was lonely, fat, depressed, and, to be truthful, suicidal. Food became my only friend, my best friend. In 10 years, I gained over 250 pounds, reaching nearly 500 pounds and wearing size 62 pants. I developed sleep apnea, heart problems, and limb numbness.

I had to try something drastic, so I applied to become one of the first candidates for weight-loss surgery. I had the surgery, but was given very inadequate warnings about the side-effects: throwing up, gas, withdrawal, *and,* that it was not a miracle cure. However, over three years, I lost 300 pounds and had two reconstructive surgeries. Things were good. Again, this was short-lived.

The problem with weight-loss surgery is that it is *not* a miracle cure and you can still gain weight. I started gaining weight again, and before I knew it, I was up almost 100 pounds. I was in horrible despair. Hopelessness was all I felt. My mother suggested that I join Weight Watchers. I told her that I had tried that before, and then she said the words that changed my life forever.

"Matt," she stated. "You have not tried Weight Watchers. You tried their program *your* way. You did not try their pro-gram *their* way." I decided to re-join. I remember eating three Hostess Fruit Pies on the way to the Weight Watchers meeting.

> *I remember eating three Hostess Fruit Pies on the way to the Weight Watchers meeting.*

This time, I surrendered. I gave in to *their* program. I did the mental and the physical work. Soon, I was losing weight again in a healthy and lasting fashion. I dropped down to 190 pounds. By learning to eat properly, exercise, and think about everything that I put into my mouth, I have kept my weight steady for eight years, and now I have my "dream job" as a motivational leader for Weight Watchers. It has *not* been easy, and I fight every day, but I write this to say that if I can do this, you can, too. There is no bigger food addict than me, but I learned that there is hope. Motivation and mental prep-aration can take you further than you ever imagined.

EXTRAORDINARY REFLECTION

Matthew decided that he had to take a drastic measure (sur-gery in his case) to make a positive change in his life. What drastic changes might you have to make in your life to bring about positive change in the areas of health and wellness?

- Determine whether there are an equal number of items in each column.
- Match what you know first.
- Cross off information that is already used.
- Use the process of elimination for answers you might not know.
- Look for logical clues.
- Use the longer statement as a question; use the shorter statement as an answer.

Strategies for True–False Questions

True–false tests ask if a statement is true or not. True–false questions can be some of the trickiest questions ever developed. Some students like them; some hate them. There is a 50/50 chance of answering correctly, but you can use the following strategies to increase your odds on true–false tests:

- Read each statement carefully.
- Watch for key words in each statement, for example, negatives.
- Read each statement for double negatives, such as "not untruthful."
- Pay attention to words that may indicate that a statement is true, such as "some," "few," "many," and "often."
- Pay attention to words that may indicate that a statement is false, such as "never," "all," "every," and "only."
- Remember that if any part of a statement is false, the entire statement is false.
- Answer every question unless there is a penalty for guessing.

Strategies for Multiple-Choice Questions

Many college instructors give multiple-choice tests because they are easy to grade and provide quick, precise responses. A multiple-choice question usually asks you to choose from among two to five answers to complete a sentence. Some strategies for increasing your success in answering multiple-choice questions are the following:

- Read the question and try to answer it before you read the answers provided.
- Look for similar answers; one of them is usually the correct response.
- Recognize that answers containing extreme modifiers, such as *always, every,* and *never,* are usually wrong.
- Cross out answers that you know are incorrect.
- Read all the options before selecting your answer. Even if you believe that A is the correct response, read them all.
- Recognize that when the answers are all numbers, the highest and lowest numbers are usually incorrect.
- Recognize that a joke is usually wrong.
- Understand that the most inclusive answer is often correct.
- Understand that the longest answer is often correct.
- If you cannot answer a question, move on to the next one and continue through the test; another question may trigger the answer you missed.
- Make an educated guess if you must.
- Answer every question unless there is a penalty for guessing.

Strategies for Short-Answer Questions

Short-answer questions, also called fill-in-the-blanks, ask you to supply the answer yourself, not to select it from a list. Although "short answer" sounds easy, these questions are often very difficult. Short-answer questions require you to draw from your long-term memory. The following hints can help you answer this type of question successfully:

- Read each question and be sure that you know what is being asked.
- Be brief in your response.
- Give the same number of answers as there are blanks; for example, _____ and _____ would require two answers.
- Never assume that the length of the blank has anything to do with the length of the answer.
- Remember that your initial response is usually correct.
- Pay close attention to the word immediately preceding the blank; if the word is "an," give a response that begins with a vowel (a, e, i, o, u).
- Look for key words in the sentence that may trigger a response.

Strategies for Essay Questions

Most students look at essay questions with dismay because they take more time. Yet essay tests can be one of the easiest tests to take because they give you a chance to show what you really know. An essay question requires you to supply the information. If you have studied, you will find that once you begin to answer an essay question, your answer will flow more easily. Some tips for answering essay questions are the following:

- More is not always better; sometimes more is just more. Try to be as concise and informative as possible. An instructor would rather see one page of excellent material than five pages of fluff.
- Pay close attention to the action word used in the question and respond with the appropriate type of answer. Key words used in questions include the following:

discuss	illustrate	enumerate	describe
compare	define	relate	list
contrast	summarize	analyze	explain
trace	evaluate	critique	interpret
diagram	argue	justify	prove

- Write a thesis statement for each answer.
- Outline your thoughts before you begin to write.
- Watch your spelling, grammar, and punctuation.
- Use details, such as times, dates, places, and proper names, where appropriate.
- Be sure to answer all parts of the question; some discussion questions have more than one part.
- Summarize your main ideas toward the end of your answer.
- Write neatly.
- Proofread your answer.

   Learning how to take a test and learning how to reduce your anxiety are two of the most important gifts you can give yourself as a student. Although tips and hints may help you, don't forget that there is no substitute for studying and knowing the material.

Strategies for Taking Online Exams

Many of the techniques used for taking online exams are the same as those that you will use to take a traditional exam. As with traditional exams, the same is true for online exams: ***There is no substitute for studying.***

Do you find it easier or harder to take tests online?

Depending on your learning management system and instructor, the rules for an online exam may vary. You may have a time requirement, and it may be that some instructors have set the exam so that after a limited time period, the question is gone and you cannot come back to it. You will need to find out their rules before the exam.

Some instructors allow you to use your text and notes for an online exam, but the questions are usually more complex and higher on Bloom's Taxonomy scale. You will have to understand the material in much more depth than for an in-class exam.

The following tips will assist you in taking an online exam:

- If at all possible, find out what the exam will cover. Is it comprehensive or on a specific chapter?
- Read the directions carefully.
- Read the questions carefully.
- Ask about the time limit for each question and whether you will be able to come back to the question. Manage your time well for an online exam.
- Find out if you have to answer the questions in sequence.
- Find out if you can change an answer once you have clicked on or entered your response.
- Make sure that you have a strong network connection wherever you are taking the exam so that you are not disconnected in the middle of the exam.

- Understand the method of submission, whether through the learning management system, e-mail, or some other means.
- If at all possible, practice using the testing feature in the learning management system before you actually have to take an exam.
- Once you begin your exam, do not close the window for any reason.
- If allowed, write down all formula, dates, definitions, and rules that you may need for the exam. Have all materials with you before you log onto the computer to begin the exam.
- If possible, save a copy of your exam before you send it, then click "save" and "send."

CHANGING IDEAS to Reality

REFLECTIONS ON NOTE TAKING AND TESTING

Just as reading is a learned skill, so are memory development, studying, and learning how to take tests. You can improve your memory, but it will take practice, patience, and persistence. You can improve your study skills, but it will take time and work. And, you can increase your ability to do well on tests but it will take a commitment on your part to study smarter and put in the time and dedication required. By making the decision "I can do this!," you've won the battle; for when you make that decision, your studying and learning becomes easier.

Your challenge is to focus on developing excellent memory techniques, study patterns, and test-taking abilities while earning the best grades you can. When you have done this, you can look in the mirror and be proud of the person you see without having to be ashamed of your character or having to worry about being caught cheating or wondering if you really did your best.

Knowledge
in Bloom

REDUCING TEST ANXIETY

Utilizes Level 6 of the Taxonomy (See Bloom's Taxonomy at the front of this text)

Explanation: Now that you have read and studied this chapter and, no doubt taken a few tests this semester, you have a better understanding of what happens to you physically and mentally during an exam. Below, you will find listed six of the common physical or mental symptoms of anxiety reported by students while testing.

Process: Beside each symptom, **create a list** of at least three concrete, doable, realistic strategies to overcome this physical or emotional anxiety symptom before or during a testing situation.

Symptom	How to Reduce It
Fatigue	1. 2. 3. Choose one of the above and write a SMART goal statement to personally address this symptom.
Frustration	1. 2. 3. Choose one of the above and write a SMART goal statement to personally address this symptom.
Fear	1. 2. 3. Choose one of the above and write a SMART goal statement to personally address this symptom.
Anger	1. 2. 3. Choose one of the above and write a SMART goal statement to personally address this symptom.
Nervousness/ nausea	1. 2. 3. Choose one of the above and write a SMART goal statement to personally address this symptom.
Uncertainty/ doubt	1. 2. 3. Choose one of the above and write a SMART goal statement to personally address this symptom.

SQ3R MASTERY STUDY SHEET

EXAMPLE QUESTION (FROM PAGE 233) Why are mnemonics important?	**ANSWER:**
EXAMPLE QUESTION (FROM PAGE 238) Discuss three strategies for studying math.	**ANSWER:**
AUTHOR QUESTION (FROM PAGE 228) What is the difference between short-term and long-term memory?	**ANSWER:**
AUTHOR QUESTION (FROM PAGE 229) Discuss the five steps in VCR3.	**ANSWER:**
AUTHOR QUESTION (FROM PAGE 237) What is H2 FLIB and how can it help you?	**ANSWER:**
AUTHOR QUESTION (FROM PAGE 240) Discuss the steps in establishing a study group.	**ANSWER:**
AUTHOR QUESTION (FROM PAGE 246) Discuss one strategy for each type of testing situation.	**ANSWER:**
YOUR QUESTION (FROM PAGE ____)	**ANSWER:**
YOUR QUESTION (FROM PAGE ____)	**ANSWER:**
YOUR QUESTION (FROM PAGE ____)	**ANSWER:**
YOUR QUESTION (FROM PAGE ____)	**ANSWER:**
YOUR QUESTION (FROM PAGE ____)	**ANSWER:**

Finally, after answering these questions, recite this chapter's major points in your mind. Consider the following general questions to help you master this material.

- What is it about?
- What does it mean?
- What is the most important thing you learned? Why?
- What are the key points to remember?

chapter eleven

PROSPER

MANAGING YOUR MONEY AND DEBTS WISELY

"Don't tell me where your priorities are. Show me where you spend your money, and I will tell you what they are." —James W. Frick

PROSPER

Why read this chapter?

Because you'll learn...

- To manage your money and avoid credit card trouble
- To identify the types of financial aid available to you
- How to protect yourself against identity theft

Because you'll be able to...

- Appraise your FICO score and keep it healthy
- Construct and use a budget
- Protect your credit cards and other vital information from identity theft

Scan and QUESTION

Take a few moments, **scan this chapter** and on page 274, write **five of your own questions** that you think will be important to your mastery of this material. You will also find five questions listed from your authors.

Example:

☑ **What are the types of financial aid?** (from page 254)

☑ **How does a grant differ from a loan?** (from page 254)

MyStudentSuccessLab

MyStudentSuccessLab is an online solution designed to help you acquire and develop (or hone) the skills you need to succeed. You will have access to peer-led video presentations and develop core skills through interactive exercises and projects.

Name: Jeffrey Steele

Institution: Graduate! Wor-Wic Community College, Salisbury, MD

Major: Nursing

At the age of 20, Jeff Steele found himself a college dropout and homeless. Growing up in rural Ohio, Jeff was a bright student who graduated from high school after his sophomore year and enrolled at a local university. However, he had a problem. "No one had explained to me how financial aid worked, and my parents couldn't afford my schooling," he laments. To meet his steep tuition bills, Jeff started working full-time as a busboy while also working part-time in his residence hall on campus.

For two years, Jeff managed to work these jobs while also attending school full-time. However, the stress and strain of this lifestyle started to take its toll. As Jeff puts it, "With the heavy curriculum and my overworked body, I didn't last long."

Before the start of his fifth semester in college, Jeff received a letter from the college that would change his life. "I could no longer attend until I paid my tuition," he remembers. "I was officially a college dropout."

Kicked out of his dorm room, Jeff found himself homeless, helpless, and severely depressed. He slept for two months at a local bus stop before saving up enough money to get his own apartment. However, after a year he still felt powerless. "I knew I had to try and attempt my college education again," he remarks.

Seeking to gain access to another chance at higher education, Jeff enlisted in the United States Air Force. This was the first step toward bettering his life. "My military life gave me a chance to earn back my confidence and re-establish my strengths."

After serving a four-year tour of duty in Germany, Jeff relocated to Maryland to be closer to family. This is where Jeff made a decision that would change his life forever— he enrolled at Wor-Wic Community College with a major in nursing.

"In finding Wor-Wic Community College, I found the help I needed to reach my goals. The faculty and staff were quick to respond to my needs," Jeff says. He learned from the college's veterans coordinator that he could use his GI Bill benefits to pay for the costs of college. His nursing advisor helped to establish his career goals, and the director of student activities helped him gain leadership skills. Jeff became active on campus, helping to organize special events and even starting a new student organization.

"Wor-Wic not only gave me an education that I could afford, it has made me a better person all-around. The people of my community college have helped me gain back the dignity and confidence I lost after my first attempt at a college education," he says gratefully.

An interview conducted and written by Ryan Messatzzia, Academic and Disabilities Counselor, Wor-Wic Community College, Salisbury, MD.

Jeff graduated from Wor-Wic Community College with honors and gained employment at a local hospital while also continuing to pursue a Bachelor's degree in Nursing. "My education has given me a purpose for my life," Jeff states, calling his current position "the perfect job."

Despite many trials and tribulations, Jeff persevered. And thanks to his college experience Jeff can now call himself a "college graduate" and a "registered nurse."

THINK a b o u t *it*

1. Finances derailed Jeff's first attempt at a college education. What financial hurdles will you have to overcome to continue your studies? What plans are you making now to overcome potential financial hurdles you might face?

2. Jeff enlisted in the military to gain financial assistance for college. What avenues are you willing to pursue to acquire the money to complete your degree?

TAKING CONTROL OF YOUR FINANCES

How Can Financial Management Affect Your Future and Your Life?

You may be wondering why a chapter focusing on personal finance is found in a student success text. The answer is quite simple. We have known many students over the years who were academically capable, socially skilled, and managed their time and goals well. However, they were forced to leave their studies because they got into financial trouble. They did not know how to earn money, manage money, save money, or live within their means. This chapter is included to help you do all of these things so that you can get your education.

Most college students have had little to no training in managing finances. Many are ill prepared to make sound financial decisions and find themselves in trouble and have to leave school. It is not unusual for college graduates to accumulate significant college loan and credit card debt, as well as car loans and other financial obligations, by the time they graduate. We do not want this to happen to you. Learning to manage your finances and debts wisely will certainly be one of the most important lessons you learn—and one that you will need to carry with you throughout your life and career.

Financial literacy is understanding information about financial matters and being able to make appropriate decisions relative to financial areas, such as real estate, taxes, student loans, and retirement. One of the first steps in financial literacy is learning the difference between "*standard of living*" and "*quality of life*." According to Sycle and Tietje (2010), your standard of living is determined by tangible things, such as your ability to buy a nice car, own a fine home, wear designer clothes, eat in famous restaurants,

What would make your quality of life better?

and go out when you please. This would be considered a "high" standard of living. Conversely, if you live paycheck to paycheck, you have a "low" standard of living. However, there are many people who have a "low" standard of living, but have an extremely high quality of life. "There are probably people living off the land in a Central American jungle who are more satisfied and content than some millionaires living in Los Angeles. Money doesn't necessarily buy you quality of life" (Syckle & Tietje, 2010).

Quality of life is determined by the things that do not cost a great deal of money, such as love, the affection of your children, your leisure activities, and the ability to enjoy quiet times with friends and family. Money *may* improve your quality of life, but there are many rich, unhappy, sad people.

The reason you need to know the difference is that many people think that the more money you make, the happier you are. This may be true if you also have the intangible things that improve your quality of life. But possessions alone seldom make anyone happy. You can live well and have a high quality of life on almost any budget if you know how to manage your finances properly, and that is what this chapter is all about—managing your money so that you can have the quality of life that you want and deserve.

PRACTICING DISCIPLINE AT THE RIGHT TIME

Can You Mind Your Own Business?

The time to learn to take care of your business and finances is right now so you can hit the ground running when you graduate. You might already be working in a full-time position with an opportunity to participate in a 401K program. Many people neglect to enroll because they don't understand and they don't want to appear ignorant by asking. You may feel that you simply can't afford to enroll and allocate that money to a retirement fund. The truth? You really can't afford not to enroll! Your future depends on it. Even if you are a typical student who is struggling to make ends meet and can't invest right now, this is the time to prepare for what comes ahead. We highly encourage you to make up your mind that you are going to be financially secure and that you are going to master the keys to saving money.

Some important tips for preparing for the future *right now* include:

- Practice *delayed gratification*. This is the first key to personal wealth accumulation. Even though it will probably require changing your habits, learn to develop this habit now.

- Take a *personal finance course* as soon as possible. You will be able to put the information into practice much sooner if you take the course early in your college career.

- If you plan to operate any kind of business, *take accounting and tax law courses*. Even if you plan to run a dance studio or a physical fitness center, this applies to you.

- *Save your change every day*. You will be surprised how quickly it adds up. You can put it in savings or invest it. You may even need it to pay the rent one month.

- *Write down everything you spend*. Where can you cut costs? In what ways are you wasting money? At the end of this chapter, you will find a worksheet entitled, **Tracking Your Expenditures and Spending Habits.** Use this sheet to track all of your spending for three days, then analyze your habits and develop a change plan. You'll be amazed at where your money goes.

- *Apply for every type of financial aid* possible to assist with your education. You may not be awarded every type, but every cent helps. The following section will help you with this.

How many credit cards do you currently have? Do you use them wisely?

FINANCIAL AID

Is There Such a Thing as Pennies from Heaven?

Nearly two out of every three students are going into debt to go to college, owing an average of more than $22,500. Today, student load debt has passed $1 *trillion*—more than all credit cards and auto loans combined. Senior citizens in America still owe over $36 billion in student loan debt (Platt, 2012; Yerak, 2012). Chances are good that you have already borrowed money or might need to in the future. Therefore, understanding financial aid, scholarships, loans, and grants is very important as you make decisions that will impact you for a long time. If you have to borrow money to attend school, we think you should; on the other hand, we urge you to be very frugal—even stingy—when it comes to borrowing money. A day of reckoning will come, and for many people, it's like getting hit by a freight train when they realize what this debt means to them. Because they are relatively uninformed about personal finances, many people make bad financial decisions. Many students don't have a clue as to the impact of large student loans and other debts on their future well-being.

The most well-known sources of financial assistance are from federal and state governments. Federal and state financial aid programs have been in place for many years and are a staple of assistance for many college students. Figure 11.1 shows sources of aid.

Each year, over $170 billion of financial aid is available. Not every school participates in every federal or state assistance program, so to determine which type of aid is available at your school, you need to contact the financial aid office—today!

One of the biggest mistakes students make when thinking about financial aid is forgetting about scholarships from private industry and social or civic organizations. Each year, millions of dollars are unclaimed because students do not know about these scholarships or where to find the necessary information. Speak with someone in your financial aid office regarding all types of scholarships.

Federal Financial Aid Types and Eligibility

The following are types of federal financial aid. See Figure 11.2 for eligibility requirements.

Pell Grant. This is a need-based grant awarded by the U.S. Government to qualified undergraduate students who have not been awarded a previous degree. Amounts vary based on need and costs and your status as a full- or part-time student. For the 2011–2012 school year, the full award amount was $5,550. This figure changes yearly and also may change due to congressional mandates and spending.

Federal Supplemental Educational Opportunity Grant (FSEOG). This is a need-based grant awarded to institutions to allocate to students through their financial aid offices. The

Figure 11.1   Types of Aid

Type	Description
Federal and state loans	Money that must be repaid with interest—usually beginning six months after your graduation date.
Federal and state grants	Money you do not have to repay—often need-based awards given on a first-come, first-served basis.
Scholarships (local, regional, and national)	Money acquired from public and private sources that does not have to be repaid. Often, scholarships are merit based.
Work study programs	Money earned while working on campus for your institution. This money does not have to be repaid.

Figure 11.2 Student Eligibility for Federal Financial Aid

To receive aid from the major federal student aid programs, you must:

- Fill out a FAFSA on a yearly basis (Free Application for Federal Student Aid at www.fafsa.ed.gov)
- Have financial need, except for some loan programs
- Hold a high school diploma or GED, pass an independently administered test approved by the U.S. Department of Education, or meet the standards established by your state
- Be enrolled as a regular student working toward a degree or certificate in an eligible program; you may not receive aid for correspondence or telecommunications courses unless they are a part of an associate, bachelor, or graduate degree program
- Be a U.S. citizen
- Have a valid Social Security number
- Make satisfactory academic progress
- Sign a statement of educational purpose
- Sign a statement of updated information
- Register with the Selective Service, if required
- Some federal financial aid may be dependent on your not having a previous drug conviction.

Source: Adapted from *The Student Guide: Financial Aid from the U.S. Department of Education.* U.S. Dept. of Education, Washington, DC, 2011–2012.

amount varies between $100 and $4,000 per year, with an average award of about $750. Priority is given to students who demonstrate exceptional need.

Academic Competitiveness Grant (ACG). The ACG became available in 2006 for first-year college students who graduated high school after January 1, 2006, and second-year students who graduated high school after January 1, 2005. Students must be eligible for the Pell Grant to be considered for the ACG. Grants are awarded to first-year students who completed a rigorous high school degree (as established by state and local educational agencies), and to second-year students who maintain a 3.0 GPA.

SMART Grant. The SMART Grant (or National **S**cience and **M**athematics **A**ccess to **R**etain **T**alent Grant) is awarded to at least half-time students during the third and fourth years of undergraduate study or fifth year of a five-year program. Students must also be eligible for the Pell Grant to receive a SMART Grant, and must be majoring in physical, life, or computer sciences, technology, an international language deemed necessary to national security, mathematics, or engineering. Students must maintain a 3.0 GPA in coursework required for the major.

Stafford Loan (formerly known as the Guaranteed Student Loan). The Stafford Direct Loan Program is a low-interest, *subsidized loan*. You must show need to qualify, and you must have submitted a FAFSA application to be eligible. The government pays the interest while you are in school, but you must be registered for at least half-time status. You begin repayments six months after you leave school.

Unsubsidized Stafford Loan. This Stafford Loan is a low-interest, *non-subsidized loan*. You *do not* have to show need to qualify. You are responsible for principle and interest payments beginning six months after graduation or six months after you drop below a half-time status. Interest begins accruing from the time the loan is disbursed to the school. Even though the government does not pay the interest, you can defer the interest and the payment until six months after you have left school.

Have you allotted enough time in your schedule to fill out your financial aid application completely and accurately?

Federal PLUS Loan. This is a federally funded, but state administered, low-interest loan to qualified *parents of students* (biological and adopted parents qualify) in college. The student must be enrolled at least half time. Parents must pass a credit check and be U.S. citizens. Payments begin 60 days after the last loan payment. Students are responsible for repaying the loan if parents default.

Work Study. Work study is a federally funded, need-based program that pays students an hourly wage for working on (and sometimes off) campus. Students earn at least minimum wage.

Hope Scholarship Tax Credit (HSTC). According to FinAid.org, the HSTC provides a federal income tax credit based on the first $4,000 in postsecondary education expenses paid by the taxpayer during the tax year. The amount of the credit is 100 percent of the first $2,000 in qualified expenses, and 25 percent of the second $2,000. You can apply for the HSTC for four years. The HSTC is subject to congressional changes.

Perkins Loan. This is a loan for students who demonstrate exceptional need in which the amount of money you can borrow is determined by the government and the availability of funds. The interest rate is relatively low and repayment begins nine months after you leave school or drop below half-time status. You must be enrolled at least half time and you can take up to 10 years to repay the loan.

Tips for Applying for Financial Aid

- You *must* complete a FAFSA (Free Application for Federal Student Aid) to be eligible to receive *any* federal or state assistance. ***If you are considered a dependent,*** *you and your parents* must apply for and obtain a PIN number to complete the FAFSA. Because much federal and state money is awarded on a first-come, first-serve basis, it is advisable to complete your application as soon after January 1 as possible—even if you have to use the previous year's tax returns and update your application later. Your college's financial aid office can assist you with this process. You can also log onto www.fafsa.ed.gov to learn more.

- ***Do not miss a deadline.*** There are *no* exceptions for making up deadlines for federal financial aid!

- *Read all instructions* before beginning the process, always fill out the application completely, and have someone proof your work.

- If documentation is required, submit it according to the instructions. Do not fail to do all that the application asks you to do.

- Never lie about your financial status.

- Begin the application process as soon as possible. Do not wait until the last minute. Some aid is given on a first-come, first-served basis. Income tax preparation time is usually financial aid application time.

- Talk to the financial aid officer at the institution you will attend. Person-to-person contact is always best. Never assume anything until you get it in writing.

- Take copies of fliers and brochures that are available from the financial aid office. Private companies and civic groups will often notify the financial aid office if they have funds available.

- Always apply for admission as well as financial aid. The college gives many awards to students who are already accepted.

- If you are running late with an application, find out if there is an electronic means of filing.

- Always keep a copy of your tax returns for each year.

- Apply for everything possible. You will get nothing if you do not apply.

See Figure 11.3 for some tips for applying for financial aid online.

Figure 11.3 Online Financial Aid Tip Guide

Consider the following online resources for learning more about and applying for different types of financial aid.

FAFSA (Free Application for Federal Student Aid)
The "must go to place" for beginning your financial aid process. You (and your parents if you are a dependent) must complete the FAFSA to receive **any** federal aid.
http://www.fafsa.ed.gov

Federal Student Aid Portal
The U.S. Government source for higher education funding.
http://studentaid.ed.gov/PORTALSWebApp/students/english/index.jsp

Finaid! The Smart Student™ Guide to Financial Aid
Great website for financial aid tools, advice, support, military aid, calculators, and various guidelines.
http://www.finaid.org

FASTWEB—Paying for School Just Got Easier
A site dedicated to helping you find scholarships. You fill out a profile and the website notifies you when a scholarship that matches your interests becomes available.
http://www.fastweb.com

Pay for College
This site offers assistance in finding different types of aid, college costs, loans, and financing.
http://www.collegeboard.com/student/pay

ed.gov (The United States Department of Education)
A website dedicated to helping you find various types of aid and helping you understand payment options and guidelines.
http://www2.ed.gov/finaid/landing.jhtml?src=ln

Financial Aid Finder—Student Scholarship Search
A website/blog that continually tracks and posts available scholarships and information. Click on "Find a Scholarship."
http://www.financialaidfinder.com/student-scholarship-search/

Financial Aid Info
A website clearinghouse that guides you to many different financial aid websites.
http://www.financialaidinfo.org/useful-student-aid-websites.aspx

STUDENT LOANS

A Day of Reckoning Will Come—Will You Be Ready?

The high cost of college makes tuition out of reach for many families. For many students, the only way they can attend college is with student loans. If this is the only way you can go to college, borrow the money—but borrow no more than you absolutely must. Try not to borrow anything but tuition and perhaps books and supplies. Get a job, budget, cut out extras, work in the summers, attend college via a cooperative program, enroll in online courses, live at home or find a roommate—do everything possible not to borrow more money than you absolutely must.

Many students are finding it necessary to extend their student loans over a period of 30 years just to keep their heads above water; of course, if one does that, the interest paid is also higher. For example, a student who takes 30 years to pay off a $20,000 loan at 6.8 percent will pay about $27,000 in interest plus the principle (for a total of $47,000), compared to $7,619 of interest (for a total of $27,619) on a loan paid off in 10 years (Block, 2006). You will have to repay the money that you have borrowed. Period! **Bankruptcy will not even relieve you of this debt** because student loans are not subject to bankruptcy laws; so again, don't borrow any money you don't absolutely need. Consider the following examples in Figure 11.4.

Because of the **College Cost Reduction and Access Act of 2007,** your federal student loan may be forgiven after 10 years of full-time employment in **public service,** such as the military, law enforcement, public health, public education, or social work, to name a few. However, you must have made 120 payments as a part of the Direct Loan Program. Only payments made after October 1, 2007, count toward the required 120 monthly payments.

Figure 11.4 Total Interest

Amount of Money Borrowed	Your Interest Rate (average)	Total Years to Repay (20 years is the average)	Your Monthly Payment	Total Interest Paid (your cost to borrow the money)
$ 5,000	3.5%	10	$ 49.44	$ 932.80
		20	$ 29.00	$ 1960.00
		30	$ 22.45	$ 3082.00
$10,000	3.5%	10	$ 98.89	$ 1866.80
		20	$ 58.00	$ 3920.00
		30	$ 44.90	$ 6164.00
$15,000	3.5%	10	$148.33	$ 2799.60
		20	$ 86.99	$ 5877.60
		30	$ 67.36	$ 9249.60
$20,000	3.5%	10	$197.77	$ 3732.40
		20	$115.99	$ 7837.60
		30	$ 89.81	$12331.60
$30,000	3.5%	10	$296.66	$ 5599.20
		20	$173.99	$11757.60
		30	$134.71	$18495.60

YOUR CREDIT HISTORY

Do You Know the Score?

Many students don't even know they have a credit score, yet this score is the single most important factor that will determine if you get approved for a mortgage, car loan, credit card, insurance, and so on. Furthermore, if you get approved, this credit score will determine what rate of interest you will have to pay. You can order one free credit report online by accessing the website www.annualcreditreport.com. There are also sites where you can access your credit score such as www.freecreditscore.com and www.freescoreonline.com. Some websites may not charge you for your credit *report* but they will charge you for your credit *score*. The website www.creditkarma.com is a very easy and totally free site.

Range of Scores and What FICO Means for You

This information may seem trivial right now, and you might not want to be bothered with more information, but the truth is, you must pay attention to this because your FICO score has long-lasting implications for almost everything you want to do. The sooner you understand the importance of this score and take steps to keep it healthy, the better off you will be.

Your credit score is referred to as a FICO score. FICO is the acronym for **Fair Issac Corporation,** the company that created the widely used credit score model. This score is calculated using information from your credit history and files. The FICO score is the reason it matters if you accumulate large debts, if you go over your credit card limits, or if you are late with payments—these offenses stick with you and are not easily changed. Based on this score, you can be denied credit, pay a lower or higher interest rate, be required to provide extensive asset information in order to even get credit, or sail right through when you seek a loan.

FICO scores range from 300 to 850. A good score is considered 720 or above. The lower your FICO score, the higher the interest rate you will have to pay because you will be considered a poor risk. So what's the big deal about a few points? Study the chart in Figure 11.5 to see how important your FICO score is when you start to finance a house or seek credit for other reasons.

> "Just about every financial move you make for the rest of your life will be somehow linked to your FICO score."
>
> —Suze Orman,

Figure 11.5   The Impact of Your FICO Score on Purchasing A House

Consider the following interest rates based on varying FICO scores. The following figures are based on purchasing a new home for $150,000. with a 30 year, fixed interest loan.

FICO Score Range (Ranging from best to worst)	Average Interest Rate you can expect to pay	Estimated Monthly payment	Estimated TOTAL Interest paid
760-850	5.78%	$ 879.00	$166,440.
799-759	6.00%	$ 900.00	$174,000.
660-699	6.28%	$ 927.00	$183,720.
620-659	7.09%	$1008.00	$212,880.
580-619	8.58%	$1162.00	$268,320.
500-579	9.49%	$1261.00	$303,960.

Using the table above, analyze the data.

What is the **monthly payment** difference for someone with a 660–699 FICO score and a 760–850 score? _____ $_____

What is the difference **in interest paid** for someone who has a 660–699 FICO score and someone who has a 760–850 score? $_____

Using your current FICO Score, what would **your monthly payment** be? $_____

Using your current FICO Score, what would **your total interest payment** be? $_____

Level 4 Analyze

Tips for Keeping Your Credit Score Healthy

- Obtain a copy of your credit report and correct any inaccuracies. Clean up any errors in your personal information: incorrect addresses, social security numbers, and employer information. Below, you will find the three major credit reporting agencies and their contact information:
  - Equifax: www.equifax.com, 1-800-685-1111
  - Experian: www.experian.com, 1-888-397-3742
  - TransUnion: www.transunion.com, 1-800-888-4213
- Review any negative credit information and correct errors. The credit reporting agencies have 30 days to investigate and respond to your inquiry. If they cannot verify a negative item within 30 days, they must remove it from your report.
- Keep all your credit card balances under 35 percent of the total credit limit available. For example, if you have a $500 limit, you should never have a balance larger than $175. To go over will lower your FICO score and might cause the credit card company to raise your interest rate.
- Call your creditors and ask them to lower your credit rate! This will dramatically, and immediately, lower your payments, and reduce your overall debt.
- Call and ask your creditors to remove any fees—late fees, over-the-limit fees. If you are a good customer, they will usually do this—but they won't do it unless you ask.
- Do not open up several credit cards at once. Multiple inquiries bring your credit score down.

> "Your credit past is your credit future."
>
> —Steve Konowalow

- Don't close credit cards if they are in good standing. The best thing for your credit score are old accounts with good credit history. Just lock them up and don't use them!
- Set up automated payments to make sure you pay your bills on time. One late payment has an extremely negative impact on your score.
- Be careful about transferring balances. If you do this too often, it will lower your FICO score. (Adapted from Trudeau, 2007)

B IS FOR BUDGETING

Where Does My Money Go?

Most people have no idea where their money goes. Many just spend and spend, and then borrow on credit cards to pay for additional expenses for which they have not budgeted. Knowing how much money you have and exactly how you spend it is a very important step toward financial security. It is easy to pay more attention to buying than to budgeting, watching your credit score, or controlling your credit card debt. This section will help you set up your own budget and take control of your finances.

One of the main reasons to budget is to determine the exact amount of money you need to borrow to finance your college education. Poor planning while in college can easily result in a lower standard of life after you graduate and begin paying back enormous loans. Deciding how much to borrow will impact your life long after you have completed your degree. You should also remember that you *will* be required to repay your student loans, even if you do not graduate. As previously mentioned, even bankruptcy won't eliminate student loans.

When budgeting, you must first determine how much income you earn monthly. Complete the following chart.

Source of Monthly Income	**Estimated Amount**
Work	$_____
Spouse/partner/parental income	$_____
Scholarships/loans	$_____
Savings/investments	$_____
Alimony/child support	$_____
Other	$_____
Total Income	$_____

Next, you must determine how much money you spend in a month. Complete the following chart.

Source of Monthly Expenditure	**Estimated Amount**
Housing (mortgage or rent)	$_____
Utilities (water, gas, power, etc.)	$_____
Phone (home and cell)	$_____
Text/data usage charges	$_____
Internet access	$_____
Car payment	$_____
Car insurance	$_____
Fuel	$_____
Transportation (train, bus, etc.)	$_____
Clothing	$_____
Food	$_____
Household items	$_____
Personal hygiene items	$_____
Healthcare and/or health insurance	$_____
Entertainment/fun	$_____
Pet care	$_____
Savings	$_____
Other	$_____
Total Monthly Expenditures	$_____

**Total Monthly Income $_____ minus Total Monthly Expenses $_____ =
$_____**

If the amount of your total expenditures is smaller than your monthly income, you are on your way to controlling your finances. If your total expenditures figure is larger than your monthly income, you are heading for a financial crisis. Furthermore, you are establishing bad money management habits that may carry over into your life after college.

Now, consider your education and the costs associated with everything from books to supplies to childcare. Using the **Economic Readiness Assessment** in Figure 11.6, do the research to determine how much your education (tuition, books, room, board, etc.) will cost you next semester. You will have to go to the bookstore (or online) to research the cost of your texts, and you may need to refer to your college catalog for rules regarding some of the other questions. You can also use the Internet to answer a few of the questions, but it is important that you answer them all.

Figure 11.6   Economic Readiness Assessment

In the spaces below, please read the question carefully, respond with Yes or No, and then answer the question based on your financial research for **next term**. Be specific. You may have to visit the financial aid office, bookstore, or other campus resource center to answer the questions.

Question	Answer	Response
I know exactly how much my tuition will cost next term.	YES NO	Answer: $_____
I know the additional cost of lab fees, technology fees, and other fees associated with my courses (if any).	YES NO	Answer: $_____
I know how much my textbooks will cost next semester.	YES NO	Answer: $_____
I know how much my transportation will cost next semester (car payment, gas, insurance, bus passes, etc.).	YES NO	Answer: $_____
I know how much I need to spend on supplies for next semester.	YES NO	Answer: $_____
I know how much childcare will cost next semester.	YES NO	Answer: $_____
I know where my GPA must remain to keep my financial aid.	YES NO	Answer: _____
I know how much money I can borrow through financial aid in one academic year.	YES NO	Answer: $_____
I know how much money I need to manage my personal budget in a single term.	YES NO	Answer: $_____
I have estimated miscellaneous and unexpected costs that might occur during the semester.	YES NO	Answer: $_____
I know what a FAFSA is and how and when to apply.	YES NO	Answer: _____
I know how a drug arrest could affect my financial aid.	YES NO	Answer: _____
I know the scholarships available to me, and how, when, and where to apply for them.	YES NO	Answer: _____
I know how and where to apply for work study.	YES NO	Answer: _____
I know how a felony charge affects my ability to get a job after graduation.	YES NO	Answer: _____

Level 4 Analyze

Level 6 Create

After completing your budget list, evaluating ways to cut spending, and taking a careful look at your college expenses, outline what you need to do to cut or control your expenses and develop a budget plan that includes your living expenses, unexpected items, college costs, and a moderate savings plan. You will probably need to also consider your **Spending Habits Chart** at the end of this chapter to give more informed responses.

**Figure 11.7   Balancing Your Checkbook—
A Quick Guide**

Keeping a balance of your daily, weekly, and monthly expenditures is an important step in getting a handle on your finances. One way to do this is to balance your checkbook or bank account after every purchase.

Notice Check 286 and how it was recorded in the check register. You might also consider downloading your bank's check register app or use Excel to electronically balance your checkbook. Whatever method you use, work hard to keep your balances up to date to avoid overdraft charges, which are sometimes over $30 to $50 per check.

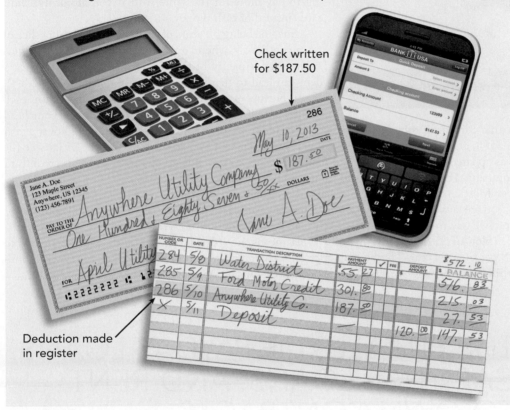

Check written for $187.50

Deduction made in register

CREDIT CARDS

Why Is Living on Borrowed Money the *Worst* Kind of Debt?

Credit card debt—one of the worst kinds of debt—is rising rapidly among college students as they struggle to pay tuition, buy books, and cover day-to-day living expenses. According to a Nellie Mae study (2010), 76 percent of all undergraduate college students have at least one credit card and carry an average balance of almost $2,500. As a result of over-the-top credit card marketing, terrible credit card terms and conditions, and an economy that no longer provides as many well-paying jobs with good benefits as it once did, graduates are facing overwhelming odds to achieve financial health, in large part as a result of the credit card debt from their undergraduate years (Williams, 2008).

> "If you can eat it, wear it, or drink it, it is not an emergency."
>
> —Kim Rebel,

Can you imagine paying for a piece of pizza for 12 years?

Studies show that credit card shoppers, in general, are less price sensitive and more extravagant. When you pay with plastic, you lose track of how much you are spending. According to the article, "Live Without Plastic" (Rosato, 2008), after McDonald's started accepting credit and debit cards in 2004, diners who paid with plastic spent $7.00 a visit on average, compared to $4.50 when they paid in cash. The article also suggests that you are less aware of what you spend if you use plastic. For example, 68 percent of students who paid cash for their books knew how much they spent. Conversely, only 35 percent of students using plastic knew what they spent. Rosato also reports that you are willing to pay more for the same stuff if you are using credit cards instead of cash money.

Imagine being 30 years old and still paying off a slice of pizza you bought when you were 18 and in college. Sounds crazy, but for plenty of people, problems with credit card debt can lead to that very situation (College Board, 2008). If you borrow excessively and only pay the minimum each month, it will be very easy to find yourself over your head with credit card problems. Take the case of Joe. Joe's average unpaid credit card bill over a year is $500, and his finance charge is 20 percent. He pays a $20 annual fee, plus a $25 late fee (he was up late studying and forgot to mail in his check). Joe ends up owing $145 to his credit card company, and he still hasn't paid for any of his purchases (College Board, 2008).

Most credit card companies charge a very high rate of interest—18 to 21 percent or higher. If you are late with a payment, the interest rate can go even higher. For every $1000 you charge, you will pay from $180 to $210 each year (Konowalow, 2003). Don't be fooled by the advertising ploy of "1.5 percent interest." This means 1.5 percent each month, which equates to 18 percent per year. The best practice is to charge no more than you can pay off each month while avoiding high interest rates. Consider the tips in the chart in Figure 11.8.

THE PITFALLS OF PAYDAY LOANS, CAR TITLE LOANS, AND RENT-TO-OWN CONTRACTS

Did You Know There's Someone Lurking on Every Corner to Take Your Money?

Many unsuspecting consumers have been duped into signing car title loans, payday loans, or rent-to-own contracts that result in very high monthly payments and penalties. Some were told by their title loan broker before they signed the contract that they could make a partial payment if they needed to and this would be OK. Unfortunately, the unsuspecting victims find out too late that their car will be repossessed due to one late or partial payment. Others realize too late that on a loan of $400, they must pay back over $500 that month. According to some reports, payday and title loan lenders have been charging as much as 250 to 350 percent interest on an annualized basis. In some instances, interest rates as high as 900 percent have been charged due to poor government regulatory policies. Some states have recently enacted laws to prevent this.

Payday loans are extremely expensive compared to other cash loans. For example, a $300 cash advance on the average credit card, repaid in one month, would cost $13.99 in finance charges at an annual interest rate of almost 57 percent, which is very high. By comparison,

Figure 11.8 **Important Facts You Need to Know about Credit Cards**

What You Don't Know Can Wreck Your Credit Rating and Ruin Your Life

Listed below are some of the most important things you can learn about managing credit card debt. Some of them will make you angry, while others don't seem legal, but they happen all the time.

- ✓ Understand that credit cards are nothing more than high interest loans—in some cases, very high! The system is designed to keep you in debt.

- ✓ Be aware that companies often add on new fees and change policies after customers have already signed up.

- ✓ If you fall behind on payments to one creditor or if your credit score drops for any reason, your rates can be raised on all your credit cards.

- ✓ Banks can and will abruptly switch your due date, so pay attention. Always check your bill to see if any fees or charges have been added.

- ✓ Avoid cards that charge an annual just for the privilege of carrying the card. This fee can be as high as $100–$400 per year. If you charge this fee, it will be automatically added to your card and then you begin paying interest on the fee.

- ✓ Be sure your card allows for a grace period before interest is charged.

- ✓ Carry only one or two credit cards so you can manage your debt and not get in over your head. Do not accept or sign up for cards that you don't need.

- ✓ When you accept a card, sign it right away and keep records of your credit card numbers (in a secure location) and the phone number to contact in case they are lost or stolen. If you lose your card, report it immediately to avoid charges.

- ✓ Avoid the temptation to charge. You should use credit cards only when you absolutely must and only when you can pay the full amount before interest is added. "Buy now, pay later" is a dangerous game.

- ✓ When you pay off a card, celebrate and don't use that as a reason to charge again. Lock that card in a safe place and leave it there.

- ✓ Each month, always try to pay more than the minimum payment due.

- ✓ Send the payment at least five days in advance. Late fees now represent the third-largest revenue stream for banks.

- ✓ Call the credit card company and negotiate a better rate. If they won't give you a better rate, tell them you are going to transfer the debt.

- ✓ If you have several credit card debts, consolidate all the amounts on the card where you have the lowest balance. Don't cancel your cards, because it helps your credit score if you have cards on which you have no debt. Just don't use them again!

- ✓ Do not leave any personal information (credit cards, Social Security numbers, checking accounts) in places where roommates or other students have access to them. Purchase a metal file box with a lock and keep it in a secure place.

- ✓ Consider using a debit card. Money is deducted directly from your bank account and you cannot spend more than you actually have.

- ✓ If you have already gotten into credit card trouble, get **reputable** counseling. One of the best agencies is the National Foundation for Credit Counseling (NFCC).

- ✓ Be aware that using a credit card carelessly is similar to a drug addiction. Credit card use is habit forming and addictive!

- ✓ Ask yourself these questions: "If I can't pay this credit card in full this month, what is going to change next month? Will I have extra income or will I reduce my spending enough to pay for this purchase?" If the answers are "No," you don't need to make the purchase.

- ✓ Realize that you are building your future credit rating even though you are a student.

> *Once you get a credit card, immediately write, "CHECK ID" across the back in red, permanent ink.*

Successful Decisions

AN ACTIVITY FOR CRITICAL REFLECTION

Jonathon enjoys school. He has made new friends, has great relationships with his instructors, and is managing to keep his grades up. But he's already got a major problem—keeping up with his expenses. He is spending much more money than he has coming in. He has one part-time job where he works 25 hours per week. It would be very difficult to work more because of his schedule at school, his family commitments, and the amount of time he has to study for his math class.

To compound these problems, he has met a great girl, and he has tried hard to impress her by taking her to expensive clubs and dinners. Their first date cost him a bundle. He didn't have the funds, so he charged everything on his new credit card. Jonathon is getting very stressed about his money situation. He's having trouble sleeping well. To top it off, his new girlfriend is talking about taking a weekend trip together. He knows that he will have to pay the majority of the bills on the trip. He is very worried because he has already maxed out one credit card and has heavy charges on the other one. Jonathon has learned that if he charges $1000 on his card and only makes the minimum payments, it will take 15.5 years to pay it off. He doesn't want to disappoint his girlfriend and fears losing her if he doesn't go on the trip, but, clearly, he has to make some changes.

What are two things you would advise Jonathon to do right away?

_____

_____

List two other suggestions for Jonathon to help him get control of his expenses.

_____

_____

however, a payday loan that costs $17.50 per $100 for the same $300 would cost $105 if renewed one time, or 426 percent annual interest (Payday Loan: Consumer Information, 2008). As bad as credit card debt is, it pales in comparison to the pitfalls of payday loans.

SMALL COSTS ADD UP!

How Much Money Will You Throw down the Drain in 10 Years?

Many people pay more money for convenience. If you are on a tight budget, you might want to give up some of the conveniences so you can hold onto more of your money. Although we want you to really live and enjoy life, we also want you to take a hard look at where your money goes. Those dimes, quarters, and dollars add up quickly. In fact, small-amount money drains for the typical person can add up to $175,000 over a 10-year period (Digerati Life, 2008). What if you could hold onto some of that money and invest it? What would that money be worth to you when you are 65 and want to retire? Is having sausage biscuits and orange juice from a fast-food restaurant really worth $3.50 a day, or $1277.50 if you have one *every day for one year*? Did you ever stop to think that if you spend $3.50 every day on fast food, or coffee, or whatever, for **10 years,** that you would be spending $12,775?

The 10-Year Plan

According to the website, The Digerati Life (2008), prime causes of money drain are:

- **Gum**—a pack a day will cost you $5488 in 10 years.
- **Bottled water**—One bottle a day will cost you almost $5500 in 10 years. (Most bottled water comes from no special source and is no better than tap water.)

- **Eating lunch out daily**—If you only spend $9, this will cost you over $35,000 in 10 years. If you can eat lunch at home, you will save thousands of dollars.
- **Junk food, vending machine snacks**—This will cost you at least $4000 in 10 years if you are a light snacker, and they are empty calories.
- **Unused memberships**—Those gym memberships that look so enticing and, for many people, go unused will total over $7500 in 10 years.
- **Expensive salon visits**—Fake nails, along with the cost of the salon visit, can cost over $30,000 in 10 years. Is that really how you want to spend your money?
- **Cigarettes**—Not only will this terrible habit kill you and make people want to avoid you, it will cost you over $25,000 in 10 years if you smoke a pack a day.

These are just a few of the drains that take our money and keep us from being wealthy when we are older. Maybe you want to splurge at times and go for the convenience, but day in and day out, you can really save a lot of money if you budget your time and do some of these things for yourself.

Examine the information about *The Latte Factor*™ in Figure 11.9 and apply it to your own spending habits.

Figure 11.9 The Latte Factor

In his book, *The Finish Rich Notebook* (2003), Bach states, "How much you earn has no bearing on whether or not you will build wealth." As a rule, the more we make, the more we spend. Many people spend far more than they make and subject themselves to stress, exorbitant debt, fear, and an ultimate future of poverty.

Bach uses the Latte Factor to call people's attention to how much money we carelessly throw away when we should be saving and investing for the future. He uses the story of a young woman who said she could not invest because she had no money. Yet, almost every day she bought a large latte for $3.50 and a muffin for $1.50. If you add a candy bar here, a drink there, a shake at the gym, you could easily be spending $10 a day that could be invested.

If you take that $10 per day and invest it faithfully until retirement, you would have enough money to pay cash for a home and a new car, and have money left over. This is the power of compound interest! If you are a relatively young person, you will probably work many years more, so you could retire with an extra $1 million in addition to any other savings you might have accumulated.

The point is that most of us have the ability to become rich, but we either lack the knowledge or the discipline to do so. Remember the Latte Factor as you begin your college career and practice it, along with other sound financial strategies, if you want to become a millionaire.

Calculate your own Latte Factor. For example, if you buy one diet soda each morning at $1.81, then your Latte Factor is $685.84 per year. ($1.81 × 7 days/week × 52 weeks/year).

My daily "have to have it" is _____.

It costs $_____ per day.

My Latte Factor is $_____.

PROTECT YOURSELF FROM IDENTITY THEFT

Why Might Your College Be Ground Zero?

"Amid all the back-to-school activities and tasks that students face, one of the most important is to protect their identities. You have such busy schedules that you may unknowingly expose yourself to identity theft and fraud, particularly when you're making online purchases or engaging

DID YOU Know?

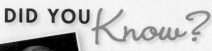

CAN YOU imagine being worth over $62 billion and still living in the same home that you bought in 1958 for $31,500? Well, **Warren Buffett**, one of the world's wealthiest people, does just that in Omaha.

Born in 1930, Mr. Buffett, a native Nebraskan, is not only one of the world's wealthiest people, a savvy investor, a successful businessman, and a financial intellectual, but also one of the most philanthropic. He recently announced that he was leaving 83 percent of his wealth to the Bill and Melinda Gates Foundation.

Having always been "financially smart," he filed his first income tax return at the age of 13 so that he could deduct the cost of his bicycle as a business expense. At age 15, he and his friend spent $25 to purchase a pinball machine, which they placed in a barber shop. A few months later, they owned three machines in different locations.

He applied to Harvard in 1950, but was denied entrance. He attended and graduated from Columbia University and began working as a stockbroker. His first real business venture, the purchase of a Texaco gas station, did not work out very well. He decided to enroll in a public speaking course and began teaching an investment class at the University of Nebraska.

He later became a major shareholder in the firm Berkshire Hathaway, which purchased major shares in The Washington Post Company, ABC, Geico, Dairy Queen, and Coca-Cola. The most he has ever taken as an actual salary from all of his ventures and investments is $100,000 per year. It was reported in 2006 that Mr. Buffett does *not* carry a cell phone, does not have a computer at his desk, and drives his own car.

Upon his death, his children will *not* inherit much of his wealth. He has been quoted as saying, "I want to give my kids just enough so that they would feel that they could do anything, but not so much that they would feel like doing nothing." (Adapted from Forbes, Wikipedia, and About.com)

in social-networking web sites. We're all living in an extremely open environment where free flow of information is the norm, as opposed to the exception," said Adam Levin, co-founder of Identity Theft 911 (Yip, 2008). Because students tend to move often, their mail service may be interrupted if they don't follow through with change-of-address cards. By the time their information catches up to them, they may have already suffered from identity theft. "All these things make this group vulnerable," said Thomas Harkins, chief strategy officer of Secure Identity Systems (Yip, 2008).

People who may steal your identity are roommates, relatives, friends, estranged spouses, restaurant servers, and others who have ready access to information about you. They may steal your wallet, go through your trash, or take your mail. They can even legally photocopy your vital information at the courthouse if, for example, you have been divorced. The Internet provides thieves many other opportunities to use official-looking e-mail messages designed to obtain your personal information. Do not provide personal information over the Internet no matter how official the website might look. Reputable businesses will not inquire about your personal information in this manner.

It is very difficult, if not impossible, to catch identity thieves. While you may not be liable, you still have to spend your time filing expensive legal affidavits, writing letters, and making telephone calls to clear your good name.

How to Minimize Identity Theft Risk

Criminals are very clever, and many are adept at using electronic means to steal your information. According to a variety of financial sources, there are a number of ways to avoid having your identity stolen:

- Carry only the ID and cards you need at any given time.
- Do not make Internet purchases from sites that are unsecured (check for a padlock icon to ensure safety).
- Do not write your PIN number, Social Security number, or passcode on any information that can be stolen or that you are discarding. Do not keep this information in your wallet or exposed in your living space.
- Try to memorize your passwords instead of recording them on paper or in the computer.
- Buy a shredder and use it.
- Avoid providing your Social Security number to any organization until you have verified its legitimacy.
- Check your credit file periodically by requesting a copy of your report.
- Do not complete credit card applications at displays set up on campus. This exposes your personal information to people you don't know.
- Use your home address as your permanent mailing address, rather than a temporary address while in school.
- Do not provide personal information on a social network that can be used by an identity thief. You don't know these people!
- Carry your wallet in your front pocket instead of your back pocket.
- Place security freezes on your credit scores. This prevents anyone from looking at your credit report except for companies that already have a financial relationship with you.

Lenders who can't pull your credit report are unlikely to grant new credit to someone else in your name.

- Opt out of pre-approved credit offers, which are easy for identity thieves to steal. This stops credit bureaus from selling your name to lenders.
- Don't use obvious passwords like your birthday, your mother's maiden name, or the last four digits of your Social Security number.

(Adapted from; Consumer Report, 2012; Consumer Response Center brochure, 2003; Identity Theft and Fraud, Yip, P. (2008).

How careful are you when it comes to protecting your financial and medical records?

BATTLING THE BIG "IFS"

Do You Know What to Do When You Need Something?

Below, you will find some helpful tips for managing some important financial decisions in your life and protecting yourself when things get tough.

If You Need to Purchase a Car:

- Do not purchase a new car. We know it is tempting, but the value will plummet 20 to 40 percent the moment you drive off the lot. It is just not worth it! Purchase a two- to three-year-old car from a reputable dealer.
- *Don't* fall in love with a car before you know everything about it. Love is blind when it comes to people . . . and cars, too!
- Purchase an extended warranty, *but* read the terms carefully.
- Always ask for a "Car-fax" and a title search, and make the dealer pay for them.
- Check to see if your state has a "lemon law," and if so, read it carefully.
- Don't be pressured into a sale by lines, such as: "this is our last one like this," or "I've got several people interested in this car." Let the other people have it.
- Make sure the vehicle has passed the smog test if one is required in your state.

If You Need to Save on Fuel:

- Consider carpooling.
- Make sure your car is in good running condition and that your tires are inflated properly. Get your car tuned up often.
- Drive slower and at a constant speed, when possible. Driving 74 mph instead of 55 mph increases fuel consumption by as much as 20 percent.
- Check your car's air filter and fuel filter and replace them if they are dirty.
- Do not use "Jack Rabbit" starts. Accelerate easily after red lights and stop signs. "Flooring it" costs money.
- When stuck in traffic, try to drive at a steady pace and not stop and start. Watch how the large trucks do this—they seldom come to a complete stop.
- Plan your trip so that you can make the most number of right turns, thus saving time at traffic lights. Also, combine your errands so that you can make fewer trips.

from ORDINARY to Extraordinary

Leo G. Borges Founder and Former CEO, Borges and Mahoney, San Francisco, CA

Tulare, California, is still a farming community today. In 1928, when I was born, it was totally agricultural and an exceptionally rural, detached part of the world. My parents had immigrated to California from the Azore Islands years earlier in search of a better life—the American dream. My father died when I was three years old, and when I was 11, my mother passed away. Even though I lived with and was raised by my sisters, aloneness and isolation were the two primary feelings I had growing up. We were orphans. We were poor. We were farm kids. We were considered Portuguese, not Americans. Every day, someone reminded us of these realities. However, one positive thing remained: My mother always told us that we could be anything or have anything if we believed in it and worked hard for it.

I left home at 17 to attend a program in advertising in San Francisco. Later that year, I moved to Los Angeles and began working for a major advertising firm. From there I enlisted in the Coast Guard, and when my duty was over, I worked for an oil company and then a major leasing firm. In each position, I worked my way up the ladder, always tried to do my very best, and proved that I was capable of doing anything, regardless of my background.

When I was in my early forties, my best friend, Cliff, and I decided to start our own business. We were tired of working in "middle management" and knew that we could be successful if we worked hard. After much research and consulting with companies across the country, we determined that we would start a company in the water treatment business.

You may be asking yourself, "What experience did an advertising agency, an oil company, and a leasing firm give me to start a business in water treatment?" The answer is none. However, Cliff was an excellent accountant, and I was an excellent salesman. We found a third partner who was one of the leading water treatment experts in the world and we were off. It was not easy, and we had to eat beans for many meals, but Borges and Mahoney, Inc., was born.

Our first office was a small storefront in San Francisco. Through the development of superior products, expert advice to clients, and outstanding customer service, we grew and grew, finally moving to our largest location in San Rafael, California. By the time we sold our business some 20 years later, we had 15 full-time employees and annual revenues in the millions of dollars.

To this day, I attribute my success to the fact that I was determined to show everyone—my sisters, cousins, aunts and uncles, former coworkers, friends and foes—that I would never let my past, my heritage, my economic background, or my history hold me back. I knew that I could be a success. Through hard work, determination, and surrounding myself with supportive, brilliant people, I proved that the American dream my parents sought years earlier is truly possible for anyone who works hard, believes in him- or herself, and doesn't give up. It is possible for you, too

> We were orphans. We were poor. We were farm kids. We were considered Portuguese, not Americans.

EXTRAORDINARY REFLECTION

Mr. Borges states that through hard work, determination, and surrounding himself with supportive, brilliant people, he and his partner, Cliff, were able to become very successful in business and beyond. Whom can you call upon in your life to offer you support and provide you solid, smart advice? What questions do you need to ask them?

- Clean out your car. Carrying around just a few extra pounds in the trunk or back seat costs fuel. For every 100 extra pounds of weight in your car, fuel efficiency is decreased by two percent.
- Stick with the wheels and tires that came with your car. If you are using larger wheels and tires than recommended, this creates more drag and weight on your car and costs you more fuel.
- Use the telephone. Often, many things can be accomplished without personal visits.

If You Feel the Urge to Make an Impulse Purchase:

Do you work hard to control your spending every day, especially your impulse purchases?

- Use the 72-hour rule. Wait 72 hours to make any purchase over $50.
- If you still feel the need to purchase the item after 72 hours, consider your budget and how you are going to pay for it.
- Consider waiting until you can pay cash for the item, or consider putting the item on layaway. Do not charge it!
- Purchase the item later as a reward to yourself for getting all A's in your classes.
- Think about how purchasing this item will affect your family's budget.
- Make as few trips out shopping as possible to lower your temptation to purchase things you can't afford and don't need.

If Your Grocery Bill Is Out of Control:

- Shop with a calculator or your smart phone's caculator app and enter each item as you place it into your cart. This will give you a great idea of what you're spending.
- Create a menu for each day of the week and shop only for the items on your list. Do not shop when you are in a hurry, tired, or after working all day.
- Consider purchasing generic brands—often they are the same product with a different label.
- Clip coupons. They actually work. Go online to your favorite product's website and print off their online coupons. Try to shop where stores double or triple the coupon's value.
- Consider cooking in bulk and then freezing leftovers for later in the week.
- Look for placement of the product in the store. Items at chest level are the most expensive. Look up and down on the shelves to find less expensive items.
- Do not shop for convenience items, such as pre-made meals, bakery items, or boneless chicken breasts. Purchase an entire chicken and cut it up. You'll save a lot of money this way.
- Buy in bulk at one of the major warehouse stores. Often this can save a lot of money if you are buying for a large family.

If Your Child Wants Something That Other Children Have:

- Use Freecycle. Log onto www.freecycle.org, a non-profit organization made up of over 4600 groups with nearly six million members who give things away in many towns.
- Consider giving your children a small allowance and have them save for the items they want to buy.

- Make the purchase a reward when your child passes a test or does something productive.
- Try to shop "out of season" when things are cheaper, for example, buy coats in the summer time.
- Keep an eye out for bargains all year long, such as school supplies—don't wait until school is about to start and things are more expensive.
- Consider shopping at thrift stores or yard sales. Often, items can be purchased at a fraction of the original price and they are in great condition.
- Trade with other parents. Perhaps they have an item that their child has outgrown and is still in great shape.
- Ask others to purchase certain items for your child's birthday or other holidays. Directed gift giving is a great way to save money.

If Your Credit Cards Are Lost or Stolen:

- Contact your local police immediately.
- Notify your creditors immediately and request that your accounts be closed.
- Ask the card company to furnish copies of documents that show any fraudulent transactions.
- Refuse to pay any bill or portion of any bill that is a result of identity theft.
- Report the theft or fraud to the credit reporting agencies.

CHANGING IDEAS to Reality

REFLECTIONS ON FINANCIAL RESPONSIBILITY

Although many young people fail in the management of their personal finances, there is no reason that you cannot manage your financial business well. You should think about personal finance and the management of money and investments as basic survival skills that are very important to you now, as well as for the rest of your life.

Since only 10 percent of high school students graduate from high school with any kind of instruction in personal finance, learning to budget your money, make wise investments, and avoid credit card debt are priority needs of all students. As you move toward establishing yourself in a career, it is important to remember that to get what you want out of life, a significant part of your success will depend on your ability to make sound money decisions. We hope you will learn to make money work for you instead of you having to work so hard for money because of poor decisions made early in life. As you become a good money manager, the following tips will assist you:

- Don't get caught in the credit card trap.
- Know exactly how you are spending your money.

- Protect your credit rating by using wise money-management strategies.
- Learn all you can about scholarships and grants.
- Understand the regulations about repaying student loans.
- Don't borrow any more money than you absolutely have to.
- Ask for your credit score at least once a year and be sure you have a good one.
- Use only one or two credit cards.
- Try to pay off your credit card each month before any interest is charged.
- Write down your credit card numbers and keep them in a safe place in case your cards are lost or stolen.
- If you get into credit card trouble, get counseling.
- Learn everything you can about investments and retirement plans.

Knowledge in Bloom

IDENTIFYING, ANALYZING AND IMPROVING YOUR MONEY MANAGEMENT SKILLS

Utilizes Levels 1–6 of the Taxonomy (See Bloom's Taxonomy at the front of this text)

PROCESS: It is never too early to study and evaluate your financial habits and map out your financial future. In this exercise, you will be asked track *every cent* that you spend over a three-day period. This includes things as large as a house payment and as small as a bottle of water. At the end of three days, you will be asked to evaluate and critique your spending habits and develop a plan to improve your financial future. You will need to be honest with yourself and identify current financial practices and concerns.

TRACKING EXPENDITURES AND SPENDING HABITS CHART

Over the course of the **next three days, write down *every cent* you spend**, including fuel, food, bottled water, childcare, newspapers, etc.—every cent. After three days, analyze your spending habits and determine at least five ways that you can cut expenses.

DAY #1	DAY #2	DAY #3
Total for Day #1 $_____	Total for Day #2 $_____	Total for Day #3 $_____

SQ3R MASTERY STUDY SHEET

EXAMPLE QUESTION (FROM PAGE 254) What are the types of financial aid?	**ANSWER:**
EXAMPLE QUESTION (FROM PAGE 254) How does a grant differ from a loan?	**ANSWER:**
AUTHOR QUESTION (FROM PAGE 252) What is the difference between standard of living and quality of life?	**ANSWER:**
AUTHOR QUESTION (FROM PAGE 259) What is a FICO score and why is it important to your future?	**ANSWER:**
AUTHOR QUESTION (FROM PAGE 263) What are some of the dangers of credit card debt?	**ANSWER:**
AUTHOR QUESTION (FROM PAGE 267) How can you avoid identity theft?	**ANSWER:**
AUTHOR QUESTION (FROM PAGE 267) What is the Latte Factor and how can you use it to manage your finances more effectively?	**ANSWER:**
YOUR QUESTION (FROM PAGE ____)	**ANSWER:**
YOUR QUESTION (FROM PAGE ____)	**ANSWER:**
YOUR QUESTION (FROM PAGE ____)	**ANSWER:**
YOUR QUESTION (FROM PAGE ____)	**ANSWER:**
YOUR QUESTION (FROM PAGE ____)	**ANSWER:**

Finally, after answering these questions, recite this chapter's major points in your mind. Consider the following general questions to help you master this material.

- What is it about?
- What does it mean?
- What is the most important thing you learned? Why?
- What are the key points to remember?

chapter twelve

PRESENT

SPEAKING WITH PURPOSE, PASSION, AND POWER

"There are always three speeches for every one you actually give—the one you practiced, the one you gave, and the one you wish you gave." —Dale Carnegie

PRESENT

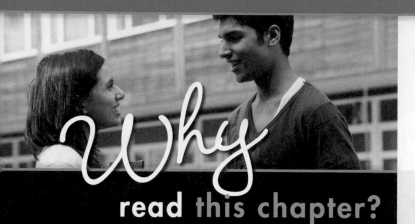

Why read this chapter?

Because you'll learn how to...

- Identify informal and formal communication styles
- Evaluate the most effective medium and message, based on the audience
- Deliver three types of presentations

Because you'll be able to...

- **Revise** communications to suit different audiences
- **Analyze** a message for its tone and content
- **Identify** speaking skills that need improvement and **outline** a plan to improve these skills

Scan and QUESTION

Take a few moments, **scan this chapter** and on page 296, write **five of your own questions** that you think will be important to your mastery of this material. You will also find five questions listed from your authors.

Example:

☑ **List two ways that speaking in a digital world differs from typical speaking settings.** (from page 279)

☑ **Contrast effective PowerPoint slides with ineffective slides.** (from page 286)

MyStudentSuccessLab

MyStudentSuccessLab is an online solution designed to help you acquire and develop (or hone) the skills you need to succeed. You will have access to peer-led video presentations and develop core skills through interactive exercises and projects.

Name: Biatriz Portillo

Institution: Graduate! University of Northern Colorado, Greeley, CO

Major: Business Accounting

Biatriz Portillo comes into lunch with that familiar brilliant smile and the fast pace that has left her frazzled throughout her college experience, but also has allowed her to accomplish a lot of things, including graduating in four years with a business degree, studying abroad, consistently working over 30 hours per week, and managing many volunteer and student activities. She has always impressed me with her drive, her commitment to do what is right, and her amazing ability to seek out new opportunities. Biatriz and I have been through many ups and downs. As she sits before me, I see a composed woman who accepts herself and has a confidence in her abilities. She has glimmers of the first-year student that I met, but college has certainly changed her and her life.

As the youngest in a family with eleven children, it was hard for Biatriz to leave her parents and attend the University of Northern Colorado. "My parents were supportive, but they had never been to college. They didn't understand why I had to go to UNC and not just attend the local college." Biatriz, who had always been good at school, considered it her natural next step. Her

An interview conducted and written by Jana Schwartz, Director, Center for Human Enrichment Student Support Services Program, University of Northern Colorado

older sister, the only other sibling who attended college, served as her mentor and role model. "I saw my sister graduate from college when I was 12. I remember sitting in the stands and thinking, 'That will be me!' I never let that thought fade away. I also remember her coming home and taking me places my parents couldn't afford or giving all of us gifts. She was not struggling like the rest of my siblings and my parents. She was living the good life and I wanted that."

Although coming to college seemed like the obvious next step, it didn't make the transition easy. When Biatriz, an A student throughout high school, earned a C on her first test in Principles of Accounting, she was devastated. She became concerned that maybe she was not "college material," but the professor pulled her aside and told her that she was going to have to study—and study hard—in college. Academic transitions were not the only transitions she had to make. "School came easy to me, but the emotional side of college was difficult. The Student Support Services program helped me and I learned to use those services often."

Her decision to leave home and focus on herself was difficult. Her family experienced two situations that required the family to pull together financially to support her parents. Biatriz, who was already working 30 hours/week to support her own studies, did not have the resources to support her parents. "That was a really hard time for me to focus on myself. I felt so guilty and so irresponsible. All of my other siblings were helping out,

277

but not me. My sister kept telling me 'Don't worry, just finish college.' But, I just felt so guilty."

Biatriz reflects on her growth over the past four years and shares this advice with students: "Don't get so caught up in who or what you are supposed to be. You will learn a lot about who you are as a person in college, and it is okay for some of your original goals or thoughts to change. Look at everything as an opportunity for growth." Biatriz did just that. She attended advising sessions, sought out resources, used tutoring, and even took a significant risk and studied abroad for a semester in Brazil. "Everyone should study abroad—you will learn so much about another culture—but mostly you will learn so much about yourself. Oh, and find someone to vent to! The SSS staff were those people for me. They helped me out by listening to me and just giving me a place to go for support."

Biatriz is graduating with her Bachelor's degree and has earned a position with one of the top five accounting firms in the state. She has largely accomplished her starting goal. "With the salary I will be earning, I will be financially stable. That was my first goal when I came to college. Since I now have accomplished that, my goals have changed. Now I ask myself 'How can I give back?'"

THINK
a b o u t *it*

1. Biatriz looked up to and emulated her sister. Who do you admire and look up to in your life? Why? How can they be a mentor to you?

2. Biatriz mentions that she wants to "give back." How will your education help you give back to your community?

> *"Words are, of course, the most powerful drug used by mankind."*
> *—Rudyard Kipling*

THE ENORMOUS POWER OF WORDS

Why Is It Important to Know How to Master the Power of Words?

Words are among the most powerful forces in existence when used by a skilled orator or writer. When people are able to get others to do what they want them to do, they usually employ words, not physical power. Words can inspire, comfort, teach, encourage, persuade, and sell. They can also be used to manipulate, misinform, and spread propaganda. Words can lift us up and bring us together. They can tear us apart and create fear and despair. They can twist our thinking, cause us not to use common sense, and even control our behavior. Words can change our opinions, make us act foolish, lead us to join a cause, and touch our emotions.

Words have started wars, led people into battle, stirred entire nations to do the right thing—or the wrong thing. "Words influence how we think, and our thoughts determine our actions. There is a powerful connection between the words we use and the results we get. Poorly chosen words can kill enthusiasm, impact self esteem, lower expectations and hold people back, while well-chosen ones can motivate, offer hope, create vision, impact thinking and alter results" (Russell, 2004). To underestimate the power of words is to do so at your own peril.

Spoken words are powerful and can literally change the course of your life if you learn to use them effectively. From job interviews and leading teams, to working effectively with others, words can be your best friend or your worst enemy.

How can the power of words affect others' actions and thoughts?

SPEAKING PUBLICLY

Is It Time To Scream or Shine?

"If I had wanted to speak in front of people, I would have taken a public speaking course," you might be saying at this moment. Relax. You are not alone about **glossophobia**—the fear of speaking publicly. In fact, "far above the fear of death and disease, comes fear of standing in front of a crowd" (Eggleston, 2012). Fear of public speaking ranked ahead of fear of sickness, insects, financial troubles, deep water, and even death! Most people would rather die than speak in front of a group!

So, why do we include a chapter on public speaking in a first-year success text? You probably won't like the answer, but the simple truth is that you are going to be asked to speak and make presentations in many of your classes; from history to chemistry, from engineering to computer programming, speaking is a way of life for today's college students and today's employees. The more you know about researching and writing speeches and delivering presentations, the more confident you are going to feel in every class. We can't overemphasize the importance of mastering the spoken word now and in the future!

What steps can you take to reduce your own anxiety over speaking publicly?

SPEAKING PUBLICLY IN A DIGITAL WORLD

Does Oral Communication Still Matter?

During the past decade, sweeping changes have been implemented as the world changed from analog to digital technology that marked a period of development that is comparable to the Industrial Revolution. This new age, often referred to as the Information Age, brought with it cell phones, computers, fax machines, iPads, and numerous social media technologies that have vastly changed our world. Most of us feel lost without new technologies at our fingertips. Some children spend more time playing with their avatar pet on a virtual website than they do with their real pets. Many people are addicted to their cell phones, constantly texting their friends. So has the power of speech lost its effectiveness in this brave new digital world? The answer is a resounding "No!"

The ability to speak fluently and persuasively is as important today as it has ever been. As a matter of fact, employers today rank oral communication skills the number one most important skill needed for the world of work (Shindell, 2011). The difference between making a speech today and fifteen years ago is that you will most likely be required to use some type of technology to complement your spoken words. Remember, however, any technology used will not replace the spoken word—it will enhance it.

Today you may be required to interact with coworkers who belong to a virtual work team using Skype, GoToMeeting, WebX, and other such software. You will almost certainly be required to make presentations in class and at work using PowerPoint or Prezi. Your reputation as an effective team member will depend on your ability to articulate your ideas and defend your positions. When you enter the workplace, you will be required to interact effectively with coworkers in meetings and with customers and clients on the telephone and face-to-face. You will also most likely be required to make oral presentations in most of your classes and beyond. The requirement to be able to speak powerfully will continue to gain importance as technology intensifies the important role of spoken messages in the workplace.

> *"If all my talents and powers were to be taken from me, and I had the choice of keeping but one, I would unhesitatingly ask to be allowed to keep the power of speaking, for through it, I would quickly recover the rest."*
>
> —Daniel Webster

> *"Give me the right words and the right accent, and I will move the world."*
>
> —Joseph Conrad

Have you ever looked around your class and really studied the diversity of your peers?

Analyzing Your Audience

Have you ever listened to someone speak about a topic that was so technical that you understood very little of it and could have passed out due to boredom? It could be because the speech was poorly written, but it may be that the boring technical speech was unappealing to you because it was written for a different audience. If you don't understand your audience, it is unlikely that you will be able to write and deliver a presentation that maintains their attention, informs or persuades them, or asks them to act on your advice. Although your immediate speech will be written for your instructor or class, there will be instances in the future when it will be advantageous to complete an analysis of your audience to assist you in learning more about the diversity or similarities of your audience. You will also want to do this for your class. Figure 12.1 will guide you in developing a comprehensive audience analysis.

Using your classroom setting as your audience, write a brief analysis of this audience. You may have to make some educated guesses based on observation and keen listening skills. You may also have to interview them or issue a questionnaire to learn more about them. As a basis for your understanding, you will want to seek

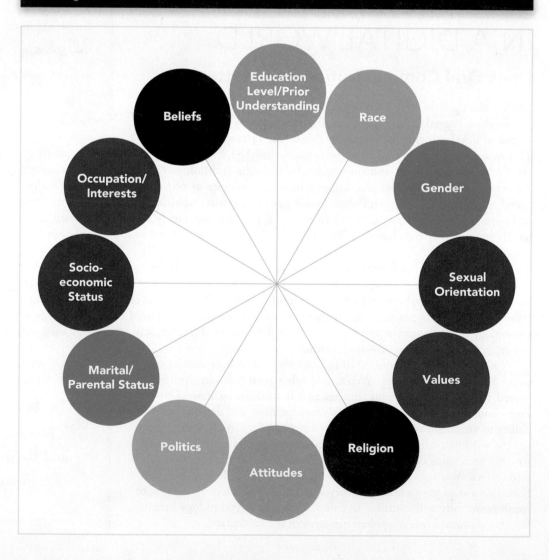

Figure 12.1 **Audience Demographic Wheel**

answers to the 12 factors in the demographic wheel. You may also need to answer questions, such as: "What do I know about them?" "What do I need to find out?" "What do they expect?" "What would interest them?" and "What does my analysis mean to my speech?" Some answers will be obvious, such as gender and age. You can also make some inferences about your audience based on classroom discussions and conversations.

Analyze your classroom audience and summarize in the space below.

_____

_____

_____

_____

_____

Level 4 Analyze

SELECTING THE MAIN IDEAS AND ISSUES FOR A PRESENTATION

Why Is Organization Important?

At this point, you need to carefully select and narrow your topic. You are not ready to begin writing your presentation until you have a topic, so at this stage you should just start writing down ideas and thoughts. Some experts on writing suggest that you choose a topic on which you are an expert. This is not always possible based on the assignment or audience, but it helps if you know a good bit about the topic you choose. To begin, list ideas nonstop for 5–10 minutes without worrying about grammatical correctness or structure. Step away from this list for a few minutes, then come back and see if you have any additional ideas.

When you have your list, group your ideas into clusters that seem to go together. Review what you have written and decide which topic relates best to the assignment and/or audience. Which one do you know the most about? Which topic would be most interesting to you? Often students say, "I can't think of anything to speak about." Basically, that's bull. We all care deeply about something. Consider this exercise. When was the last time you got angry? What aroused it? What caused you to feel this way? This could be your topic. When was the last time you felt passion, real dynamic passion? Here is a topic for you. When was the last time you felt really frustrated and agitated? There is a topic. When was the last time you were scared, really frightened about something? There is a topic. When was the last time you learned how to do something new? There is a topic. Your best topics will come from your emotions and experiences and your desire to explain your anger, passion, fears, or other feelings. Some tips for topic selection are listed below.

Tips for Topic Selection

- Know what type of speech you will be writing and/or delivering (informative, demonstrative, persuasive, etc.).
- Think about your talents, interests, and experiences, and what appeals to you most.
- Determine if your topic is appropriate to you and your audience.
- Decide if you can adequately cover a speech on this topic in the allowed length of time.

- Build your speech around an interesting theme.
- Analyze your audience and their interests. Why will they want to hear your remarks?
- Be sure you can deliver a speech on this topic in a reasonable length of time.

Now, you are ready to decide on the main issues and major details that you plan to share with your audience. Main issues are the major points of your speech.

Organizing the Body

One of the most effective ways to begin composing your speech is to create a rough outline of the points you would like to cover. As you begin to outline, remember that your organizational pattern should guide you through this phase.

Assume you are writing a speech on date rape. Your outline might look similar to this:

I. Introduction
  A. Thesis statement
  B. Overview of the speech

II. The problem of date rape
  A. What is date rape?
  B. Facts and statistics supporting its prevalence
  C. Laws relative to date rape

III. Where does date rape happen and why?
  A. Where are the settings that this typically happens?
  B. What are the usual circumstances that cause date rape?
  C. Who does it typically happen to?

IV. How to prevent date rape
  A. Avoid excessive drinking and drugs
  B. Be responsible for watching your drink
  C. Get to know people before you are with them alone
  D. Go out in groups
  E. Check on each other
  F. Pay your own way

V. What to do if date rape happens
  A. Report it to campus security or the police
  B. Do not destroy evidence
  C. Report it to the proper college authorities
  D. Press charges if advised

VI. Conclusion

Once you have developed your outline, you can begin to research and write your speech.

CREATING EFFECTIVE INTRODUCTIONS AND CONCLUSIONS

Why Are the First Thirty Seconds So Important?

Communication experts suggest that you have only *thirty seconds* in which to gain your audience's attention (Moyer, 2012). If you do not do so, it is unlikely that you will gain their attention for the remainder of the presentation. In Figure 12.2, you will find a variety of techniques used to help you start your speech by creating an effective introduction.

Figure 12.2 Creating Effective Introductions

- Telling a story or creating a vivid, visual illustration
- Using startling facts or statistics
- Referring to an incident with which the reader is familiar
- Asking rhetorical yet pertinent questions
- Using novel ideas or striking statements
- Using quotations
- Using humor or humorous stories
- Using a powerful visual aid or demonstration

Using the topic of date rape, choose one technique, or a combination of the techniques we've discussed, and compose a draft of an introduction.

_____

_____

_____

_____

_____

_____

Level 6 Create

Writing Conclusions

Conclusions are very important to the overall quality of your speech. They are designed to leave the audience wanting more and remembering your words. Figure 12.3 features several techniques to help you construct an effective conclusion.

Figure 12.3 Techniques for Concluding a Speech

- Summarize and re-emphasize the main points.
- Make a final appeal for action or a challenge.
- Refer to the introduction you used (story, quote, or joke); this is parallelism.
- Complete the opening story.
- Re-emphasize the impact of your topic.
- Use a vivid analogy or simile.
- End powerfully! You want your reader to remember your topic and your compelling points.
- If possible and appropriate, leave your audience on a high note—laughing, and feeling special or highly motivated.

(continued)

Level 6 Create

Figure 12.3 Techniques for Concluding a Speech (Continued)

Write the draft of a memorable, creative conclusion on the topic of date rape.

_____

_____

_____

_____

_____

THREE MAJOR TYPES OF FORMAL PRESENTATIONS

Does It Take Information to Persuade or Persuasion to Inform?

The chances are very good that you will encounter the following three types of formal presentations in your classes. There is also a very good chance that you will be required to deliver all three types in one situation or another in the workplace. While all three types are similar in some ways, they have distinct requirements in order to deliver them effectively.

Informative Speaking

The secret to making effective ***informative presentations*** is to present information in an interesting, clear, and memorable way. Regardless of how fluent you are or how many big words you use, you have not communicated unless your audience understands. Remember, you are simply trying to convey information to them—you are not trying to persuade them to accept your position in an informative presentation. Consider the following questions as you prepare to make an informative presentation:

- Have I researched my topic thoroughly and would I be able to answer audience questions about my topic?
- What can I do to make this topic clearer to my audience?
- Do I need a visual that explains my words more clearly?
- What attention-getting devices can I use to communicate my ideas more effectively?
- How can I simplify my ideas to make them more understandable?
- Am I talking too fast or too slow?

- Can I relate new information to information the audience already understands?
- How can I tailor my presentation to this particular audience's interests? Can I touch on something in their lives, such as money or health?
- What word pictures can I use to effectively paint a mental picture or describe a smell?
- Do my nonverbal actions and gestures match my words in a powerful way?
- Is my presentation audience-centered rather than speaker-centered?

Possible Topics for Informative Speeches

- Global Warming
- The San Diego Zoo
- Traveling to Europe
- Invention of the Computer
- Steve Jobs

Demonstrative Speaking

Demonstrative presentations certainly inform, but go further in that they are used to explain how to do something or to teach how something works. An effective demonstrative speech is a visual speech and must incorporate physical activity or the use of objects or visual aids, such as charts, diagrams, pictures, maps, or graphs *with* your words. Consider the following questions as you prepare to deliver a demonstrative presentation:

- Am I using the proper type of physical object for this presentation?
- Is it legal to bring the objects required for this presentation onto campus?
- Are my physical objects large enough for my audience to see?
- How can I make the demonstration significant and interesting to my audience?
- Have I chosen clear, vivid word choices that complement my demonstration?
- Are my words and accompanying aids appropriate for my presentation?
- Can I give my audience ingredients or materials that they can use to participate in the demonstration as I share my directions?
- During the presentation, am I paying attention to my audience to ensure that they are following and understanding?

Possible Topics for Demonstrative Speeches

- How to change the oil in a car
- How to grill a chicken
- How to construct a website
- How to balance a checkbook
- How to caulk a tub or shower

Persuasive Speaking

Persuasive presentations differ from others in that you are not simply trying to inform an audience or show them a demonstration; you are trying to get them to do something – to take action! You are trying to motivate an audience to follow your wishes, which means that you may have to change or alter their thinking, their wishes, their beliefs, their values, and/or their behaviors. Although informative and demonstrative speeches differ from persuasive speeches, many of the same principles discussed in the informative and demonstrative presentations apply. The difference is that you are not only informing and/or demonstrating, you are going one step further and trying to get your audience to do what you want them to do, even if it is contrary to what they want to do. Consider the following questions as you prepare to deliver a persuasive presentation:

- Have I clearly defined my purpose and exactly what I am trying to persuade people to do?
- Have I identified my central argument? In other words, with what exactly do I want my audience to agree?
- How can I establish credibility with my audience without sounding boastful?
- What can I say that encourages my audience to accept me as trustworthy?
- Does my research support my argument?
- Did I provide evidence that what I am saying is factually based?
- If possible, did I establish common ground with my audience?
- Am I using non-threatening language and demeanor?
- Am I using any unethical strategies to get others to do what I want them to do, such as manipulation and coercion?
- Am I practicing honest and forthright practices as I try to persuade people?
- Have I used positive appeals? For example, if you were running for the city council, you might promise a better educational system for people's children.
- Have I thought about my audience's responses to what I am presenting and how I might counter specific negative comments?
- Have I thought about my audience's values and how I might have to change them to persuade them to do what I want them to?
- Does my presentation include a statement that gets the audience to take action? If my audience does nothing, I have not persuaded them.

Possible Topics for Persuasive Speeches

- Persuading the audience to give blood
- Persuading the audience to vote
- Persuading the audience to conserve water
    - Persuading the audience to recycle
    - Persuading the audience to volunteer at an animal shelter twice per week

How can using a visual aid, such as PowerPoint, help you get your point across more effectively?

CREATING POWERFUL VISUAL PRESENTATIONS

Do Visuals Really Help My Cause?

You can hardly take a class today or go to work in any position that does not require you to use PowerPoint or Prezi to make presentations. Even elementary school children are using this software. Used effectively, this software can greatly enhance your spoken words. Used poorly, the same software can be boring and deadly.

PowerPoint continues to be the most popular presentation software, but Prezi has introduced an exciting package as well. You absolutely need to know PowerPoint, but you are also highly encouraged to review the up-and-coming Prezi presentation package at http://prezi.com.

Almost everyone has had to develop a slide presentation while they were in school, and all of us have tried to stay awake during a long, boring, tedious, computerized presentation. This is an area of technology and communications that you need to be able to do well. While entire books have been written on making effective slideshows, we are going to share a few major points with you in this chapter:

- Your first slide sets the stage, so be sure it gets attention in a positive way and includes your name, your course, and the title of your presentation.

- Use real pictures instead of clip art because they are more interesting and professional. If you can use photos that fill the entire slide, the visual is more appealing.

- Avoid wordiness! Never put every word you are going to say on a slide and then proceed to read to your audience. This is deadly! Nothing is worse than one slide after another that is filled with many points typed in a size 12 font that no one can see. Words in the body should be at least 18 points, and preferably larger. Titles and headings should be at least 4 points larger than the body.

- Light text on a dark background is more difficult to read than dark text on a light background.

- Present no more than one concept per slide.

- Try not to use more than three or four bullet points per slide, and use animation to introduce them one point at a time.

- Number your points to show order, and use bullets to emphasize certain points.

- Use no more than one or two fonts, and avoid the fancy, hard-to-read styles.

- Use simple, clear graphs and charts that complement your remarks. Photos, graphs, and diagrams can often be used to explain a concept better than words.

- If you use a handout to complement your slideshow, distribute it at the end of the presentation because people will be focused on reading the handout instead of paying attention to your slideshow.

Figure 12.4 illustrates a slide that is boring and has too much information. Figure 12.5 illustrates an interesting and appealing slide.

Figure 12.4   Slide with Too Much Information

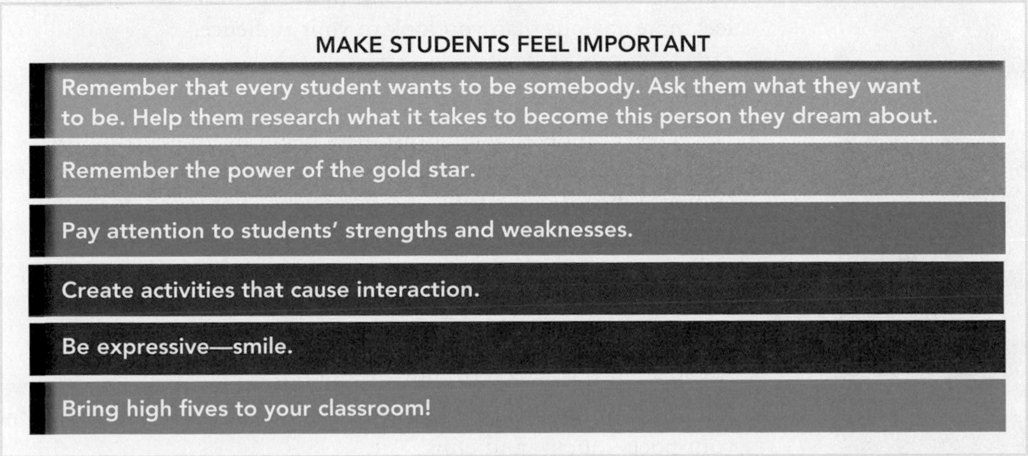

MAKE STUDENTS FEEL IMPORTANT

Remember that every student wants to be somebody. Ask them what they want to be. Help them research what it takes to become this person they dream about.

Remember the power of the gold star.

Pay attention to students' strengths and weaknesses.

Create activities that cause interaction.

Be expressive—smile.

Bring high fives to your classroom!

Figure 12.5 Visually Appealing Slide

the **FUTURE** is
purchased by
the **PRESENT**

REDUCING ANXIETY

Is It Possible to Relax, Have Fun, and Walk Tall?

The day has finally come for you to speak in public—actually, it may have arrived way too early to suit you. If you have prepared using the steps outlined in this chapter, you have every reason to believe you are going to do well. Try to look at this presentation as an opportunity to practice a skill that will serve you well all your life. You may feel nervous, but you need to remember that no one else knows that but you if you don't tell them or show them. Below, you will find some helpful tips to help overcome performance anxiety.

- Be prepared! Nothing trumps preparation in overcoming anxiety. If you know what you're talking about, you'll have more confidence. ***Be the expert*** on your topic.

- Walk to the front of the room, turn and face your audience, and establish eye contact before you start speaking. Take a few deep breaths on the way to the front. Do not begin speaking while walking to the podium or the front of the room. Remember, you'll feel more anxious than you look to your audience.

- Use your anxiety as a positive. Extra adrenaline can increase your energy level.

- Never, ever, under any circumstances begin by apologizing for your presentation. Remember, your introduction must grab your audience! Begin powerfully and positively! "I'm sorry" is neither powerful or positive.

- When rehearsing for your presentation, try to re-create the physical environment in which you will be speaking. Be certain to rehearse aloud.

- If you are using a lectern, don't lean on it.

- Remove temptations to fidget with things, such as keys, change in your pocket, pens, and clips.

How can speech anxiety impact your career decision?

Successful Decisions
AN ACTIVITY FOR CRITICAL REFLECTION

Mike is taking a First-Year Experience course that requires him to make an oral presentation. Although his class is small and he has gotten to know many of his classmates, he is terrified at the thought of making this speech. The date for his speech is two weeks away, and he needs to get moving, but he seems to be immobilized by his fears of speaking in front of a group.

Mike's fear of making oral presentations goes back to the eighth grade, when one of his teachers required him and his peers to make a speech. Mike didn't prepare very well. When it was his time to present, he panicked and forgot his speech. His classmates laughed at him, and his teacher rebuked him in front of his peers. He was humiliated! Mike has hated making presentations since that day, and has avoided speaking in front of a group at all costs. He has built this bad event up in his mind until he cannot face the thought that this could happen again.

The time has come for him to get over this fear and move on. He knows that he has to overcome this fear because he will be making presentations all through college and later when he goes to work.

What suggestions would you make to Mike to help him focus on getting this task done and being able to get up and make this presentation? What advice would you give him for getting over his fears?

1. _____
   _____

2. _____
   _____

3. _____
   _____

- Practice eye sweep. Begin by looking at your audience on the left side of the room and gradually move your eyes around the room so everyone feels they are being addressed.

- Don't indicate in any way that you can't wait for this to be over. If you show that you want it to be over, your audience will want it to be over, too!

- Watch your timing! Don't ramble around after you have made your points. Stick to your outline.

- Don't concentrate on the evaluation. If you have prepared and do your best, you will be evaluated fairly.

- Enjoy yourself. The more you act like you are enjoy doing this, the quicker you will actually begin to have fun speaking. "Fake it 'til you make it!"

> "The trouble with talking too fast is that you might say something you haven't thought about yet."
>
> —Ann Landers

SPEAKING BEYOND THE LECTERN

Why Is Informal Communication Important to Success?

There will be times in your life when you are required to communicate orally with others beyond the lectern. It may be that you are required to lead a meeting via teleconference, introduce a speaker at a conference, or simply answer the telephone at your company. While these situations may not seem as significant as a "formal speech," have no doubt that speaking to one customer on the telephone can be as important as speaking to one thousand people at the lectern. Consider the following informal speaking situations and tips and how they can impact your career.

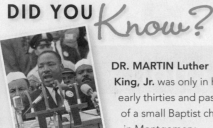

DID YOU *Know?*

DR. MARTIN Luther King, Jr. was only in his early thirties and pastor of a small Baptist church in Montgomery, Alabama, when he was thrust into the national spotlight as a leader of protests against segregation.

He is considered one of the most powerful, effective, and persuasive speakers in American history. His oratory skills helped wake up a nation, and indeed the world, to the injustices, inequities, and discrimination against people of color. His words helped change the direction of this nation.

The movements and marches he led brought significant changes in the fabric of American life through his courage and selfless devotion. He was arrested over twenty times, traveled 6,000,000 miles, and spoke over 2500 times wherever there was injustice or protest. His ability to prepare and deliver powerful speeches, along with his bravery and personal sacrifice, changed the world.

Dr. Martin Luther King, Jr. and Coretta Scott King had four children, all of whom are involved in different aspects of civil rights. He was awarded the Nobel Peace Prize at the age of 35, the youngest man to ever receive the award.

Introducing a Speaker

At some time in your career, you will most likely be asked to introduce a speaker. Often instructors have students introduce peers and guest speakers for classes or conferences, so it is important to know how to do it right. People who introduce speakers frequently have not even read the biography and present a stumbling, bumbling, rambling introduction that discredits the speaker along with the introducer. Providing a strong, carefully crafted introduction sets the stage for the speaker and establishes his or her credibility with the audience, along with your own. Your job is to prepare the audience and to excite them about the speaker's remarks. So how do you effectively introduce a speaker?

- Put excitement in your voice and show your enthusiasm for the speaker.
- Memorize the opening lines so you can look at your audience.
- Tell the audience the general topic of the presentation.
- Give them some clues as to why this is important to them.
- Share with the audience why this particular speaker is highly qualified to deliver this speech.
- Be sure you know how to pronounce the speaker's name and any other difficult words in the introduction.
- Tell enough about the speaker's credentials to persuade the audience of his or her credibility, but don't bore them with every detail.
- If you know personal things about the speaker that might be interesting, you might share one or two of those. For example, you might say, "Dr. Morgan has just returned from his tenth trip to China, where he completed his landmark study on rapidly developing Chinese tourism, so he brings us first-hand information on the Chinese tourists bound for the US." Or you might say, "Mrs. Smith is an accomplished researcher on the topic of ADHD, but her greatest accomplishments, according to Mrs. Smith, are her three grandchildren."
- Wait at the lectern and shake hands with the presenter, which indicates you are turning the program over to the speaker.

Making the Pitch and Selling Your Ideas and Opinions

Have you ever known your idea and opinion was the right one, but you were so ineffective in presenting it that no one listened? Having a good idea is one thing—getting it accepted is something else altogether. You may not like it, but you are being judged right along with your ideas. Your personal brand is on display, so it is important that you prepare and use the right voice and the right strategy to get your ideas heard. Selling ideas is an active sport—not passive. It includes informative, demonstrative, and persuasive techniques. You have to tell and show to convince.

Your voice can add "money in the bank" to your career, and it can be a great tool in expressing your ideas and opinions and getting them accepted. One of the ways you sell your ideas and opinions is with your speaking voice, so you need to check your *voice appeal*. Your researched idea, your voice, and your complementary body language are your best tools for selling your personal ideas because together they have a powerful effect on people. If you have a pleasant, appealing voice that is pitched low, you will likely have people listen to you. On the other hand, if you use a loud, squeaky, monotonous, nasal tone, people will be turned off. If you use the right tone, modulation, and inflection, coupled with sincere, honest body language, you are much more likely to persuade someone that you have a good idea. Your voice, your gestures, and your facial expressions become your tools for success. Study the following checklist below to help sell your ideas.

- Know what you are selling. If you don't believe in your product or idea, no one else will believe it.

- Don't just talk. This is your opportunity to **_perform_** and grab positive attention for yourself.

- Express your main points up front. Don't lose your audience with too much superfluous information that puts them to sleep.

- Find a hook that grabs their attention. What do they already know and like? How can you attach your idea to something they already understand and embrace?

- When you are selling a new idea, you are trying to confirm what they already believe, not prove them wrong. No one likes to be wrong!

- Use a pleasant and well-modulated tone of voice that shows confidence and excitement for your idea or product.

- Use simple language that everyone understands. Avoid jargon.

- Avoid nasal, whining, croaky, or otherwise unpleasant tones.

- Speak with confidence and own what you are saying.

- Express your ideas boldly, demonstrating a professional image.

- Be sure your body language matches your voice quality and enthusiasm.

- Ask for something when you get to the end of your presentation. If you don't want them to do something, why are you talking and trying to persuade them?

Telephone Etiquette

Everyone knows how to answer and talk on the telephone. Right? **_Wrong!_** Of course, everyone can talk on the phone, but many people make a poor impression for a variety of reasons. Since you probably spend a great deal of time on the telephone, you need to pay special attention to how you are being perceived. The most important thing to remember is this: We communicate 8 percent of our message with our words, 35 percent with our tone of voice, and 57 percent with our body language. When you are on the phone, you lose your most important communication tool, your body language! All you have going for you are your words, your tone of voice, and your fluency. In person, you might say something that is sarcastic in a kidding way and the other person probably wouldn't be offended. On the phone, however, the person can't see your wink that indicates this is a joke, and the same message might become offensive. Study the following tips for making a good impression on the telephone.

1. Put a smile in your voice even when you answer the phone, and use a pleasant, congenial tone of voice; identify yourself clearly. Remember, your voice and your words are all you have to make a good impression on the telephone.

2. Remember that you are representing your personal brand when you answer the phone. The objective is to make a good impression. A very important thing for you to remember is this: your personal, outgoing message is a positive or negative reflection on you and your brand. "What up??!!" might be funny to your friends, but a professional caller or employer would find this immature.

3. Avoid speaking too loud or too soft. Do not slur your words.

4. Do not eat, drink, or chew gum while talking on the telephone. This is rude behavior, and it makes a very poor impression.

5. If you are working and you answer the phone, address the caller properly. Call the person by his or her name and title if appropriate. For example, you might say, "Good morning, Dr. Manning."

6. Listen very carefully to what the caller is saying. If you are taking a message, repeat information if necessary, such as return phone numbers, amounts of money, or addresses.

What does your personal outgoing phone message say about you?

from ORDINARY to Extraordinary

Dr. Wayne A. Jones, Assistant Professor and Thurgood Marshall Pathways Fellow—Department of Political Science and Public Administration, Virginia State University, Petersburg, VA

I come from a fine family. My mother is a retired social worker, college professor, and community activist, and my father is a retired Presbyterian minister and college professor. They provided a safe, structured environment and always encouraged me to do well. Clearly, I had the foundation to do well in school. However, I have not always followed my parents' advice to look out for my best interests. This was especially true for my senior year in high school. The outcome was that I did not graduate. So at 18, I started working and got my own apartment, and things were OK. At least, so I thought.

I have always been interested in anything that has wheels on it. If it has wheels, I want to drive it! I drove a school bus for a few years, and then I drove an ambulance. Additionally, I had a part-time job driving a taxi. One day, however, I saw our local bookmobile and I wanted to drive it, as it was different from anything that I had previously operated. I applied to do so, but found out that I had to have a high school diploma to be able to drive the bookmobile. At 19, this became my reason for going back to get a GED. Now, I could master driving yet another "thing" with wheels. It was not, however, as exciting as I thought it would be.

With my GED in hand, my parents encouraged me to begin my college studies. Subsequently, I enrolled at Virginia Commonwealth University. After only one year, I decided that college was not for me. I did not return for a third semester. In 1975, I began working for the police department in Chesterfield, VA. I was only the second African American police officer on the force. I held this position for four years.

My desire for wheels was still with me. I left the police department and began working for The Virginia Overland Transportation Company as a safety supervisor/bus driver. A short time later, I was promoted to operations manager. With this experience under my belt, I went to work for a larger bus company in Richmond, VA, driving a city transit bus.

I left the second bus company after a year to drive for a local construction company. This work, however, turned out to be very "seasonal," and I found myself frequently without income. This company also operated trash trucks, so I asked to be allowed to drive one of their trash trucks so that I could have a steady income and overtime, too. So, there I was in my early 30s, without a college degree, driving either a dump truck or trash truck. There was not a lot to look forward to.

My grandmother called me one day and asked me why I didn't go back to college. "You are far from dumb," I remember her telling me. I tried to explain to her that I was making decent money and I really liked the company I was working for and would not quit my job. I told her that if I went back to college part time, it would take me at least eight years to get a bachelor's degree. "I'll be too old by then," I told her.

7. If you answer the phone and the caller is upset or irate, remain calm and keep your voice soft. Do not meet anger with anger. If you are at work, try to solve the problem to the caller's satisfaction or excuse yourself and get a supervisor who has the authority to make the right decision.

8. If you have a job, do not engage in personal calls at work. If you have to make a personal call, make it quick. Tell your friends not to call you at work.

9. Give your undivided attention to the caller. Do not allow yourself to be distracted by others around you. If someone tries to talk to you while you are on the phone, excuse yourself from the caller for a moment and inform the other person that you are on an important call and cannot talk now.

She posed a question to me, the answer to which was a turning point in my life. "Son," she asked, "how old will you be in eight years if you do not go back to college?" That was my wake-up call. I enrolled at John Tyler Community College with no idea of what I wanted to become. The start of my second semester would bring a devastating event, as my grandmother died unexpectedly of cardiac arrest. Her final gift to me was her wonderful words of wisdom.

So, there I was, working full time, going to college full time, attending classes several nights a week, and studying on the nights when I did not have classes. One night, I received another phone call that changed my life again. My parents called me and told me that they wanted to talk with me about my education. To my surprise, they asked me to quit work and concentrate on my studies. "Grandma had a vision," my mother told me. "She knew that you were going to do great things." They told me that if I quit, they would help with my bills until I finished college. I agreed to take their help.

I transferred from John Tyler Community College and enrolled again at Virginia Commonwealth University. I completed my Bachelor's degree. My GPA was not great upon graduation. I took the Graduate Record Exam (GRE) and scored very badly. I was turned down for the graduate program in public administration. I was now 35. I met with the chair of the department and said to him, "Just give me a chance, I know I can do this." After some conversation, he agreed to give me that opportunity. I completed my Masters of Public Administration in only 18 months. Then, I applied to the doctoral program in public administration at VCU. The chairman of the doctoral program reviewed my GRE scores and basically told me that based upon them I should not have been able to obtain a Master's degree. I then applied to

> *In just a few short years, I went from driving a trash truck to being a university professor.*

the doctoral program in higher education administration at The George Washington University for their Ph.D. program. They accepted me provisionally. However, I again rose to the occasion, and only five years later, I graduated with a 3.85 GPA. My dissertation won the *Outstanding Dissertation of the Year Award* in 2000 from the George Washington University chapter of Phi Delta Kappa.

While working on my Master's degree, I obtained a position as adult day coordinator for a local non-profit agency. Eventually, I would become the agency's executive director. It was during this time that the thought of becoming a college professor came to mind. I saw an ad in the local newspaper for an adjunct teaching position at Richard Bland College instructing a class of advance placement high school students in United States government. It was through this part-time position that I found the love of my life—teaching. I later applied to become a full-time faculty member at Virginia State University, and today, I teach freshman studies and public administration classes.

It may seem like a lifetime to an outsider, but in a few years, I managed to go from driving a trash truck to being a university professor. With hard work, dedication, and help from those around you, you too can change your life and find your dream job. I wish you much luck in your search.

EXTRAORDINARY REFLECTION

Dr. Jones was brave enough to take an enormous risk, quit his full-time job, accept help, and reach his goals. Who do you have in your life that you can depend upon for support (maybe not monetary support, but crucial support of your goals, dreams, and educational plans)? Why?

10. Avoid leaving long-winded messages that someone has to wade through. If you want your message to be acted on, make it clear and brief. Let the person know exactly how to reach you. Speak your telephone number slowly and repeat it once.

Developing a Powerful Telepresence

Teleconferencing with people on programs such as Skype, WebEx, or Go-to-Meeting has become quite common in recent years. Chances are, you are already using a telepresence program to talk with friends and relatives around the country, and perhaps around the world. In case you have not yet used one of the many programs available, you need to know that teleconferencing

Have you mastered the techniques of video conferencing?

allows you to do everything from participating in a remote job interview to sharing photos with your friends. Use the following tips to improve your teleconferencing techniques:

- Since your friends and perhaps coworkers or even an interviewer can see you, you need to take a little more care with your personal appearance before signing on. Hair, grooming, makeup, and dress are important when using this technology.

- If this is an important event, such as an interview, you need to be sure to have good lighting in the room. You should angle your webcam to a position that allows you to look directly into it.

- If you are participating in a telepresence session, such as an interview, be sure the background in the room is appropriate. Your desk should be orderly and no offensive photos or posters should be visible.

- If interviewing, you want to avoid clothes with bright colors, because the lighting can make your skin look weird. Avoid busy patterns.

- If you have agreed on a time to meet, respect the other person's time by being online at the prescribed time.

- Be sure the camera is not angled to pick up a lot of extraneous movement in the background. Background noise and movements are very distracting.

- Try to sit still and not wiggle around too much in your chair, because it is distracting. Look directly into the camera when speaking.

- Use your normal speaking voice. It is not necessary to shout or talk slower than usual.

Video conferences are used frequently in the business world today, as well as in private homes. They are a great way to save time and money, and they are a really cool way to communicate with friends and family.

CHANGING IDEAS to Reality

REFLECTIONS ON ORAL COMMUNICATIONS

As you learn to speak well, you will be following a tradition that has been practiced by scholars for thousands of years. Effective speechmaking principles can be traced to Plato, Socrates, Cicero, and Quintilian. By learning to construct and deliver your own presentations, you are becoming accomplished in skills that will serve you well all your life.

Learning to present effective presentations will help you succeed in every class you take. While you further hone your communications abilities, you will want to practice the following points:

- Use a logical organization pattern.
- Speak on subjects that you know.
- Always rehearse aloud and often.
- Take every opportunity to speak in public.
- Use a keyword outline.
- Analyze the audience and relate to them.
- Learn to use technology and visual aids to complement your presentations.

Knowledge in Bloom

IDENTIFYING PROBLEM SPEAKING SKILLS AND DEVISING A PLAN FOR IMPROVEMENT

Utilizes Levels 1–6 of the Taxonomy (See Bloom's Taxonomy at the front of this text)

Process: The exercise will require you to use critical thinking and research skills to design a plan for improving your speaking skills and abilities.

Using the list below, identify those problems that you think you have in delivering presentations by circling the number beside the problem. Add additional problems using the blank lines.

1. Extreme anxiety about speaking in front of a group.
2. Not being able to identify a good topic.
3. Inability to narrow the topic to a manageable scope.
4. Fear of speaking without writing out every word and reading it.
5. Inability to write a compelling, interesting introduction.
6. Ineffective use of audiovisual aids.

7. Ineffective use of PowerPoint or Prezi.
8. Not being able to relate to my audience.
9. Presenting in a rambling, disjointed manner.
10. Inability to finish strongly using a summary and powerful ending.
11. Anxiety in using a telepresence program
12. Unfamiliarity with introducing a speaker
13. _____
14. _____

Now, choose the top three problem areas that seem to give you the most trouble. In the space below, summarize why you think you have problems with these areas.

Problem One:

_____

_____

_____

Problem Two:

_____

_____

_____

Problem Three:

_____

_____

_____

Now, research these three areas using the Internet or other references and decide on a plan as to how you can overcome these three major problems by applying knowledge you have uncovered through your research.

When you have designed your plan for overcoming these three problem areas, practice the techniques you discovered and create a simulated environment as though you are presenting to a group or using a telepresence program.

SQ3R MASTERY STUDY SHEET

EXAMPLE QUESTION (FROM PAGE 279) List two ways that speaking in a digital world differs from typical speaking settings.	**ANSWER:**
EXAMPLE QUESTION (FROM PAGE 286) Contrast effective PowerPoint slides with ineffective slides.	**ANSWER:**
AUTHOR QUESTION (FROM PAGE 280) Discuss two factors of audience demographics.	**ANSWER:**
AUTHOR QUESTION (FROM PAGE 282) Discuss two means by which you could write an effective introduction.	**ANSWER:**
AUTHOR QUESTION (FROM PAGE 283) Discuss two means by which you could write an effective conclusion.	**ANSWER:**
AUTHOR QUESTION (FROM PAGE 284) Name three important steps in writing an informative speech.	**ANSWER:**
AUTHOR QUESTION (FROM PAGE 288) How can you reduce speaking anxiety?	**ANSWER:**
YOUR QUESTION (FROM PAGE ____)	**ANSWER:**
YOUR QUESTION (FROM PAGE ____)	**ANSWER:**
YOUR QUESTION (FROM PAGE ____)	**ANSWER:**
YOUR QUESTION (FROM PAGE ____)	**ANSWER:**
YOUR QUESTION (FROM PAGE ____)	**ANSWER:**

Finally, after answering these questions, recite this chapter's major points in your mind. Consider the following general questions to help you master this material.

- What is it about?
- What does it mean?
- What is the most important thing you learned? Why?
- What are the key points to remember?

chapter thirteen

COMMUNICATE

COMMUNICATING INTERPERSONALLY, APPRECIATING DIVERSITY, AND MANAGING CONFLICT

"Words can destroy relationships. What we call each other ultimately becomes what we think about each other, and what we think about each other matters."
—Jeanne J. Kirkpatrick

COMMUNICATE

Why read this chapter?

Because you'll learn...

- About the steps in the communication process
- How computer-mediated communication relates to interpersonal communication
- How to deal with difficult people

Because you'll be able to...

- Understand and use nonverbal communication more effectively
- Understand the dimensions of diversity and how they affect relationships
- Navigate and learn how to manage conflict more effectively

Scan and QUESTION

Take a few moments, **scan this chapter** and on page 320, write **five of your own questions** that you think will be important to your mastery of this material. You will also find five questions listed from your authors.

Example:

- ☑ **What are the six elements of the communication process?** (from page 300)
- ☑ **What is self-disclosure, and why is it important for healthy relationships?** (from page 306)

MyStudentSuccessLab

MyStudentSuccessLab is an online solution designed to help you acquire and develop (or hone) the skills you need to succeed. You will have access to peer-led video presentations and develop core skills through interactive exercises and projects.

Name: Gregg Gudelinis
Institution: Graduate! Suffolk County Community College, St. Joseph's College, and Long Island University, Long Island, NY
Major: Elementary Education

Gregg Gudelinis graduated high school in the summer of 2000. He always wanted to be a teacher and knew that he wanted to stay on Long Island. Gregg chose to attend a community college because of the cost, smaller classes, and more personalized help. "I chose Suffolk County Community College because it was right around the corner from my home and many of my friends were already attending and had a great deal of positive feedback about the college and its professors."

Gregg knew that it was important for him to stay in college because he would need a degree for his career choice. He took a freshman seminar course in his first semester at Suffolk and believes the class is what helped motivate him to start working on his goals. "Freshman Seminar gave me the tools necessary for success, such as time management, study skills, transitioning from high school to college, and learning about all of the recourses my college had to offer. The course also helped me to grow up and prepare for my future."

Gregg believes that because all of his classes at the college were smaller, he received the individual attention

An interview conducted and written by Nancy Gerli, Instructor, SUNY Suffolk County Community College, Long Island, NY

he needed to stay in school and work toward his goal of becoming a teacher. Once Gregg graduated from SCCC, he went on to continue his studies at St. Joseph's on Long Island, where he received his BA in elementary education, and then his Master's degree in Literacy from LIU. In the fall of 2008, I was going through resumes to find adjunct teaching faculty for my developmental reading and freshman seminar courses. Gregg Gudelinis was one of the faculty members I interviewed and then hired part time. He told me he got his start at Suffolk and was happy to be back, now in the capacity of teacher.

After Gregg was at the college for a few weeks, he came to me to discuss his classes and his students. He told me that he was surprised at how many students had to overcome great obstacles in order to attend college. They shared stories with him about their struggles and the lack of support from family and friends, and the many other hardships they had to endure. Gregg was truly touched by these students and realized just how lucky he had been. He had the support of his family, and never had to deal with any of the hardships that some of his students have shared with him. It was at that point Gregg realized that he needed to give back to his students.

"I realized how lucky I was to have such a supportive family, and it was because of this support and guidance that I was able to achieve my goals. So many of my students don't have that support or guidance and are desperately looking for someone to care."

Because of this, Gregg decided he was going to do whatever he could to help his students succeed. Gregg was only part time, but was sure to be accessible to his students both in and outside the classroom. He stayed longer than required to tutor, advise with schedules, and just talk with students. In the spring of 2009, a full-time reading coordinator position became available. Gregg interviewed for the position and was chosen. Now Gregg is able to touch many more lives and help many more students. Gregg is rarely in his office alone; students are with him getting help with homework, seeking advice, or just talking.

"I feel that I can make a difference in so many students' lives now. I know the help and guidance I received at SCCC has helped me be a better teacher and mentor to my students. It is because of the guidance and motivation of the teachers at SCCC when I was a student that I want to become the best teacher I can be for my students."

THINK about it

1. How did attending college help Gregg achieve his goals?

2. What qualities do you look for in a teacher? Who were some of your best teachers and why?

THE COMMUNICATION PROCESS

How Does Communication Work?

Look around in any store, at any red light, in any restaurant, and, often, in any classroom, and you will see someone on a cell phone. Increasingly, they are not talking, rather texting. Technology is one of the dominant forms of communication in today's world. Does texting count as communication? You bet it does. Does writing an e-mail count as communication? Yes, it does, too. We are living in a world where communication through technology is a way of life that is here to stay. This chapter is included to help you understand the communication process face to face or using technology, how to communicate more effectively, how to appreciate the diverse nature of your institution and work environments, and how to manage the inevitable conflicts that arise from time to time.

Communication is not something we do **to people**, rather it is something that is done **between people**. Communication can take on a variety of forms, such as oral speech, the written word, body movements, electronic messages, and even yawns. All of these actions communicate something to another person. As you begin thinking about communication, it is paramount that you know this: If you are in the presence of another person, communication cannot be stopped.

Basically, the communication process involves **six elements**: the source, the message, the channel, the receiver, barriers, and feedback. Consider Figure 13.1.

Barriers (represented by the lines in Figure 13.1) are things that can interfere with the source, the message, the channel, or the receiver. Barriers can occur anywhere within the communication process, and can include things like external noise (others talking, cell phones, and traffic), internal noise (self-talk, doubt, and questioning), interference, and poor communication habits. Your emotions, past experiences, social norms, communication expectations, and prejudices can also be barriers to effective communication. Think about a time when your feelings for someone interfered with your ability to listen to them objectively. This is a perfect example of a barrier. **Feedback** is the verbal and nonverbal responses given to you by the receiver.

"I see communication as a huge umbrella that covers and affects all that goes on between human beings."

—Joseph Adler

Figure 13.1 **Six Elements of Communication**

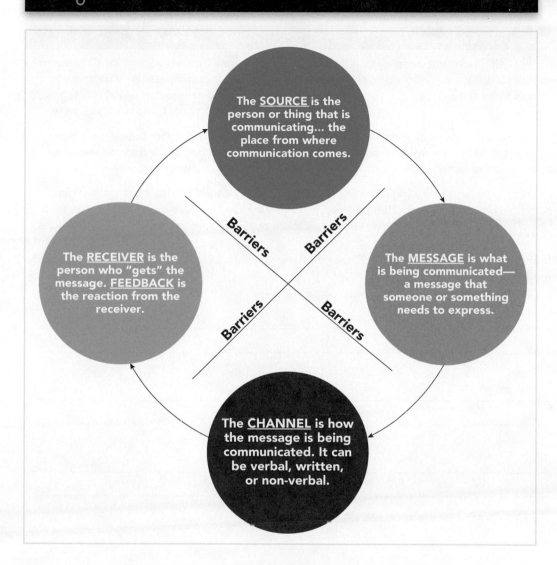

What Is the Role of Interpersonal Communication in Everyday Life?

Interpersonal communication is a part of the greater communication spectrum. It is "a dynamic form of communication between two (or more) people in which the messages exchanged significantly influence their thoughts, emotions, behaviors, and relationships" (McCornack, 2007). The messages in interpersonal communication are not necessarily static like the words in a book, a written letter, or a text message; they are fluid and constantly changing, potentially causing your relationships to change along with them. Texting and e-mails are components of interpersonal communication, as well as computer-mediated interpersonal communication, which we will discuss later in this chapter.

Steven McCornack, in his book, *Reflect and Relate* (2007), suggests that there are three *interpersonal communication goals,* as shown in Figure 13.2: *self-presentation goals, instrumental goals*, and *relationship goals*.

Later in this chapter, we will discuss how to use interpersonal communication to your best advantage in understanding and learning from others, building lasting relationships, and dealing with inevitable conflicts both in person and through technology.

Figure 13.2 Interpersonal Communication Goals

Type of Goal	Explanation	Example
Self-Presentation Goals	Goals that help us present ourselves to others in a particular fashion and help others see us as we wish to be seen	If you want a new acquaintance or love interest to see you as a caring, compassionate person, you will use words and actions that reveal yourself as caring, trustworthy, honest, and compassionate.
Instrumental Goals	Goals that help us present information in such a way as to get what we want or need from another person, to possibly win approval	If you wanted to borrow your best friend's tablet, you would remind him or her that you are always careful and respect other's property.
Relationship Goals	Goals that help us build meaningful, lasting, and effective relationships with other people	If your friend loaned you her tablet, you might write a thank you note or buy a small gift as a token of your appreciation to show your gratitude.

Take a moment and identify one way that you could use each of the interpersonal communication goals to help you succeed in college and establish strong relationships.

Self-Presentation Goal

I can use this to _____

_____

Instrumental Goal

I can use this to _____

_____

Relationship Goal

I can use this to _____

_____

THE STORY OF ONE WILD BOY

Why Is Interpersonal Communication Important?

You do *not* have a choice—if you are in the presence of another human being, you are communicating. Period! Smiling is communication. Reading a newspaper is communication. Turning your back to the wall and hiding your face from everyone is communication. Silence is communication. It is just the law of nature—if you are around one or more people, you are communicating with them. With that said, understanding the impact of your communication is paramount.

Consider this: nothing in your life is more important than effective communication. **Nothing!** Your family is not. Your friends are not. Your career is not. Your religion is not. Your money is not. "*Why?*" you may ask. "*That's a harsh, drastic statement.*" We make this assertion because without effective communication, you would not have a relationship with your family and friends. You would not have a career or money or even religious beliefs. Communication is that important. In fact, it is so important that communication gives us our identity. That's right. Without communication and interaction, **we would not even know that we were human beings**.

Take into account the ***true story*** of the Wild Boy of Aveyron. It may sound like this story was taken from *The National Enquirer,* but it was not. This story has been documented in many science, psychology, sociology, and communication texts over the years. In January of 1800, a gardener in Aveyron, France, went out one morning to collect vegetables for the day. To his surprise, he heard this unusual moaning and groaning sound. Upon further inspection, he found a "wild boy" squatting in the garden eating vegetables as an animal might do. This boy showed no signs or behaviors associated with human beings. He appeared to be 12–14 years old, but stood just a little more than four feet tall. He had scars and burns on his body and his face showed traces of smallpox. His teeth were brown and yellow and his gums were receding. It can only be assumed that when he was an infant, he was abandoned in the woods and left to die. It has also been suggested that someone may have tried to kill him as an infant because of the long scar across his trachea (Lane, 1976).

When he was found in 1800, he could not speak and barely stood erect. "***He had no sense of being a human in the world. He had no sense of himself as a person related to other persons***" (Shattuck, 1980). Because of his lack of communication and contact with other humans, he had no identity, no language, no self-concept, and no idea that he was even a human being in a world of human beings. Of course, he had no religious beliefs or relationships with other human beings. That is how **powerful** communication is in our world today—it gives us our identity. It lets us know we are *human*! It helps establish our place and purpose in the world.

THE ROLE OF NONVERBAL BEHAVIOR IN INTERPERSONAL COMMUNICATION

How do our communication and language affect our self-image?

Can We Communicate Without Words?

Nonverbal communication is any and all communication other than words—and it is constant. We cannot escape our body language or the body language of others. Why is it important to study nonverbal communication? Because there can be so many interpretations of a single nonverbal clue, we must understand that not every action is equal or carries the same message. We must consider everything, from cultural traditions to unconscious acts, to fully grasp what may be intended by a look, a smile, a touch, or how close we stand to someone. We must consider that many of our nonverbal clues are accidental. Think about how many interpretations there can be from a pat on the shoulder. It could mean "congratulations," or "welcome back," or "way to go," or "I'm sorry," or "Hey, friend" (Lane, 2008).

Nonverbal clues mean different things to different people and in different cultures, and can be interpreted in vastly different ways. One's facial expressions are among the most telling of our nonverbal clues. "One research team found that some facial expressions, such as those conveying happiness, sadness, anger, disgust, and surprise, were the same in 68 to 92 percent of all cultures examined" (Beebe et al., 2008).

Proximity is also a strong nonverbal clue. Maybe you are not overly fond of a person who has approached you and you decide to keep your distance from him or her. Conversely, when a person approaches you that you consider to be your friend and confidant, you may move closer to him or her. The rules surely vary from culture to culture, but consider the diagram in Figure 13.3, The Classification of Spatial Zones, as described by interpersonal expert Edward T. Hall (1966).

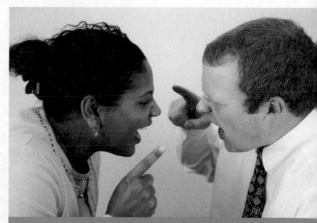

How do your physical actions influence your message?

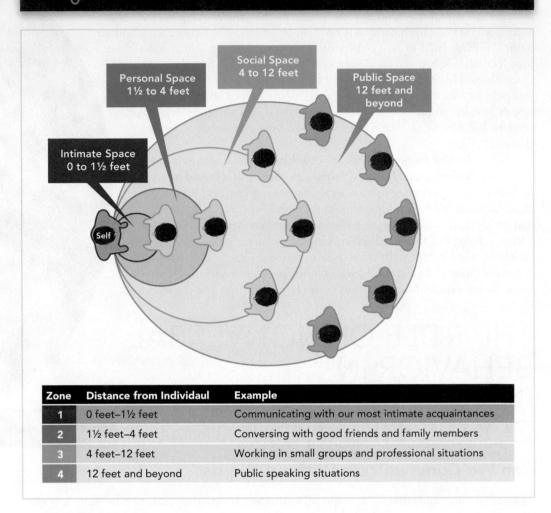

Figure 13.3 **The Classification of Spatial Zones**

Zone	Distance from Individaul	Example
1	0 feet–1½ feet	Communicating with our most intimate acquaintances
2	1½ feet–4 feet	Conversing with good friends and family members
3	4 feet–12 feet	Working in small groups and professional situations
4	12 feet and beyond	Public speaking situations

Consider the chart in Figure 13.4, describing more common nonverbal clues. As you study each action and example, try to determine what it would mean to *you* based on *your* thoughts and cultural traditions.

OMGUROTT (OH MY GOD, YOU ARE OVER THE TOP)

Why Is Studying Computer-Mediated Communication Important in Today's Society?

Believe it or not, there was a time not too long ago when there was no such term as ***computer-mediated communication*** (CMC). There were no e-mails, Blackberries, iPhones, tablets, text messages, blogs, tweets, Facebook pages, or instant messages. OMG, YKM! No, we're not kidding you. As a matter of fact, it was not until a few years ago that the study of interpersonal communication even mentioned CMC; it was not considered to be a part of interpersonal communication at all. It was believed that interpersonal communication had to take place *in person*.

Today, CMC is widely considered a vital sub-category of interpersonal communication studies. "There is some evidence that those wishing to communicate a message to someone,

Figure 13.4   Nonverbal Communication

Nonverbal Action	Examples	What They Could Mean
Eye contact	Looking directly at someone Avoiding eye contact Fixed gaze	
Posture	Slumping Standing very erect Leaning forward when seated	
Facial expressions	Smiling/frowning Squinted eyes Blank stare	
Clothing/emblems	Well dressed and pressed Wrinkled and sloppy "Smelly"	
Artifacts	Jewelry Tattoos Body/facial piercings	
Gestures	Waving arms Fingers pointed toward person Crossed arms	
Touch	Patting someone on the back Firm handshake Weak handshake	

such as a message ending a relationship, may select a less-rich communication message—they may be more likely to send a letter or an e-mail rather than share the bad news face-to-face" (Beebe et. al., 2008). Technology has become an integral part of our communication strategies.

Some may ask, can CMC really be considered "interpersonal" when you are not meeting face to face with another person? The answer is yes. Why? Because in today's rich CMC environment, we can **infer or imply emotions** as we send and receive electronic communication. For example, we use symbols such as ☺ to indicate happiness or humor, and ☹ to indicate that we are sad or upset. We use abbreviations such as LOL (for laugh out loud). We even SCREAM AT OTHERS or SPEAK WITH EMPHASIS when we use all capital letters in our communication. Additionally, many people have cameras connected to their computers so the sender and receiver can see each other's facial expressions on the screen. Therefore, emotions can be conveyed through CMC, although there are not as many nonverbal clues to view and interpret as in face-to-face communication (Lane, 2008). Because we cannot see all the nonverbal clues associated with face-to-face communications, we are more likely to misunderstand the message when using CMC.

The fact that we are not face to face does not seem to negatively affect our communication efforts via technology. Several studies suggest that CMC relationships differ very little

> "The information superhighway is clearly not just a road for moving data from one place to another, but a roadside where people can pass each other, occasionally meet, and decide to travel together."
>
> —*Beebe, Beebe, and Redmond*

> *"Good communicators don't use the same approach in every situation. They know that sometimes it's best to be blunt and sometimes tactful, that there is a time to speak up and a time to be quiet."*
>
> —Ronald Adler

from those who meet face to face. Further research also suggests that CMC relationships may even be stronger than face-to-face relationships because people using CMC ask more pointed and direct questions, reveal more about themselves, and communicate more frequently (Tidwell & Walther, 2002; Walther & Burgoon, 1992). Think about the last time you revealed something online that you may have never revealed to that person face to face.

There can be a downside and some challenges to CMC, however. For years, communication experts have worried about the effects of electronic communication on the entire communication process, especially traditional interpersonal communication. In today's technologically advanced world, we do not have to speak to anyone if we don't want to. We purchase gasoline at the pump, pay for groceries at self-checkout, use automated tellers to get money, go to Amazon or iTunes to purchase our music and books, search eBay for sale items, and text others rather than pick up the phone or visit. Social isolation is a major concern and you have to work hard to guard against becoming **emotionally detached** and **technologically reclusive.**

SELF-DISCLOSURE AND INTERPERSONAL COMMUNICATION

Are You Willing to Let Others into Your Life?

Self-disclosure is how much you are willing to share with others about your life, your goals, your dreams, your fears, and your setbacks. Often, self-disclosure determines the *quality* of your interpersonal relationships. The level of self-disclosure is up to you, and it can vary from **insignificant** facts ("I had dinner at O'Toole's last night" or "I'm a Leo"), to **informational** facts ("I'm majoring in History" or "I have two children"), to **highly significant** facts ("I'm fighting ovarian cancer" or "I'm going through a divorce"). True self-disclosure must present new information about the parties involved.

Irwin Altman and Dalmas Taylor (1973) state that self-disclosure is "showing ourselves to others on a conscious and unconscious level." They use the analogy of an onion and suggest that you think of your life with multiple layers. As you know, an onion has layer after layer, each hidden beneath the other. The outer layer is different from the inner layers and is only the covering of what lies inside—much like our clothes are a covering for what is inside us. The skin of an onion is easily peeled away. The further you peel into the onion, the smaller it becomes and the more protected those inner layers are. We too have many layers, and we can choose to "peel" them away or keep them all intact.

Consider Figure 13.5. What would you be willing to reveal (peel away) about yourself, and to whom would you feel comfortable revealing this information?

> *"Confiding a secret to an unworthy person is like carrying grain in a bag with a hole in it."*
>
> —Ethiopian Proverb

Everyone has more than three layers, but this figure gives you a good example of how you can peel away layers to let others know you more intimately. By self-disclosing and getting past your outer layers, you can enrich the quality of your relationships with others and also strengthen your own self-concept. You must, however, self-disclose (tell the truth) to yourself before you can ever self-disclose to others. Without personal and interpersonal self-disclosure, you cannot have mature, intimate, well-developed, sincere interpersonal relationships, because your inner life remains hidden.

Figure 13.5 **The Third Layer**

Outer (Public) Layer or Insignificant Fact: What would you be willing to reveal?

_____

_____

_____

To whom? _____

Second Layer or Informational Fact: What would you be willing to reveal?

_____

_____

To whom? _____

Third Layer or Highly Significant Fact: What would you be willing to reveal?

_____

_____

_____

To whom? _____

RELATIONSHIPS WITH FRIENDS

How Can You Strengthen the Ties That Bind?

Level 1 Remember

Think about your best friend. How did you meet? In class? Through another person? By chance? What was the force that brought you together? More importantly, what is the "glue" that holds you together? If you compare your relationships with your closest friends, you will probably recognize that honest communication, self-disclosure, and trust are paramount in these relationships. You can't choose your family, but you can, and do, choose your friends.

So, why are friendships important? Friendships can bring a plethora of joys, including comfort, understanding, a loyal confidant, and a listening ear. They give you someone to talk with about happiness and sorrow, and someone to laugh with when things are funny. You can share your hopes and dreams and fears with good friends. Take a moment and list the qualities that you like in your close friends. Consider the emotional, intellectual, spiritual, and physical aspects of friendship.

> "The worst solitude is to be destitute of sincere friendship."
> —Francis Bacon

_____

_____

_____

When making new friends, consider adding people to your life who:

- Treat you kindly, fairly, and equally
- Bring new and different ideas and experiences to your life

- May be very different from friends you have had in the past
- Have ambition and courage and are outgoing and adventurous
- Have healthy work habits and strong ethics, and take pride in his/her character
- Enjoy learning new things
- Have found their goals and mission in life

APPRECIATING DIVERSITY

How Can You Strengthen Your Relationship with People from Diverse Backgrounds?

As we have discussed, if you are in the presence of another person, *you are communicating*. It is inescapable. Well, it is also inescapable that we all live in a diverse world with people from different socio-economic, cultural, religious, and ideological backgrounds. The American culture is one of the most diverse of any on earth! We are a nation of immigrants that still welcomes people from all over the world to our shores.

This fact is one of our greatest strengths, because in this country, ideas from all over the world come together in an environment that allows anyone to pursue his or her dreams and ambitions. On the other hand, all this diversity is accompanied by the problems of throwing so many people from diverse cultures together and expecting them to function together as one society. In a society such as ours, it is almost inevitable that prejudice will arise. However, by understanding what it means to live in a diverse society, we can learn how to communicate more effectively and, hopefully, learn more about the cultures and traditions of others.

> *"I am not a citizen of Athens or Greece, but of the world."*
> —Socrates

What Are Ethnocentrism and Xenocentrism?

Many people truly believe that they are not prejudiced against any group and that they have no stereotypes in their thought processes about certain groups of people. If we dig deep enough, however, we would find that most of us have some kind of prejudices, and that we all discriminate in some ways. Because many of us have lived in rather homogeneous neighborhoods and primarily hang out with people "like us," we tend to be *ethnocentric*, believing that our particular ethnic background is superior, and tending to stay with "our kind."

Ethnocentrism suggests that we tend to fear people from other ethnic backgrounds, or we lump them together and view them **as a group,** rather than **as individuals**. We don't think that their culture, religion, or race could possibly be as important or worthwhile as our own. Think about the ramifications to your own life if you were judged by "your group" of people instead of as an individual—if everyone judged you *as a woman,* and not as Suzanne; if everyone judged you *as a Northerner,* and not as Joe; if everyone judged you *as a Pentecostal,* and not as Raymond; if everyone judged you *as a lesbian,* and not as Sandra.

> *"We don't see things as THEY are, we see things as WE are."*
> —Anais Nin

Think about the negative terms many people use to describe just a few practices from cultures other than those found in the United States.

"People in England drive on the **wrong** side of the road."

"The Islamic language is written and read **backward**."

"Europeans use the **wrong kind** of money."

"Africans dress **funny**."

Have you ever made a snap judgment about something unfamiliar to you?

"Asians eat **weird** things."

"Arabs listen to **strange** music."

Ask yourself this: "Is it really wrong?" "Is it really backward?" "Is it really weird?" or are these customs simply *different* from your own? You know the true answer.

Xenocentrism is the opposite of ethnocentrism in that one believes that other cultures are superior to one's own culture and that one's own culture has very little value or nothing to offer. Some people use xenocentrism as an "overcorrection" for their ethnocentrism. This can be just as dangerous as ethnocentrism, because once again, we cut ourselves off from learning from everyone and everything we encounter. All people, places, cultures, religions, races, genders, and orientations have something to offer. It does not mean that we have to accept and embrace every idea or characteristic from every person or every culture, but being an educated citizen does mean learning to listen, evaluate, analyze, and then make our decisions.

Take a few moments to complete Figure 13.6. As you consider each statement, respond with honesty and sincerity.

Figure 13.6 Getting a Grasp on Ethnocentrism

Read each statement very carefully, and then, based on *your* personal feelings, experiences, and upbringing, circle the number on the scale that best reflects your opinion as to whether this behavior or action is "good" or "bad."

STATEMENT	BAD		NEUTRAL		GOOD
1. Looking at someone when you talk to them.	1	2	3	4	5
2. Eating any type of food with your bare hands.	1	2	3	4	5
3. Having a pierced eyebrow.	1	2	3	4	5
4. Smelling someone as a greeting.	1	2	3	4	5
5. Eating someone's cremated ashes as a tribute to him or her.	1	2	3	4	5
6. Being late for an appointment.	1	2	3	4	5
7. Participating in an arranged marriage.	1	2	3	4	5
8. Believing in more than one god.	1	2	3	4	5
9. Eating cows.	1	2	3	4	5
10. Eating pigs.	1	2	3	4	5
11. Eating dogs.	1	2	3	4	5
12. Eating horses.	1	2	3	4	5
13. Having sex before marriage.	1	2	3	4	5
14. Chewing food with your mouth open ("smacking" your food).	1	2	3	4	5
15. Believing that money is a good thing.	1	2	3	4	5
16. Requiring that women cover all body parts except their eyes.	1	2	3	4	5
17. Staring at someone.	1	2	3	4	5
18. Moving away or out of your parents' home.	1	2	3	4	5
19. Shaking hands with your right hand.	1	2	3	4	5
20. Taking a bath every day.	1	2	3	4	5
21. Duty and country should always come first.	1	2	3	4	5
22. Calling a person by their first name.	1	2	3	4	5
23. Everyone should have a chance to be educated.	1	2	3	4	5
24. Nose rings are OK.	1	2	3	4	5
25. Tattoos are OK on any part of the body.	1	2	3	4	5
26. Using profanity to express one's self.	1	2	3	4	5

(continued)

Figure 13.6 **Getting a Grasp on Ethnocentrism (*Continued*)**

STATEMENT	BAD		NEUTRAL		GOOD
27. Having more than one wife at a time.	1	2	3	4	5
28. Having "barnyard" animals live in your home.	1	2	3	4	5
29. Believing that all citizens have a right to know "the truth" about what the government does.	1	2	3	4	5
30. Showing no emotions to others.	1	2	3	4	5
31. Having healthy self-esteem.	1	2	3	4	5
32. Believing in fate.	1	2	3	4	5
33. Believing that the arrangement of furniture in your home can help determine your health and happiness.	1	2	3	4	5
34. Always finish what you start regardless of the cost or consequences.	1	2	3	4	5
35. Hard work is more important than fun.	1	2	3	4	5
36. Honesty is always the best policy.	1	2	3	4	5
37. Participating in a nomadic lifestyle.	1	2	3	4	5
38. Mercy or honor killing.	1	2	3	4	5
39. Marrying children under the age of 16.	1	2	3	4	5
40. Lying to protect someone's feelings.	1	2	3	4	5

ANALYSIS: Now that you have circled a response for each statement, work with a group of students in your class or online to determine how your answers are different from or similar to theirs. This can be of significance when your responses vary by at least two numbers on the scale. (Example: If you responded with a 5 on #30 and your partner(s) responded with a 1, this is a major difference.) After you have discussed your responses with each other, write a brief statement about what conclusions can be drawn from this experience.

_____

_____

_____

_____

CONFLICT IN RELATIONSHIPS IS INEVITABLE

Why Is It Important to Learn How You Deal with Conflict?

Many people intensely dislike conflict and will go to extreme measures to avoid it. On the other hand, some people seem to thrive on conflict and enjoy creating situations that put people at odds with each other. While in college, you certainly will not be sheltered from conflicts. In fact, on a college campus where a very diverse population lives and learns together, conflict is likely to arise on a regular basis. The simple truth is, conflict is pervasive throughout our culture, and you simply cannot avoid having some confrontations with other people. Therefore, you should not try to avoid conflict; rather, you can use it to create better relationships by exploring workable solutions—hopefully win-win solutions.

Consider the Chinese symbol for *conflict* in Figure 13.7. You will see that it is made up of two different symbols: **danger** and **hidden opportunity**. Why? Because when you are engaged in a conflict, you have the potential to enter into *dangerous* territory. Violence, alienation, and irreparable damage could occur. However, you also have the *hidden opportunity* to grow,

Figure 13.7 Chinese Figure for Conflict

Danger   Hidden Opportunity

learn, and strengthen your relationships. Just because conflict in relationships is inevitable does not mean that it has to be permanent, dangerous, or destructive.

Conflict can occur in any relationship, whether it is with family members, your girlfriend or boyfriend, your best friend, a roommate, a spouse or partner, your children, or a total stranger. Some of the causes of *relationship tensions* include:

Jealousy	Honesty	Emotions
Dependency	Culture	Sexual orientation
Outside commitments	Opinions/values/beliefs	Perceptions
Personality traits or flaws	Affiliations	

Dealing with Conflict

Conflict does not happen in just one form. Conflict can be personal or situational. There are several ways that people deal with issues. They include:

Blowing your lid	This involves screaming, uncontrolled anger, hurling insults and an unwillingness to listen.
Shunning	This involves shutting the other person out and being unwilling to engage in any type of communication or resolution.
Sarcasm	This involves using stinging remarks to make the other person feel small, unimportant, insignificant, or stupid.
Mocking	This involves using past experiences or words to "mock" or ridicule the other person; laughing at them; or poking fun at them or the situation.
Civility	This involves sitting down and logically, rationally discussing the issues or problems and trying to come to a win-win solution. (Adapted from Baxter, (1993)

THE FACES OF CONFLICT

Uggggg!! How Do I Deal with Negative, Nasty, Difficult People?

We've all encountered them from time to time—*difficult* people who are negative, angry, unhappy, destructive, argumentative, sad, depressed, and judgmental. They are people who seem to walk around with a black cloud above their heads and seem to enjoy causing interpersonal conflict. They are likely to pop up everywhere—at work, in class, in traffic, in restaurants, and even in places of worship. They cannot be avoided. Figure 13.8 profiles the most common types

Successful Decisions

AN ACTIVITY FOR CRITICAL REFLECTION

In a meeting of the American Institute of Architecture Students, John made a suggestion that the council sponsor a fund raiser to secure funds to send the officers to a design workshop. His suggestion included having all members of the council participate in raising the funds, even though only the officers would get to attend. This suggestion set Barry off and he began to talk very animatedly with a loud, intimidating voice about how this would be unfair to everyone who worked and didn't get to attend the workshop. He stood up and towered over John and continued to use abusive language.

Rather than fuel Barry's argument, John remained calm, and in a very quiet and controlled, but firm voice, said, "Barry, I understand your feelings, but what you need to realize is that next year you will be an officer, and all of us will be working to send you and your team. Why don't we move to another agenda item and come back to this one after we have all had time to collect our thoughts."

In your own words, what two suggestions would you give John to help further control the situation at hand?

1. _____

2. _____

of negative, difficult people. Perhaps you recognize some of them. Read the descriptions and try to develop two to three strategies to effectively deal with each type of difficult person. In developing your strategies, you may have to rely on others in your class for assistance, pull from your past experiences (what worked and what did not), and do some research on your own.

Learning to manage conflict and interact with difficult people are very important steps in developing sound communication practices and healthy relationships. If you can learn to stay calm, put yourself in the other person's shoes, and try to find mutually beneficial solutions, you will gain admiration and respect from your friends, family, peers, and colleagues. As you consider conflicts in your life and relationships, take a moment and complete the Conflict Management Assessment in Figure 13.9 to determine your awareness of issues related to conflict and how to manage conflict.

Figure 13.8 **Types of Difficult Behaviors and People**

Types of difficult behaviors by difficult people	Description	What can you do to effectively deal with them?
Gossiping	Doesn't do a lot of work and would rather spread rumors and untruths about others to make themselves feel better.	_____ _____ _____
Manipulating	The person who constantly tries to negotiate every aspect of life: "I'll do 'X' for you if you do 'Y' for me."	_____ _____ _____

Types of difficult behaviors by difficult people	Description	What can you do to effectively deal with them?
Showing Off	They usually talk more than they work; they know everything about every subject and are not willing to listen to anything or anybody new.	_____ _____ _____
Goofing Off	Usually do very little and what they do is incorrect; they pretend to be involved, but spend time looking busy more than actually being busy.	_____ _____ _____
Standing By	They do not get involved in anything or any cause, but then complain because something did not go their way.	_____ _____ _____
Complaining	May produce work and be involved, but complains about everything and everybody and seems to exist under a rain cloud; nothing is ever good enough for them.	_____ _____ _____
Dooming and Glooming	The person who is so negative they make death look like a joy ride; they are constantly thinking about the "worst case" scenario and don't mind voicing it.	_____ _____ _____

Standards for Dealing with Difficult People and Managing Conflict

- Check your own behavior before anything else. Don't become the same type of difficult person as the ones with whom you are dealing. Fighting fire with fire will only make the flame hotter. Learn to be the "cool" one.
- Don't take the other person's attitude or words personally. Most of the time, they don't know you or your life.
- *Avoid* physical contact with others at every expense.
- If you must give criticism, do so with a positive tone and attitude.
- Remember that everyone is sensitive about themselves and their situations. Avoid language that will set someone off.
- Do not verbally attack the other person; simply state your case and your ideas.
- Allow the other person to save face. Give the person a way to escape embarrassment. People may forgive you for stepping on their toes, but they will never forgive you for stepping on their feelings.
- If you have a problem with someone or someone's actions, be specific and let them know before it gets out of hand. They can't read your mind.
- If someone shows signs of becoming physically aggressive toward you, get help early, stay calm, talk slowly and calmly to the other person, and, if necessary, walk away to safety.
- Allow the other person to vent fully before you begin any negotiation or resolution.

Figure 13.9 Conflict Management Assessment

Read the following questions carefully and respond according to the key below. Take your time and be honest with yourself.

1 = **Never** typical of the way I address conflict
2 = **Sometimes** typical of the way I address conflict
3 = **Often** typical of the way I address conflict
4 = **Almost always** typical of the way I address conflict

1. When someone verbally attacks me, I can let it go and move on.	1 2 3 4
2. I would rather resolve an issue than have to "be right" about it.	1 2 3 4
3. I try to avoid arguments and verbal confrontations at all costs.	1 2 3 4
4. Once I've had a conflict with someone, I can forget it and get along with that person just fine.	1 2 3 4
5. I look at conflicts in my relationships as positive growth opportunities.	1 2 3 4
6. When I'm in a conflict, I will try many ways to resolve it.	1 2 3 4
7. When I'm in a conflict, I try not to verbally attack or abuse the other person.	1 2 3 4
8. When I'm in a conflict, I try never to blame the other person; rather, I look at every side.	1 2 3 4
9. When I'm in a conflict, I try not to avoid the other person.	1 2 3 4
10. When I'm in a conflict, I try to talk through the issue with the other person.	1 2 3 4
11. When I'm in a conflict, I often feel empathy for the other person.	1 2 3 4
12. When I'm in a conflict, I do not try to manipulate the other person.	1 2 3 4
13. When I'm in a conflict, I try never to withhold my love or affection for that person.	1 2 3 4
14. When I'm in a conflict, I try never to attack the person; I concentrate on their actions.	1 2 3 4
15. When I'm in a conflict, I try to never insult the other person.	1 2 3 4
16. I believe in give and take when trying to resolve a conflict.	1 2 3 4
17. I understand *and use* the concept that kindness can solve more conflicts than cruelty.	1 2 3 4
18. I am able to control my defensive attitude when I'm in a conflict.	1 2 3 4
19. I keep my temper in check and do not yell and scream during conflicts.	1 2 3 4
20. I am able to accept "defeat" at the end of a conflict.	1 2 3 4

Number of 1s _____   Number of 2s _____   Number of 3s _____   Number of 4s _____

If you have more 1s, you do not handle conflict very well and have few tools for conflict management. You have a tendency to anger quickly and lose your temper during the conflict.

If you have more 2s, you have a tendency to want to work through conflict, but you lack the skills to carry this tendency through. You can hold your anger and temper for a while, but eventually, it gets the best of you.

If you have more 3s, you have some helpful skills in handling conflict. You tend to work very hard for a peaceful and mutually beneficial outcome for all parties.

If you have more 4s, you are very adept at handling conflict and do well with mediation, negotiation, and anger management. You are approachable; people turn to you for advice about conflicts and resolutions.

© Robert M. Sherfield, Ph.D.

- Try to create "win-win" situations where everyone can walk away having gained something.
- Determine if the conflict is a "person" conflict or a "situation" conflict.
- Ask the other person or people what he/she needs. Try to understand the situation.
- Realize that *you* may very well be "in the wrong."
- When dealing with conflict and other people, ask yourself, ***"If this were my last action on earth, would I be proud of how I acted?"***

from ORDINARY to Extraordinary

Maureen Riopelle, President and Founder, Mary's Circle of Hope—The Mary Maguire Foundation, Milford, OH

Things could not have been going better! I was a star basketball player recruited by hundreds of colleges, and was a top pick by the University of Iowa. My dream of going to college, becoming an Olympic athlete, and later being a sportscaster was so close I could see it all happening. But, life has a funny way of turning on a dime.

I had suffered knee problems for many years, and most doctors attributed it to "growing pains." I continued to play sports in high school despite the pain. When I got to the University of Iowa, at the urging of my coaches I finally saw a few specialists, but the diagnosis was inconclusive. They knew my knee was in serious disrepair and that I had lost over 35% of the range of motion, they just couldn't figure out why.

After the surgery, my knees actually began to worsen. They feared a massive infection, and after more tests, another surgery was scheduled. It was then determined that the plica in my knees had hardened and formed so much scar tissue it seemed to almost form another "bone" in my leg. I was told that I would probably have to have surgery every two years to repair the damage, and that I only had a 50/50 chance of ever walking again.

In a relatively brief period of time, I went from a college basketball standout and Olympic hopeful to losing my scholarship, dropping out of college, potentially facing the rest of my life on crutches or in a wheelchair. I had five surgeries in seven months, and I spent that summer in a wheelchair and on crutches, but within a year, I was walking on my own again. Within a year and half, I walked my first 5K.

I attribute my recovery to my drive and determination. When necessary, I am the most stubborn person you'll ever meet. When I was told that I would not walk, run, or play basketball again, I took it as a *personal challenge* to prove

> In a brief period of time, I went from a college basketball standout and Olympic hopeful to losing my scholarship, dropping out of college, potentially facing the rest of my life on crutches or in a wheelchair.

everyone wrong—*"I'll show you."* I eventually went back to college and graduated with a 4.0 GPA. After graduation, I began working, and life was moving along. Little did I know that within a few short years, I would again have to call upon that teenager who years earlier had told herself, *"I'll show you."*

One morning I found a lump in my breast and immediately met with my doctor, who scheduled a mammogram. After the test, I was told that everything was fine. But there was a little voice in my head that said, "You need to ask someone else. Get a second opinion." This little voice saved my life. I did, indeed, have breast cancer, and it had even spread to my lymph nodes. My determination and strong will to live and beat the odds became my salvation once again. After surgery and treatment, there are no signs of cancer.

Both of these experiences, while trying and frightening, have led me to my real calling in life—founding *Mary's Circle of Hope—The Mary Maguire Foundation*, a non-profit organization dedicated to the support of women cancer survivors. We help provide financial assistance, health, fitness, and nutritional assistance, empowerment retreats and workshops, and additional services that help a woman go from surviving to thriving. Being able to help others thrive in the face of adversity has become my passion and focus in life. Visit us at www.marymaguirefoundation.org.

EXTRAORDINARY REFLECTION

Ms. Riopelle suffered a major setback with her health, causing her to lose her scholarship and drop out of college for a time. What advice would you give to someone who is facing a major, life-threatening health problem with regard to persistence, internal motivation, positive thinking, and determination?

> "It is said about geese that if one is shot or has to fall out of formation, another goose will follow and stay with him until he is OK or until he is dead. Good team members look after each other this way."
>
> —Robert McNeish

DID YOU Know?

DITH PRAN was born in 1942, in Cambodia. He learned English and French and worked for the U.S. Government as a translator, then on a British film crew, and as a hotel receptionist. In 1975, after meeting a *New York Times* reporter, he taught himself how to take pictures.

After U.S. forces left Cambodia, he stayed behind to cover the fall of Phnom Penh to the communist Khmer Rouge. Having stayed behind, he was forced to stay when foreign reporters were allowed to leave. From this point, Dith witnessed many atrocities and had to hide the fact that he was educated or knew any Americans. He pretended to be a taxicab driver.

Cambodians were forced to work in labor camps and Dith was not exempt. He endured four years of starvation and torture before Vietnam overthrew the Khmer Rouge and he escaped the camp. He coined the term "the killing fields" because of the number of dead bodies he encountered during his escape. He later learned that his three brothers and fifty members of his family were killed during the genocide.

Dith escaped to Thailand in 1979, fearing for his life because of his association with Americans and his knowledge of what had happened. He moved to America in 1980. In 1984, the movie, "*The Killing Fields*," was released detailing the horrors and triumphs of his life. He died of pancreatic cancer in 2008.

BECOMING A GREAT TEAM MEMBER

How Can I Work with Different Types of People?

Teams are created for the purpose of providing a framework in which individuals can work together to be more productive, to make better decisions, and to reach common goals. Usually, team members take ownership of decisions and planning, and they share the workload. Highly effective teams take pride in each other and in their collective team.

Perhaps Maxwell (2002) described a team best: "A team is one voice with many hearts." A team is a small number of people who work together to achieve a common mission, who appreciate and celebrate diverse talents and skills, and who hold each other accountable for the end result. Teams need a clear purpose and carefully delineated goals and objectives in order for all members to get on the same page and to move in the same direction. Teams work best when everyone carries his or her load; there is no place for freeloaders on a good team. Members of strong teams are free to disagree and respectfully express their opinions without fearing repercussions. Leadership of effective teams changes according to the task or goal at hand; sometimes a member leads, and other times, he or she follows. This will be true in your study groups, in class project teams, and in campus organizations in which you are in involved.

Types of Teams

Teams are typically formed to meet a certain goal and to perform a particular purpose. While there are many types of teams, several are fairly typical:

- **Problem-solving teams** are usually assigned the responsibility of improving quality, the work environment, and work processes.
- **Cross-functional teams in many organizations** are typically comprised of members from diverse areas who are charged with the responsibility of developing new ideas, managing complex projects, and spearheading innovation. In college classrooms, students from different majors with different skill sets are often assigned to the same team and must capitalize on the diversity of skills and knowledge.
- **Virtual teams function in ways that are similar** to face-to-face teams except they are physically located apart from each other; they must, therefore, rely on technology to communicate and to share workloads. They might suffer from the lack of social interaction and the absence of body language. In some cases, they must overcome time and space constraints brought about by problems such as working in different time zones.

Effective teams don't just happen; to be effective, team members must be carefully chosen and brought together to accomplish a particular goal or mission. Team members must be carefully prepared if a team is going to function as a well-oiled machine. If you are assigned to a preexisting team (a biology study group already working) and have no choice in the team's make-up, you can still follow the tips and advice in Figure 13.10 **to establish positive relationships and useful teams.**

Figure 13.10 — Best Practices for Forming Effective Teams

1. Determine, understand, and contribute to the mission of the team.
2. Start by making a list of the knowledge and skills the team will need to accomplish the mission.
3. Choose people because of their knowledge, skills, and expertise—not because you like them or they "seem like you." If the team is already established, or if the team is appointed by a professor, work hard to get to know the strengths that other members bring to the table.
4. Provide clear expectations of what is expected as the end result.
5. Make sure that you and other members have a clear, detailed understanding of what is expected of each individual and ensure that the workload is adequately divided and covered. Provide sufficient training, orientation, and social mixing to allow team members to learn about each other and to get comfortable with each other.
6. Provide the team a comfortable, environmentally satisfactory place to work, along with the right technology to accomplish the job.
7. When team members are successful, provide incentives to properly reward them.

To become a good team member, one has to be willing to learn and to grow, to compromise, to lead and to take a back seat. Some best practices for participating as a member of a team can be found in Figure 13.11.

Certainly, you must have a great leader to accomplish major goals, but great leaders cannot lead without great team members. According to Maxwell (2002), "Team players are enlargers, meaning they have the ability to see their teammates in the best light and make those around them better." If you are an enlarger, you believe in your teammates and want the best for them. You delight in seeing them grow. If you are a good, solid team player, others will work better

Figure 13.11 — Best Practices for Participating Team Members

1. When you join a team or are appointed to a team, make up your mind to be a participating member who gives his or her best throughout the project.
2. Be sure you understand the mission, the objectives, and what end result is expected.
3. Be sure you understand exactly what is expected of you personally and exceed those expectations.
4. Be committed to your teammates; try to appreciate each person's skills and knowledge, as well as their differences.
5. Work hard to establish trust among your team members. Two-way trust is essential for teams to function.
6. Try to be open to working with members of the team who are very different from you and who may not work in the same manner as you do.
7. Work in a cooperative manner with other members of the team; be able to compromise when most members agree.
8. Listen carefully to the ideas and opinions of other team members.
9. If you have a disagreement with a team member, talk to that person; don't let bad feelings mushroom because of a simple misunderstanding. Be able to admit your mistakes.
10. Offer your opinions and suggestions in an inoffensive manner; don't be a know-it-all.
11. Be willing to share leadership responsibilities.
12. Practice effective techniques for giving and receiving praise, feedback, and criticism.
13. In the beginning, establish procedures and guidelines for removing a team member who is inhibiting the success of the overall team.
14. If the team members plan a social event, make every effort to participate.

because of you and your contributions to the team. Good team members who are also good followers care about their colleagues, and they have a burning desire to succeed together. A good team member is committed to giving his or her all to making their team succeed.

REFLECTIONS ON INTERPERSONAL COMMUNICATION AND CONFLICT MANAGEMENT

In today's fast-paced, ever-changing, cell phone–addicted, text message–crazy, pay-at-the-pump, "don't have to talk to anyone unless I want to," action-packed world, it is easy to forget that communication is paramount in so many areas of your life. From building healthy and meaningful relationships with your fellow students, to talking to your instructors, to managing conflict, few tools will ever give you the power to effect change more than effective interpersonal communication skills.

By working to improve your interpersonal communication skills, your appreciation of diversity, and your conflict management abilities, you will begin to see how the relationships in your life begin to change and improve. Properly nourished and cultivated relationships will grow from superficial, insignificant encounters to powerful, meaningful bonds where trust, honesty, and maturity are commonplace.

MANAGING CONFLICT IN INTERPERSONAL RELATIONSHIPS

Utilizes Levels 1–6 of the Taxonomy (See Bloom's Taxonomy at the front of this text)

Explanation: Read the following brief case study. After you have familiarized yourself with the situation, work through each level of Bloom's Taxonomy to discuss, analyze, and solve the conflict.

Case: Suzanne is a nice person. Most of the time, she is very affectionate and passionate toward me. She is supportive of my career, and most of the time we get along well. However, it seems that when something goes wrong or she gets angry or stressed, I am the person who receives the brunt of her aggression, regardless of the cause. She can become very verbally abusive sometimes, yelling, screaming,

cursing, and hurling insults. Sometimes, I just get the "silent treatment." On certain occasions, she has used personal and private information that I shared with her to hurt me or insult me. She has never physically abused me, but I sometimes worry that the verbal aggression may turn into physical aggression. I'm not sure what to do or what to make of this situation.

Procedure: Answer the following questions related to the case from each level of Bloom's Taxonomy. Be specific and use the information from this chapter, your own experiences, and outside research to aid in your responses.

Bloom Level	Question	Response
Level 1 Remembering	In your own words, define the conflict(s) and the cause(s).	
Level 2 Understanding	Identify at least three major problems with this interpersonal relationship.	
Level 3 Applying	What solutions would you offer to both parties?	
Level 4 Analyzing	Compare and contrast this interpersonal relationship with a "healthier," more mature, productive relationship.	
Level 5 Evaluating	Develop a brief argument as to why you think this relationship is more the norm than the unusual.	
Level 6 Creating	Develop/design a plan you would use to make this situation better. List at least five positive steps to bring about change.	

SQ3R MASTERY STUDY SHEET

EXAMPLE QUESTION (FROM PAGE 300) What are the six elements of the communication process?	ANSWER:
EXAMPLE QUESTION (FROM PAGE 306) What is self-disclosure and why is it important for healthy relationships?	ANSWER:
AUTHOR QUESTION (FROM PAGE 300) What are barriers to communication?	ANSWER:
AUTHOR QUESTION (FROM PAGE 304) What is computer-mediated communication (CMC)?	ANSWER:
AUTHOR QUESTION (FROM PAGE 306) In your own words, define "technological recluse."	ANSWER:
AUTHOR QUESTION (FROM PAGE 308) Compare and contrast ethnocentrism with xenocentrism.	ANSWER:
AUTHOR QUESTION (FROM PAGE 313) Discuss at least two strategies for managing conflict.	ANSWER:
YOUR QUESTION (FROM PAGE _____)	ANSWER:
YOUR QUESTION (FROM PAGE _____)	ANSWER:
YOUR QUESTION (FROM PAGE _____)	ANSWER:
YOUR QUESTION (FROM PAGE _____)	ANSWER:
YOUR QUESTION (FROM PAGE _____)	ANSWER:

Finally, after answering these questions, recite this chapter's major points in your mind. Consider the following general questions to help you master this material.

- What is it about?
- What does it mean?
- What is the most important thing you learned? Why?
- What are the key points to remember?

LIVE

DEVELOPING YOUR PLAN FOR WELLNESS AND PERSONAL RESPONSIBILITY

"The concept of total wellness recognizes that our every thought, word, and behavior affects our greater health and well-being." —Greg Anderson

LIVE

Why read this chapter?

Because you'll learn how to...

- Understand holistic wellness and how to care for your body, mind, and soul
- Identify and understand the signs of depression and anxiety
- Understand the responsibility of eating well and tracking your food intake

Because you'll be able to...

- Make intelligent decisions regarding alcohol and drugs (legal, illegal, and prescription)
- Identify the risks associated with smoking and the steps to quit
- Describe the dangers of sexually transmitted diseases and protect yourself

Scan and QUESTION

Take a few moments, **scan this chapter** and on page 339, write **five of your own questions** that you think will be important to your mastery of this material. You will also find five questions listed from your authors.

Example:

☑ **What does it mean to have a holistic approach to health?** (from page 324)

☑ **Why is it important to know about depression and anxiety?** (from page 325)

MyStudentSuccessLab

MyStudentSuccessLab is an online solution designed to help you acquire and develop (or hone) the skills you need to succeed. You will have access to peer-led video presentations and develop core skills through interactive exercises and projects.

How
COLLEGE CHANGED MY LIFE

Name: Kerie Francis Grace

Institution: Graduate! The University of Nevada–Las Vegas, Las Vegas, NV

Major: Sociology

Pregnant at the age of 17, Kerie Francis Grace decided to drop out of high school. She "didn't have any work skills and couldn't write." According to Kerie, she knew that a service job would probably be her "only option." Not wanting to go back to high school, which had bored her anyway, she got her GED after having her son and taking a prep class at a community college in Arizona.

She stayed at home with her son until he was about four years old. While she wanted to stay home with him, they "didn't have the money to do that" and she wanted to go to school so that she could contribute to the household finances. She understood that, without an education, the only job that would probably be available to her would be as a store clerk. When the family moved to Las Vegas, the College of Southern Nevada (CSN) had "space for me," Kerie related, offering evening and once a week classes that fit in with her growing family, which now included her daughter. She attended CSN as a part-time student when her children were young, but moved on to full-time status at UNLV once they got a little older.

Her first major was nursing, and Kerie planned to become a midwife, something very near and dear to her

An interview conducted and written by Deanna Beachley, Adjunct Instructor, The University of Nevada–Las Vegas, and Professor of History and Woman's Studies, The College of Southern Nevada

(both of her children were delivered by midwives). She changed her major when she discovered that she had an affinity for the social sciences, much more than the physical sciences. She ended up with a major in sociology. "I found my home in the social sciences," Kerie stated. Sociology and learning how our society works became a great "outlet for expression" for Kerie. She completed her AA degree in sociology at CSN, and then completed her Bachelor's degree in sociology at UNLV. She found that in sociology she could study medical practices in this country, which would enable her to investigate midwifery, which is what she focused on in her master's thesis. She is now completing her last comprehensive exam to be an A.B.D. student, which means that all she will have left to complete her Ph.D. is writing her dissertation. Many of her friends from the early days do not understand why she went to school, or why she has stayed in school and received all of these degrees.

One thing that enabled Kerie to remain focused on her studies were odd jobs, including doing some research for a professor and being a personal shopper. As a graduate student, Kerie received a research assistantship and a teaching assistantship, which enabled her to contribute to the family income without sacrificing her education.

Reflecting on her educational journey, Kerie recognizes that "I came into school with nothing," but "I have skills now that no one can take away from me." She has developed and constantly uses critical thinking skills. She has also developed good writing skills, as well

323

as time management skills. She never missed a class because she was afraid of missing something.

Kerie gives a great deal of credit to her success in school to her family. Their support was critical for her staying in school. They are proud of her. As a non-traditional student, it was sometimes awkward and difficult to be one of the older students in class, but she is much more comfortable with that now than she was when she started school in 1996. Kerie also credits good teachers with helping her achieve her goals. Finding a good role model was significant to her. She found one of her female community college professors who modeled "who I wanted to be when I grow up," as she put it. She now teaches several classes a semester at CSN and UNLV, including an upper division medical sociology class that

many pre-med students take. She is getting better and better in the classroom. She has sharpened her skills as a teacher. "I want to be there, even if I'm sick; I don't want students to miss out. So, I go to class to share things with students, about race, class, gender, and political economy, things that help open their eyes and cause them to rethink things." A few days after completing this interview, Kerie let me know that she received the UNLV Sociology Department's Outstanding Teaching Award, which is a testament to her abilities in the classroom and the skills that she was able to attain in the course of her educational path. As a capable woman, she is now independent in a way that she never would have been able to be without that education, and "no one else can take it away."

THINK about *it*

1. Kerie states that she "found a home" in the social sciences. Have you found your academic home? If so, where is it? Why?

2. Kerie is interested in midwifery because of her personal experiences. What personal experiences have shaped your career plans? How?

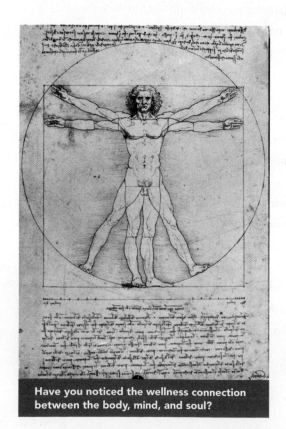

Have you noticed the wellness connection between the body, mind, and soul?

A HOLISTIC APPROACH TO WELLNESS

Why Care for Your Mind, Soul, and Body?

As a college student, you are changing and growing in many ways, including intellectually, emotionally, and physically. Now, we will ask you to continue your pattern of change and growth to include practices that will make you healthy in all aspects of your life. In this chapter, you will find an overriding theme—you have to take care of yourself and you have the power to do so! This can mean everything from eating properly and getting enough exercise, to avoiding binge drinking and prescription drugs, to protecting yourself sexually. You will encounter situations where you have to make decisions on a daily basis. It is imperative to your health and academic success that you choose wisely!

"In many ancient systems of medicine (such as in China) treatment has been made with the view that mind, body, and soul are linked together as a whole and should not be seen as isolated from each other. Mind, body, and soul healing focuses on the interactions between the brain, mind, body and the ways in which emotional, mental, social, spiritual, and behavioral factors affect us as a whole" (Tarkovsky, 2006). As far back as 400 BC, Hippocrates recognized the spiritual impact on healing, so this idea that wellness is holistic is nothing new. But it does have some new spins to it.

What is meant by "the mind?" If your mind is in balance with your body and soul, you should be using your mind's power to your best advantage, thinking clearly and making good decisions. If your body is exhausted and your soul is depressed, your mind will not function well.

What is meant by "the soul?" In the context of wellness, the soul and spirituality are important in the ability to develop healthy relationships, to communicate well with diverse others, and to express yourself using creativity.

What is meant by "the body?" For your body to be in balance with your mind and soul, you must exercise properly, get sufficient rest, engage in sports and physical activity, and have good eating habits and nutrition that fuel your body. If your body is functioning poorly, your mind and soul will, too.

Maintaining a healthy body, mind, and soul can be one of the most exciting and challenging aspects of your college career, as well as the rest of your life. If you achieve balance among all three of these important categories, you should feel optimistic, confident, and anticipative about what lies ahead for your future.

THE MIND'S EFFECT ON WELLNESS

How Strong Are the Hidden Powers of the Mind?

The mind is an incredibly complex organ. The health industry has not even begun to tap the awesome power the mind has over a person's physical health. Very basic studies have shown that the mind is a vital link to physical health. Your emotions and mental thoughts play a tremendous role in how you approach your overall wellness program. Your emotional well being impacts all aspects of your general wellness and therefore is the platform for all health. People who are mentally healthy possess these qualities. They:

- Have a positive sense of self-worth
- Are determined to make an effort to be healthy
- Can love and have meaningful relationships
- Understand reality and the limitations placed on them
- Have compassion for others
- Understand that the world does not revolve around them

How can having a positive attitude help you feel better and perform at your best?

SILENT PROBLEMS OF THE MIND

Can Depression and Anxiety Disorders Be Controlled?

Depression is a term used to describe feelings ranging from feeling blue to utter hopelessness. The use of "I'm depressed" to mean "I'm sad" or "I'm down" is a far cry from the illness of clinical depression. Depression is a sickness that can creep up on an individual and render that person helpless if it is not detected and properly treated.

There are several major types of depressions. They include

Situational Depression	**Situational depression** involves feelings of sadness due to disappointments, bad news, daily frustrations, or "people problems."
Clinical Depression	**Clinical depression** is major depression and is characterized by the inability to enjoy life, loss of interest in things you once loved doing, self-hatred, feelings of utter worthlessness, and suicidal thoughts. Clinical depression is diagnosed when these feelings last at least two weeks. (See Figure 14.1.)
Bipolar/Manic Depression	**Bipolar (or manic) depression** entails people who suffer excessive mood swings from extreme sadness to intense mania (elation). The mood swings can happen slowly or suddenly. This type of depression is extremely complex and a difficult disorder to treat. It can be treated, however.
Dysthymia	**Dysthymia** is classified as mild to moderate depression and can last a long time—two years or more. There are times that you can't remember not being depressed and it is hard to enjoy life, family, or friends.
Seasonal Depression	**Seasonal depression** is caused by the weather or by the changing seasons of the year. Some people are depressed by rain, and others are depressed by a lack of sunshine.
Psychotic Depression	**Psychotic depression** occurs when a severe depressive illness has a co-existing form of psychosis. The psychosis could be hallucinations, delusions, or some other break with reality" (WebMD, 2012).
Postpartum Depression	**Postpartum depression,** sometimes called "the baby blues," occurs after the birth of a child. It can be a very serious condition where the mother avoids the child or even wants to cause harm to the child. It can occur up to a year or more after birth.

Some common signs of situational or mild depression include the following (WebMD, 2012):

- Persistent sadness and unexplainable, lingering fatigue
- Inability to find joy in daily activities that once brought you joy
- No interest in work, school, activities, and sex
- Sleep disorders, such as insomnia and awakening early in the morning
- Withdrawal from friends and family
- Feelings of hopelessness and worthlessness, and a desire to die

Anxiety

According to the Anxiety Disorders Associations of America (2012), anxiety disorders are the most common mental illness in America—with more than 13 percent of American adults suffering from some form of anxiety disorder. Learning to cope with anxiety allows you to focus and maintain balance in your health and academic welfare. There are several ways to proactively approach dealing with anxiety: relaxation techniques, such as yoga, music or dance therapy, and meditation, cognitive behavior therapy, other forms of therapy, and medication.

Figure 14.1 **Are You Clinically Depressed?**

Changes in Eating Habits	You experience an increase or decrease in appetite; you have a weight gain or loss of more than 5% in a month; you find yourself binging on unhealthy foods; you begin to abuse drugs and/or alcohol.
Changes in Attitude	You experience negative feelings about the future; you see no hope; there seems to be a dark cloud over everything; you find yourself feeling pessimistic more than optimistic; you have thoughts of suicide or death.
Change in Activity / Energy Levels	You experience a loss of energy; your normal activities are harder to accomplish; you are constantly tired throughout the day; you see no value in setting and working toward goals; you lose interest in sex.
Changes in Temperament	You experience extreme highs and extreme lows; you do not feel like your "normal" self; you find yourself constantly agitated; you are more short-tempered and agitated than usual; your tolerance level is very low.
Changes in Self-Esteem	You experience feelings of worthlessness; you negatively judge yourself and your abilities; you easily find fault with others; you feel "empty."
Changes in Concentration and Memory	You experience loss of memory; you find it hard to concentrate; you find it difficult to remember small details and tasks; you are more indecisive than usual.
Changes in Sleep Patterns	You experience difficulty sleeping or you find that you cannot sleep enough.
Changes in Physical Conditions	You experience constant aches and pains; you have headaches more often than usual; you have digestive problems; you cry for no reason.
Changes in Relationships	You experience negative changes in personal and work relationships; you begin to cut off people who once mattered to you; you prefer to be alone.

If you are feeling depressed or your anxiety has reached a level where you cannot control it, but your depression seems minor or situational, try some of these helpful hints for picking yourself up out of the blues:

- Get physical exercise because it causes the release of endorphins, which help to stimulate you and give you a personal high.
- Spend time talking with a good friend; share your thoughts and feelings.
- Control your self-talk. If you're feeding yourself negative words, change to positive thoughts.
- Do something special for yourself: take a long walk in the park, watch a favorite movie, listen to music, or visit a friend.
- Nurture yourself by doing things you love and enjoy and that bring you peace.
- *Never* be afraid or ashamed to seek professional assistance.

THE SOUL'S EFFECT ON WELLNESS

Is Your Well Running Dry?

The world is a tough place to be at times. You read the newspapers and see all the bad things that are happening around us. You listen to the evening news and hear about murder, war, gas prices, negative politics, and so on. You feel the pressures of trying to work, struggling to pay bills, finding time to exercise and eat right, studying for difficult tests, writing papers, keeping relationships going, communicating with others—the list of stressors goes on and on. According to Housden (2007),

> "The poorest man would not part with health for money, but the richest would gladly part with all their money for health."
>
> —Charles Caleb Colton

"We are usually preoccupied with being useful—doing something with an outcome in mind, rather than being open to where we are at this moment."

But in the midst of all these worldly concerns, you need to take time to find peace and joy. For at least a few minutes every day, you need to turn loose all these pressures that weigh you down and cause you to feel defeated and overwhelmed. You need to nurture and feed your soul. The soul can be nurtured in many ways—having solid, meaningful relationships; participating in something, such as a play, that gives you a creative outlet; talking to someone who makes you laugh and forget your problems at least temporarily; watching an uplifting movie; or communicating with new and diverse types of people. Just as your body needs to be fed a healthy diet of good, nutritious food, your soul needs to be nourished with activities and thoughts that bring you joy, comfort, and peace. See Figure 14.2 for more ways to nurture your soul.

Figure 14.2 Ways to Nourish Your Soul

- Commune with nature by taking a hike or just sitting in the park.
- Volunteer doing something you love.
- Ride a bike on a beautiful fall day.
- Go for a drive in the country.
- Stop everything and laugh with a friend.
- Walk on the beach.
- Row in a river or lake.
- Have friends over who lift you up and make you feel good about yourself.
- Experiment with your creative side—write a poem, act in a play, learn to play an instrument.
- Roll on the grass with a little child and giggle like she does.
- Look around you and count your blessings.

THE BODY'S EFFECT ON WELLNESS

Can You Believe You Ate the Whole Thing?

Eating has become Americans' favorite hobby. Rather than eating to live, many of us live to eat. We socialize around food—dinner and a movie, pizza and a beer with friends, and so on. Research has shown that most people have no idea as to how much they have eaten, what it contained, how it was grown, or what effect the food had on their health. Dr. Phil McGraw (2007), well-known talk show host, states, "Food is the most powerfully addictive substance in the world because you can't abstain from it." He goes on to say, "It's not chocolates or potato chips that sabotage diets (try fear, old attitudes, tempting environments)." What we eat and why we eat it is more complicated than it appears at first glance. For many first-year students, however, weight gain happens simply because they don't pay enough attention to what they are eating, they do not exercise, or they change their nutrition habits when they arrive on campus.

Some points that might be helpful as you work on changing your diet to maximize your overall health:

- Choose lean cuts of meat or baked or broiled poultry or fish
- Eat a variety of foods, making sure you are getting the right variety and amount of nutrients

How many times per week do you binge on junk food?

- Choose whole-grain breads and cereals
- Drink non- or low-fat milk and eat low-fat cheese
- Drink at least six glasses of water a day
- Severely limit unhealthy foods, fast-food restaurants, and eating binges
- Snack on fruits instead of potato chips. Apples, for example, have no fat.
- Stay away from super-size meals unless you want a super-size body!

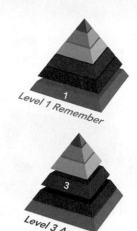

To help you develop healthier eating habits, consider this activity. For three days write down everything you eat or drink—snacks, wine, meals—every bite and sip. Complete the **Three-Day Food Tracking Sheet** located at the end of this chapter. This exercise will assist you in keeping track of your food intake.

WHAT YOU DO TODAY MAY IMPACT YOU FOR YEARS TO COME

What Is Your Responsibility to Ensure Wellness?

The following section will simply provide you with information that you can study and use to make intelligent decisions about drinking, drug usage, smoking, and sexual behavior. The only thing we ask is that you consider carefully this fact: Everything you put into your body and do with and to your body has a direct effect, either positively or negatively, on your overall wellness. As with many things, the choice is yours.

Drugs and Alcohol

First, you need to know that alcohol *is* a drug—it is addictive, and many people of all ages get hooked. According to Learn About Alcohol (2012), Americans spend over 197 million dollars per DAY on alcohol and there are over 12 million alcoholics currently struggling with the disease. Although it is legal for people over 21, it is a drug, just as cocaine and ecstasy are drugs. Drugs can basically be divided into two categories—legal and illegal. It may sound strange, but drugs run the gamut from caffeine to crystal methamphetamine. The decision to use a drug, legal or illegal, is yours and it is personal. However, every drug—from tobacco to roofies—has ramifications and health consequences. If you choose to use certain drugs, you are literally gambling with your life. Figure 14.3 provides a better understanding of many legal and prescription drugs.

How Can Prescription Drugs Negatively Impact Your Health?

More Americans today are addicted to prescription drugs than to illegal drugs, and college campuses are only a microcosm of the country. Nonmedical use of prescription drugs for either recreational purposes or for purposes other than their prescribed intent has reached epidemic proportions. The three classes of prescription drugs most commonly abused are pain medications, anti-anxiety and sleep medications, and stimulants. All of these medications have had a history of being overprescribed, and if students don't come to campus with pills or prescriptions from their homes, many acquire them through the Internet or other means. These drugs, because of their familiarity to the user, can

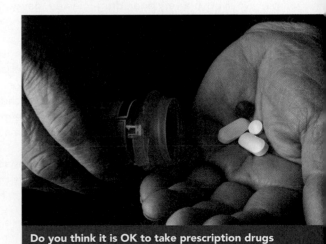

Do you think it is OK to take prescription drugs for recreational use because a doctor prescribed them?

from ORDINARY to Extraordinary

Catherine Schleigh, Customer Service Coordinator, Kinkos–FedEx, Inc., Philadelphia, PA

I don't like to speculate, but I would say that few college students in America had to take a bus two and a half hours each way to attend classes five days a week. I did. I would also speculate that few college students became the primary care giver for his or her mother at the age of seven. I did. I might also speculate that few people feel as lucky, proud, and honored to simply hold his or her head high and say, "I made it." I am. My name is Catherine Schleigh, and despite my past family history and personal struggles, I am a first-generation college graduate and hold a professional position with a major corporation in one of the most wonderful cities in America.

Growing up, I had no real family to speak of. My dad left my mom and me when I was young, and from the age of seven, I was left to care for my mother, who is a diagnosed paranoid schizophrenic. Growing up, I received no help, no support, and no encouragement from her or any member of my family. Often, she would not take her medications (or the medications had been improperly prescribed) and she would be physically, emotionally, and verbally abusive to me. It was hard to watch her talk to herself or invisible people. We lived in a very poor, drug-infested, gang-populated area of Philly, and many times, I could not see how I would ever survive.

I managed to complete high school, and I began attending Job Corp, studying business. From there, I began my college studies, majoring in business administration. I had to work very hard, and the adjustment from high school to college was massive. I had to learn how to motivate myself, but the most important thing I learned was that there are people in this world who will help you if you let them.

Some of my instructors did not understand my situation at first. I cried a lot in class, did not have my projects completed from time-to-time, and basically lived the life of an introvert. Once everyone learned that I was caring for my mother, traveling five hours a day to class, and struggling just to eat, they became my family. They taught me that I had to put my education first. They taught me that, without an education, I would most likely have to work in dead-end jobs for the rest of my life. I began to really look at all of the people in my neighborhood and I made a committed decision that I was not going to fall prey to the temptations of alcohol, sex, unemployment, and drugs.

As I began to succeed in classes, my self-esteem became healthier. I began to understand how to support myself, take pride in my successes, and help others in any way possible. I still struggle with my mother as she seeks therapy and better medical care, but I also know that I must take care of my own life and keep working toward my own goals. My life is my first priority.

Today, I am an honors graduate. I completed my Bachelor of Arts degree in business administration with a GPA of 3.50. At the graduation ceremony, I was presented an award by the faculty and staff for my dedication and hard work, and for overcoming all odds to obtain my degree. I hope in some small way that my story can help you "hold on" and reach your dreams. Happiness and success are possible for you.

> *I was left to care for my mother, who is a diagnosed paranoid schizophrenic.*

EXTRAORDINARY REFLECTION

Ms. Schleigh had no family support. As a matter of fact, her father was gone and she was the primary caregiver for her mother. How has your family support (or lack of support) affected your studies? Do you think it is important to have your family's support to succeed?

Figure 14.3 Commonly Used and Abused Legal Drugs and Dangerous Prescription Drugs

Name	Use	Sources	Negative Effects
OxyContin (Roxicodone)	A synthetic opioid used to combat post-operative and chronic pain	Prescribed by physician	Feeling of being detached; *highly* addictive; can be deadly if overused or crushed to inhale; can be fatal if mixed with alcohol
Lortab (Hydrocodone)	Narcotic pain reliever used to combat chronic pain	Prescribed by physician	Excessive amount can damage liver or cause death; highly addictive
Vicodin	Narcotic pain reliever	Prescribed by physician	Can suppress breathing; may be habit forming; dangerous if taken with alcohol
Over-the-Counter Drugs	Weight loss, alertness, sleep aids, body building, depression, pain relief, laxatives, diet medications, sleep enhancers, stimulants, herbal medications, nasal sprays, cough medications, pain relievers	Can be purchased without a prescription at any store that sells over-the-counter medications	Addiction, organ damage, nausea, vomiting, reduced absorption of vitamins and minerals, liver damage
Tobacco/Nicotine	Stimulant, relaxation, social acceptance, curb appetite, increase alertness	Cigarettes, cigars, pipes, snuff, chewing tobacco, nicotine gum	Highly addictive, increased heart and respiratory rate, increased blood pressure, increased risk of cancer, strokes, lung disease, gum disease, birth defects, and cardiovascular disease
Alcohol	Relaxation, mood enhancer, overcome depression, overcome shyness, social acceptance, relieve tension, celebrate, bonding	Found in beer, wine, liquor, medications, and some foods	Liver disease, memory loss, blackouts, false euphoria, depression, hangovers, birth defects, loss of balance, mental impairment, increased suicide rate, death
Caffeine	Alertness, pleasure, energy, reduce fatigue	Coffee, tea, chocolate, some soft drinks, medications, energy drinks and pills	A stimulant, increased anxiety, highly addictive, increased urination, irregular heartbeat, indigestion

be more dangerous, and therefore more addictive. Casual use may unwittingly escalate into a full-blown, difficult-to-shake addiction.

Several drugs need to be discussed separately. These drugs are more commonly called "cocktail drugs" or "club drugs," because they are most commonly found in dance clubs, raves, and other places where people are interacting and inhibitions are low. Club drugs include ecstasy, sextasy, roofies, and crystal meth.

Sextasy is a mixture of ecstasy and Viagra. *Ecstasy* alters one's senses, but can hinder sexual functioning. To increase sexual functioning, many people have begun also taking Viagra, whose real purpose is to treat impotence and assist prostate cancer patients. The mixture can cause serious problems! "Doctors warn that combining the two drugs can cause heart problems or erections that don't subside for more than four hours, possibly leading to anatomical damage" (Leinwood, 2002).

Roofies and GHB are very common in the club scene and can be slipped into a drink (alcoholic or not) with little trouble. Because they are usually odorless and colorless and have a very quick effect on the body, they rapidly alter your alertness and ability to function. We encourage you to guard your drink carefully if you are at a party or club. Letting your guard down may be a serious mistake!

How much care do you actually take to protect yourself when you are out with friends?

Crystal meth is one of the fastest growing drugs in this country—and one of *the* most addictive and dangerous. It is used as a stimulant, and can be smoked, sniffed, or injected. Some of the *many* negative side effects include seizures, hallucinations, high blood pressure, depression, anxiety, heart attacks, rotting teeth, and malnutrition.

BINGE DRINKING

Is It Really That Bad to Drink a Lot Only Once a Week?

It's common knowledge that many college students drink way too much. Although some control their drinking and use good judgment, many totally lose control. Some say to themselves, *"Hey, I only drink once a week, and after a week of studying, writing papers, and taking texts, I deserve one night off."* When you drink many drinks in one evening, this is called binge drinking and it can be exceedingly dangerous to you and others. *Binge drinking* is classified as having three to five drinks within a three- to four-hour period. This type of drinking can be extremely detrimental to your liver, your memory, your digestive system, and your health in general, not to mention your grades and academic career. It can also be dangerous to your overall well-being. One young woman commented after a night of binge drinking, "I got totally wasted and couldn't remember getting home. The taxi could have taken me anywhere" (Steinke, 2007).

"One of five women between the ages of 18 and 44 is said to be a binger, which is particularly disturbing because health experts are finding that alcohol takes a harsher toll on women than men; even relatively small amounts can cause damage. Women cannot drink as much as

Successful Decisions

AN ACTIVITY FOR CRITICAL REFLECTION

One of your new friends, Miriam Forsythe, has been going to a club in a popular area of town. College students hang out there after games, concerts, and campus events. "Party night," as it is known on campus, is Thursday, and you and Miriam plan to attend. Miriam had many dating restrictions when she was growing up, and is very inexperienced in taking care of herself, but she is enjoying her new-found freedom. In fact, you are somewhat worried about Miriam because she seems to be ignoring her classes and focusing only on having fun. She slept in this Thursday morning and cut classes so that she would be rested for "party night."

Miriam has "flipped out" over Max, a senior who spent time with her at the club last Thursday night, and she is hoping that she will see him there tonight. You have heard that Max has quite a reputation as a "ladies man," and you aren't sure that Miriam can take care of herself. When you try to talk to her about

it, she brushes you off, and in so many words, tells you to mind your own business. When the two of you arrive at the club, she immediately hooks up with Max and ignores you for the rest of the evening. You look for her but are never able to locate her. Around midnight you decide to go home with a group of friends. You look around for Miriam, but she is nowhere to be found. At 3:30 am, Miriam staggers into your room, disheveled, drunk, and crying. She tells you that Max raped her in his apartment.

Describe the steps that you would take to help your friend.

1. _____

2. _____

3. _____

men because their bodies are smaller and their bodies have more fat and less water content. Water dilutes alcohol, and fat retains it so a martini stays in a woman's body far longer than in a man's" (Steinke, 2007). This fact, of course, doesn't mean that men can be careless about how much alcohol they consume.

In their breakthrough work, *Dying to Drink,* Harvard researcher Henry Wechsler and science writer Bernice Wuethrich explore the problem of binge drinking. They suggest, "Two out of every five college students regularly binge drink resulting in approximately 1,400 student deaths, a distressing number of assaults and rapes, a shameful amount of vandalism, and countless cases of academic suicide" (Wechsler & Wuethrich, 2002). Many college students say they drink because it makes them relax, become better conversationalists, or act funnier than they typically are. Excessive drinking and all its the ramifications and consequences is a heavy price to pay to be funnier. If you are participating in binge drinking, this is one activity you need to change before it brings serious consequences.

SMOKING CESSATION AND HOW TO DO IT

Is It Really Good to Be a Quitter?

Cigarrette smoking is one of the most prevelant health problems in the world today. Nicotine is one of *the* most addictive substances known to man, and according to the American Heart Association, it has historically been one of the hardest addictions to break. Smoking affects your brain, and the more you smoke, the more you need to smoke. Many who have tried to quit state that stopping smoking is the single hardest thing they have ever tried to do, *but,* it can be done. It will take much effort and perhaps longer than you hoped, but it is possible. Consider the benefits of stopping smoking on one's health, as outlined in Figure 14.4.

How Addicted Are You?

Consider the following questions (adapted from HealthCoach4Me, 2012). Answer them carefully and honestly to determine the level of your addiction.

Check the statements that apply to you:

_____ Do you tend to smoke within a half hour after you wake up?

_____ Do you find it hard not to smoke where smoking is not allowed?

_____ Do you smoke 10 or more cigarettes a day?

_____ Do you smoke 25 or more cigarettes a day?

_____ Do you smoke more during the morning than during the rest of the day?

_____ Do you smoke when you're sick?

_____ Do you smoke when engaged in social activities, such as at parties, at dinners, and when drinking?

_____ Do you associate smoking with certain places and activities?

_____ Do you want to smoke when you see others smoking?

_____ Does your mood change when you smoke or are not allowed to smoke?

_____ Have you tried to stop smoking in the past but failed?

The more checkmarks you have, the more you rely on nicotine. Even if you did not check any statements, it will still take hard work to quit smoking.

Have you or someone you know tried to stop smoking? Was it easy or difficult? Did they need medical help to stop?

Figure 14.4 The Effect of Stopping Smoking on the Body

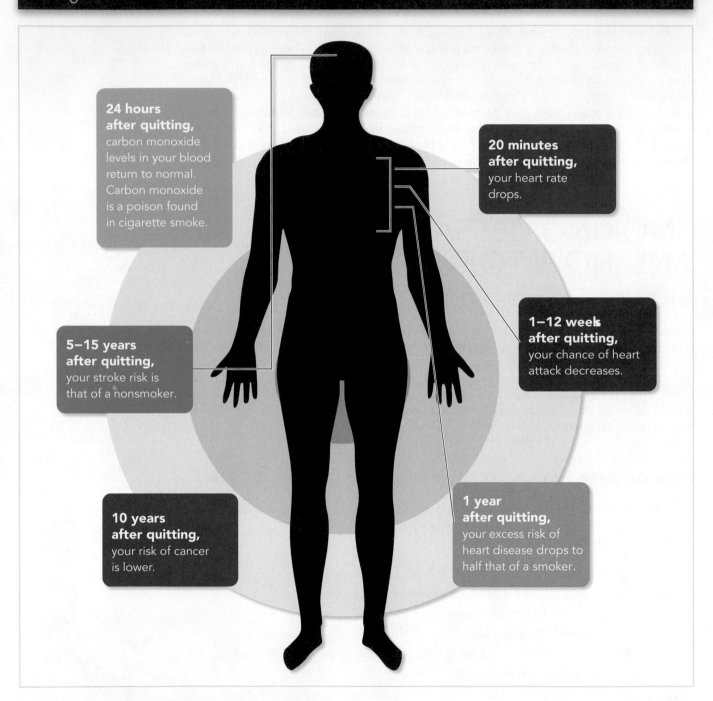

24 hours after quitting, carbon monoxide levels in your blood return to normal. Carbon monoxide is a poison found in cigarette smoke.

20 minutes after quitting, your heart rate drops.

5–15 years after quitting, your stroke risk is that of a nonsmoker.

1–12 weeks after quitting, your chance of heart attack decreases.

10 years after quitting, your risk of cancer is lower.

1 year after quitting, your excess risk of heart disease drops to half that of a smoker.

Source: HealthCoach4Me (2012).

You Can Stop!

As you begin to prepare to stop smoking, you may need a plan. Some people can do it "cold turkey," but others need to develop a step-by-step plan to guide them along. Consider these tips from the U.S. Surgeon General's Office (2012):

- Pay attention to *why* you smoke and think about your reasons for quitting.
- Tell your friends and family you're planning to quit; ask for their help and support.
- Stop buying cigarettes.

- Think about what you'll do with the extra money when you stop buying cigarettes.
- Make a list of people to reach out to when you need help.
- Buy a stop-smoking aid; some people need them.

SEXUALLY TRANSMITTED DISEASES

Can It Happen to You?

Sexually transmitted diseases (STDs) are diseases that are generally transmitted through vaginal, anal, or oral intercourse. Although they are most commonly spread through sexual contact, some can be transmitted through related nonsexual activities (for example, human immunodeficiency virus (HIV) can be contracted by using contaminated needles, and crabs can be contracted through contact with contaminated bed linens or towels). Study Figure 14.5 for a more complete look at sexually transmitted diseases.

STDs AND BIRTH CONTROL

Do You Know What You Need to Know?

Figure 14.6 is provided to give you information about the most common birth control methods and their effectiveness in preventing STDs.

DID YOU Know?

GREG LOUGANIS was born in 1960, adopted by his Greek American parents, and was raised in California. In 1976, at the age of 16, he placed second in the Summer Olympics in Montreal, Canada. In 1982, he won two world diving titles, and in 1984, he won two gold medals at the Los Angeles Olympic Games. In 1988, he won two more gold medals at the Seoul, Korea, Olympic Games, even though he suffered a concussion after hitting his head on the springboard. This feat earned him the ABC's *Wide World of Sports* "Athlete of the Year" honor for 1988.

In 1994, Louganis announced that he was gay, and in 1995, he published an autobiography revealing that his partner had abused and raped him for years, and that he was HIV positive. He received much criticism for not revealing his HIV status after his diving accident in 1988. He was advised by an HIV expert that his minor bleeding posed no danger to other athletes. Regardless, after his disclosure, he lost every major company endorsement except Speedo.

Today, Greg Louganis is a gay rights activist, TV commentator, and actor. In 1997, Mario Lopez portrayed him in the movie, *Breaking the Surface: The Greg Louganis Story.*

Figure 14.5 **Sexually Transmitted Diseases**

STD	Transmission	Symptoms	Diagnosis	Consequences
AIDS/HIV	Sexual contact (vaginal, oral, and anal) Infusion with contaminated blood (sharing needles, etc.) From mother to fetus Breast feeding	People may go years without symptoms. When symptoms appear, they may include flu-like symptoms, fever, weight loss, fatigue, diarrhea, and cancer.	Bodily fluids, such as blood, urine, or saliva reveal HIV antibodies; two tests include the Western Blot and the ELISA; a new "20-minute test" is now available at many doctors' offices	Transmission to sexual partners; many health-related issues, such as heart problems, gastroenterological issues, and death
Chlamydia	Sexual contact (vaginal, oral, and anal) By touching one's eye after touching infected genitals From mother to child	Women: sometimes no symptoms; painful urination, occasional vaginal discharge, bleeding between periods Men: discharge from penis, painful urination	A cervical smear for women; extract of fluid from the penis for men	Rapid progression if undiagnosed or untreated; cancer; pneumonia; death

(continued)

Figure 14.5 Sexually Transmitted Diseases (*continued*)

STD	Transmission	Symptoms	Diagnosis	Consequences
Gonorrhea	Sexual contact (vaginal, oral, and anal) From mother to child	Women: vaginal discharge, painful urination, bleeding between periods Men: discharge from penis, painful urination	Medical examination from discharge or culture	Transmission to sexual partners; various inflammations; possible sterility in men and women
Genital Warts	Sexual contact (vaginal, oral, and anal) Other types of contact, such as infected towels or clothing	Women: single or multiple soft, fleshy growths around anus, vulva, vagina, or urethra; itching or burning sensation around sexual organs Men: burning around sexual organs; single or multiple soft, fleshy growths around anus or penis	Medical examination	Transmission to sexual and nonsexual partners; precancerous conditions; cannot be cured
Herpes (Simplex Virus Types I and II)	Sexual contact (vaginal, oral, and anal) Touching Kissing Sharing towels, toilet seats	Single or multiple blisters or sores on genitals, generally painful, but disappear without scarring, reappear	Medical examination; culture and fluid inspections	Transmission to sexual and nonsexual partners; cannot be cured
Hepatitis (Viral A, B, C, and D Types)	Sexual contact, especially involving the anus Contact with infected fecal matter Transfusion of contaminated blood Severe alcoholism Exposure to toxic materials	Can be asymptomatic; mild flu-like symptoms, fever, abdominal pain, vomiting, and yellowish skin or eyes; loss of appetite; whitish bowel movements; brown urine	Medical examination of blood for hepatitis antibody; liver biopsy	Transmission to sexual and nonsexual partners; severe liver problems or failure; cancer of the liver; death
Syphilis	Sexual contact (vaginal, oral, and anal) Touching an infected chancre	Four stages: (1) painless red spots later forming a sore; (2) skin rash or mucous patches; (3) latent stage, no symptoms; (4) complications leading to possible death	Primary stages by medical examination of fluid from a chancre; secondary stage by blood test, VDRL	Transmission to sexual and nonsexual partners; death (although seldom advances this far today)

Adapted from Powell (1996), Donatelle & Davis (2002).

Figure 14.6 Birth Control and STD Protection

Type	Usage	Prevention of STDs		
		Yes*	No	Not Necessarily
Abstinence	Refraining from *all sexual activity*—vaginal, anal, oral, and outercourse; 100 percent effective	X		
Outercourse	Oral genital sex and mutual masturbation			X
The Pill	Oral contraceptive; the most widely used form of birth control		X	
The Male Pill	Oral contraceptive; newly developed for male use		X	
The Patch	Called the Ortho-Evra patch, it is a transdermal method of dispensing similar medicine as in the pill; each patch lasts for one week		X	
The NuvaRing	A clear, flexible vaginal ring that is self-inserted in the vagina and releases a low dose of hormones; lasts for one month		X	
Diaphragm	Round, flexible disk inserted into the vagina to cover the cervix		X	
IUD	Intrauterine device; must be inserted into the uterus by a physician		X	
Male Condom	A sheath, generally latex, worn over the penis to prevent sperm from entering the vagina	X		
Female Condom	A loose-fitting sheath inserted into the vagina to prevent sperm from entering the uterus	X		
Spermicides	Inserted into the vagina to kill sperm; comes in foams, jellies, suppositories, and creams		X	
Withdrawal	Also called coitus interruptus; the penis is withdrawn from the vagina before ejaculation		X	
Rhythm Method	Abstaining from sexual intercourse during the time in the menstrual cycle when ovulation occurs		X	
Norplant	Silicone tubes surgically embedded in a woman's upper arm to suppress fertilization		X	
Sterilization	Male and female surgery; male version is called vasectomy; female versions are called tubal sterilization, tubal ligation, and hysterectomy		X	
Cervical Cap	Much like the diaphragm, it is fitted into the vagina by a doctor; it is meant to be used with a spermicide and can provide up to 48 hours of protection		X	

* Only total abstinence is 100% effective in preventing sexually transmitted diseases.

CHANGING IDEAS to Reality

REFLECTIONS ON HEALTH AND WELLNESS

Your understanding of wellness and the gift of a healthy body during your college education and beyond is a wonderful beginning to a bright future. During this chapter you have been given the opportunity to think about the role the mind, body, and soul have in your overall approach to wellness. You've looked at the importance of personal responsibility regarding your approach to relationships, alcohol, and drugs. College is a time when you have an opportunity to reflect on the great questions in life and enjoy wonderful relationships, but this can only take place if your body, mind, and soul are healthy.

Our wish for you is that you carefully develop your wellness plan and take personal responsibility for your total health. We urge you to make wise decisions, as some choices have very bad consequences. No matter what you may have done in the past, there is always an opportunity to change, mature, and become more responsible for your own well-being.

Knowledge in Bloom

BRINGING WELLNESS INTO YOUR LIFE

Utilizes levels 1–6 of the Taxonomy (See Bloom's Taxonomy at the front of this text)

Throughout this chapter, we have tried to give you information that will be useful to you as you think about your overall wellness. The following activity will ask you to look at your life in more detail. You will be asked to identify one area of wellness in the mind, soul, or body that you would like to improve.

The area of wellness I want to improve is _____ _____

Level 1—Remember Identify what you need or want to change about your wellness and why.	
Level 2—Understand Research your options for making the desired change and seek advice and assistance from a variety of sources.	
Level 3—Apply Demonstrate how these sources would be helpful.	
Level 4—Analyze What conclusions could be drawn about your life if these changes are not made?	
Level 5—Evaluate Predict how your wellness will be enhanced by employing this change in your life.	
Level 6—Create Design a plan to bring about this wellness change in your live. Consider using one of the goal setting charts from Chapter 1.	

SQ3R MASTERY STUDY SHEET

EXAMPLE QUESTION (FROM PAGE 324) What does it mean to have a holistic approach to health?	**ANSWER:**
EXAMPLE QUESTION (FROM PAGE 325) Why is it important to know about depression and anxiety?	**ANSWER:**
AUTHOR QUESTION (FROM PAGE 324) Define the "holistic" approach to wellness.	**ANSWER:**
AUTHOR QUESTION (FROM PAGE 327) Discuss three symptoms of depression.	**ANSWER:**
AUTHOR QUESTION (FROM PAGE 329) Why are prescription drugs as dangerous as non-prescription drugs?	**ANSWER:**
AUTHOR QUESTION (FROM PAGE 331) Compare and contrast OxyContin to alcohol.	**ANSWER:**
AUTHOR QUESTION (FROM PAGE 337) In your opinion, rank the top three forms of birth control. Justify your answer.	**ANSWER:**
YOUR QUESTION (FROM PAGE _____)	**ANSWER:**
YOUR QUESTION (FROM PAGE _____)	**ANSWER:**
YOUR QUESTION (FROM PAGE _____)	**ANSWER:**
YOUR QUESTION (FROM PAGE _____)	**ANSWER:**
YOUR QUESTION (FROM PAGE _____)	**ANSWER:**

Finally, after answering these questions, recite this chapter's major points in your mind. Consider the following general questions to help you master this material.

- What is it about?
- What does it mean?
- What is the most important thing you learned? Why?
- What are the key points to remember?

THREE-DAY FOOD TRACKING SHEET

For the next **three days,** track *everything you consume through your mouth*; nutritious food, junk food, water, alcohol, carbonated drinks, fruits, chewing gum, etc. After you have tracked your food, answer the questions at the bottom of this exercise.

DAY ONE	DAY TWO	DAY THREE

After you have a complete list of what you ate for three days, analyze your eating habits and determine what you are eating that should be dropped or curtailed. What is missing from your diet that you need to be healthy? Visit www.mypyramid.gov to assist you in this exercise.

DEVELOP A FIVE-POINT PLAN TO BRING ABOUT THIS CHANGE IN YOUR LIFE.

Be certain to use action verbs in your goal statements.

1. _____

2. _____

3. _____

4. _____

5. _____

PLAN

FOCUSING ON YOUR FUTURE AND PROFESSIONAL CAREER

"No one can tell you what your life's work is, but it is important that you find it. There is a part of you that already knows; affirm that part." —Willis W. Harman

Why read this chapter?

Because you'll learn...

- Ways to make yourself a desirable employee
- How to write cover letters and resumes
- Important tips for having a dynamic interview

Because you'll be able to...

- Implement the DOCTOR system to write a powerful cover letter and resume
- Use the REWARDS system to prepare for an interview
- Write a compelling thank you note

Scan and QUESTION

Take a few moments, **scan this chapter** and on page 378, write **five questions** that you think will be important to your mastery of this material. In addition to the two questions below, you will also find five questions from your authors.

Example:

☑ **Why is it important to write an excellent resume?** (from page 358)

☑ **What does DOCTOR stand for?** (from page 358)

MyStudentSuccessLab

MyStudentSuccessLab is an online solution designed to help you acquire and develop (or hone) the skills you need to succeed. You will have access to peer-led video presentations and develop core skills through interactive exercises and projects.

How

Name: Zack Karper

Institution: Honor Graduate! The Art Institute of Philadelphia

Major: Digital Film and Video Production

"My childhood was filled with trouble. It is hard to think of it, much less speak of it. I had little direction and no future. I did not respect authority, began missing school, and fell into the 'wrong' crowd. My life was headed in a direction where the ending was not going to be good."

It was surprising to learn that Zack Karper, a mild-mannered young man with a thirst for knowledge, looked at his childhood as being anything but pleasant. Zack finally realized he needed to change his life for the better. That was when he learned about The Patane Foundation's Dream Camp. It was there he found the change he desperately needed. Zack's experience with the camp left a lasting impression that will never be forgotten.

"I was then asked, and decided to attend, The Patane Foundation's first 'Dream Camp' for challenged youth, and my life changed forever. At the camp, I found support, advice, guidance, love, and a sense of my own future. I also learned how to produce movies and eventually found that not only was I good at it, but that I loved it!"

An interview conducted and written by Lya Redmond, Coordinator of Disability Services and Developmental Studies, The Art Institute of Philadelphia, Philadelphia, PA

Zack's experience at the camp influenced his decision to pursue his new-found interest in filmmaking as a career. "After camp, I decided to enroll at The Art Institute of Philadelphia to major in Digital Film and Video Production, never realizing that soon I would return to the camp that changed my life to be a part of the change in others' lives. Today, I am head of the newly named Buggle Productions, Dream Camp Foundation's video production division. We film all of the foundation's nonprofit activities."

Like many first-time college students, Zack encountered challenges adjusting to college life. Zack candidly talked about his biggest challenge as a college student. "The biggest challenge in attending college was adapting to a new life and being on my own." He did not give up on his dream to be a filmmaker. Instead, he developed strategies that helped him to maximize his educational experience. "I had to learn how to manage my day and leave enough time for rest and sleep. I learned how to create lists and plan out my days. I posted the lists so that I could see them daily. This helped me develop a schedule that worked for me."

Zack chose to stay in college because he knew his education in digital film and video production was going to help prepare him for the future and better his life. He had the freedom to physically work on projects while constantly learning. College also helped Zack understand who he is as a person and how he worked best, whether independently or with others. Zack explained that college provided him with basic life skills in a non-judgmental environment, where he was able to make mistakes and learn from them.

"During my time at The Art Institute of Philadelphia, I learned how to push myself and get out of my comfort zone. I learned how to actually do things and not just talk about doing things. I did not waste my time on partying and mindless activities. I began to explore new avenues and seek new skills that would carry me into the future. By learning how to step outside my comfort zone, I learned how to become who and what I wanted to be. I was no longer trying to be the person others wanted me to be. By stepping outside my comfort zone and focusing on my career and my future, my life began to change."

Zack achieved and maintained outstanding grades, as well as enhanced his natural talent for producing quality films, which have earned accolades at film festivals both in the United States and abroad.

"I never dreamed that I could be an award-winning filmmaker. But, with hard work and perseverance, I won awards at school, nationally, and internationally. Some of my films have received recognition and won awards at film festivals in Colorado, New Jersey, California, and even at the International Youth Film Festival in England!"

Zack's experience at The Art Institute has taught him many lessons that he has shared with other students, but there is one lesson he constantly conveys to the young people with whom he works. "The biggest lesson that I learned in college was to treat every project, whether a paper, a speech, or a film, as if it was your baby. Nurture it. Care for it. Feed it. Make it great and never raise it halfway. Give your baby your all. Today, as head of video production at Buggle Productions, I live my dream of working in film and I get to help troubled kids who were in the same shoes I was in. I get to make a difference!"

THINK a b o u t *it*

1. Zack mentioned that he had some things in his past to overcome. What areas of your past will you have to overcome to be successful in your chosen field?

2. Zack has won many awards for his work in documentary filmmaking. What are your hopes and dreams for your future? What do you hope to accomplish with your education and degree?

What changes do you foresee coming in your chosen career field in the next five years?

PLANNING FOR THE FUTURE

What Are You Going to Do for the Rest of Your Life?

"What are you going to do for the rest of your life?" is an overwhelming question for anyone, especially in a dramatically changing, global, technology-driven environment. What was true last year—and sometimes even last week—is no longer true. While many things that worked for your parents and grandparents are still important and relevant today—things like ethics, integrity, hard work, education, honesty, and teamwork—many practices that were true in their time are no longer valid. Your grandfather may have gone to work for a company and stayed there all his life. Employers were loyal to employees, and employees were loyal to the

company. Work stayed pretty much the same this year as it was the last. All that has changed. You will have many different jobs during your lifetime—in fact, you will most likely have three or four different careers, and what constitutes your work will be constantly changing.

> "The four great questions: Why are you here? Where have you been? Where are you going? What difference will you make?"
>
> —Hal Simon

STRATEGIES TO SUCCESSFULLY PREPARE FOR YOUR FUTURE

What 10 Baby Steps Will Become Giant Steps Tomorrow?

You might consider what you are doing today and the rest of your college career as baby steps that will lead to giant steps in being prepared for the future. The following strategies (adapted from Orndorff, 2008) will help you as you move toward your transition goals, whether they are moving to the sophomore class or to the world of work.

1. Make good grades. Grades do matter! While everyone can't graduate with a 4.0, you need to be one of those who earns a respectable GPA. Not only do good grades show that you have gained knowledge in certain areas, they indicate a work ethic and a sense of responsibility that employers are seeking. Your grades can also affect your transition to other undergraduate and graduate institutions.

2. Come to grips with your abilities, interests, values, and personal characteristics. You might be telling people you want to be a corporate attorney or a businesswoman. Do you really know what these careers entail? How many years of education are required? What kind of GPA does it take to get into a really good business school? Specifically, what do you want to do? Where will the jobs be? What kind of preparation does it take? Do you have the ability and perseverance to become what you dream about?

3. Fine tune your computer skills. Most first-year students today have good computer skills, but these skills need to be very strong. Your skills need to include the ability to work with spreadsheets, databases, word processing systems, social media networks, and PowerPoint. Before you graduate, other software programs may become important. Learn to develop web pages, and create your own website that reflects a professional, career-oriented person.

> "A study has shown that first- and second-year students spend more time deciding on a movie to watch than on what they might want for a career, even though a movie lasts two hours and a career lasts a lifetime."
>
> —Bob Orndorff

4. Hone your communication, speaking, and writing skills. By now, you are tired of hearing this, but it's true. Enroll in classes that are writing and speaking intensive, even if you hate the thought of it. Many recruiters point out the weaknesses of applicants' writing and speaking skills. Good communication skills could be a major asset to you in a job search in the future.

5. Actively engage in exploring career options. Your career—and variations of it—will last a lifetime. Doesn't that fact make it evident that you need to spend some time "trying on" careers to see if one might be a good fit? Read about careers in professional journals in your library, go to the career counseling center, talk to people who are in the career that interests you, and attend career fairs and job expos. Finding the "right" major and career requires hard, intensive work.

6. Get involved and stay active. Job recruiters are looking for people who are leaders, who understand teamwork, who have shown by their involvement that they can manage time and make things happen. Select one or two activities or organizations and become actively engaged. Work your way to the top. You'll learn valuable skills, and it will look great on your resume! Go to job interviews with excellent experiences on your resume.

7. Give back to your community. Here again, recruiters consider service learning a great asset. Many times students look at community service as just another task, but after it's over, they realize the benefits they have derived from helping someone else. Many careers have been jumpstarted by an outstanding service learning project that showcased a person's talents. You'll get more than you give by participating in service learning.

8. Spend your summers working in internships, preferably ones that carry college credit. Once you have decided on a direction that interests you, explore the field by actually working in it. If you begin as a first-year student working for a company that interests you, perform well, and go back every summer, the chances are good that a job will be waiting for you when you graduate. Many students transition from an internship to a career position.

9. Expand your cultural and international knowledge. This is a great time to learn everything you can about people from different backgrounds. Make friends with people from international backgrounds, explore different cultures, and learn to appreciate and celebrate diversity.

10. Take advantage of your campus career center. Few students really take full advantage of their career center. The counselors there may not have all the answers, but they can start you in the right direction by offering advice on trends, requirements, and changes in certain fields. Check out the center on your campus, and soon!

THE SOPHOMORE YEAR

Is It Possible to Prepare for a Successful Transition?

> *"You are the way you are because that's the way you want to be. If you really want to be any different, you will be in the process of changing right now."*
> —Fred Smith

Since you are enrolled in this course, you already know that colleges and universities spend considerable amounts of time teaching you such things as how to improve your study habits, how to manage your time and money, and how to organize your work successfully when you are a first-year student. Rarely, however, will you be given much information about how to transition successfully into your **sophomore year,** or how to navigate through this next step. You might say—and rightfully so—*"I'm still trying to get through my first year. I don't have time to think about my sophomore year."* But it is never too early to plan for the future, for your next step. It is advisable to set aside some time to think about what comes next and begin preparing to successfully take the steps to make this next venture a successful reality. Even if you begin your second year and are still classified as a first-year student, these steps can help you move toward your goals faster.

- **Begin with the end in mind.** Think about how happy you are going to be when you finish your sophomore year and you are about to enter your junior year or the workforce. All the way through this venture—and any venture—work hard today, but focus on the end result and enjoy the great opportunity that you have to learn and grow.

- **Formulate a clear vision about what you want your life to be.** This may not happen overnight or even for a few weeks or months, but you should begin embracing certain thoughts, ideas, and pictures of what you want your life to be. It may sound strange, but having a visual picture of what you want actually helps you move toward it. Each transition can be looked at as another step toward getting to this beautiful vision you have created in your head.

> *"Training teaches people what to do. Education teaches people what to be."*
> —Nido R. Qubein

- **Begin now to explore options about career interests you would like to pursue.** Researchers are discovering that students really begin to zero in on how they want to spend their lives during their sophomore year (Reynolds, Gross, & Millard, 2005). Choosing a major requires you to use your decision-making skills to determine if you have the ability and discipline to pursue certain majors and careers. While you do not want to rush this important decision, research shows that sophomores with a high degree of certainty as to what major they want to declare tend to perform better academically (Graunke & Woolsley, 2005).

■ **Look inside yourself and get in touch with your inner feelings about school, work, family, and community.** You will most likely never have another time when you will be as free to focus on yourself as you do right now. Even if you have a family and children, you are free to focus on you while you are in class, and perhaps between some classes.

■ **Beware of the "sophomore slump."** Although it is hard to pinpoint exactly what the "sophomore slump" really is, second-year students often find themselves confused about what they want to do, stressed because of hard decisions that need to be made, depressed because they are getting less attention in college than they did in high school, or simply tired from working, trying to spend time with family, and maintaining good grades all at the same time. This condition might become an issue as early as the second semester of your first year, so be prepared to combat it. Some ways to deal with the "sophomore slump" include:

■ Interact with faculty and advisors and try to make a strong connection with at least one of them.

■ Try to make connections with at least one or two fellow students with whom you have something in common.

■ Realize that you may become less motivated, and that finding a major and a purpose can help you get back on track.

■ If you are not doing well in a particular subject, get help as quickly as you can—talk to the professor, hire a tutor, start a study group, or connect with a study partner—don't wait until it is too late!

DID YOU Know?

MAYA ANGELOU was born in St. Louis, MO, in 1928. As a young girl, she was raped by her mother's boyfriend, and did not speak again for four years. By the time she was in her twenties, she had been a cook, streetcar conductor, cocktail waitress, dancer, madam, high school dropout, and an unwed mother.

Today, Dr. Angelou is a world-renowned poet, civil rights activist, historian, screenwriter, and director. She is only the second poet **in history** to write and deliver an original poem at a presidential inauguration (Clinton).

She has won three Grammy Awards in the spoken word category, and has been nominated twice for Broadway's prestigious Tony Award.

THE SUCCESSFUL TRANSITION PLAN FOR FIRST-YEAR STUDENTS

How Can I Prepare for My Future?

It is never too early to begin thinking about your future—whether it is graduating, transferring to another institution, or entering the world of work. Developing a *four-year plan* may be a little overwhelming at this stage of your college career, but it will pay big dividends in saved time, reduced frustrations, and well-designed career and educational objectives. Consider the tips in Figure 15.1 as you build a blueprint for your four-year degree.

Figure 15.1 **The Four-Year Plan**

First Year

■ Explore campus organizations and get involved in activities that interest you. If you already know your major, you can work in organizations that enhance your career options. Employers are interested in graduates who have been actively involved in their chosen field.

■ Identify academic centers where you may get help in improving your grades. A solid GPA is important when you seek internships, part-time jobs, and full-time work later on. A solid GPA is also important for scholarships and graduate school.

■ Establish study groups for your courses and secure study partners for difficult courses.

■ If you need developmental/remedial work, start it now.

(continued)

Figure 15.1 The Four-Year Plan (continued)

- Develop a cover letter and resume using the information found in this chapter. This will change as you grow and progress, but it is good to have one on hand if you need it.
- Establish relationships with advisors and professors who know your work first-hand and can be a reference for you for scholarships, internships, part-time employment, etc.
- Begin searching now for a part-time position or a summer job. Competition is stiff during difficult economic times, and many jobs are promised early.
- Attend job fairs, even if you aren't looking for a job right now. Job fairs give you practice talking to people about work, and give you a chance to meet people who might be able to tell you more about a career you are interested in.
- Try to identify a major that you like, that you can successfully pursue, and that meets your financial expectations.
- Visit the career center at your college.
- Take a personal finance course as an elective.

Second Year

- Don't let the "sophomore slump" impact your grades. Keep your GPA as high as possible.
- If you have not been working, try to find a part-time job that relates to your career interest. Try to limit your hours so work does not impact your grades.
- Explore career options and interests in the library, at career fairs, and using Internet resources.
- Try to increase your range of responsibilities in campus activities to gain more leadership experience.
- Gain exposure and experience through job shadowing and volunteering if you have time.
- Explore possible internships or cooperative programs in your field.
- Expand your relationships with professors who can serve as references.
- Update your resume.

Third Year

- Visit all the offices on campus that relate to your needs—financial aid, career counseling, academic enrichment center, etc.
- Find a part-time job that relates to your major.
- Quickly build relationships with professors and advisors who can assist you and serve as references.
- Work hard to keep your GPA as high as possible as you get closer to the time to look for a job and/or pursue graduate school.
- If you want to attend graduate school, begin exploring options.
- Find out the right place on campus that can help you with practice interviews.
- Attend all career fairs to practice your skills and to learn more about career options.
- Seek assistance from a prominent professor in getting an internship in your major to build your experience.
- Assemble new study groups and study partners.
- Update your resume.
- Consider study abroad programs or an international field study if you can afford it or if you can get a scholarship.
- Try to build an interviewing wardrobe of at least two suits and accessories.
- If you haven't had one yet, take a speech course.

Fourth Year

- Get very serious about finding a career in your chosen profession **now**!
- Seek advice from a knowledgeable professor relative to your resume. How can you improve it? What is missing that you can do now?
- Participate in all job fairs and career fairs.
- Network with anyone and everyone you know who might be able to help you locate a good job in your field.
- Hone your online job search skills.
- Select a few companies and conduct a complete search about each one.
- If you get an interview, find out everything you can about the company.
- Make a list of questions that you want to ask an interviewer.
- Determine the areas where you are willing to move if asked to do so by an employer.
- If you plan to go to graduate school, find out what entrance exams you need to take and begin taking practice tests to prepare. See if there is a course you can enroll in to prepare for the test.
- Apply early for graduate school.
- Seek assistantships early!

Source: Adapted from Career Center at The University of South Carolina (n.d.).

DEVELOPING YOUR CAREER SELF-STUDY PLAN

What Factors Shape the Future?

More people than you can imagine have trouble deciding what they want to be when they "grow up." Studies indicate that more than 20 percent of all first-year college students have not declared a major. That's all right for the time being, but before long you will need to make a decision, as this choice affects your selection of classes, co-curricular activities, and possible internships. If you delay selecting a major for too long, you may lose credit hours and take unnecessary courses.

The questions that follow are designed to help you make the decision regarding what you want to do with the rest of your life—your career.

What Is Your Personality Type?

You can best answer this question by taking a personality inventory, such as the Golden Personality Type Profiler (you can access this inventory through MyStudentSuccessLab at www .mystudentsuccesslab.com). This question is important, because your personality may very well indicate the type of work in which you will be successful and happy. For example, if you are a real people person, you probably will not be very happy in a job with minimal human contact and interaction.

Describe your personality type. _____

_____

How will your personality type affect your career path? _____

_____

What Are Your Interests?

Understanding your specific interests may help you decide on a career. If you love working on cars, you might consider becoming a mechanical engineer. If you love to draw or build things, you might be interested in architecture or sculpting.

What are your major interests? _____

_____

How can these interests be transferred to a career choice? _____

_____

Do You Enjoy Physical or Mental Work?

Many people would go crazy if they had to spend as much as one hour per day in an office. Others would be unhappy if they had to work in the sun all day or use a great deal of physical strength. The answer to the following questions will greatly narrow your list of potential career choices. For example, if you are an outdoor person who loves being outside in all kinds of weather, then you should probably avoid careers that are limited to indoor work. You should also consider whether you have any physical limitations that might affect your career choice.

Do you enjoy physical or mental work or both? Why? _____

_____

What does this mean to your career path? _____

_____

What Is Most Important? Money? Service? Independence? Or a Combination?

Most people, if asked, "Why do you work?" would respond, "For the money." There is nothing wrong with wanting to make money in your profession, but not all professions, regardless of their worth, pay well. Some of the hardest and most rewarding work pays the least. You have to decide whether to go for the money or do something that is personally challenging and rewarding to you. Many times, you can find both!

Is your major goal in choosing a profession money or something else? What? _____

_____

What does your goal mean to your career path? _____

_____

Where Do You Want to Live?

Although this question may sound strange, many careers are limited by geography. If you are interested in oceanography, you would be hard-pressed to find a job living in Iowa; if you love farming, New York City would be an improbable place for you to live. If you like small towns, you might not be happy in Atlanta. Some people simply prefer certain parts of the United States (or the world) to others. You need to ask yourself, "What climate do I really enjoy?" "Where would I be the happiest?" "Do I want to live near my family or away from them?"

Where do you eventually want to live? Why? _____

_____

What does your preference mean to your career path? _____

_____

Do You Want to Travel?

Some jobs require travel; some people love to travel, some hate it. Ask yourself whether you want to be away from your home and family four nights per week, or whether you want a job that does not require any travel.

Do you enjoy travel? Do you want to do a lot of traveling? _____

_____

What does this mean to your career path? _____

_____

What Motivates You and What Do You Value?

Do you value relationships, possessions, money? Are you motivated by love, security, challenges, or power? Once you have identified what you value and what motivates you, you can identify careers that closely match your personal value system and eliminate careers that don't motivate you. If you have to constantly compromise your values just to get a paycheck, you may be unhappy and motivation will be hard to find on a daily basis.

What do you truly value in your life? What motivates you? _____

_____

How might these two things affect your career decisions? _____

_____

What Are Your Skills?

Are you especially good at one or two things? Are you good with computers, a good manager of money, a good carpenter, a good communicator? Employers still stress the importance of three basic skills: writing, speaking, and listening. If you have these skills, you are ahead of the pack. If not, you need to enroll in a class that will help you to become better at all three.

What are your skills? What do you do well? _____

_____

How could your strongest skills help you make a career decision? _____

_____

Do You Like Routine?

The answer to this question will narrow your choices tremendously. If you like routine, you will want a career that is conducive to routine and provides structure. If you do not like routine and enjoy doing different things each day, certain careers will be unrealistic for you.

Do you like routine or do you prefer variety? Why?

_____

How does this affect your career path?

_____

Dream Job

Using the answers you provided to the previous questions and a variety of additional resources, such as websites, job shadowing, and interviews, write a description for your dream job—the job you would have if you could do anything in the world.

_____

_____

_____

_____

_____

HELP ME: I'M UNDECLARED

What Is the Roadmap for Exploring and Deciding?

Being undeclared is not a fatal disease. It is not a disgrace or a weakness. It is a temporary state of mind, and the best way to deal with it is to stop, think, and explore. You should not declare a major because you are ashamed to be undeclared, and you shouldn't allow yourself to be pressured into declaring a major. Instead, you can take measures to work toward declaring a major and being satisfied with your decision. It is better to be undeclared than to spend several semesters in a field that is wrong for you, wasting credit hours that won't count toward a degree. On the other hand, the sooner you declare a major, the less likely you are to take courses that do not count toward your eventual decision. While you need to take your time and make a good decision, you don't have forever!

> " Though no one can go back and make a brand new start, anyone can start from now and make a brand new ending."
> — Carl Bard

Important Steps to Career Decision Making

Step 1—Dream! If money were not a problem or concern, what would you do for the rest of your life? If you could do anything in the world, what would you do? Where would you do it? These are the types of questions you must ask yourself as you try to select a major and career. Go outside, lie on the grass, and look up at the sky; think silently for a little while. Let your mind wander, and let the sky be the limit. Write your dreams down. These dreams may be closer to reality than you think.

Step 2—Go to the career center and/or talk to your advisor. Academic advisors are there to help you, but don't be surprised if their doors are sometimes closed. They teach, conduct research, perform community service, and sometimes advise hundreds of students. Always call in advance and make an appointment to see an advisor. When you have that appointment, make your advisor work for you. Take your college catalog and ask questions, hard questions. Your advisor will not make a career decision for you, but if you ask the proper questions, he or she can be of monumental help to you as you make your career decisions. Also consider visiting your campus career center. These centers usually provide free services; the same types of services in the community could cost from $200 to $2,000. The professionals in the career center can provide information on a variety of careers and fields, and they can administer interest and personality inventories that can help you make career and other major decisions.

> *"It's a sad day when you find out that it's not an accident, or time, or fortune, but just yourself that kept things from you."*
>
> —Lilian Hellman

Step 3—Use electives. The accreditation agency that works with your school requires that you be allowed at least one free elective in your degree program. Some programs allow many more. Use your electives wisely! Do not take courses just to get the hours. The wisest students use their electives to delve into new areas of interest or to take a block of courses in an area that might enhance their career opportunities.

Step 4—Read, read, read! Nothing will help you more than reading about careers and majors. Ask your advisor or counselor to help you locate information on your areas of interest. Gather information from colleges, agencies, associations, and places of employment—then read it! If you know the job you want, read trade journals in that field.

Step 5—Shadow. Shadowing describes the process of following someone around on the job. If you are wondering what engineers do on the job, try calling an engineering office to see whether you can sit with several of their engineers for a day over spring break. Shadowing is the very best way to get firsthand, honest information regarding a profession in which you might be interested.

Step 6—Join pre-professional organizations. One of the most important steps you can take as a college student is to become involved in campus organizations and clubs that offer educational opportunities, social interaction, and hands-on experience in your chosen field. Pre-professional organizations can open doors that will help you make a career decision, grow in your field, meet professionals already working in your field, and, eventually, get a job.

Step 7—Try to get a summer practicum, internship, or job in your field of interest. Work in your field of interest to gain practical experience and see if it really suits you. Some programs require a practicum or internship, and this experience often leads to your first full-time job.

THE FUTURIST

How Can You Prepare for a Job That Doesn't Exist Yet?

As crazy as it sounds, learning to prepare yourself for careers and jobs that do not yet exist may be the skill that separates you from the unsuccessful, the unhappy, and the unemployed. As you read this, you may be thinking, *"How do you expect me to prepare and train for something that isn't out there, a career for which there is no major, a job for which no one is hiring?"*

Consider that, before 2005, there were no careers or positions such as Facebook page designer, and social media marketing experts did not exist. Just a few years ago, few people ever held the position of teleconference coordinator. And, it was not even twenty years ago that colleges began offering online, distance education as we know it today. There were no bloggers, Tweeters, Googlers, or Wiki writers. However, it is safe to say that developments such as Facebook, Skype, distance education, and social media are among the most sweeping societal and economic changes since the Industrial Revolution—and yet, these fields did not exist a few years ago. Today, these fields employ millions.

> *"Sixty percent of Apple's sales are from products that did not exist three years ago."*
>
> —Horace Dediu

So, how did Mark Zuckerburg (Facebook), Niklas Zennstrom (Skype), and Jones International University (the first fully accredited online university) become so lucky? How did they know where the future was headed? Was it luck? Did they have a crystal ball that actually worked? No one knows for sure, but you can rest assured that anyone who has ever forged a brave new world studied trends and current problems, surrounded themselves with brilliant people, had boundless courage, and never succumbed to the idea of defeat.

Eli Whitney and Catherine Greene (inventors of the cotton gin), Alexander Graham Bell (inventor of the telephone), Willis Carrier (inventor of the first electric air conditioner), Alexander Bain (inventor of the fax machine), Mary Anderson (inventor of the windshield wiper), and Art Fry and Spencer Silver (inventors of Post-It Notes) all helped change the way we work and live. They developed and honed skills that prepared them for an ever-changing, dynamic, unpredictable future. You can develop your skills and talents, too.

Skills to Develop for a Brighter, More Competitive Future

- Learn everything that you can about technology.
- Develop a keen sense of curiosity and observation.
- Look beyond today and try to see what is coming—move from "sunset careers" to "sunrise careers."
- Read articles, books, and reports by futurists and industry scholars.
- Study emerging trends and data (nationally and internationally).
- Keep up with world affairs.
- Study today's problems; the solutions are tomorrow's careers.
- Sharpen your oral, written, and online communication skills.
- Develop boundless courage and a strong will.
- Surround yourself with the smartest, most well-read, trend-setting people that you can find—build and maintain a professional network of successful people.
- Develop professional relationships outside your current major, field, or industry.
- Think globally by working with diverse cultures and learning to speak languages other than your own.
- Seek and capture opportunities for international, global exposure and travel.
- Prepare yourself for lifelong learning—try to work for a company that provides continuous educational development opportunities.
- Learn to accept and embrace fast-paced change.

THE JOB SEARCH PACKAGE

How Can You Sell Yourself and Get Your Foot In the Door?

There is going to come a time when you will need to show, tell, and write to others about your skills, talents, and qualifications. It may be for a summer job, an internship, or a full-time position in your desired field. The remainder of this chapter will help you prepare a **dynamic job search package** that will help you land the attention of employers seeking skilled associates.

Remember the old saying, "*You are what you eat*"? When searching for a professional position, you could change that to read, "**You are what you write**." Most likely, the people conducting the job search have never met you and know nothing about you except what you provide to them. A carefully crafted resume communicates your past history (skills and experience) that makes you the ideal candidate for their position. Your resume and cover letter are the first marketing pieces when a recruiter is determining whether or not to interview you. Just as a well-designed and written cover letter and resume can be a wonderful first step, a poorly designed and written cover letter and resume can doom you before you ever leave your house. A good thing to remember is this: A cover letter and resume get you the interview; the interview gets you the job. Although there is no single way to develop your job search package, and formats may vary from discipline to discipline, this chapter outlines the key components of resumes and cover letters and discusses how to develop both for the best results.

Often, applicants ignore or gloss over the cover letter. This is not a wise decision. A cover letter is basically an expansion of your resume. A cover letter gives you the chance to link your resume, skills, and experience together with your interest in *a specific company's* position. You will need to write many cover letters to make this connection work properly; in other words, you most likely need to write a cover letter designed for each job for which you apply. Your cover letter will often be the stepping-stone to get an employer to even look at your resume. Consider it "a teaser" if you will, to all of your talents and experience. Just as you would never send someone a greeting card and not sign it, you would never send a resume and not tell the person or committee *why* you sent it. Your cover letter tells why.

WRITE A POWERFUL AND CONCISE COVER LETTER

I've Got A Resume. Do Cover Letters Really Matter?

Careful preparation must be done *prior to starting* the interview process. Whenever you send your resume to a company, whether it is in response to a posted advertisement or requested, you must send a cover letter with it. Cover letters are extremely important; in fact, most recruiters say that they read four times as many cover letters as they do resumes, because if the cover letter does not "strike a chord," then they never look past it to the resume.

Carol Robbins (2006), career development expert, author, and speaker, states, "*During my 25 plus years that I've been involved in career development, I have found that of all the paperwork associated with job searching, cover letters give job searchers the most difficulty.*" The information presented below will help you overcome anxiety associated with writing your cover letter or resume.

As you begin your cover letter and resume process, consider the general tips in Figure 15.2.

Figure 15.2 Successful Cover Letters and Resumes

- Both your resume and cover letter *must be typed*. There are no exceptions to this rule. Ever! Seriously, **ever**!

- Your cover letter and resume must be printed on the same *type and color* of *fine-quality paper*. Cheap paper sends the message that you don't care. This is not the place or time to pinch pennies; buy excellent quality, 100 percent cotton stock, resume paper.

- Check your printer and be sure that the print quality is impeccable. Never send a cover letter or resume with smudges, ink smears, or poor print quality.

- When you print your cover letter and resume, be certain that the watermark on the paper is turned in the correct direction. Hold it up to the light and you will see the watermark embedded in the paper. This may sound silly and picky, but people notice attention to detail.

- Do not fold your cover letter or resume. Purchase a packet of 9 x 13 envelopes in which to send your materials.

- Do not handwrite the address on the envelope. Use a label or type the address directly on the envelope. Remember, first impressions are important.

- Never send a generic photocopy of a cover letter or resume, even on the finest paper.

- Layout, design, font, spacing, and color must be considered when creating your cover letter and resume.

- Unless you are specifically asked to do so, *never* discuss money or salary history in either your cover letter or resume; this could work against you. When asked for a salary history, use ranges.

- Your resume and cover letter *must* be error-free. That's right, not one single error is acceptable, including grammar, spelling, punctuation, layout/spacing, dates, or content.

- Each cover letter must be signed in black or blue ink.

Simply put, the cover letter's purpose is to get the interviewer to read your resume. It sets the tone for who you are, what you have to offer, and what you want. *"It screams—ever so politely—that you have the intelligence, experience, and soft skills to be the answer to an employer's staffing problem"* (Britton-Whitcomb, 2003). The cover letter should say to the reader, "You have an opening and a detailed description of what you need and I can fill your opening and be the person who gets the job done—and done well."

Consider the following **four steps to success** when writing your cover letter:

1. **An effective cover letter will be** *personally addressed and job specific.* If at all possible (and yes, it is possible with just a little research), address your letter to a specific person. Avoid at all cost the dreaded "Dear Sir or Madam" or "To Whom It May Concern." In most cases, a phone call to the company will provide the name of the person, their title, and their address. Always verify spelling, even with common names. This single step can set you apart from lazy jobseekers. Also, make *sure* you spell the company's name correctly.

2. **Once your letter is correctly addressed, your first paragraph should be an "attention grabber" and should answer the question, "Why am I writing?"** Susan Britton-Whitcomb, author of *Resume Magic* (2003), calls this "the carrot." This simply means that your first paragraph has an interesting fact, an appeal, or maybe even a quote—something that makes the reader (hopefully, your future employer) read further. Your first paragraph should also have a transition statement that makes the reader want to read on. For example, your last statement might read, *"With a degree in Medical Assisting and four years experience at Desert Medical Center, I know that I can make a valued contribution to Grace Care Center."*

3. **Your second (and maybe third) paragraph(s) should clearly state why you are qualified for the position you are seeking.** Use your cover letter to highlight those areas of your experience that specifically qualify you for the job. Your cover letter is not the time to list all of your qualifications, but should indicate the two or three components that most qualify you for the position and closely match the position announcement. You may also include specific attributes that may not be on your resume. The key word to consider here is your "value." Relate your education, experience, and talents to the company's needs. Mention facts and statistics of how you've been successful in the past. Remember, *"Employers are not interested in you for your sake, but rather because of what you can bring to the organization. This might sound harsh, but businesspeople have an obligation to improve the success of their organization. If you consistently show how you can help them do this…they will be much more motivated to talk to you"* (Farr & Kursmark, 2005).

4. **Your final paragraph should address the question of "Where do we go from here?"** Do not be ambiguous here by saying something trite like "I hope to hear from you in the near future," or "If you have any questions, please do not hesitate to call me." Remember, *your* job search is none of their business, nor is it their responsibility. Be proactive by stating that *you will be following up* with a phone call to discuss your resume and experience(s) in more detail. Make sure that once you have told them that you are going to call that you actually do call.

Your final paragraph should also continue to express what you can do for the company. You should end your letter with a statement about your qualities and their needs, such as, *"Mr. Thompson, I will call you on Monday, January 24, at 11:30 am, to discuss how my past experiences can help streamline operations and continue superior patient care at Grace Care Center."*

Don't forget to **sign your letter.** Figure 15.3 provides a sample cover letter, and indicates the correct format and spacing to the left of the letter's content.

Figure 15.3   Sample Cover Letter with Formatting Information

Your name and address ⟶
Your name should be larger
and/or in a different font to
draw attention (then double space)

The date (then double space) ⟶

The specific person, title, and
address to whom you are writing
(then double space) ⟶

The formal salutation followed by a
colon (then double space) ⟶

Paragraph 1 (then double
space) ⟶

Paragraph 2 (then double
space) ⟶

Paragraph 3 (then double
space) ⟶

BENJAMIN SHAW

1234 Lake Shadow Drive   (123) 555-1234
Maple City, PA 12345   ben@online.com

January 3, 2012

Mr. James Pixler, RN, CAN
Director of Placement and Advancement
Grace Care Center
123 Sizemore Street, Suite 444
Philadelphia, PA 12345

Dear Mr. Pixler:

Seven years ago, my mother was under the treatment of two incredible nurses at Grace Care Center in Philadelphia. My family and I agree that the care she was given was extraordinary. When I saw your ad in today's *Philadelphia Carrier*, I was extremely pleased to know that I now have the qualifications to be a part of the Grace Care Team as a Medical Assistant.

Next month, I will graduate with an Occupational Associate's Degree from Victory College of Health and Technology as a certified Medical Assistant. As my resumé indicates, I was fortunate to do my internship at Mercy Family Care Practice in Harrisburg. During this time, I was directly involved in patient care, records documentation, and family outreach.

As a part of my degree from Victory, I received a 4.0 in the following classes:

- Management Communications
- Microsoft Office (Word, Excel, Outlook, PowerPoint)
- Business Communications I, II, III
- Anatomy and Physiology I, II, III
- Medical Coding I, II
- Principles of Pharmacology
- Immunology I, II, III, IV
- Urinalysis and Body Fluids
- Clinical Practicum I, II, III

This, along with my past certificate in Medical Transcription and my immense respect for Grace Care Center, makes me the perfect candidate for your position.

I have detailed all of my experience on the enclosed resumé. I will call you on Monday, January 24, at 11:30 a.m., to discuss how my education and experiences can help streamline operations and continue superior patient care at Grace. In the meantime, please feel free to contact me at the number above.

Sincerely,

Benjamin Shaw

Benjamin Shaw

Enclosure: Resumé

UNDERSTAND THE DO'S AND DON'TS OF MEMORABLE RESUMES

How Do You Sell Yourself In A World of Fierce Competition?

"*Eight seconds*." That is all the time you have to gain the attention of your potential employer. According to Susan Ireland, author and consultant (2003), "*In eight seconds, an employer scans your resume and decides whether she will invest more time to consider you as a job candidate. The secret to passing the eight-second test is to make your resume look inviting and quick to read.*"

A resume is the blueprint that details what you have accomplished with regard to education, experience, skills acquisition, workplace successes, and progressive responsibility and/or leadership. It is a painting (that *you* are able to "paint") of your professional life. It is the ultimate advertisement of *you*! Your resume must create interest and, hopefully, a **desire** to find out more about you!

As you begin to develop your resume, make sure to allow plenty of time. Plan to enlist several qualified proofreaders to check your work. We cannot stress strongly enough the need for your resume to be perfect. A simple typo or misuse of grammar can disqualify you from the job of your dreams. Don't allow a lack of attention to detail to stand between you and your future career.

Further, your resume must be 100% completely accurate and truthful. Do not fabricate information or fudge dates to make yourself look better—it will only come back to haunt you in the long run. Dennis Reina, organizational psychologist and author of *Trust and Betrayal in the Workplace*, states, "*I think that what you put in a resume absolutely has to be rock-solid, concrete, and verifiable. If there are any questions, it will immediately throw both your application and your credibility into question*" (Dresang, 2007). People have been fired from positions after they were hired because they misrepresented themselves on their resume, cover letter, or application.

As you begin to build your resume, remember to "call in the **DOCTOR**."

DVisual **design** and format are imperative to a successful resume. You need to think about the font that you plan to use, whether color is appropriate (usually, it is not), the use of bullets, lines, or shading, and where you are going to put information. You also need to pay attention to the text balance on the page (centered left/right, top/bottom). The visual aspect of your resume will be the first impression—"make it pretty" (Britton-Whitcomb, 2003).

OWriting a clear and specific **objective** can help get your foot in the door. The reader, usually your potential employer, needs to be able to scan your resume and gather as much detail as possible, as quickly as possible. A job-specific objective can help. Consider the following two objectives:

Before: **Objective:** To get a job as an elementary school teacher in the Dallas Area School District

After: **Objective:** To secure an elementary teaching position that will enable me to use my 14 years of creative teaching experience, curriculum development abilities, supervisory skills, and commitment to superior instruction in a team environment.

CClarity is of paramount importance, especially when including your past experiences, education, and job responsibilities. Be certain that you let the reader know exactly what you have done, what specific education you have gained, and what progress you have made. Being vague and unclear can cost you an interview.

TWhen writing your resume, you may be tempted to fudge a little bit here and there to make your resume look better. Perhaps you were out of work for a few months and you think it looks bad to have this gap in your chronological history. Avoid the urge to fudge. Telling the absolute **truth** on a resume is essential. A lie, even a small one, can (and usually will) come back to haunt you.

OBefore you begin your resume, think about the **organization** of your data. Several model resumes are provided in this chapter; however, there are several other formats you might select. It is most important that you present your information in an attractive, easy-to-read, comprehensive format.

Reviewing your resume and cover letter is important, but having someone else review them for clarity, accuracy, spelling, grammar, placement, and overall content can be one of the best things you can do for your job search.

The basic tips in Figure 15.4 will help you as you begin building a dynamic resume. Remember, the job market is highly competitive. Your job is to write a resume that is solid, appealing, and comprehensive yet brief. The idea is to get someone to read it and make them want to know more about you.

Figure 15.4 Resume Guidelines

General Resume Tips and Advice

- Do not date stamp or record the preparation date of your resume in any place.
- Limit your resume (and cover letter) to one page each (a two-page resume is appropriate if you have more than 10 years' experience).
- Use standard resume paper colors, such as white, cream, gray, or beige.
- Use bullets (such as these) to help profile lists.
- Avoid fancy or hard to read fonts.
- Use a standard font size between 10 and 14 points.
- Do not staple anything to your resume (or cover letter).
- Try to avoid the use of "I" or "me" or "my" in your resume (if you must use them, do so sparingly).
- Avoid contractions, such as "don't," and do not use abbreviations.
- Use action verbs, such as "designed," "managed," "created," "recruited," "simplified," and "built."
- Avoid the use of full sentences; fragments are fine on a resume, but not in a cover letter.
- Use the correct verb tense—use past tense (such as "recruited") except for your current job.
- Do not include irrelevant information that does not pertain to this particular job search.
- Choose a format that puts your "best foot" or greatest assets forward.

What to Include or Avoid

Contact information (name, complete mailing address, phone and cell numbers, fax number, e-mail address, webpage URL)	MUST include
Education, degrees, certificates, advanced training (include dates and names of degrees)	MUST include
Current and past work history, experience, and responsibilities	MUST include
Past accomplishments (this is *not* the same thing as work history or responsibilities)	MUST include
Specific licensures	MUST include
Specific career objective (different for each position for which you apply)	SHOULD include
Summary or list of qualifications, strengths, and specializations	SHOULD include
Special skills (including special technical skills or multiple language skills)	SHOULD include
Volunteer work, public service, and/or community involvement	SHOULD include
Internships, externships, and/or extracurricular activities	SHOULD include
Awards, honors, certificates of achievement, special recognitions (at work or in the community)	SHOULD include
Military experience	CONSIDER including
Professional/pre-professional memberships, affiliations, and/or associations	CONSIDER including

(continued)

Figure 15.4 **Resume Guidelines (*continued*)**

Publications and presentations	CONSIDER including
Current *business* phone number and/or address (where you are working at the moment)	DO NOT include
"Availability" date/time to begin work	DO NOT include
Geographic limitations	DO NOT include
Personal hobbies or interests	DO NOT include
Personal information, such as age, sex, health status, marital status, parental status, ethnicity, or religious affiliations	DO NOT include
Photos	DO NOT include
Salary requirements or money issues	DO NOT include (unless specifically asked to provide a salary history)
References	DO NOT include, but have the information ready on a separate sheet of paper that matches your resume

TYPES OF RESUMES

What Are the Major Differences?

There are different types of resumes, but they can mainly be classified as chronological resumes, functional resumes, accomplishment resumes, or a combination. Your job package may also contain a portfolio. You might also consider submitting a video resume or a resume that can be easily scanned and sent electronically. Each type of resume is described below and several are modelled on the following pages.

- A **chronological resume** organizes education and work experience in a reverse chronological order (your last or present job is listed first).

- A **functional resume** (Figure 15.5) organizes your work and experience around specific skills and duties.

- An **accomplishment resume** allows you to place your past accomplishments into categories that are not necessarily associated with an employer, but show your track record of "getting the job done." This type of resume is usually reserved for those with previous work experience.

- A **video resume** is a resume that showcases your experiences and talent through a brief (3–5 minute) video recording. A video resume might be used to supplement a traditional resume and show your creative and technological skills. Some employers, however, will not accept video resumes because they can lead to claims of bias.

- A **scannable resume** (Figure 15.6) is a resume with very little formatting that uses a clear font, such as Courier, Arial, or Times New Roman. These resumes may appear to be less visually appealing, but they are easier to read once scanned. You may be asked to send your resume as a PDF. A PDF file basically takes a snapshot of your document exactly as it was prepared and ensures that your electronic resume remains just as you designed it.

- An **electronic (or plain text) resume** (Figure 15.7) is one that can be easily sent online and scanned electronically for **keywords and skills** based on the company's needs and job advertisement. It is saved in **American Standard Code for Information Interchange** (ASCII) format. When designing your electronic resume, consider the spacing, formatting, and fonts. Avoid italics, bullets (use asterisks instead), and columns. Align the text on the left. Do not indent with tabs or use parentheses or brackets. To save your current or future resume as an electronic or plain text resume, simply click "Save As," and in the "Save as type" box, select "Plain Text." Then re-open your file and make adjustments, corrections, and additions.

- A **portfolio** is a binder, website, CD-ROM, flash drive, or cloud file that showcases your very best work. It details your projects, awards, certificates, certifications, degrees, transcripts, military experience, and major accomplishments. Your portfolio should always be specific to the position for which you are applying.

ONLINE APPLICATIONS

How Can I Make a Strong Electronic Impression?

Often, employers will ask you to complete an **online application** instead of submitting a resume or cover letter. Some will require all three. Employers have found that online applications are easier to disseminate to the right people at the right time. The following tips will help you complete a successful online application and make a strong, lasting impression.

- Verify the existence and authenticity of the company before you complete an online application.
- Complete an online job application package with sites such as Monster.com, Careerbuilder.com, or LinkedIn.com before you begin filling out company-specific online applications, as they may ask for a link to your material.
- **Read** the instructions. Mistakes on an online application are as bad as mistakes on a hard-copy resume or cover letter.
- Download the application as a hard copy and fill it out by hand before you complete the application online. This gives you the opportunity to polish your wording and check the accuracy of your dates, names, and numbers.
- Use **keywords** found in the company's job announcement in your online application so the computer will select your application.
- If possible, examine sample online applications from the company before completing your application.
- Complete all fields (boxes) of the online application.
- Do not provide any personal information in an online application, such as mother's maiden name, bank account information, or credit card numbers. No reputable company will ask for these.
- As with your resume, strive for truth and accuracy in dates, names, locations, skills, and accomplishments. Your online application should match your resume.
- As with a resume, tailor your online application to the specific job for which you are applying.
- Send references only if requested.
- Keep a file (hard copy or electronic) of all online applications, materials sent, dates on which they were sent, attachments, and the actual job announcements.
- Re-read your application for spelling and grammar. If possible, have someone read the application with you before you submit it.
- If at all possible, follow up your online application with a personal e-mail or phone call to the employer.

Figure 15.5 Functional Resume

BENJAMIN SHAW

1234 Lake Shadow Drive, Maple City, PA 12345   (123) 555-1234   ben@online.com

OBJECTIVE: To work as a medical assistant in an atmosphere that uses my organizational abilities, technical skills, people skills, compassion for patients, desire to make a difference, and impeccable work ethic.

SKILLS:

Bilingual (English/Spanish)	Data Protection
Claims Reimbursement	Client Relations
Highly organized and motivated	Problem-Solving Skills
Expert in Word, Excel, PowerPoint	Team Player
Priority Management Skills	Delegating Ability
Strategic Planning	Budget Management

PROFESSIONAL PREPARATION:

Occupational Associate's Degree—Medical Assistant
Victory Health Institute, Harrisburg, PA
May 2013 (with honors)

Certificate of Completion—Medical Transcription
Philadelphia Technical Institute
December 2010

Vocational High School Diploma—Health Sciences
Philadelphia Vocational High School
August 2005

PROFESSIONAL EXPERIENCE:

January 2012–Present	Medical Assistant Intern Mercy Family Care Practice, Harrisburg, PA
February 2006–December 2012	Medical Transcriptionist The Office of Brenda Wilson, MD, Lancaster, PA
March 2001–February 2006	Ward Orderly Wallace Hospital, Lancaster, PA
August 1999–March 2001	Administrative Assistant Ellen Abbot Nursing Care Facility
References:	Provided upon request

Figure 15.6 Scannable Resume

BENJAMIN SHAW

1234 Lake Shadow Drive, Maple City, PA 12345   ben@online.com
(H) 123-456-7890 (C) 123-456-1232

OBJECTIVE

Seeking a position as a medical assistant in an atmosphere that uses my organizational abilities, communication skills, computer expertise, compassion for patients, desire to make a difference, and impeccable work ethic.

PROFESSIONAL EXPERIENCE

January 2012–Present

Medical Assistant Intern
Mercy Family Care Practice, Harrisburg, PA

- Responsible for completing patient charts
- Take patients' vitals
- Assist with medical coding

February 2006–December 2012

Medical Transcriptionist
The Office of Brenda Wilson, MD, Lancaster, PA

- Interpreted and typed medical reports
- Worked with insurance documentation
- Served as Office Manager (1/05–12/06)

March 2001–February 2006

Ward Orderly
Wallace Hospital, Lancaster, PA

- Assisted nurses with patient care
- Cleaned patient rooms
- Served patient meals

EDUCATION

Occupational Associate's Degree—Medical Assistant
Victory Health Institute, Harrisburg, PA
May 2012 (with honors)

Certificate of Completion—Medical Transcription
Philadelphia Technical Institute
December 2010

Vocational High School Diploma—Health Sciences
Philadelphia Vocational High School
August 2005

Figure 15.7 Electronic (Plain Text) Resume

BENJAMIN SHAW   E-mail: ben@online.com
Box F-123 Pittsburgh, PA 12345 Phone: 555-123-4567

OBJECTIVE
Seeking a position as a medical assistant in an atmosphere that uses my organizational abilities, communication skills, computer expertise, compassion for patients, desire to make a difference, and impeccable work ethic.

QUALIFICATIONS SUMMARY
Health management, client relations, order processing, data protection, interpersonal skills, accounting, marketing, health policy, claims reimbursement, problem solving, leadership, responsible, management skills

----

COMPUTER SKILLS
Word, PowerPoint, Excel, Outlook, Publisher, Prezi, HTML/Web publishing, Facebook, and Twitter

----

PROFESSIONAL EXPERIENCE
January 2012–Present
Medical Assistant Intern
Mercy Family Care Practice, Harrisburg, PA
*Responsible for completing patient charts
*Take patients' vitals
*Assist with medical coding and billing

February 2006–December 2012
Medical Transcriptionist
The Office of Brenda Wilson, MD, Lancaster, PA
*Interpreted and typed medical reports
*Worked with insurance documentation
*Assisted with medical coding
*Served as Office Manager (5/08–12/12)

EDUCATION
Occupational Associate's Degree, Medical Assistant
Victory Health Institute, Harrisburg, PA
May 2012 (with honors)
Certificate of Completion, Medical Transcription
Philadelphia Technical Institute
December 2006

RELEVANT COURSES AND SKILLS
Human Anatomy & Physiology I, II, III
Public Health Policy
Organizational Health Care
Human Resource Management
Bilingual (English and Spanish)
Excellent Client Relations
Treatment Procedure Guidelines

Successful Decisions

AN ACTIVITY **FOR CRITICAL REFLECTION**

$\mathcal{R}$ichard had never held a professional job. He had only held a series of odd jobs for friends and family members. When it came time for Richard to begin applying for a full-time position, he was unsure who to ask to serve as his references.

He began to think about his past part-time job, and decided that his old boss at the gas station, James Cartman, might help him. His boss was a friend of his father, and he only worked for him for two months during class break, but he knew that he had done a good job for Mr. Cartman.

Richard stopped by the gas station to ask if he could use Mr. Cartman's name on his applications. Mr. Cartman told Richard that he would be happy to speak about his work ethic and reliability. Now, Richard only needed two more people.

How could Richard locate two more people to serve as his references?

_____

_____

Should Richard contact these people by phone, e-mail, Facebook, or another method? Justify your answer.

_____

_____

Figure 15.8 **Selecting References**

In the space provided in Figure 15.8, list three people you could ask to serve as references for you (or who could write you a reference letter). Once you have identified these three people, list the skills that each person could speak to on your behalf. Think about this carefully, as it is important to choose references who can speak to your many qualifications, not just one or two. Choose people who know you in different areas of success.

Level 1 Remember

Level 5 Evaluate

Person	Qualification She/He Can Write About
JoAnna Thompson	My oral communication skills My attention to detail My ability to get along with others
Beau DeTiberious	My ability to form a team My ability to motivate team members My ability to meet deadlines
Person 1 _____	_____ _____ _____
Person 2 _____	_____ _____ _____
Person 3 _____	_____ _____ _____

NETWORKING

Is "Who You Know" More Important Than "What You Know?"

It will be important for you to develop a network among the people you know who may work for a company in which you have an interest. People on the inside have an advantage in helping you get your foot in the door. What about your dad's co-worker? Your wife's friend? What about a graduate who is your friend and knows your work style, and may be working for a company in which you have an interest? Use every method you have to get the interview. Some important networking opportunities include:

- Attending events and conferences on and off campus
- Joining professional organizations in your field of study
- Shadowing professionals in your field
- Volunteering within your community
- Working in externships or internships in your field
- Contacting family and friends about opportunities
- Logging onto websites and job search social networking sites, such as:
  - www.monster.com
  - www.career.com
  - www.careerbuilder.com
  - www.yahoohotjobs.com
  - www.indeed.com
  - www.craigslist.org
- Talking to your instructors
- Working with headhunters or recruiters
- Contacting a temp agency in the city in which you hope to work
- Working with your school's counselors and career officers
- Interviewing and connecting with guest speakers who came to your class

THE INTERVIEW

How Do You Make the Impression of a Lifetime?

Remember the "*eight seconds rule*" for making an impression? Consider this: during the interview process, you have even less time. A judgment is made immediately about you based on your dress, your grooming, your stance, your handshake, and your overall visual impression. Right or wrong, the interviewer will form an immediate first opinion of you—just as you will form an immediate first impression of your interviewer.

There are several ways your potential employer might choose to conduct the interview. In today's globally connected world, the standard face-to-face interview may not be the first choice of an employer, especially if they have to pay for your travel expenses to have you visit the office. Your interview may take one of the following forms.

In Person—This type of interview takes place face-to-face with one person or with a group of people. The interview usually happens at the place of business.

Electronic—With so many electronic ways to communicate, some employers are interviewing potential employees over the Internet, using Skype, Go To Meeting, WebEx, or another networking site.

Social—You may have an interview where you are asked to join the members of the interview team at a restaurant or outside the business location.

Phone—Because of the high cost of bringing in someone to an interview, many employers will conduct the first interview over the phone. If you do well and they are impressed, they will then bring you in for an in-person interview.

As you begin to prepare for your interview, consider the mnemonic **REWARDS**. If you confidently *carry REWARDS* with you to an interview, you will most likely *get* rewards after the interview, such as a job offer, benefits, and a career in which you can grow and prosper.

R = Rapport

Rapport is basically your "relationship" (intended or unintended) with another person—the emotional alliance you establish with someone. Consider how you come across to others. Rapport involves your verbal and nonverbal communication efforts. You should strive to establish a positive relationship with potential employers and future colleagues.

E = Education and Training

Be confident about what you know and eloquently promote your abilities, skills, and talents to the interviewer. Remember, if you don't promote yourself, it is unlikely that anyone else will.

W = Willingness

Project a sense of willingness to learn new things, to become a team member, to assist the company with growth and new projects, and to keep up with advancements and changes in the modern world of work. Potential employers enjoy seeing an attitude of willingness and engagement.

A = Appearance

Dress for success. Pay close attention to your grooming, your hygiene, your hair, your clothing, and yes, even your shoes and socks (or hosiery). It all matters—and it is all noticed. Never make the mistake of thinking that appearance is not important. You also want to consider dressing for a specific type of job. Careers in health studies may require a different type of interview dress than careers in aviation maintenance, engineering, or business.

In the past, what preparations have served you best in getting ready for an interview?

R = Response

Project positivity and optimism in your responses to the questions asked in the interview. Even if you have to talk about your weaknesses or past experiences of conflict and turmoil, put a positive spin on them. Let the interviewer know that you have learned from adversity.

D = Demeanor

Project an aura of confidence (not cockiness), intelligence, professionalism, and positivity. Carrying yourself with confidence during the interview will not go unnoticed. Pay attention to your handshake, your eye contact, your posture, your mannerisms, and your facial expressions.

S = Sincerity

No one likes phony people, especially a potential employer. Be yourself and strive to be sincere in your answers, your emotions, and your passion.

Getting Prepared

Just as you prepare for exams, you will need to prepare for the interview. Please do not make the common mistake of thinking that your degree or past work experience will get you the job. It may, but more often than you would believe, it is the interview and the relationship that you establish that day that gets you the offer. Your experience and credentials are important, but nothing is more important than you, how well you are prepared for this day, and how well you represent yourself. As you prepare for your interview, consider the following sound advice:

Days before the interview:

- Prepare extra copies of your resume to take to the interview. Though one person typically conducts interviews, some employers designate several people to sit in on the interview process.

- Place your extra resumes, references, and other job search information in a professional portfolio (leather binder) or nice folder. Avoid carrying loose papers, and never carry a backpack to an interview.

- Prepare a typed reference sheet and take several copies to the interview.

- Using the research that you have done on the company, make a list of questions that you want to ask the interviewer. Never attend an interview without asking questions yourself. You are interviewing them, just as they are interviewing you. Interviewers are much more impressed if they think you have researched the company and if you have questions to ask.

- Have a friend or colleague sit with you and ask you questions that you might anticipate. Have them throw a few "surprise questions" your way, too.

- Make sure you know how to get to the interview site. Make a dry run if you have to. Being late for your interview will be the "kiss of death" for that job.

- Be sure you have enough gas to reach your destination if you are driving yourself. What is the availability for parking? Will you need to allow time for finding a parking space?

The day of, and on the way to, the interview:

- Bring a pen, paper, and calendar with you to the interview. These can be kept in your portfolio.

- Know where your items are located so that you do not have to search for them during an interview. Fumbling around makes you look unorganized and unprepared.

- Be certain that your clothes are clean and pressed, and your shoes are spotless and shined.

- Arrive at the interview at least 15 minutes early.

- If you are a smoker, **do not** smoke in the car on the way to the interview, and try to avoid smoking in your interview clothes. Often, the smell of cigarette smoke lingers for hours and clings to your clothing. For many, this is an immediate turn-off. Some employers will find a way not to hire a smoker because of increased insurance premiums paid for smokers.

- Do not carry any type of food or drink into the interview with you.

- Before you enter the building, **turn off** your cell phone, pager, Blackberry, iPod, tablet, and any other electronic device, except your hearing aid, pacemaker, or other life-assisting device. Turn them off! Period! There is *no* excuse for your cell phone to ring during an interview. No one, including you, is that important.

During the interview:

- Establish eye contact and work to develop an immediate rapport.

- Offer a firm handshake to everyone in the room.

- Speak with clarity and enunciate your words.

- Ask where to sit if you are not told upon entering the room.

- Enter with a positive and upbeat attitude.

- Jot down the names of everyone in the room as they are introduced to you. You may even draw an impromptu "seating chart" to remind you of who's who in the room.

- Refer to people by their names if you address them during the interview.

- Answer every question asked, as long as the question is legal.

- You don't have to be deadly serious or stodgy, but it is advisable to avoid jokes or off-color humor during the interview process.

- **Never** downgrade or talk badly about a past job or employer. This will only come back to haunt you.

- If at all possible, do not discuss any aspect of your personal life, such as children, marriage, family, etc.

- **Never** ask about money or company benefits during an interview, especially during the *first* interview, unless the interviewer approaches the topic. Let them lead this discussion. If you are asked about salary requirements, respond with this question: "What is the range for this job?" In negotiations of any kind, you want the other person to offer information first. If you think you are highly qualified, respond with a salary amount close to the top of the range by saying, "Based on my qualifications and experience, I would consider a salary of $ _____."

After the interview:

- Shake hands with everyone in the room and thank them for the opportunity to meet with them. Let them know that you were honored to have the opportunity. Humility goes a long way.
- Politely let them know that you enjoyed the interview and that you are very interested in the position.
- Ask each person in the room for a business card. This provides you with their correct name spelling, address, and e-mail address for use in future correspondence.
- Don't linger around the site unless you are told to wait—this makes you look desperate.
- *Always* follow up with a personalized thank you note.

General Tips:

- Remember the cardinal rule of interviewing: Interviewers are not interested in what the company can do for you; they are interested in what you can do for the company. Therefore, you must present your case on why you want to work for the company and the contributions you are prepared to make.
- Be truthful in every aspect of the job search: the application, your resume, your cover letter, your portfolio, your references, your question responses, your salary history, and yes, your interest in the position.
- Be nice and gracious to everyone you meet—they may be the person with whom you interview in a few moments.

ANTICIPATING THE INTERVIEWER'S QUESTIONS

Can You Answer Hard Questions with a Positive Attitude?

Richard Nelson Bolles, author of *What Color is Your Parachute* (2012), *the* most widely published job-hunting book in history (with over 10 million copies in print), makes an astounding assertion. He states, "You don't have to spend hours memorizing a lot of 'good answers' to potential questions from the employer; there are only five questions that matter." Wow—five questions!

With this statement, *do not* think that you will only be asked five questions, but rather Mr. Bolles is suggesting that with every question asked of you, the interviewer is trying to get to the heart of the matter—the five basic questions:

1. Why are you here?
2. What can you do for us?
3. What kind of person are you?
4. What distinguishes you from the nineteen other people who can do the same tasks that you can?
5. Can I afford you?

What do you have to offer an employer that is unique to you?

So, how do interviewers get to "the heart of the matter?" How do they pull the answers to these five questions from you? Ironically, they do it by asking many, many other question. This section will offer you insight into some common, and not so common, questions asked by today's employers.

It is usually customary that the interviewer will make "small talk" for a few minutes to give you time to relax and get comfortable. You should avoid answering questions with a simple "yes" or "no." Briefly elaborate on your answers without talking too much. For example, if the interviewer says, "I hope you had no trouble finding our building," you should not just answer "no." You might say something like, "Not at all. I live near here so I was familiar with the location. Actually, I had a part-time job when I was a sophomore and I brought materials to one of your managers from my department chair."

Interviewers will often say to you, "Tell me about yourself." They are not looking for your life history as much as they are gathering background information on you and observing how well you can present information. Provide highlights of your education, experience, and accomplishments. If you are just yourself and enjoy the process, this will show.

The interviewer might then ask you, "What do you know about our company?" This is a good opportunity for you to show how prepared you are. You could open your portfolio and tell the interviewer, *"When I was researching the company, I found some interesting facts on your website. I know that you are an international company based in New York and that you have over 4000 employees. I learned that you have several divisions including food processing and distribution, restaurants, and contract food sales. In fact, this information is the reason I applied for a job with you through our career center. My minor in college is Restaurant Management, and I think this company will be a great place to put my knowledge and skills to use."*

You will, of course, have to adapt your answer to your own situation. There is no way to be completely prepared for all questions an interviewer may ask. The key is to have anticipated the interviewer's questions and to be so comfortable with the message you want to convey about yourself that you sound confident and decisive. As you talk, remember to look at the interviewer and to lean forward slightly, which indicates that you are listening intently.

After a brief, "Let's-get-to-know-each-other" session, you can anticipate more direct and important questions. Some of the more common questions that you might expect include:

- Why should we hire you?
- Why are you interested in this company and in the position?
- When did you decide on a career in _____?
- Tell me about your extracurricular activities.
- What are your strengths?
- What are your weaknesses?
- Why did you leave your last job?
- Do you have a geographic preference? Why?
- Are you willing to relocate?
- Are you willing to travel?
- Do you have job experience in _____?
- What can you do for the company?
- What other companies are you interviewing with?
- Tell me about a difficult problem you have had and how you solved it.
- Tell me about a time when you worked under stress.
- What kind of accomplishment gives you the greatest satisfaction?
- What are your long- and short-range goals?
- Where do you see yourself in five years?
- What one word best describes you?
- How do you deal with difficult people?

- Describe one goal you have set over the past six months and how you went about accomplishing it.
- What is the biggest mistake you ever made? What did you learn from it?
- What subject in school gave you the most challenges? Why?
- What past experiences or courses have prepared you for this position?
- Would you prefer to work alone or with a group of people? Why?

Regardless of the question asked, your primary responsibility in the interview is to be straightforward and honest, and answer the question to the very best of your ability.

ASK INFORMED QUESTIONS

Am I Allowed to Interview the Interviewer?

You should feel free to ask the interviewer questions during the interview, but the interviewer should lead the majority of the first part of the interview. At the close of the interview, you may be asked if you have any questions. If this opportunity is not offered, you should say, "I have a few questions, if you don't mind." Asking questions of the interviewer is impressive and indicates to them that you are interviewing them as well. Some typical questions follow.

- How would you describe a typical day in this position?
- What kind of training can I anticipate?
- What is the probationary period of employment?
- What are the opportunities for personal growth and professional development?
- To whom would I report?
- Will I have an opportunity to meet some of my coworkers?
- Would you describe the training program?
- When will my first job performance evaluation take place?
- Why do you enjoy working for this company?
- How would you describe the most successful person working at this company? Why?
- What objectives do you expect a new employee to meet in the first six months?
- Can you tell me about an assignment I might be asked to do?
- What happened to the person who most recently held this position?
- What do you see as the major challenges facing this organization? Why?
- How would you describe the "culture" of the workplace in this organization?
- What does this company value?

ROUGH, TOUGH, HARD QUESTIONS

How Do You Effectively Manage Inappropriate or Illegal Questions?

Sadly, you may encounter questions that are either inappropriate or even illegal. Remember, federal and state laws may prohibit many questions that deal with your personal life, but, "*No single federal, state, or local agency or court defines for all cases which interview questions are legal or illegal. Instead, a plethora of court rulings, legislative decisions, agency regulations, and constitutional*

from ORDINARY to Extraordinary

Mark Jones
Senior Customer Service Trainer, SCANA, Columbia, SC

My proudest moment? Finally coming to the realization that I am a functional member of a highly dysfunctional family. *"I know. I know. Many people say they have a dysfunctional family,"* but in my case, it is the raw, inescapable truth. My realization may not sound like much to an outsider, but when you finally realize that you do not have to be a victim of your family or your past, it is a proud moment! I can confidently say, *"I am not like them."*

I don't have any memories of a time when my family was "normal." My mother, who has been clinically depressed my entire life, attempted suicide when I was four years old. I have never known a day when she was not heavily medicated. My father had the first of four heart attacks when I was six. My parents divorced when I was 11, and I remained with my father. My mother remarried when I was 13. When I was 15, my father died, leaving us very little. Even the mobile home in which we lived was repossessed.

My new stepfather was legally blind and has never driven a car. My mother does not drive either. They never wanted me to get my permit or drive, and fought my attempts to do so for years. They thought walking everywhere was perfectly normal. My stepfather did not have any children of his own, and did not have any parenting skills. I was treated more as a tenant than a son or stepson. As a matter of fact, I had to pay rent to live with him and my own mother. Due to my father's death, I drew a small Social Security check until I graduated from high school. Every month, much of that money had to be turned over to my stepfather. I even had to buy my own bed to sleep in. Of course, we had our share of good times, too, but I knew this situation was far from "normal"— whatever that was.

When I was in my early twenties, I begged a dear friend, Stella, to let me use her car so I could try for my driver's license. I had practically no driving experience, but somehow, I passed the test. I paid $200 for my first car in two installments of $100 each. It was a 1973 Buick LaSabre that was wrecked down one entire side and had been used in demolition donut field races—but it was much better than walking everywhere.

laws combine to produce the often confusing and frequently changing list of what you can and can't ask a job applicant" (Bell & Smith, 2004). Federal laws, including the Civil Rights Act of 1964 and the Americans with Disabilities Act of 1990, do regulate certain questions that cannot be asked during an interview.

If illegal or inappropriate questions are asked in person or on an application, it can be challenging to manage them and still retain your composure and decorum. It is up to you how much you want to tell a potential employer about your personal life or lifestyle. They can only demand an answer if the question is directly related to a legal requirement of the job such as bartending or commercial piloting to name a few. Consider the following questions that should *not* be asked during the interview, but that may be asked anyway. With some exceptions, employers should not ask you about:

- Your age
- Your marital status, your parental status, or your living situation
- Your race or national origin
- Your sexual orientation
- Your religious affiliation

This was a turning point in my life. I was in my early twenties and working in a local grocery store. I enrolled in the university right after high school, but I had to drop out because I could not get a grant and did not make enough money to pay tuition. I later enrolled in the local community college, but after one semester, I realized I could not afford this either.

Basically, I had to make a hard, life-altering decision. I did not want to live my life in debt as my father had done, so I made up my mind that I would have to take a few steps back to eventually go forward. I began to look for a job that offered educational benefits. I scanned the phonebook for hospitals, utility companies, banks, and government agencies that offered this benefit. Every Monday night, their job lines would be updated, and I would call, fill out an application, and wait. Nothing!

Finally, I learned how to properly fill out an application. I would call the job line many times and write down every word in their advertisement. Then, I would craft my application and letter based on *their needs,* not *my experiences.* I had to learn to apply for a job as if I already had it. After two years and many attempts to secure a suitable position, a utility company hired me—*and* they had educational benefits. Finally, I could go back to school and get another car! I began working toward my degree, and after six long, hard years, I graduated with a Bachelor of Science in Business Management. It was

> *I paid $200 for my first car—a 1973 Buick LaSabre that was wrecked down one entire side and had been used in demolition donut field races.*

not easy, as I am sure you know. I had to take some courses online, and I was in class every Friday night for years and years.

During my time in college, I worked my way up in the company, and today, seventeen years later, I am a senior trainer for SCANA, an $11 billion, Fortune 500 utility holding company founded in 1846. I design training programs and development materials for new hires, system enhancements, and employee upgrades.

I look back on my childhood and early adulthood and I am proud of the fact that I did not let my past or my family dictate my future. I survived. I refused to succumb to their life. I knew that I had to have my own life with my own fate. You can have this, too! Never let your past or your family tell you what you're capable of doing. Take chances. Take risks. And, if you have to take a step backward to go forward, never be ashamed to do that, too.

EXTRAORDINARY REFLECTION

Mr. Jones came from a family that did not support him financially, emotionally, or educationally. What advice would you give to someone who might be experiencing the same type of environment? Does your family have to play a role in your life for you to be successful?

- Your political affiliation
- Your physical limitations or your mental/emotional limitations
- Your physical attributes
- Your financial status
- Your personal habits
- Your *arrest* status (remember, arrest and conviction are different)
- Your affiliations
- Your military status
- Your school and/or college records

Basically it comes down to money. It is very expensive to hire, train, and retain an employee in today's workforce. An employer wants to know as much about you as possible, and they basically want to know if you are qualified, if you will get along with others, and if you will be at work when you say you will be there.

How would you handle an illegal question during an interview?

WIN, LOSE, OR DRAW, ALWAYS SAY "THANK YOU" IN WRITING

Do I Have to Say Thank You Even if I Don't Get the Job?

Indeed, it is safe to say that failing to send a thank you note is *"the most overlooked step in the entire job search process"* (Bolles, 2012). Yes, this is a mandatory step for every interview, and it is mandatory that you send one to every person who interviewed you. Period. In today's high-tech and fast-paced world, this one act will set you apart from the thousands who interview on a daily basis. And yes, you must send a thank you letter even if you *do not* get the job. "When do I send the thank you note?" you might ask. *Immediately after the interview.*

Sending a simple thank you note does many things—it lets the employer know that you have good manners, that you respect other people's time and efforts, that you are considerate, that you really do care about the position, and that you have positive people and communication skills. Yes, all of that from a card and stamp that can cost less than $2.

In Figures 15.9 and 15.10, you will find examples of two thank you notes. Review them and consider using them as a template when writing your own notes.

Figure 15.9 Sample Thank You Note—After the Interview

BENJAMIN SHAW
1234 Lake Shadow Drive
Maple City, PA 12345
ben@online.com

January 20, 2013

Mr. James Pixler, RN, CAN
Director of Placement and Advancement
Grace Care Center
123 Sizemore Street, Suite 444
Philadelphia, PA 12345

Dear Mr. Pixler,

Thank you for the wonderful opportunity to meet with you and the team at Grace Care Center on Monday. Your facilities are amazing, and the new wing is going to be a remarkable addition to your center.

I enjoyed learning more about the new position in Medical Assisting, and I think that my qualifications and experiences have prepared me for this challenging opportunity. I would consider it an honor to answer any further questions that you might have or to meet with you again if you consider it necessary.

I look forward to hearing from you at your convenience. If you need any additional information, you can reach me at 123-555-1234.

Thank you,

Benjamin Shaw

Benjamin Shaw

Figure 15.10 Sample Thank You Note—After a Position Rejection

BENJAMIN SHAW
1234 Lake Shadow Drive
Maple City, PA 12345
ben@online.com

January 20, 2013

Mr. James Pixler, RN, CAN
Director of Placement and Advancement
Grace Care Center
123 Sizemore Street, Suite 444
Philadelphia, PA 12345

Dear Mr. Pixler,

Thank you for the opportunity to meet with you and the team at Grace Care Center on Monday. I enjoyed learning more about your center and the planned addition.

While I was not offered the position, I did want to let you know that I appreciate your time and I would like for you to contact me if you have any future openings where you feel my qualifications and experiences would match your needs. Grace is an incredible facility, and I would consider it an honor to hold a position there.

If you need to contact me in the future, you can reach me at 123-555-1234.

Thank you for your time and assistance, and best wishes to you and your colleagues.

Sincerely,

Benjamin Shaw

Benjamin Shaw

CHANGING IDEAS *to Reality*

REFLECTIONS ON CAREER AND LIFE PLANNING

This is your one lifetime! You need to prepare to do something you love. No matter how much money you make, you won't be happy unless you are doing something that matters to you, something that allows you to keep learning and becoming, something that provides you opportunities to give back—perhaps the best gift of all.

As you reflect on this chapter, keep the following pointers in mind:

- Learn how to make yourself a desirable employee.
- Set yourself apart with a dynamic cover letter and resume.
- Select references who can speak to your many talents and skills.
- Learn to promote and sell yourself in an interview.
- Send thank you notes after your interview.
- Present yourself in a professional, educated manner.

PREPARING YOUR RESUME

Utilizes Levels 1–6 of the Taxonomy (See Bloom's Taxonomy at the front of this text)

YOUR RESUME WORKSHEET

Now, it is your turn. After reviewing the information for resume writing and the example resumes, begin compiling information to build your own chronological resume using this template or an online template.

PERSONAL INFORMATION

Name

_____

Address

_____

_____

Phone Number(s)

_____

E-mail address

_____

Website

_____

WORK EXPERIENCE (EMPLOYMENT HISTORY)

1. (most recent)
Company name

_____

Your position and duties

_____

_____

2. (next most recent)
Company name

_____

Your position and duties

_____

Your duties/job responsibilities

_____

_____

_____

EDUCATION AND TRAINING (LIST YOUR CURRENT OR MOST RECENT JOB FIRST)

Name of institution

_____

Name and date of degree(s)

_____

Honors/recognition

_____

_____

ADDITIONAL TRAINING

Name of institution

_____

Name and date of certificate or training program

_____

_____

SPECIAL SKILLS, QUALIFICATIONS, COMMUNITY OR COLLEGE SERVICE

List any skills and qualifications that you possess that may be of interest to an employer. List the *exact* skill so that these words can be picked up from a scannable resume. Example: Word, PowerPoint, Excel, etc.

_____

_____

_____

_____

REFERENCES

List the names, addresses, and phone numbers of at least three people whom you could ask to serve as a reference for you.

1. _____

2. _____

3. _____

Locate a position for which you would like to apply. Practice writing a job-specific objective.

_____

_____

_____

_____

_____

SQ3R MASTERY STUDY SHEET

EXAMPLE QUESTION (FROM PAGE 358) Why is it important to write an excellent resume?	**ANSWER:**
EXAMPLE QUESTION (FROM PAGE 358) What does DOCTOR stand for?	**ANSWER:**
AUTHOR QUESTION (FROM PAGE 360) What are the three major types of resumes?	**ANSWER:**
AUTHOR QUESTION (FROM PAGE 361) What is a portfolio? What should it include?	**ANSWER:**
AUTHOR QUESTION (FROM PAGE 365) Why do references matter?	**ANSWER:**
AUTHOR QUESTION (FROM PAGE 365) How do you select a reference?	**ANSWER:**
AUTHOR QUESTION (FROM PAGE 374) Why do you need to write a thank you note, even if you do not get the position?	**ANSWER:**
YOUR QUESTION (FROM PAGE ____)	**ANSWER:**
YOUR QUESTION (FROM PAGE ____)	**ANSWER:**
YOUR QUESTION (FROM PAGE ____)	**ANSWER:**
YOUR QUESTION (FROM PAGE ____)	**ANSWER:**
YOUR QUESTION (FROM PAGE ____)	**ANSWER:**

Finally, after answering these questions, recite this chapter's major points in your mind. Consider the following general questions to help you master this material.

- What is it about?
- What does it mean?
- What is the most important thing you learned? Why?
- What are the key points to remember?

Adler, R., Rosenfeld, L., & Proctor, R. (2010). *Interplay: The Process of Interpersonal Communication* (11th ed.). New York: Oxford University Press.

Altman, I., & Taylor, D. (1973). Social Penetration: The Development of Interpersonal Relationships. New York, NY: Holt.

Anderson, L., & Bolt, S. (2008). *Professionalism: Real Skills for Workplace Success.* Upper Saddle River, NJ: Pearson/Prentice Hall

Anxiety Disorders Associations of America. (2012). "Depression: Understanding the Facts." Retrieved August 8, 2012, from www.adaa.org/understanding-anxiety/depression.

Bach, D. (2003). *The Finish Rich Notebook.* New York, NY: Broadway Books.

Baxter, L. A. (1993). Conflict Management: An Episodic Approach. *Small Group Behavior, 13*(1), 23–42.

Beebe, S., Beebe, S., & Redmond, M. (2008). *Interpersonal Communication: Relating to Others* (5th ed.). Boston, MA: Allyn and Bacon.

Begley, S. (2011, March 7). "I can't think." *Newsweek.*

Bell, A., & Smith, D. (2004). *Interviewing for Success.* Upper Saddle River, NJ: Prentice Hall

Block, S. (2006, February 22). Students Suffocate Under Tens of Thousands in Loans. *USA Today.*

Bolles, R. N. (2012). *What Color Is Your Parachute? A Practical Manual for Job-Hunters and Career-Changers.* Berkeley, CA: Ten Speed Press.

Boolean Searching on the Internet: A Primer in Boolean Logic. Retrieved April 13, 2012, from www.internettutorials.net/boolean.asp.

Bosack, J. (1978). *Fallacies.* Dubuque, IA: Educulture.

Branden, N. (1994). *The Six Pillars of Self-Esteem.* New York, NY: Bantam.

Briggs-Myers. (1998). *Introduction to Type: A Guide to Understanding Results on the Myers-Briggs Type Indicator,* 6th ed. Gainesville, FL: Center for Applications of Psychological Type.

Britton-Whitcomb, S. (2003). *Resumé Magic: Trade Secrets of a Professional Resumé Writer.* Indianapolis, IN: JIST Works.

Buscaglia, L. (1982). *Living Learning, and Loving.* New York: Fawcett Columbine.

Career Center at The University of South Carolina. (n.d.). "Four Year Student Plan." Retrieved August 8, 2012, from www.sc.edu/career/Pdf/fouryearstudentplan.pdf.

College Board. (2008). "College Prices Increase in Step with Inflation: Financial Aid Grows But Fewer Private Loans Even Before Credit Crisis." Retrieved from www.college board.com/press/releases/201194.html.

"College Dropout Rate Climbs as Students Face Challenges; Life Coach Offers College Tips to Success." (2007, September 12). Retrieved from http://newsblaze.com/story/20070912020000800001.mwir/topstory.html.

Collins, J. (2001). *Good to Great: Why Some Companies Make the Leap and Others Don't.* New York: Harper Business.

Consumer Report, 2012; Retrieved on August 3, 2012 from http://www.consumerreports.org/cro/2012/02/debunking-the-hype-over-id-theft/index.htm

Consumer Response Center brochure,(2003); Identity Theft and Fraud,

Cooley, C. (1981). *The Social Self in American Thought.* New York, NY: Garland Press.

Coopersmith, S. (1981). *The Antecedents of Self-Esteem.* Palo Alto, CA: Consulting Psychologists Press.

Daly, J., & Engleberg, I. (2006). *Presentations in Everyday Life: Strategies for Effective Speaking.* Upper Saddle River, NJ: Allyn and Bacon.

The Digerati Life. (2008). "Lost Money: How Money Drains Add Up to $175,000 in 10 Years." Retrieved September 5, 2008, from www.thedigeratilife.com/blog/index.php/2008/07/31/lost-money-how-money-drains.

Donatelle, R., & Davis, L. (2002). *Health: The Basics.* Upper Saddle River, NJ: Prentice Hall.

Dresang, J. (2007, April 23). Liar! Liar! Won't Get Hired. In age of easy information, resume fibs can sabotage hunts for work. *Las Vegas Review Journal,* reprinted from *Milwaukee Journal Sentinel.*

Dunn, R., and Griggs, S. (2000). Practical Approaches to Using Learning Styles in Higher Education. New York, NY: Bergin & Garvey.

Eggleston, P. (2012). "Fear of Public Speaking." Retrieved April 17, 2012, from www.theegglestongroup.com/writing/fearspk1.php.

ERIC Digest. (2010). "Nontraditional College Students." Retrieved April 3, 2010, from www.ericdigests.org/1992-3/college.htm.

Farr, M., & Kursmark, L. (2005). *15 Minute Cover Letter: Write an Effective Cover Letter Right Now.* Indianapolis, IN: JIST Works.

Futrell, M. H. (2007). *A Nation of Locksmiths: Transitioning Our Educational System to Guarantee All of America's Children a Quality Education.* Washington, DC: National Committee of Teaching and America's Future.

G. T. Doran, "There's a S.M.A.R.T. Way to Write Management's Goals and Objectives," Management Review 70, no.11 (1981: 35-36).

Gamble, T., & Gamble, M. (1998). *Public Speaking in the Age of Diversity.* Boston: Pearson.

Gardner, H. (1983). Frames of Mind: The Theory of Multiple Intelligences. New York, NY: Basic Books.

Girdano, D., Dusek, D., & Everly, G. (2009). *Controlling Stress and Tension* (8th ed.). Boston: Benjamin Cummings.

The Goddess Path. (2009). "Mnemosyne, the Goddess of Memory." Retrieved from www.goddessgift.com.

Goleman, D. (2006). *Emotional Intelligence: Why It Can Matter More Than IQ,* 10th Anniversary Edition. New York, NY: Bantam.

Graham, S. (2009). *Identity: Passport to Freedom.* New York, NY: Success Books.

Graunke, S. S., & Woosley, S. A. (2005). An Exploration of the Factors That Affect the Academic Success of College Sophomores. *College Student Journal, 39*(2), 367–376.

Hall, E. (1966). *The Hidden Dimension.* Garden City, NY: Doubleday.

Hansen, R., & Hansen, K. (2012). What Do Employers Really Want? Top Skills and Values Employers Seek from Job Seekers. Retrieved April 3, 2012, from www.quintcareers.com/job_skills_values.html.

HealthCoach4Me. (2012). "Quit Smoking." Retrieved July 14, 2012, from www.healthcoach4me.com/en/health-library/quit-smoking.html.

Heath, C., & Heath, D. (2010). *Switch: How to Change Things When Change Is Hard.* New York: Crown Business.

Housden, R. (2007). Taking a Chance on Joy. *O's Guide To Life: The Best of the Oprah Magazine.* Birmingham, AL: Oxmoor House.

Ireland, S. (2003). *The Complete Idiot's Guide to the Perfect Resumé.* Indianapolis, IN: Alpha.

James, W. (2011). *The Collected Work of William James.* Amazon Digital Services.

Jung, C. (1921). Psychology Types. In *Collected Works of C. G. Jung* (Volume 6; R. Hull, Translator). Princeton, NJ: Princeton University Press. (Reprinted 1976)

Kabani, S. H. (2010). *The Zen of Social Media.* Dallas, TX: BenBella Books.

Kay, A. (2011, May 30). What Employers Want: 5 More Skills to Cultivate. *USA Today Online.* Retrieved April 5, 2012, from www.usatoday.com/money/jobcenter/workplace/kay/2011-05-30-skills-employers-want-part-ii_N.htm.

Kiewra, K., & Fletcher, H. (1984). The Relationship Between Note Taking Variables and Achievement Measure. *Human Learning, 3,* 273–280.

Kirszner, L. G., & Mandell, S. R. (1995). "Avoiding plagiarism." *The Holt Handbook* (4th ed.). Fort Worth: Harcourt and Brace, pp. 606–611.

Konowalow, S. (2003). *Planning Your Future: Keys to Financial Freedom.* Columbus, OH: Prentice Hall.

Lane, H. (1976). *The Wild Boy of Aveyron.* Cambridge, MA: Harvard University Press.

Lane, S. (2008). *Interpersonal Communication: Competence and Contexts.* Boston, MA: Allyn and Bacon.

Learn About Alcoholism. (2012). "Statistics on Alcoholism." Retrieved August 9, 2012, from www.learn-about-alcoholism.com/statistics-on-alcoholics.html.

Leher, J. (2010). *How We Decide.* New York, NY: Mariner Books.

Leinwood, D. (September 23, 2002). Ecstasy-Viagra Mix Alarms Doctors. *USA Today,* p. D4.

Maslow, A. (1943). A Theory of Human Motivation. *Psychological Review, 50,* 370–396.

Maxwell, J. (2002). *The 17 Essential Qualities of a Team Player.* Atlanta, GA: Thomas Nelson Publishers.

McCornack, S. (2007). *Reflect and Relate: An Introduction to Interpersonal Communication.* Boston: Bedford/St. Martin's Press.

McGraw, P. (2007). "9 Things Weight Loss Winners Know (That You Don't)". *O's Guide to Life: The Best of the Oprah Magazine.* Birmingham, AL: Oxmoor House.

MindTools. (2011). *The Ladder of Influence: Avoiding Jumping to Conclusions.* Retrieved May 2, 2011, from www.mindtool.com.

Moyer, L. (2012). "How to Get Your Audience's Attention in Thirty Seconds." Retrieved February 25, 2012, from www.sermoncentral .com/article.asp?article=a-Larry_Moyer_08_06_07&ac=true.

Nellie Mae (2010). "How Undergraduate Students Use Credit Cards. Retrieved on August 2, 2012 from http://static.mgnetwork.com/rtd/ pdfs/20090830_iris.pdf

Nelson, D., & Low, G. (2003). *Emotional Intelligence: Achieving Academic and Career Excellence.* Upper Saddle River, NJ: Prentice Hall.

Nobel Foundation. (1993). *Nelson Mandela—Biography.* Retrieved from http://nobelprize.org/nobel_prizes/peace/laureates.

Ormondroyd, J., Engle, M., and Cosgrave, T. (2001). *How to Critically Analyze Information Sources.* Cornell University Libraries. Retrieved from www.library.cornell.edu.

Orndorff, Bob. (2008). "Top Ten Career Strategies for Freshmen and Sophomores." Retrieved November 18, 2008, from www.jobweb .com/parents.aspx?id=50.

Owen, L. (1997). New Views of Learning: The Eighth Intelligence—Naturalistic. Retrieved August 1, 2012, from www4.uwsp.edu/ education/lwilson/learning/natintel.htm.

Pauk, W. (2007). *How to Study in College* (8th ed.). New York: Houghton Mifflin.

Paul, R., & Elder, L. (2006). *A Miniature Guide to Critical Thinking: Concepts and Tools.* Dillon Beach, CA: Foundation for Critical Thinking.

Payday Loan: Consumer Information. (2008). Retrieved February 12, 2009, from www.paydayloaninfo.org.

Platt, J. (2012). "Is Student Loan Debt Threatening Our Economic Recovery?" Retrieved April 10, 2012, from www.mnn.com/money/ personal-finance/stories.

A Profile of This Year's Freshmen. (2011, February 4). *The Chronicle of Higher Education,* p. 22.

Reynolds, P., Gross, J., & Millard, B. (2005). *Discovering Life Purpose: Retention Success in a Leadership Course at Indiana Wesleyan University.* Bloomington, IN: Indiana Project on Academic Success, Smith Center for Research, Indiana University.

Robbins, C. (2006). *The Job Searcher's Handbook* (3rd ed.). Upper Saddle River, NJ: Prentice Hall.

Rosato, D. (2008, July). Life Without Plastic. *Money,* pp. 91–95.

Russell, N. S. (2004). "Words, Words, Words." Retrieved October 7, 2008, from www.careerknowhow.com/improvement/words.htm.

Scholarship Watch (2012). Financial Aid. org. Retrieved on August 3, 2012 from Financial Aid http://www.naas.org/scholarships/tag/ finaid-org/

Shattuck, R. (1980). *The Forbidden Experiment: The Story of the Wild Boy of Aveyron.* New York, NY: Farrar, Straus & Giroux.

Shindell, B. (2011). "Ten Skills Employers Are Looking For. Good Job Hunting." Retrieved February 25, 2012, from www.coursepark .com/blog/2011/01/top-10-skills-employers-are-looking-for.

Smilkstein, R. (2003) *We're Born To Learn: Using The Brain's Natural Learning Process to Create Today's Curriculum.* Thousand Oaks, CA: Corwin Press.

Smith, B. (2007). *Breaking Through: College Reading* (8th ed.). Upper Saddle River, NJ: Pearson Education.

Snyder, C. R., & Lopez, S. (2007). *Positive Psychology: The Scientific and Practical Explorations of Human Strength.* Thousand Oaks, CA: Sage Publications.

Steinke, R. (2007). Women on the Rocks. *O's Guide to Life: The Best of the Oprah Magazine.* Birmingham, AL: Oxmoor House.

Sycle, B., & Tietje, B. (2010). *Anybody's Business.* Upper Saddle River, NJ: Pearson.

Tarkovsky, S. (2006). "Mind, Body, and Soul: The Key to Overall Wellness and Health." Retrieved September 11, 2006, from http://ezinearticles. com/?Mind,-Body,-and-Soul---The-Key-to-Overall-Wellness-and-Health.

Texas A&M University. (n.d.). "Improve Your Memory." Retrieved January 5, 2009, from www.scs.tamu.edu/ selfhelp/elibrary/ memory.asp.

Tidwell, L., & Walther, J. (2002, July). Computer-Mediated Communication Effects on Disclosure, Impressions, and Interpersonal Evaluations: Getting to Know One Another a Bit at a Time. *Human Communication Research, 28,* 317–348.

Tieger, P., & Barron-Tieger, B. (2007). *Do What You Are: Discover the Perfect Career for You Through the Secrets of Personality Type* (3rd ed.). Boston, MA: Little, Brown.

TimMcGraw.com (n.d.). "About Tim." Retrieved from www .timmcgraw.com/#about-tim.html.

Trudeau, K. (2007). *Debt Cures They Do Not Want You to Know About.* Pueblo, CO: Equity Press.

Turnitin.com. (n.d.). Retrieved September 30, 2008, from www .turnitin.com/static/home.html.

UC Berkeley—Teaching Library Internet Workshop. (2005). Evaluating Web Pages: Techniques to Apply and Questions to Ask. Retrieved from www.lib.berkeley.edu/TeachingLib/Guides/ Internet/Evaluate.htm.

U.S. Bureau of the Census, Department of Labor. (2011). *Education and Training Pay.* Washington, DC: U.S. Government Printing Office.

U.S. Bureau of Labor Statistics. (2011). "American Time Use Survey." Washington, DC: Department of Census. Retrieved April 16, 2012, from www.bls.gov.

U.S. Surgeon General's Office. (2012). "Preventing Tobacco Use among Youth and Young Adults." Retrieved August 9, 2012, from www.surgeongeneral.gov.

Waitley, D. (1997). *Psychology of Success: Developing Your Self-Esteem.* Boston: Irwin Career Education Division.

Wallechinsky, D. & Wallace, A. (2005). *The New Book of Lists: The Original Compendium of Curious Information.* New York, NY: Conongate Press.

Walther, J., & Burgoon, J. (1992). Relational Communication in Computer-Mediated Interaction. *Human Communication Research, 19,* 50–88.

WebMD. (2012). Depression Health Center. Retrieved April 26, 2012, from www.webmd.com/depression/guide/depression-symptoms-and-types.

Wechsler, H., & Wuethrich, B. (2002). *Dying to Drink: Confronting Binge Drinking on College Campuses.* New York, NY: Rodale Press.

Wetmore, D. (2008). "Time Management Facts and Figures." Retrieved December 1, 2008, from www.balancetime.com.

Wikipedia. (n.d.). "Tim McGraw." Retrieved from www.wikipedia.org/ wiki/Tim_McGraw.

Williams, E. (2008, June 26). "Students Need Help Combating Credit Card Debt. Testimony Before the House Financial Services Subcommittee on Financial Institutions and Consumer Credit." Retrieved September 2, 2008, from www.americanprogress.org/is-sues/2008/06/williams_testimony.html.

Wingfield, B. (2007, October 9). Help Unwanted: The Worst Jobs for the 21st Century. Forbes.com. Retrieved April 5, 2012, from www.forbes.com/2007/10/08/jobs-employment-economics-biz-wash-cx_bw_1009worstjobs.html.

Woolfolk, A. (2009). *Educational Psychology* (11th ed.). Upper Saddle River, NJ: Merrill.

Yerak, B. (2012, April 21). Student Loan Debt Seen as Growing Debt to Economy. *The Seattle Times.*

Yip, P. (2008, August 31). College Campuses Are Ripe for the Picking. *The State,* p. B22.

Zen Habits. (2008). "Simple Living Manifesto: 72 Ways to Simplify Your Life." Retrieved from http://zenhabits.net.

Zupek, R.(2011). Top 10 Reasons Employers Want to Hire You. CareerBuilder.com. Retrieved April 3, 2012, from www.cnn. com/2009/LIVING/worklife/11/02/cb.hire.reasons.job/index.html.

PHOTO CREDITS

INDEX

Abstinence, 337
Academic advisement centers, 61
Academic advisors, 60, 352–353
Academic Competitiveness
    Grant (ACG), 255
Academic freedom, 53–55
Academic misconduct, 59–60
Accomplishment resumes, 360
Acronyms, as mnemonic devices, 234
Action(s)
    in change, 10, 21
    in goal setting, 19
    values in, 40
Action-oriented listeners, 208–209
Active learning, 158, 192
Active reading, 182–183
Ad baculum, 118–120
Ad hominem, 118–119
Ad populum, 118–119
Ad verecundiam, 118–119
Adams, Jennifer, 50
Addiction
    to drugs and alcohol, 329–333
    to technology, 74
Adler, Joseph, 300
Adler, Ronald, 206, 306
Adult students, 63–64
Advisors, academic, 60, 352–353
AIDS, 335
Alcohol abuse, 329, 331, 332–333
Altman, Irwin, 306
American Psychological Association (APA)
    style, 93
Americans with Disabilities Act
    of 1990, 372
America's Got Talent (TV show), 10
Amygdala, 106–107, 115, 147
Analysis
    in critical thinking, 114–115
    in note taking, 215
Anderson, Alencia, 130
Anderson, Greg, 321
Angelou, Maya, 347
Anti-anxiety medications, 329
Anxiety disorders, 326–327
APA (American Psychological Association)
    style, 93
Appearance, in job interviews, 367
Arguments, fallacious (false), 118–120
Artifacts, 305
Associate of Applied Science (AAS) degree,
    53, 54
Associate of Arts (AA) degree, 53, 54
Associate of Science (AS) degree, 53, 54
Attendance, expectations in college for, 15
Attitudes
    developing new, 35–36
    expectations in college for, 16
    values in, 40
Audience, in public speaking, 280–281
Auditory learning style, 165–170

Babysitters, 236
Bachelor of Applied Science (BAS) degree,
    53, 54
Bachelor of Arts (BA) degree, 53, 54
Bachelor of Fine Arts (BFA) degree, 53, 54
Bachelor of Science (BS) degree, 53, 54
Bacon, Francis, 307
Bandwagon arguments, 118–119
Bard, Carl, 8, 352

Barriers
    to interpersonal communication,
        300–301
    to listening, 209–211
Beggars, 135
Behavior(s). *See also* Etiquette
    and aspirations, 21
    difficult, 312–313
    self-defeating, 35–36
Behaviorism, 159
Belonging, sense of, 44
Binge drinking, 332–333
Biological stressors, 150
Bipolar depression, 326
Birth control, 335, 337
Bizarreness effect, 233
Bloom, Benjamin, 159
Bloom's Taxonomy
    campus resources, 68
    change implementation model, 22–25
    conflict management, 318–319
    evaluating sources, 124–125
    guiding statement, 46
    information literacy, 98–99
    listening skills, 221–223
    money management skills, 273
    oral communication, 295
    personal life profile, 176–177
    reading for comprehension, 197–200
    reducing test anxiety, 247
    resume writing, 376–377
    stress management, 151–152
    wellness, 338
Bly, David, 66
Body
    effects of stress on, 146–148
    in holistic approach to wellness,
        324–325, 328–329
Body language, 290, 291, 303–304, 305
Bolles, Richard Nelson, 369
Boolean logic, 79–80
Borges, Leo G., 270
Boys in the Band, The (Crowley), 55
Brain teasers, 108–110
Brain workouts, 160–161
Branden, Nathanial, 44
Briggs, Katharine, 171
Briggs-Myers, Isabel, 171
Britton-Whitcomb, Susan, 356
Brodsky, Joseph, 191
Bronner, Nathaniel, Jr., 59
Brown, Les, 37
Budgeting, 260–263
Buffett, Warren, 268
Buscaglia, Leo, 7, 8, 45
Byron, Luke, 94–95

Caffeine, 331
Cantor, Joanne, 70
Car buying, 269
Car title loans, 264
Career centers, 346, 352–353
Career planning
    for jobs of future, 353–354
    personality type in, 174–175, 349
    self-assessment in, 349–352
    steps in decision making, 352–353
    strategies for, 5–6, 345–346
Carnegie, Dale, 275
Case studies, 159
Categorical organization, 92

Cause–effect organization, 92
Census Bureau, U.S., 11
Certainty
    lack of, tolerating, 111–112
    sin of, 115–117
Cervical cap, 337
Change, personal, 1–26
    in attitudes, 35–36
    global economy and, 4–7
    goal setting in, 10–11, 18–20
    implementation model for, 22–25
    motivation in, 30–31
    in self-discipline, 132
    success through, 7–11
Change, technological, 73
Character, taking pride in, 41–42
Chavez, Cesar, 112
Cheating, 59
Checkbook, balancing, 263
Chicago Manual of Style (CMS) style, 93
Children
    in financial management, 271–272
    studying with, 236–237
Chlamydia, 335
Choices. *See* Decision making
Chronic muscle pain, 148
Chronicle of Higher Education, The, 11
Chronological organization, 92
Chronological resumes, 360
Churchill, Winston, 45
Cigarette smoking, 331, 333–335
Circlers, 134
Citation styles, 92–93, 97
Civil Rights Act of 1964, 372
Civility, 57–58, 311
Classes
    developmental/remedial, 60–62
    distance learning, 86–87
    elective, 353
    etiquette in, 57–58
    language spoken in, 56
    note taking in, 212–221
    participation in, 15
Clayton, Bill, 17
Clinical depression, 326, 327
Clothing, 305
Club drugs, 331–332
CMS (Chicago Manual of Style) style, 93
Cocktail drugs, 331–332
Cognitive mental action, 157
Collaboration, online, 82. *See also* Teams
College. *See also* Education
    expectations in, 15–16, 53–55
    four-year plan for, 347–349
    "second term slump" in, 66
    sophomore year of, 346–347, 348
College Cost Reduction and Access Act of
    2007, 258
College culture. *See* Culture of college
College degrees, types of, 53, 54
Collins, Jim, 8
Colton, Charles Caleb, 328
Comfort zone, 12
Communication. *See also specific types*
    forms of, 300, 302
    importance of, 6, 302–303, 345
    process of, 300–302
Communication programs,
    collaborative, 82
Community service, 345–346
Compare/contrast organization, 92

Compassion, in creative thinking, 122
Competence, in self-esteem, 44
Competition, in creative thinking, 123
Complaining, 313
Comprehension, reading, 186
Computer labs, 61
Computer skills, importance of, 345
Computer-mediated communication
    (CMC), 304–306
Concentration, 186, 230
Conclusion, in presentations, 283–284
Condoms, 337
Conflict, 310–314
    causes of, 311
    dealing with, 311–314
    opportunities in, 310–311
Confucius, 159
Conrad, Joseph, 279
Conscience, 58
Conscious learning, 157
Contaminated people, 39
Content-oriented listeners, 208–209
Cookies, 77
Cooley, Charles, 44
Coopersmith, Stanly, 44
Cornell system, 216–217, 218, 219
Cornerstones for Lifetime Success, 34–45
Cortisol, 147
Cosby, Bill, 18
Counselors, academic, 60, 352–353
Courage, in creative thinking, 122
Cover letters, resume, 354–357
Crabs, 335
Crafts, for children, 236
Cramming, 237–238
Creative thinking, 120–123
Credibility, expectations in college for, 16
Credit cards, 263–265
    in credit score, 260
    lost or stolen, 272
    problems with debt on, 263–264
    tips for using, 260, 265
Credit history, 7, 258–260
Critical thinking, 101–127
    creative thinking in, 120–123
    decision making in, 115–117
    emotional intelligence in, 106–108
    fact *vs.* opinion in, 118
    on faulty arguments, 118–120
    importance of, 6, 104–105
    list of steps in, 105
    looking at things differently in,
        108–110
    problem solving in, 112–115
    questions and uncertainty in, 110–112
Cross-functional teams, 316
Crowley, Mart, 55
Crystal meth, 332
Cultural diversity, 308–310
    ethnocentrism and, 308–310
    in nonverbal communication, 303
Culture of college, 48–69
    adult students in, 63–64
    basic truths about, 12–18
    ethics in, 58–60
    expectations in, 15–16, 53–55
    golden rule in, 57–58
    grades in, 55–56, 62–63
    persistence and, 51, 66–68
    policies and procedures in, 51–52
    student services and, 60, 61